2024

How Trump Retook the White House and the Democrats Lost America

Josh
DAWSEY

Tyler
PAGER

Isaac
ARNSDORF

HUTCHINSON
HEINEMANN

Hutchinson Heinemann

UK | USA | Canada | Ireland | Australia
India | New Zealand | South Africa

Hutchinson Heinemann is part of the Penguin Random House group of companies
whose addresses can be found at global.penguinrandomhouse.com

Penguin Random House UK,
One Embassy Gardens, 8 Viaduct Gardens, London SW11 7BW

penguin.co.uk
global.penguinrandomhouse.com

Penguin
Random House
UK

First published in the US by Penguin Press 2025
First published in the UK by Cornerstone Press 2025
001

Printed and bound in India by Manipal Technologies Limited

The authorised representative in the EEA is Penguin Random House Ireland,
Morrison Chambers, 32 Nassau Street, Dublin D02 YH68

A CIP catalogue record for this book is available from the British Library

ISBN: 978–1–529–15482–5 (hardback)
ISBN: 978–1–529–15483–2 (trade paperback)

Penguin Random House is committed to a sustainable future
for our business, our readers and our planet. This book is made
from Forest Stewardship Council® certified paper.

MIX
Paper | Supporting
responsible forestry
FSC
www.fsc.org
FSC® C018179

CONTENTS

Part Three

SHAKEUP

INTRODUCTION

— January 10, 2025 —

Donald Trump, wearing a white golf shirt and a red hat that said TRUMP WAS RIGHT ABOUT EVERYTHING, bounded between rooms of his Florida pleasure palace. The president-elect was running late between meetings, after spending hours on the links. The afternoon was warm and sunny, ten days before his second inauguration, and the Mar-a-Lago Club teemed with visitors. A group of women in matching red dresses boarded a charter bus outside. A stretch Cadillac Escalade limousine idled by the front door. Foreigners wearing name tags filled the golden lobby. Congresswoman Lauren Boebert passed through carrying a shimmering short dress. Roger Stone luxuriated on a white sofa holding an unlit cigar. "You're the One That I Want" from the *Grease* soundtrack blasted over the sound system. Trump's body man, Walt Nauta, who'd been charged alongside him with hiding and lying about classified documents, rambled through the lobby meeting fans. Trump's personal lawyer, Boris Epshteyn, who'd been accused of demanding payoffs in exchange for recommending people to Trump for administration posts, was still around making introductions.

Tech executives, political operatives, and club members wandered the halls, hoping for a handshake or an autograph—or maybe an ambassadorship, an inauguration ticket, or a favor for a friend. Trump had been musing to members that maybe he should raise the club's initiation fee, which was already more than half a million dollars. He had fundraising dinners almost every night with business executives and finance titans lavishly praising him and trying to influence him on issues like vaccines and the corporate tax code.

"Zuckerberg is in there," Trump whispered slyly, pointing to another room. The Facebook founder was mediating a lawsuit that Trump had brought to challenge his suspension from the social media platform after the January 6, 2021, riot in the U.S. Capitol. Elon Musk, who would appear shortly, was in a different room nearby. "We've had everybody here," Trump said. "We've had Google, we've had Facebook, we've had Bill Gates, we had Tim Cook, Apple—we've had all of them."

They weren't coming empty-handed. They came bearing seven-figure checks for his inauguration. Amazon, Meta, Microsoft, OpenAI, Uber, Toyota, Ford, GM, Pfizer, Goldman Sachs. His advisers said they did not have enough time and perks to accommodate all the new admirers. "I used to have a list," Trump said. "And I always ask them, 'Would you have been here if I lost? Would you have been here if I lost?' It's funny. They know the answer is no, but they don't want to really say it. And it would be no if I were them too."

He settled in a dining room with a curved glass panorama overlooking the ocean, helped himself to fried shrimp dipped in tartar sauce, and pondered how different his life would be now if he'd lost the election. Friends and politicians would have abandoned him. He would have faced multiple criminal trials. He might have lived out his golden years behind bars. Friends told him, "You were either going to win or your life was really going to be very unpleasant." Miserable, even. He couldn't disagree.

He was feeling especially triumphant on this afternoon, having appeared earlier that morning by video link in a New York court for sentencing. He had been convicted of thirty-four felony counts for paying hush money to a porn star before the 2016 election. The crimes carried a penalty of up to four years in prison. But the judge, whom Trump had berated for months as biased and unfair, imposed nothing.

"Discharge, unconditional discharge," Trump marveled. "Nobody ever even heard of it. 'We are unconditionally discharging this case.' It's over. No fine. No penalty. No this. Nothing. It's actually just a total win."

An aide interrupted the president-elect to remind him he had to meet three candidates for secretary of the Air Force, and he was having dinner with lawmakers from the hardline House Freedom Caucus. "You have three interviews, sir, and you have to be at your dinner in an hour," said the aide, Sergio Gor, who published Trump's coffee-table books (*Save America* and *Our Journey Together*) and would soon become the director of the White House Presidential Personnel Office. Trump believed the biggest mistake of his first term was picking disloyal officials, and Gor was determined to disqualify candidates who had ever criticized Trump or anyone associated with him.

"I look a little bit sloppy," Trump lamented, between bites of fried shrimp. He preferred to wear a suit and tie for such meetings.

For all the hubbub around the club, it was more heavily fortified than ever before. No traffic was allowed on the oceanfront highway. Vehicles were screened by bomb detectors in a parking lot across the road. A metal detector and TSA-like bag scanner guarded the front door.

"Let me ask you," he said, taking a moment to reflect on his brush with death at a summer rally in Pennsylvania. "If that didn't happen, that day in Butler didn't happen, would the result have been . . . I think I would've won, but it might've been a little bit closer. Do you think? I don't know. I would have preferred that it didn't happen, obviously. But I cannot tell you whether or not it would've been closer."

"I think you would've won no matter what, sir," Gor said.

Gor pressed again about the Air Force interviews. Trump's son, Don Jr., walked through the room. Musk soon followed. Natalie Harp, a former One America News Network anchor who took Trump's dictation for social media posts and often carried a portable printer to show him flattering articles, sat in a corner, smiling as Trump talked.

Ever since he'd left the White House four years earlier, this club had been Trump's refuge. Here, no matter his criminal jeopardy and political isolation, the sun was always shining, the fans were always fawning, and the toasts were always MAGA. The bathrooms were decorated with magazine covers and old pictures of Trump playing golf with Arnold Palmer or marching in a parade in Manhattan. A replica of Air Force One sat out in the lobby. His office displayed a drawing of his face on Mount Rushmore.

But now the world outside the curved glass of the dining room windows was Trump's too. The four prosecutions against him had crumbled and collapsed. He had redefined the Republican coalition and created an existential crisis for the Democratic Party. He'd promised to pardon January 6 rioters, round up and deport millions of immigrants, start trade wars with allies, use government power to punish his critics, purge law enforcement agencies to install personal loyalists, relocate homeless people to tent cities, eliminate government agencies, give his biggest donor free rein to slash federal spending, even act as a dictator, if only for a day. And America said OK. Almost every county shifted right. He improved with almost every demographic. He even won the popular vote.

The acceptance and legitimacy Trump had craved his whole life was at last his to enjoy. A day earlier, he'd attended Jimmy Carter's funeral, walking into Washington not as a scourge but as a conqueror. He could ignore the speech on character by the outgoing president, and the cold shoulder from the vice president he'd defeated. Instead he sat next to Barack Obama and invited him to play golf, enticing him with descriptions of Trump's courses around the world. He was no longer an anomaly. He was being treated like an American president. He wanted to be remembered as a great one.

"Honestly, what can you say that was bad?" Trump said in the dining room. "I won. Seriously. I won against all odds. I won against the DOJ, and the whole world was against me. And I won."

There was a view popular among some political insiders that this election had been over before it started. The overwhelming majority of Americans thought the country was on the wrong track. They were fed up with inflation, immigration, and overseas conflicts, and they blamed the sitting president (and his vice president) for their feelings of economic and global insecurity.

But the true story of the 2024 campaign is not so impersonal, and the outcome was not so predetermined. According to hundreds of interviews with the people closest to the Trump, Biden, and Harris campaigns, the election hinged on accidents and individual decisions that had enormous consequences and might just as easily have gone another way. If Republicans moved on from Trump like every other defeated ex-president, or coalesced around a single alternative. If Democrats got clobbered, as expected, in the 2022 midterms, and Joe Biden never ran for reelection. If any of his advisers ever told him he shouldn't. If he faced a real primary challenge. If Trump never got indicted, or if Republicans didn't respond by rallying to him, or if the prosecutions were more successful. If Trump and Biden didn't agree to an early debate, or if Biden didn't perform so poorly. If he stayed in, or didn't endorse Kamala Harris right away. If she inherited a better campaign, or had more time to run one of her own. If Trump gave in to the chaotic impulses that defined his previous campaigns and went through with blowing up his own operation in the final stretch.

The result, however contingent, would affect nothing less than the lives of billions of people around the world and the course of human history. Biden saw Trump as an existential threat to the American way of life as a democratic, free society, and he expected a second Trump administration to be more extreme and ruthless than the first. He conceptualized his first run against Trump, in 2020, as a "battle for the soul of the nation," only to become still more horrified by the violence of January 6. He thought Trump and his movement were growing only more dangerous. He worried about losing the country he knew, but believed Trump was an aberration. Ensuring that—or failing to—would define his legacy and place in history.

Biden and his advisers constantly assessed the political winds and concluded that running for reelection was the obvious choice. They believed he governed well, and they cared that historians agreed, ranking Biden among the most successful modern presidents. They thought voters agreed too, based on the 2022 midterms, when Democrats outperformed historical patterns and widespread expectations. They drew further validation from the absence of a serious primary challenge from any of the party's many ambitious younger rising stars. They knew his age was a problem but considered it a perception, not a reality. They insisted his age never affected his ability to govern, only to campaign. They also bet that whatever discomfort voters had with Biden, their aversion to Trump would prevail.

Biden and his team dug into this bunker mentality because they had long felt counted out and underestimated. For decades they were treated like the B team, a stepping stone to a more prestigious job with Barack Obama or Hillary Clinton. Washington never believed in them. Yet they won and proved everyone wrong, hardening their resolve to defy their skeptics again.

Harris was also running against her doubters. She wanted to prove she was more than the 2019 also-ran who didn't even make it to Iowa, or the "DEI hire" that Republicans reduced her to. Her vice presidency got off to a rough start, and the press and the public largely started ignoring her; but while they weren't looking, she improved her team and skills. She wanted to demonstrate herself as an established national leader with political strengths. Then suddenly she was thrust into an extraordinary situation, and Democrats desperately hoped she could overcome all Biden's baggage if she just didn't make any more mistakes.

The election fell in a year of deep anxiety about national decline, new technology, government failure, and changing social values. Trump always drew his strength from decades of pent-up frustration with the American democratic system's failures to address the hardships and problems that people experienced in their daily lives. In 2024, his supporters saw institutions stacked against them, from the economy to culture, leading them to identify viscerally with his legal ordeal, even though they had never experienced anything like it before.

Trump recognized that the fate of his prosecutions hinged on his return to office, meaning the stakes of the election included his personal liberty. He was perhaps equally motivated by the impact on his businesses, brand, fortune, and family name. He was also running to avenge the defeat in 2020 that he could never admit or accept. And while voters showed less concern for his health than Biden's, Trump was at an age when many of his friends and peers were getting sick and dying. He increasingly talked about his mortality and legacy. He did not want his obituary to begin with "criminal" and "loser."

In that effort he had the crucial assistance of a top adviser, Susie Wiles, who had her own reputation to rehabilitate and exile to overcome. She also wanted to prove that the Minotaur could be contained—that Trumpworld could be managed, his campaign did not have to be shambolic and treacherous like the previous ones, and she did not have to finish like so many previous advisers, with a knife in her back.

It was easy to forget how vulnerable Trump had been at the start of this campaign, in late 2022. He had trouble getting big-name Republicans to come to his launch party. The excitement in the GOP was around another candidate who was supposed to be the new and improved version. There was even a moment when Trump might not have run at all.

Part One

COMEBACKS

1

Point of No Return

On the morning of August 8, 2022, Donald Trump was in his office on the twenty-sixth floor of his eponymous tower in New York. With brass letters blaring his name as loudly as any tabloid headline, the skyscraper was at once a symbol of the outerborough boy who made it and a monument to the "greed is good" eighties when it was built. To see its black glass sawtooth silhouette was to hear *The Apprentice* theme song, "For the Love of Money" by the O'Jays—*Money money money money, money*. In June 2015, the site took on a new and much greater significance, as the place where Trump launched his campaign for president with an escalator ride that changed the world. Ever since that moment, Trump's life—and to a large extent, American public life—has been dominated by constant conflict.

Trump could recount in shorthand a laundry list of "witch hunts" for his adoring fans, who would all understand him and sympathize: "They spied on my campaign; they did the Russia, Russia, Russia hoax; the Ukraine, Ukraine, Ukraine . . . Impeachment Hoax Number One; Impeachment Hoax Number Two; the January Sixth Committee of

Unselect Political Thugs . . . an attorney general, Letitia, that went out and campaigned on, 'I will get Trump.'"

That last grievance—a reference to a civil fraud investigation by the New York attorney general into Trump's family business—was the focus of his attention that Monday morning, as he met with one slice of his sprawling legal team. He was preparing for an upcoming deposition when he was interrupted by a phone call telling him the FBI was at Mar-a-Lago.

Trump was stunned. The club was closed for the season. No one was around. What was the FBI doing there? What were they taking? How many agents were there? Were they on camera? What shape would they leave his club in? He wanted to know everything.

His legal team didn't have the answers. One of his lawyers, Christina Bobb, was on her way to the scene. She was not, on paper, the attorney you would ordinarily call to deal with the FBI. A graduate of California Western School of Law in San Diego, she was more experienced as an on-air correspondent for the pro-Trump television network OAN than with federal criminal investigations. But she was based in Florida, the only Trump lawyer within a hundred miles that day, so the task fell to her.

Trump hung up and exclaimed to his lawyers in the office, "Can you fucking believe they did this?"

He called his other lawyers. He called his adult children. Some aides watched on Mar-a-Lago's surveillance cameras as the agents, dressed in khakis and polos instead of blue-and-yellow windbreakers to be less conspicuous, went in and out of Trump's office and living quarters. Other aides became obsessed with finding a mole. How did the FBI know Trump still had government documents at Mar-a-Lago?

Trump was a packrat. On flights, the seat next to him was reserved for a stack of papers the height of a small passenger: printed-out articles for him to read, which he would mark up in Sharpie with commentary or instructions for his aides to post on social media or mail to someone. When he was president, top-secret government documents could be interspersed with printed-out right-wing blog posts. In January 2021, Trump had moved out of the White House hurriedly and messily. He and a few loyal aides personally packed up the Oval Office and the residence. Briefings, memos, maps, schedules, charts, slide decks, letters, newspapers, golf shirts, a phone list, a menu, a napkin. They all wound up in boxes brought to Mar-a-Lago. As far as Trump was concerned, all of it belonged to him.

The National Archives started bothering Trump back in May 2021 to hand over the boxes. A top lawyer from the agency told Trump's team that every president took things mistakenly. But they'd never seen a situation like this, where a former president would not cooperate.

Multiple lawyers and advisers repeatedly warned Trump he should return the documents or else the FBI was going to come get them. Some had even flown down to Palm Beach to plead with him in person. Trump told them he wasn't concerned about it. "You're such a fucking yip," he told Alex Cannon, an attorney working on the case who recommended returning the files. To Trump, they were "my boxes," and he was not giving them back. For the National Archives to ask for them was just another case of official Washington trying to mess with him, and he wasn't going to roll over. He was betting the Justice Department's leaders were too cautious to confront him over a bunch of boxes.

After more than a year of his resistance, the Justice Department got a grand jury to issue a subpoena. When Trump received it, he asked his lawyer Evan Corcoran, couldn't they just tell the archives they didn't have anything classified? "What happens if we just don't respond at all?"

Corcoran went into the Mar-a-Lago storage room and found thirty-eight documents marked classified. When he told the boss, Trump suggested maybe those documents could mysteriously go missing and mimed plucking a paper out of a pile. In June 2022, a senior Justice Department official and three FBI agents came to Mar-a-Lago. Trump greeted them in the dining room, served them lunch, and told his lawyer to give them everything they needed. They left with a taped-up folder containing the thirty-eight documents that Corcoran had found. Trump would later joke that he should have been more hospitable. "I should have given them dinner."

The government lawyers didn't know that Trump and some of his employees had moved some boxes out of the storage room. He was playing a cat-and-mouse game to keep some of the boxes—*his* boxes—in his possession. He was never one to give up something for nothing.

Justice Department officials believed the subpoena had finally succeeded in getting Trump to return classified material, but a secret witness told investigators he was hiding more. They issued another subpoena for video footage, and FBI officials watched in horror as they saw boxes moved throughout the club. They realized they couldn't keep trying to negotiate if Trump was hiding stuff from his own lawyers. They had to get a search warrant. But FBI officials insisted on no fanfare. The agents would go when Trump was away. They would not wear uniforms or carry guns. Once inside, the agents were stunned by what they found.

At 6:19 p.m. on August 8, the FBI agents gave Bobb a three-page inventory of what they'd taken: eleven sets of classified documents. Some of his advisers hoped that would be the end of it, that the feds had gotten what they wanted.

Trump saw it differently. To him, the FBI's search was an escalation, a provocation, an abomination. His astonishment turned to fury, then determination. He convened a call with top allies and advisers.

He was concerned that a media outlet would report the search before he did. This was big news, and he wanted to drive attention to his Truth Social website. "I want to break the story," he said.

He also wanted people on TV defending him. One adviser wondered whether that was premature, since there was so much they didn't know. Trump said he didn't care. "I want everybody that has a voice out there," a person close to him remembered him saying. "I don't care who they are, I don't care if they're good at this or not, I want them all out there talking." The order was to attack the Justice Department and the FBI.

As those attacks spread across right-wing media, some of them resonated within the FBI's ranks. Agents across the country complained to bureau leaders that the political consequences of the search could damage the institution's reputation. The agency's top officials responded by organizing an "education session" about the case.

Trump's lawyers began trying to re-create the FBI's movements at Mar-a-Lago. They interviewed everyone around, in the off-season mostly groundskeepers and household staff. What had the agents done? What had they taken? What had they said? They reviewed video footage but found it mostly unremarkable. Over several calls, the lawyers realized they had no idea what Trump really possessed. One of Trump's longtime assistants, knowing the boss did not want a mess, drove to the club to try to put things back in order.

Steve Bannon, Trump's 2016 campaign chief, and Boris Epshteyn, his longtime lawyer and adviser, thought Trump should capitalize on the publicity around the Mar-a-Lago search to launch his campaign to take back the White House. At that point, Trump was already moving toward running, but he never fully decides something until it happens. Throughout 2021 and early 2022, he had discussed the possibility with Senator Lindsey Graham of South Carolina. Over rounds of golf in West Palm Beach, Graham argued Trump could easily win the Republican nomination and even the presidency regardless of January 6. Trump said he was not so sure he wanted to run. On other days, he signaled he was definitely running. Some family members were encouraging Trump to move on from politics. Other Republicans were less excited about his return. "There was a time, right after the election, where he was really contemplating what to do," Graham said.

Finally, the Mar-a-Lago search forced Trump's hand. "It made me more resolute," he would later say in an interview for this book. He wanted to get ahead of any possible indictments by officially declaring his candidacy, which he thought would help portray the charges as politicized. "He was not going to run until the FBI raided Mar-a-Lago," said Doug Deason, a Republican donor close to the Trump family. "He was pissed, he was stunned, he then was going to run and he was going to clean house at the DOJ." Another longtime aide said the former president saw the campaign as "running for his freedom."

The classified documents at Mar-a-Lago were not Trump's only reason to anticipate an indictment. There were multiple separate criminal and civil investigations circling him, his staff, and his businesses. Besides the documents investigation and the New York attorney general's civil fraud case, Trump's company and its CFO (though not Trump himself) were facing charges for criminal tax fraud in New York. In Washington, federal prosecutors were interviewing former White House officials before a grand jury, asking them about conversations with the former president, his lawyers, and some of his closest advisers, raising the possibility that Trump himself could be the target of a federal criminal investigation into his efforts to overturn the election. The Manhattan district attorney wound down a probe into possible tax crimes, only to reopen an investigation into hush money payments to a porn star before the 2016 election. The district attorney in Fulton County, Georgia, was investigating the Republican electors who falsely attested that Trump had won the state. When Trump learned about the special grand jury empaneled to investigate him in Georgia, he accused his lawyers of working against him. "I can't be fucking indicted by a local prosecutor," he screamed at Cannon and others. "Why haven't you shut this thing down?"

There was another reason for Trump to announce early: to get ahead of the expected challenge from Florida Governor Ron DeSantis. Conservative pundits were hailing DeSantis as the heir apparent to the MAGA movement. Asked directly if he had higher ambitions, DeSantis repeatedly sidestepped the question, never ruling out a 2024 White House bid. Trump saw that as a supreme betrayal, since his endorsement in 2018 had been instrumental in DeSantis's winning the gubernatorial primary. DeSantis had been an undistinguished congressional backbencher whose entire gubernatorial campaign was premised on winning Trump's favor; he went so far as to hang around Palm Beach hoping for a meeting. Since then, Trump and DeSantis had displayed mutual admiration: DeSantis would defend Trump on TV, and Trump would compliment DeSantis on his performance defending him on TV. They never shared any genuine personal warmth. Theirs was always a marriage of convenience. Trump became furious that DeSantis would dare to challenge him and thought he couldn't spare a minute in taking him down. "I decided to start the campaign then, much against the views of a lot of people," Trump later said in an interview.

Trump's staff told him to wait. They argued that if he declared himself a presidential candidate, he would no longer be allowed to draw on the millions of dollars stockpiled in his political action committee, and the Republican National Committee would have to stop covering his legal expenses. They warned that attacking a popular Republican governor who was currently running for reelection would backfire, and Trump would get blamed if Republicans underperformed in the midterms. He agreed to hold off. In the meantime, he would act like a candidate—traveling around the country, holding rallies, giving speeches, hiring staff, meeting with donors—and he would throw his energy and clout into backing the most fervidly loyal candidates in the 2022 Republican primaries and the midterms, those who would agree the election was stolen and who would defend Trump over January 6.

As he started preparing for a new campaign, Trump wanted to recapture the magic of his 2016 run. He could do without the periodic meltdowns and scandals, but he wanted at least some of the same spontaneity and adventure. Despite being a former president, Trump felt like an underdog and an outsider. His initial ostracism after the January 6 riot and the threat of criminal prosecution rekindled a sense of thrill—Trump against the world. He did not want a repeat of his 2020 campaign: a bloated behemoth, where he never knew what anyone did all day.

There was no question who would be in charge. Susie Wiles, his top political adviser, had mastered the role of gatekeeper and Trump whisperer like no one before. At sixty-five, Wiles spoke softly and almost never swore, but she could kill you with a look. She often wore oversize mirrored sunglasses, making her expressions all the more inscrutable, and she had a halo of silver hair as imperturbable as Trump's own coiffure. For years, she'd been a top Republican operative in Florida, and Trump credited her with winning him the state in both 2016 and 2020 (back when it was still considered competitive). Her personal politics remained a mystery to longtime associates; she'd worked for Republicans as varied as Jon Huntsman Jr. and Rick Scott. She did not have fixed policy views on many issues. She was not an election denier. She liked to win. Trump saw her as a winner. He often described her as having "good genes"; one of the reasons he liked her was that her father was Pat Summerall, the famous football announcer and former player who he knew from New York.

He called her not long after leaving the White House to invite her to dinner at Mar-a-Lago. She found him in an alarming state. He wasn't eating as much, enjoying his daily eighteen holes, or peacocking around the patio as usual. Since January 20 he'd rarely appeared in public. He had almost no one around him, and no idea how much money was left in his accounts or what legal trouble awaited him. He thought his advisers were stealing from him, or worse—betraying him by cooperating with investigators. "I don't know who's with me, who is against me," he told Wiles. "I just need this sorted out." He seemed sadder than ever, she later said.

At first, Wiles didn't agree to take the job. She feared it would be too hard, too time-consuming, and bound to end the same way it had for everyone else: with an ignominious firing. But ten days later, she came back for dinner, and this time Trump convinced her to do it, at least temporarily. He had been there for her when she was at her lowest.

Back in 2018, Wiles had lobbied Trump to endorse DeSantis, arguing that having a Republican governor in Florida would help Trump there in 2020. She went on to take charge of DeSantis's campaign and steer it to a hard-fought, narrow victory. After the election, DeSantis turned on her. As head of his transition, Wiles became concerned over DeSantis's accepting meals, gifts, and golf trips from donors and lobbyists. Wiles saw to it that DeSantis received a legal memo about Florida's state ethics rules, spelling out what he could and couldn't accept. One Saturday in early 2019, she personally went to Tallahassee to warn DeSantis and his wife, Casey, that they should be more careful. The governor and his wife denied doing anything improper and became defensive.

Not long after, some of DeSantis's unseemly arrangements to fundraise on the golf course appeared in the *Tampa Bay Times*. Wiles denied planting the stories, but DeSantis blamed her and went on a rampage. He not only fired her from his staff, he purged anyone he believed was close to her, badmouthed her to anyone who would listen, and got her publicly expelled from her day job as a lobbyist. She privately described it as the worst year of her life. She'd recently gotten divorced, and she spent many days crying in the sole company of her dog.

During the 2020 race, DeSantis pressured the Trump campaign to make a public statement disavowing Wiles. But Trump decided he wanted her help, believing she was the key to winning Florida. DeSantis tried to stop him, calling Wiles overrated. "You don't need her," the governor told the president on a phone call, offering to find him someone else to lead the campaign in Florida. Trump declined, hung up, and hired Wiles. She would always be grateful to him for that; he didn't have to do it.

Wiles spent 2021 and 2022 getting Trump back in shape to run for president again, like a trainer coaching a prizefighter. Every week, she'd drive four hours from her home near Jacksonville and crash at a hotel near Mar-a-Lago. Trump was often in a foul mood at first, screaming about the election being stolen. She was like his therapist, explaining to him why he lost various states, what challenges he would face if he ran again, and even how elections worked. She identified bad spending choices and which advisers she thought were grifting. She encouraged Trump to take a softer tone with his own aides and stop talking about the 2020 election.

Slowly, Wiles earned Trump's trust, to the point that he would often ask her opinion five or six times in a group dinner. "What do you think, Susie?" he would say with a smile. Wiles would sometimes offer a differing opinion, but she would never contradict him directly. He started deferring to her. When other advisers would tell Trump to do things, he'd reply, "Ask Susie."

The talent that made Wiles so effective in her role—a gift for smoothing over conflict while quietly getting her way—was also the reason Trump wanted her to hire a partner. He wanted an enforcer who liked to fight. "You're not tough enough," he told her. "I need an asshole."

Wiles consulted Tony Fabrizio, a veteran pollster who also worked for Trump, and he had just the asshole for her: Chris LaCivita.

Here was the man who brought you "Swift Boat Veterans for Truth," the 2004 ad campaign that smeared John Kerry's war record. The man who had swum across an icy lake to plant a campaign sign; stopped traffic on a highway to shepherd supporters to a debate; stabbed office walls with a sword; and once shot a goose while on the phone with a reporter. When Democrats later shopped opposition research on LaCivita with allegations intended to make him look ridiculous, LaCivita responded, "LOL. All true!"

He'd fought in the trenches of Operation Desert Storm and taken shrapnel through the chin. He covered those scars with a gray beard to complement his thick eyebrows and bald pate. Years ago, when a private investigator came to the bottom of his driveway in Virginia, he met him with a rifle and told him never to return. His motto was "spray and pray": spray bullets and pray they don't hit any friends. He was an experienced warrior in the public-facing functions of press, communications, and messaging, as well as the behind-the-scenes, nuts-and-bolts legwork of political field operations and delegate math. He wasn't afraid of dirty tricks either. At the 2016 Republican National Convention, when former Virginia attorney general Ken Cuccinelli tried to propose a rules change, his motion couldn't be recognized because the chair couldn't hear him. Someone had cut off Cuccinelli's microphone.

LaCivita's support for Trump was not unshakable. When Trump

supporters stormed the Capitol on January 6, LaCivita shared tweets condemning the rioters and liked a tweet calling for the Cabinet to remove Trump through the Twenty-Fifth Amendment. As Trump began to make his comeback, LaCivita removed the posts.

LaCivita had always wanted to work for a presidential campaign. He knew Wiles's formidable reputation, but they'd never worked together, or against each other, so he was game to meet her, at Fabrizio's invitation. The three of them hit it off over dinner at an Italian restaurant in Fort Lauderdale. LaCivita understood that everything involving Trump would require Wiles's blessing. They had several more dates before Wiles brought LaCivita to meet the boss.

LaCivita could hear the hushed buzz of *who's the new guy* as he sat for dinner with Wiles and Trump in the middle of the Mar-a-Lago patio. "You like lobster?" Trump asked.

"I love lobster," LaCivita answered.

He turned to the staff. "Bring Chris the biggest lobster."

They brought out a three-pounder on a giant platter, which Trump said he had to get specially made for the purpose. "People don't want to pay a hundred fifty dollars for a little pile of meat," Trump said. "I keep it in the whole shell." LaCivita appreciated that attention to detail, with the crustacean perfectly split down the back.

Trump was generally chilly toward newcomers, and he was skeptical of LaCivita at first. He questioned whether LaCivita really made the Swift Boat ads. "Everyone claims credit for that," he said. At that first dinner, he cranked up the music, making it impossible for his guests to continue talking—a sign that the conversation bored him.

Still, LaCivita got involved making ads in the 2022 midterms for the MAGA Inc. super PAC to boost the Senate candidates whom Trump endorsed. One crime-themed attack ad on Dr. Oz's Democratic opponent in Pennsylvania included bloody imagery and a nightmarish voice-over, enough to make the infamous "Willie Horton" ad from 1988 look quaint. The ads previewed the same themes the Trump campaign would use in 2024: inflation, crime, immigration. They never mentioned Trump, attesting to LaCivita's sensitivity to the former president's assets and liabilities alike. In his thirty-five years in the business, LaCivita had seen a lot of liars, cheats, morons, and maniacs. He didn't see Trump like that. To Republican friends who wondered out loud whether LaCivita knew Trump was crazy, LaCivita would respond, "Like a fox."

That fall, once Trump decided he wanted LaCivita on the campaign, Wiles invited him to another meeting, this time at Trump's golf club in Bedminster, New Jersey. She let LaCivita think the agenda was merely to discuss ideas for the next round of TV ads. But at the meeting, Trump asked LaCivita, "When can you start?" He froze, tricked and cornered. Trump went on, "Susie, make a deal with him. Let's get this thing going."

Rounding out Trump's small core team were Jason Miller, an unendingly loyal communications director and one of the few aides Trump still trusted; a speechwriting duo of Vince Haley and Ross Worthington, who worked in Trump's White House under Stephen Miller, the immigration hard-liner who remained a trusted policy adviser; and spokesman Steven Cheung, a former Ultimate Fighting Championship flak whom Trump adoringly described as having come straight from "central casting for a killer."

Trump's advisers managed to hold him back from announcing his campaign before the midterms, only to face yet another fire drill on the day before the election. His aides argued that an announcement would get drowned out by election coverage, and he would get blamed for energizing Democrats. The compromise was to say that he would be making a very special announcement a week later, on November 15, 2022, at Mar-a-Lago.

The midterms turned out to be far from the "red wave" that Trump had been banking on. Trump spent election night sitting dolefully at a banquet table in the Mar-a-Lago ballroom, watching his hand-picked candidates go down in key races. Meanwhile, on the other coast of Florida, DeSantis cruised to a 20-point victory and entered an ebullient Tampa convention hall to chants of "Two more years!" Trump's advisers privately admitted the contrast was the worst possible outcome for the former president. The next morning's *New York Post* crowned DeSantis "DeFUTURE."

Some advisers urged Trump to postpone his announcement and wait for a better moment. Privately, Trump polled his confidants on whether to delay, but publicly he held firm. "We had tremendous success," he said in a Fox News interview. "Why would anything change?"

The announcement was packed with the usual Trump superfans in their colorful costumes—the Front Row Joes who camped out for every rally in matching baseball-style jerseys; the Bikers for Trump in leather vests; the "Build the Wall" guy in a redbrick-printed suit; a group of "Vietnamese Americans for America First" women in matching red Áo dài dresses. Then came the Palm Beach crowd in their own uniforms: open-necked shirts, pastel blazers, and sockless loafers for the men; pearls and sequined gowns for the ladies; colored hair for both. There were only a handful of Republican elected officials: Madison Cawthorn, the one-term North Carolina congressman who'd antagonized his colleagues and lost his primary; and Ken Paxton, the Texas attorney general facing his own criminal indictment. Most elected officials wanted to stay away, despite repeated invitations from Trump's team.

Onstage, Trump almost looked as if he regretted going through with the announcement. He seemed to get fed up with his script, ad-libbing more and more as he went on, alternating the prepared lines with improvised reactions, as if in call-and-response with his own text. Twenty minutes in, he launched into an extended riff on trade deals; thirty minutes in, he started meandering about China and Germany and windmills. Conspicuously, he did not mention the stolen election—his constant refrain for two years. His aides argued it wasn't a winning message for another presidential campaign, and after Republicans had belly flopped so spectacularly in the midterms, he listened. But it was still Trump's passion. His heart wasn't in this speech. Even aides and allies gritted their teeth and admitted the launch was a dud. The cover of the next day's *New York Post*—a signal of where Rupert Murdoch's powerful right-wing news empire was leaning—jeered, "Florida Man Makes Announcement."

Trump fumed over the coverage and turnout. Where were all the members of Congress who'd spent months asking for his endorsement? Why didn't the networks take it live? He was supposed to do an interview with Sean Hannity on Fox News, but it fell through.

This is going to be a real struggle, Steve Bannon remembered thinking at the time.

The main impact of the announcement was to trigger the appointment of a special counsel to take over the two federal investigations into Trump. Now that Trump was a declared candidate for president, Biden's attorney general, Merrick Garland, felt he had no choice. He could have appointed a retired Republican like Robert Mueller, someone who might have approached prosecuting Trump warily. But the investigations into Trump's handling of classified documents and his role in January 6 had both already gathered extensive evidence.

The January 6 investigation was the largest in the Justice Department's history, and it was never limited to the rioters who broke into the

Capitol or the violent extremist groups who egged them on. From the beginning, the department had a team investigating possible connections to Trump and his circle, code-named "Willard," after the historic hotel near the White House, where many of those associates spent the day. The team chased leads that might have established a connection between Trump and the violence.

Most tantalizing, in early to mid-2021, prosecutors got a tip that would have been a smoking gun. The tip suggested that a close Trump aide had brokered a meeting before the attack between the then-president and the Proud Boys in Las Vegas. Investigators spent that spring and summer trying to track it down. In the end, they determined it wasn't true. There had been no meeting.

Prosecutors went on collecting grand jury testimony about what Trump knew about the various efforts to keep himself in power despite losing the election. The documents case had already produced a search warrant, meaning a judge agreed the FBI was likely to find evidence of a crime.

In Jack Smith, Garland chose a special counsel known for being aggressive and fearless. His last job was prosecuting war crimes and genocide at the International Criminal Court in the Hague. He started out his career jailing mobsters and gang leaders. He did not shrink from bringing cases that ventured into untested legal territory. He lost trials charging former Democratic Senators John Edwards and Bob Menendez, and his 2014 corruption conviction of Virginia Governor Bob McDonnell was overturned by the Supreme Court. Many federal prosecutors were elite-educated careerists who would rather not try a case they weren't guaranteed to win, a culture sometimes derided as "the Chickenshit Club." For better or worse, Jack Smith was decidedly not a member.

Garland told Smith to brief him occasionally and he would not interfere. The department's rules set a high bar for the attorney general to overrule a special counsel, and with Garland and Smith, it never came to that.

Smith took on the assignment with his characteristic zeal. The investigations sped up. He pushed the FBI for his own team of agents and set up his office in a nondescript building away from the main Department of Justice. He recruited some of the government's most accomplished prosecutors and started looking at lists of Trump's top aides.

Trump's lawyers soon told him that Smith was escalating the probes. For Trump, every legal threat presented a political opportunity. Playing the victim to a rabid Trump-hating inquisitor was a role he was comfortable in. Now he had a way to revive his favorite subject—the rigged and stolen election—by spinning it forward, portraying the criminal investigations as the latest form of "election interference." He got a mulligan for his spiritless campaign announcement, speaking to supporters at his club on the night of Smith's appointment.

"I've been going through these investigations and hoaxes and scams from the day I came down the escalator at Trump Tower, and you'd really say, 'Enough is enough,'" Trump said, back to showing the kind of fight he was known for. "I've proven to be one of the most honest and innocent people ever in our country."

Not Dead

In late March 2022, New Jersey Governor Phil Murphy, a Democrat who had just survived a closer-than-expected reelection race, attended a gathering of his state's political elite at a steakhouse in the Hard Rock Hotel & Casino in Atlantic City. The room was packed with elected officials, lobbyists, and other power brokers, as well as former Virginia Governor Terry McAuliffe, fresh off losing his own bid for another term in Richmond. McAuliffe's loss—and Murphy's uncomfortably close win—portended danger for Democrats in the November 2022 midterms. The president's party often got walloped in his first midterms, and the current president, Joe Biden, had an underwater approval rating. All signs pointed to 2022 being especially dire.

Murphy had parlayed his Goldman Sachs wealth into politics, serving as the finance chair of the Democratic National Committee and then as Obama's ambassador to Germany, winning the governorship of New Jersey in 2017. He chose not to move into Drumthwacket, the executive mansion in Princeton, but rather to stay in his own mansion on the Navesink River. He became a fixture in Washington and quickly grabbed leadership posts at both the Democratic Governors Association and the National Governors Association, serving as president of each in successive years, and fueling suspicions he might have higher ambitions.

On this night, several drinks in and wearing a blazer without a tie, Murphy used his welcome remarks to celebrate his success before turning his attention to the broader American political landscape. Like most of the people sitting in the room, he did not believe Biden would actually run for a second term. "We love the president," he said, according to one guest's recollection. "If he runs, we'll back him. If he doesn't, should I?"

The proposition wasn't as spontaneous as it might have sounded in the moment. One month earlier, Murphy's wife, Tammy, and former aides had launched a PAC and a nonprofit to tout the governor's record—a signature move for politicians seeking higher office. Aides were also making calls behind the scenes, including to top Democratic strategists, asking if they could help raise his national profile and whether they were already committed to other potential presidential candidates. Murphy and his aides expected the 2022 midterms to be the starting gun for the 2024 presidential primary. If Biden decided not to run, Murphy's aides would be poised to launch a full-fledged presidential campaign in a matter of weeks. They were not deterred by Biden's vice president and ostensible heir apparent, Kamala Harris.

On the other side of the country, aides to Gavin Newsom also saw the midterms as the right moment to nudge the California governor into the presidential race. Newsom had become a leading Democratic communicator with conservative audiences, having joined Trump's Truth Social website to troll him and regularly appearing on Fox News. His aides, predicting that Democrats would get clobbered on November 8, 2022, discussed having Newsom follow the midterms with a speech on the future of the Democratic Party and a tour of Southern states, which played an outsize role in competitive primaries. The plan didn't call for Newsom to directly say Biden should step aside. They figured he wouldn't have to; the message would be obvious.

Murphy and Newsom weren't the only politicians making plans. J. B. Pritzker, who had deployed his family's hospitality fortune to become governor of Illinois, scheduled a speech at the New Hampshire Democratic Party Annual State Convention in June—an obvious step toward competing in that state's first-in-the-nation primary. Some aides to Pete Buttigieg, the polyglot wunderkind of the 2020 primary who went on to become Biden's transportation secretary, were pushing him to consider another presidential run, even if Biden ran; Buttigieg dismissed the idea. Donors were talking up Governors Roy Cooper of North Carolina and Gretchen Whitmer of Michigan, California Congressman Ro Khanna toured the industrial Midwest, and even Senator Bernie Sanders was open to another run at the White House, despite being a year Biden's senior. Democrats were putting plans in place not only in case Biden voluntarily chose not to run but also in case Biden was unable to complete his first term, or became medically unable to run for a second.

Early in Biden's presidency, former President Barack Obama privately told allies that he did not think Biden should run again. Obama had never thought all that much of Biden's political skills. He picked Biden as his running mate in 2008 to compensate for his lack of foreign policy and Washington experience. A real bond formed between them, however, especially after Biden lost his son Beau to brain cancer in 2015. Obama delivered an emotional eulogy at Beau's funeral and later awarded Biden the Medal of Freedom. But Obama discouraged Biden from running for president in 2016, favoring Hillary Clinton, and Biden, who thought he could have beaten Trump in 2016, regretted taking Obama's advice. That made Obama's counsel unwelcome, and he knew better than to tell Biden directly not to seek reelection, even as he grew increasingly anxious about the president's age and his ability to mount a vigorous campaign against Trump, whom he feared Democrats continued to underestimate.

No one outside Biden's inner circle seriously believed he would run. He would be eighty-two by the end of his first term, and eighty-*six* by the end of a second. His political standing looked precarious: staff at the Democratic National Committee recorded a massive drop-off in enthusiasm for Biden, as measured by a shrinking community of online volunteers. Ambitious young Democrats saw a midterms thrashing as the perfect time to begin pushing Biden aside. They had no idea that Biden was secretly facing another political time bomb, which would have devastating consequences.

On October 12, 2022, Pat Moore, one of the president's personal attorneys, was sent to complete a seemingly mundane task that no one else had wanted to do: clean out Biden's private office, which had sat unused for years. The office was in the Penn Biden Center for Diplomacy and Global Engagement in Washington, one of several sinecures created by the University of Pennsylvania for Biden after his vice presidency. The center, which included a full-scale replica of Biden's West Wing office, was housed in 101 Constitution, a vanity address steps from Capitol Hill with a rooftop known for lobbyists' parties and a Charlie Palmer Steak in the lobby.

As soon as Moore opened the door, he realized his task would not be so simple. There was way too much stuff—the sitting president was a hoarder. He found drafts of speeches (including a binder of addresses Biden had given on every St. Patrick's Day dating back decades), silverware engraved with Biden's and Obama's names (handed out to donors by the Democratic National Committee), a portrait of Hillary Clinton (for reasons unclear), nearly two dozen boxes of condolence letters after Beau Biden died, and piles of challenge coins (souvenirs modeled on military missions). Moore needed to come back with some help.

On November 2, Moore returned with a new young associate to sift through the boxes. Personal files, including photographs and letters, would be sent to Biden's residence in Wilmington. Material that could be relevant to congressional inquiries, related to Biden's activities after he left the White House in 2017, would go to Moore's law office in Boston for review. In one of the boxes, the associate discovered a manila envelope marked "EYES ONLY." The folder was labeled "IRAN." The associate brought it to Moore, who had previously held security clearance because of his work in the Obama White House. He had an idea of what the folder might contain. He opened it and, as he feared, discovered documents marked "Classified."*

An experienced government lawyer, Moore knew that it was not an option to repack the box and back away slowly; he had an obligation to report the discovery through appropriate channels. He also knew, as did anyone who was remotely politically conscious, that Trump was already under investigation for mishandling classified documents. Biden had slammed Trump's treatment of national secrets as "totally irresponsible." Moore took a seat and thought to himself, *Well, this is going to be something.*

His first call was to Bob Bauer, the president's main personal lawyer, who sat at the intersection of law and Democratic politics. A professor at New York University with a gray beard and shaggy white hair, he had long been a top lawyer for Democratic candidates and the party, positioning him to serve as White House counsel for Obama.

"Are you in a place where you can talk?" Moore asked.

After Moore told him what he had discovered, Bauer consulted top

---

*Ironically, the first document he found turned out to be the most sensitive.

White House officials, including Anita Dunn. Bauer and Dunn were married, and the couple had enmeshed themselves in Biden's inner circle at the end of the Obama administration, when Biden was considering running for president and most other Obama aides dismissed him and wanted to help Clinton. Dunn and Bauer stuck with Biden after he decided to hold off in 2016, and they went on to become key players in his 2020 presidential campaign.

Dunn, a forty-year veteran of Democratic politics with a short bob of white hair, was a mercenary. She rose from an intern in Jimmy Carter's White House to a top aide to two Democratic presidents and, between stints in government, built a multimillion-dollar fortune at a political consulting firm. She held all the grudges that Biden claimed he never had; in 2020, she refused to give former Housing Secretary Julián Castro a speaking slot at the Democratic National Convention because during the primary he'd suggested Biden was senile. As a senior adviser in the White House, Dunn built a large and loyal following, in part because her political consulting firm served as a revolving door for top communications jobs.

Shortly after Moore spoke to Bauer, Biden's lawyers alerted lawyers at the National Archives and Records Administration, one of whom replied by pointing out that this was not the first time something like this had happened—a likely reference to Trump. The White House then started working with the Justice Department, confident the president and his team had not intended to take classified materials. Aides were adamant that haphazard packing by low-level staff at the end of the Obama administration was to blame (an excuse not unlike the ones Trump was making), and that once the Justice Department figured that out, the case would go away.

Some aides would advocate for publicly disclosing the discovery right away. Others worried an announcement would annoy the Justice

Department and prevent a quick resolution. They ultimately decided to keep quiet, hoping to maximize cooperation with the DOJ—and not, they insisted, because the midterm elections were only six days away. In case the details leaked, a top lawyer in the White House drafted a matter-of-fact statement explaining that classified documents had been found in Biden's personal office, and the White House was cooperating with law enforcement. The lawyer then filed the statement away in his desk drawer. Later, some aides joked that Moore should have eaten the documents and taken the secret to his grave.

Biden had never actually promised to be a one-term president. During his 2020 campaign, he called himself a "bridge" to a new generation, and people heard what they wanted to hear. His top aides remained adamant the president was the party's best candidate. His advisers understood his age would probably be his biggest challenge, but one they thought he could overcome, like he did in 2020. That attitude sometimes blinded them to how much he'd aged in the job. When David Axelrod, a former top adviser to Obama, raised the president's age as a concern in an interview with *The New York Times*, he received an angry phone call from Ron Klain, the president's chief of staff. Klain wanted to know what Axelrod was trying to accomplish. "There's no Obama out there, Axe," Klain said. "Who's going to do it if he doesn't do it?"

Biden was a man who'd first introduced himself to his in-laws by saying he wanted to be president—of the United States, he had to clarify. He ran three times over thirty years and in 2020 he finally won, even after everyone told him he was too old and he should drop out after losing Iowa and New Hampshire. Now, those same naysayers suggested he should be a one-term president. Why should he stop now? The way Biden explained it, he'd passed historic legislation, put the first Black woman on the Supreme Court, and mobilized the transatlantic alliance to counter Russia. The world was on edge, the country was divided, and America needed an elder statesman to hold it all together. Biden had finally reached the pinnacle of his career, and he believed he was doing a good job. Historically good. If polls showed Americans disagreed, Biden argued that was just because they didn't yet know about all the good he'd done. He still had two more years to show them, and he would. If he didn't run again, he would be a lame duck. He would start to wither away. His son Beau, before he died, told him: you have to stay engaged in public life.

As proud as they were of Biden's legislative accomplishments, his staff understood that none of that would matter if Biden lost to Trump. That loss would define his legacy. They also recognized that if Biden didn't run, he'd face enormous pressure to endorse his vice president, Kamala Harris. Biden's aides, and many of his supporters, didn't believe she was ready for the job—at least not yet. Her office was as dysfunctional as her presidential campaign in 2019. Staff fought with each other constantly, and then a steady stream of them departed. Harris largely stopped speaking to her first communications director after three months in office. She also had no signature achievement to tout. She botched one of her first assignments, to tackle the root causes of migration—defined by a disastrous interview with Lester Holt during which she seemed baffled by the question of why she had not visited the southern border. "I haven't been to Europe," she responded. Polling showed she was even more unpopular than Biden. The president's aides believed Trump would eat her for lunch and have American democracy for dessert.

Harris was also aware of her doubters and had been taking steps to change her trajectory. In late summer 2021, she brought on two senior advisers, Lorraine Voles and Adam Frankel, to help with organizational development, strategic communications, and long-term planning. Their roles were meant to be temporary, to help the office get back on track. Voles never left. Harris had asked Voles to diagnose the problems in her office, and Voles identified many, but also told the vice president it started at the top.

Harris's chief of staff, Tina Flournoy, had served in the same role to Bill Clinton in his postpresidency and was one of the highest-ranking Black women in Democratic politics, part of a group that called themselves the Colored Girls. But staff viewed Flournoy as indecisive and secretive, and they started leaving the office, fueling the storyline that plagued Harris throughout her political career: that no one wanted to work for her. Harris agreed staff changes were necessary, and Voles became her chief of staff. Voles, and the new team she brought in, went on to improve Harris's relationship with the West Wing. They also helped the vice president develop relationships with reporters and found issues to champion that better played to her strengths.

In May 2022, immediately after a draft opinion showing the Supreme Court was poised to overturn *Roe v. Wade* was published, Ron Klain walked down the hall in the West Wing and into Harris's office. He had a proposal for her: "If this really is where the Supreme Court comes down, we're going to set up an administration task force to deal with actions we'll take, and someone needs to lead that," he told her. "And I think you should lead that."

"Well, do you think it's going to be real?" Harris asked. "Are we going to do real stuff?"

Klain encouraged her to talk to Biden, but he started to outline various executive orders and agency-led efforts to protect access to abortion. "It's not the issue the president's most comfortable with personally, and you've got a great voice on this issue, and you should do it."

Harris had reservations. She didn't want to take on the issue just because she was the female vice president. "I don't want it to be symbolic," she said.

Klain persisted. "It's a substantive effort that needs a political leader," he said. "I can't send [Health and Human Services Secretary] Xavier Becerra to go speak to state legislatures about fighting the right."

Still, Harris wasn't sold. "Send me some paper on what we'd do."

A few days later, Klain arranged for Jen Klein, the director of the White House Gender Policy Council and the staffer who would oversee the task force, to meet with Harris to discuss the specifics of the policy work. Harris agreed to lead it. As Biden, a devout Catholic who long held personal reservations about abortion, struggled to champion reproductive rights, Harris became the administration's most forceful and effective messenger on the issue that would prove to be Democrats' advantage in the 2022 midterms.

Six days after Moore's discovery, officials set up two war rooms at the White House to track the midterm results. The most senior Biden aides gathered in the Roosevelt Room, the conference room just off the Oval Office, stocked with pizza and soda. The junior staff holed up in a conference room in the Eisenhower Executive Office Building, just across the street. The president spent most of the night in his small study next to the Oval Office, juggling calls to Democrats as the returns started to pour in. Around 10:30 that night, when it was declared that Abigail Spanberger would keep her frontline House seat in Virginia, Biden aides started to exhale. It wasn't going to be a blowout. Biden spent much of the night on the phone, mostly making congratulatory calls to newly reelected governors and members of Congress. By midnight, relief turned into jubilation, and aides started sending around a clip from Biden's interview with the *New York Times* editorial board in early 2020. "You all . . . declare me dead, and guess what?" Biden says in the video, slapping the shiny conference room table. "I ain't dead. And I'm not going to die."

In the midterms, the Democrats picked up a Senate seat and won almost every toss-up House seat, only narrowly losing their majority. For Biden, that success was the ultimate validation of his worldview. The polls had said he would lose. The press and the pundits, even many of his fellow Democrats, had counted him out. In his mind, the results had proven that they were all wrong, as they had always been about him. He was the only one who'd ever beaten Trump, and he doubted whether anyone else could again.

It was customary for the president to hold a press conference the morning after the midterms, and Biden used the occasion to claim victory. Other Democrats argued that the party beat expectations *despite* Biden, not because of him. Voters had turned out because they were outraged by the Supreme Court's decision to overturn *Roe v. Wade* and motivated to oppose the Trump-worshipping, election-denying Republican candidates. But to Biden and his closest advisers—Mike Donilon, Bruce Reed, and Steve Ricchetti, all longtime loyalists in their sixties— the midterms were just the latest example of everyone underestimating Biden to their detriment.

Biden's victory lap, however dubious, was enough to silence the young upstarts. Though other Democrats thought Biden was learning the wrong lesson from the midterms, they didn't plan to challenge him directly. Newsom never gave a big speech about the future of the Democratic Party. Murphy and Pritzker never moved forward either.

Still, Biden's top advisers recognized they could not afford to sit still: They had to act now to remove any obstacles to the nomination. The first two nominating contests were traditionally held in Iowa and New

Hampshire, and both states were historically hostile to Biden. In 2008, Biden finished fifth in the Iowa caucuses with less than 1 percent of the vote, forcing him to drop out. In 2020, he finished fourth in Iowa followed by fifth in New Hampshire—a devastating one-two punch that had some allies fearing he would again have to drop out of the race.

Losing or even narrowly winning the first two primaries would be especially humiliating for a sitting president, so Biden's team decided to shift the primary calendar onto friendlier terrain. The effort was led by Dunn, Ricchetti, and Jen O'Malley Dillon, the White House deputy chief of staff. O'Malley Dillon had risen through the party ranks as a field organizer, overseeing the battleground states for Obama's 2008 presidential campaign. She had served as the deputy campaign manager on Obama's reelection, developing a reputation as the party's best whiz at building campaigns and efficiently deploying people and resources around the country. In 2020, Dunn had recruited her to Biden's campaign after O'Malley Dillon had initially run Beto O'Rourke's primary flameout. She eventually became Biden's campaign manager, even though she was a newcomer by Biden standards.

Dunn, Ricchetti, and O'Malley Dillon capitalized on existing agita over the primary calendar, which traditionally gave an outsize role to two small, overwhelmingly white states that were increasingly mismatched with the demographics of the Democratic coalition. There was already a process under way to change the order. DNC members decided to prioritize states that held primaries (instead of caucuses), were demographically diverse, and were competitive in the general election. Those considerations doomed Iowa, which met none of them, and set off a beauty pageant among other states seeking to move to the front of the line. Nevada and New Hampshire dispatched their senators to lobby the DNC members.

On December 1, those members gathered at the Omni Shoreham

Hotel in Washington for dinner before a vote the next day on a final order. The Nevada delegation, including both its senators, Jacky Rosen and Catherine Cortez Masto, hosted a reception to try to win over members and knock out New Hampshire. But around 7:00 p.m., when the members walked back into a small conference room, they were given a printed letter from the president. He proposed his own order: He wanted South Carolina first, followed by New Hampshire and Nevada on the same day. Georgia and Michigan would go next and hold their contests in the subsequent weeks. "I feel like I just got kicked in the stomach," Rebecca Lambe, one of the Nevada officials, told a committee member after reading Biden's letter.

South Carolina, which voted for Republicans in every presidential election since 1980, hardly met the committee's criterion of being competitive. But the state's significance to Biden was obvious. It was where his 2020 candidacy was resurrected, thanks in large part to the endorsement of congressional eminence Jim Clyburn. But Clyburn hadn't lobbied for South Carolina to jump the line; he just wanted South Carolina to remain the first primary in the South. The state's representative on the rules committee was also unaware of the president's plan—her jaw went slack.

Biden also said the committee should review the calendar every four years, making very clear that this was a onetime deal to benefit himself. He didn't care what the primary schedule would look like for future Democrats. The president usually gets his way with the party's central committee, and so despite some initial protests, the committee got on board and approved Biden's proposal.*

With the calendar overhaul complete, O'Malley Dillon and Dunn set

*The final order shook out slightly differently due to Republican resistance to changing primary dates in Georgia.

out to contain the ambitious young Democrats at Biden's heels. While these elected officials publicly supported Biden, they were not shy about telling donors in private or reporters anonymously that they had serious reservations about Biden's ability to run and beat Trump. Even if he could, many of them still wanted the prize for themselves. To solve this problem, O'Malley Dillon proposed gathering the party's rising stars on a "national advisory board." The board would have no official responsibilities, but its members would be called on to travel and fundraise for Biden's campaign and appear on TV. It would include nearly all the potential challengers: Murphy, Newsom, Pritzker, Cooper, and other past or likely future contenders such as Senators Cory Booker, Elizabeth Warren, Amy Klobuchar, and Raphael Warnock, as well as Governors Josh Shapiro of Pennsylvania and Wes Moore of Maryland.

The arrangement would serve both camps: The younger Democrats could raise their profiles, while helping Biden get reelected. Not that they would have any say in the matter. When a reporter reached out to Klobuchar's office about her joining the Biden-Harris national advisory board, her aides had no idea what it was. Many of the board members had never agreed to serve and learned about their participation from reading it in the press.

Even though the midterms were a success by historical standards, the GOP still won control of the House of Representatives, which presented a problem for Biden's son Hunter. He was facing investigations into his overseas business dealings, taxes, and lying on a federal form about his drug use. Many Republicans, including incoming Oversight Committee chairman James Comer, had spent nearly two years attacking him, promising to investigate him as part of a broader effort to try to impeach his father. Neither Hunter nor Biden's other surviving child, Ashley, wanted to deter their father from running for a second term, but everyone knew the family would be put through the wringer again, distracting if not emotionally devastating the elder Biden.

At the same time, Hunter Biden was growing frustrated with his team's legal strategy. He had taken Bauer's recommendation to hire Chris Clark of Latham & Watkins to represent him in the federal investigation into his taxes. Clark advised Hunter to keep his head down, cooperate with the Department of Justice, and avoid unnecessary media attention—a strategy that Bauer supported. But Kevin Morris, a wealthy Hollywood entertainment lawyer turned benefactor who lent Hunter Biden money to pay back his taxes, had a different approach. He thought Hunter should fight back against the Republican attacks, many of them unfounded. Morris connected with David Brock, the former Republican opposition researcher turned Democratic operative, who recommended Hunter work with Abbe Lowell. Lowell, a longtime Washington lawyer known for aggressive, public fights, spent most of his career working for Democrats, like Senator Bob Menendez of New Jersey, as well as Republicans, including Ivanka Trump and Jared Kushner.

Lowell's hiring prompted Josh Levy, a lawyer experienced in congressional investigations, who had joined Hunter's legal defense on Bauer's recommendation, to leave the team. With Morris, Brock, and Lowell, Hunter shifted to a more aggressive posture, suing Fox News for publishing explicit images of him, and Rudy Giuliani for allegedly manipulating data from his laptop.* Hunter wanted to rehabilitate his tattered public reputation. He was done hiding.

---

*Hunter Biden dropped both lawsuits in June and July 2024.

Just Business

Shortly after Trump's campaign launch, his small staff all left Palm Beach for the Thanksgiving holiday. Trump took the opportunity to dine at Mar-a-Lago with Ye, the rapper formerly known as Kanye West. Ye was losing fans and business partnerships because of his anti-Semitic outbursts, but he had always been complimentary of Trump, so the former president would not turn him away. Ye brought with him Nick Fuentes, a young man Trump insisted he did not recognize, but who turned out to be a far-right internet personality known for white nationalism and misogyny. Then, on December 3, Trump responded to disclosures from Twitter, under its new owner, billionaire Elon Musk, about the platform's moderation during the 2020 campaign. "A Massive Fraud of this type and magnitude," he wrote on Truth Social, "allows for the termination of all rules, regulations, and articles, even those found in the Constitution."

"What the fuck?" Chris LaCivita said when he saw the post. "Why is he saying that?" He thought about quitting, but he decided to give Trump a chance to explain himself. The boss's case was less than compelling. He said he didn't really plan to terminate the Constitution. "That's not what I meant," he said.

"Well, that's what it says," LaCivita replied. He asked Trump to clear it up publicly, and Trump followed up with a new post denying what he had said and blaming the media for twisting his words. In less than a month on the campaign payroll, Trump was already testing LaCivita's limits. But he decided to stay, partially because he'd started to like Trump.

Susie Wiles expected the campaign to bring some level of craziness. The Ye/Fuentes dinner was too crazy. She set up new procedures to try to prevent another self-inflicted wound like that. Trump would not be left completely unstaffed again; someone from the campaign (often her) would be around him at all times.

She also needed to reduce Trump's idle time, when he was prone to posting self-sabotaging all-caps social media screeds, and instead channel his energies into activities that played to his political strengths. Since the official campaign launch, Trump had done precious little campaigning, partially because his signature mega rallies were expensive and cumbersome, and partially because it was too early in the cycle to make them count. Through December, he barely left Mar-a-Lago, except to play golf. The few interviews or speeches he gave were live streamed rather than in person.

After the disappointment of the midterms, Republican voters needed time to forget why they were mad at Trump, and he needed to find ways to remind them what they loved about him. There was such a thing as too much Trump. Wiles set out to fine-tune his level of exposure. He started recording videos communicating directly with his supporters, excoriating Biden and unveiling fresh promises for a second term. Trump became engrossed in the videos, recording them back-to-back, doing take after take, until he was sure that he'd gotten it just right.

Some advisers appreciated Trump could blow off steam on Truth Social without attracting as much attention as he used to get on Twitter.

At the start of 2023, Trump was ready to go out on the road again. The campaign experimented with smaller-scale events: an indoor theater rather than a fairgrounds. The crowds of a thousand or so were still large by the standards of any other politician, and they were much easier to stage than mega rallies. The events produced just as much press coverage and gave Trump less opportunity for incendiary improvisations. In February, the campaign added an unannounced drive-by at a McDonald's near East Palestine, Ohio, the site of a disastrous train derailment. Aides were thrilled to see how the visit generated viral cell-phone videos of the former president shaking hands and signing autographs. Trump and his team came to see the visit as a turning point, when Trump found his stride. The campaign started adding more retail visits, which looked spontaneous, though somehow word always got around so Trump fans knew to show up with hats and signs. The events showcased Trump's celebrity appeal, his knack for making someone feel special with a smile—all emphasizing a contrast with his leading rival for the Republican nomination.

DeSantis emerged from the midterms as the great shining hope of Republican politicians, operatives, donors, and even many voters who thought it was time to move on from Trump. His popularity in Florida, fueled by economic growth and his largely hands-off approach to the coronavirus pandemic, seemed to offer a rubric for bipartisan appeal. Even if Florida was not the swing state it had been in 2000, DeSantis had flipped the Democratic stronghold of Miami-Dade County. His young and telegenic family offered an alluring contrast to Biden. He was unafraid to take on the media or supposed sacred cows like Disney, one of the state's largest employers. DeSantis pitched himself as a more disciplined Trump, someone who could not only talk a big game but actually deliver policy wins, with a similar knack for defying the laws of political gravity. He was attractive to the party's grassroots activists and its richest billionaires—a rare ability to combine money with the base.

"All the callers into my show were asking about DeSantis," conservative radio host Erick Erickson recalled. The earliest primary polls at the outset of 2023 showed DeSantis trailing Trump by just 10 points. At the first cattle call of the presidential primary, held in Las Vegas by the Republican Jewish Coalition, Trump refused to share the stage after a private audience with megadonor Miriam Adelson fell through, and appeared via video feed. The top billing instead went to DeSantis, who stomped onto the stage in cowboy boots and finished by gladhanding a busload of cheering college kids.

But DeSantis didn't announce his campaign right away. He decided to take his time and focus on the upcoming state legislative session. His plan was to use the session to rack up right-wing policy wins—expanding his controversial restrictions on classroom discussions of gender and sexuality (known to its critics as "Don't Say Gay"); authorizing people to carry concealed guns without a permit; banning abortion at six weeks—and then campaign on the promise to achieve the same successes at the federal level. He was an effective governor, and that was going to be the message.

The late launch was not entirely within DeSantis's control. Florida had a "resign-to-run" law, which prevented a sitting governor from running for president. If he wanted to run while also keeping his job, DeSantis would need the state legislature to change the law. But that would have to wait until the end of the session, in May 2023, or else lawmakers would lord it over him and block him at every turn.*

---

*A DeSantis adviser denied the resign-to-run law affected the governor's plans.

In the meantime, he embarked on a book tour, a well-worn ruse for staging campaign-style promotional events without triggering federal campaign finance rules. After the first event, a February book signing at the Lake Square Mall in Leesburg, Florida, Trump saw a viral video of a small group of MAGA-capped supporters with Trump signs rallying outside in the parking lot, until a police officer came to tell them to leave. "They told me anybody wearing Trump has to go right now," the officer said in the video, posted by the pro-Trump blogger Laura Loomer. Trump called Loomer to thank her, saying she'd exposed "DeSanctimonious," as Trump started calling him, as a disloyal Trump hater.

Trump called Brian Ballard, a leading Tallahassee lobbyist who had long represented Trump in private business and was also close to DeSantis. Ballard was the one who DeSantis had pressured to oust Wiles from his firm. When Trump came to Washington, Ballard expanded his practice, becoming a favored lobbyist for Fortune 500 companies and foreign governments. Mastro's Steakhouse in Washington put a plaque above a table signaling it was always reserved for Ballard. Over the years Trump ribbed Ballard for making money off their relationship, knowing that Ballard also bundled tens of millions of dollars for Trump's political operation. But this time Trump wasn't kidding around when he pointedly accused Ballard of helping DeSantis.

Ballard said he wasn't, but he acknowledged that some other lobbyists at his firm were raising money for the governor—they had to, it was their business. Trump wouldn't hear it. "You need to put out a statement saying he's a bad governor," he said. "Charlie Crist was a better governor." Ballard said he couldn't, plus he thought DeSantis was actually doing a good job. Trump told him that DeSantis was going to lose. Ballard assured Trump he would help him soon. Within days, he resumed his role as a top fundraiser for Trump.

Wiles wasn't the only Trump adviser who had a history with DeSantis.

Deputy campaign manager Justin Caporale and Jason Miller also worked for him in the past. Wiles had a disciple named James Blair who worked with her on Trump's 2020 campaign and DeSantis's 2022 campaign. Thirty-three and hungry, with a young family in Tampa and a shaved head that gave him the look of an enforcer, Blair was fiercely loyal to Wiles. He served as DeSantis's deputy chief of staff, leaving shortly before Wiles did. Blair believed DeSantis wasn't the Republican savior that others wished he was, and started working for MAGA Inc., the main pro-Trump super PAC.

The super PAC's first round of data on the primary landscape showed a single threat to Trump: DeSantis. He was within striking distance. He had consolidated much of the Never Trump remnant of the party, galvanized online influencers, and taken the sheen off Trump. And he had convinced many Republicans that he was electable against Biden, which they feared Trump was not. They were the voters who said, "I wish he would stop tweeting."

Pollster Tony Fabrizio reviewed the results with Blair and Taylor Budowich, who rose from Don Jr.'s body man to Trump's spokesman and now CEO of MAGA Inc. "We have to squeeze him from the left and the right," Fabrizio said. "We have to firebomb him while he's still on the runway."

The goal was to reposition DeSantis from the conservative shining star to a wooden figure uncomfortable in his own high-heeled cowboy boots. "Nobody wants to vote for the guy who is a weird nerd loser," a Trump adviser said.

The campaign and the super PAC both took advantage of aides' personal experiences with DeSantis to target his insecurities—his image, his appearance, his intellect, his manners. Staff swapped anecdotes about DeSantis's relationships with lobbyists, how he treated his staff, his personal habits, his political weaknesses, how much they disliked him. Blair predicted getting under DeSantis's skin would provoke him to start making mistakes and blaming them on others. "We tried to make it as personal as possible, and they took the bait every time," said Alex Bruesewitz, an adviser to the super PAC. One aide likened it to a psychological warfare operation, designed to get inside DeSantis's head and disable him. Another adviser, paraphrasing *The Godfather*, shrugged it off as simply running a political campaign. "It's just business."

A story appeared in *The Daily Beast* alleging that DeSantis was once seen eating chocolate pudding with his fingers, and Blair wanted to turn it into an attack ad. The ad featured a reenactment of the offending dessert interspersed with clips about DeSantis's record on Social Security. Blair showed the script to Budowich, who thought it was disgusting. Blair asked Budowich to let him make it, show it to Fabrizio, and if they didn't want to air it, then he'd pay for it out of his own pocket. Fabrizio loved it. The super PAC announced a million-dollar ad buy for the spot, generating a burst of headlines. But the ad aired exactly once: After that, the PAC rotated it out for more serious spots directed at Republican primary voters. The pudding fingers ad was just for Ron. No one in the press noticed the trick.*

Trump allies found it similarly straightforward to stir up news stories for the sole purpose of piquing DeSantis. Operatives said Blair spread a rumor that the governor was taking the weight-loss drug Ozempic. (People in Tallahassee *were* saying it....) Trump allies sent a reporter screenshots of DeSantis wearing a fleece vest in ninety-degree heat, clearly to streamline his midsection. Every time DeSantis held a fundraiser, the hosts got whacked with a negative news story. A June 2023 article pitched by the super PAC knocked DeSantis for raising money from a lobbyist

---

*Trump told people he did not like the ad because it was too gross. But the pastry chef at Mar-a-Lago got in on the joke. A lawmaker who visited Trump was treated to a dessert of chocolate high-heeled cowboy boots filled with pudding. A spoon was provided.

for Anheuser-Busch, the parent company of Bud Light—the same brand DeSantis was condemning over an advertising deal with a transgender TikTok star.

DeSantis repeatedly grew frustrated with the tactics. He wanted to run a campaign about policy and attack Trump from the right, for not being conservative enough. He told aides he was so tired of discussing his attire, or his eating habits, or long-ago stories in Tallahassee.* Republican voters would not care, he argued privately.

Trump was surprised by how easy it turned out to be to mess with DeSantis. He took up the term "groomer," which DeSantis had popularized to accuse the LGBTQ community of preying on children, and used it with an old photo of DeSantis at a party with high school girls, baiting, "He would never do such a thing!" He dramatized the story of how DeSantis came begging for his endorsement "with tears in his eyes" and told reporters that if not for his endorsement, DeSantis would be working at "a law office, Schwartz, Schwartz and Schwartz" or "maybe a Pizza Hut." He recorded a Truth Social video summing up: "The problem with Ron DeSanctimonious is that he needs a personality transplant, and those are . . . not yet available!" Trump urged his team not to let up. "We want to destroy him for 2028!" In one meeting, Wiles showed Trump polling of him winning over DeSantis, and he noticed her smile as she briefed him on some of the attacks. "You might hate him more than I do," he said.

---

*A DeSantis adviser denied that the governor cared.

Inevitable

On a sunny afternoon in March 2023, a group of Republican political operatives played a round of golf at Trump's course in West Palm Beach, near Mar-a-Lago. Afterward they retired to the clubhouse grill and were surprised to learn they could sit anywhere in the small restaurant, even one table over from the former president of the United States, without any security screening. Trump was reclining in his chair, looking relaxed and carefree. After the group received burgers served on buns stamped with the owner's name and face, one of the Republicans, Michael Goldfarb, walked over to Trump.

Goldfarb was the top political adviser to Paul Singer, the hedge fund billionaire who led a network of major Republican donors called the American Opportunity Alliance. Singer and his circle were not Trump fans (never had been), but they had not thrown their money behind anyone else in the primary either. Goldfarb asked Trump to sign his cap, and Trump smiled and obliged. They made small talk for a bit, and then Trump gave Goldfarb a message for Singer. "He'll say he's against me the whole time, but we know how it's going to turn out," Trump said. "Just have him be for me now."

Goldfarb laughed and returned to his table. Before tucking back into his burger, he whispered to his companions, "He's probably right."

They had all seen the research that Republican operatives were sharing with donors, pitching them to invest in campaigns against Trump. The data wasn't compelling. In focus groups, when Trump supporters were confronted with anything negative about Trump, they'd say they either didn't care or didn't believe it. You could show them violent criminals released under his sentencing reform bill. You could show them how little wall he'd actually built on the Mexican border. They'd insist he'd done a good job, or blame the Democrats for fighting him at every turn. The party's biggest donors had spent fortunes trying to stop Trump in 2016, and all it got them was diminished access to his White House. They weren't about to throw good money after bad, at least not without proof of concept predicting a return on investment.

Donor interest in stopping Trump did not increase as the primary went on. A few months later, Singer and other top donors summoned Republican National Committee chairwoman Ronna McDaniel to Dallas for a meeting. McDaniel didn't know what they wanted to discuss but was excited to have the audience, so she rearranged her schedule to make the trip. At the meeting, Goldfarb presented a montage of clips that he said showed bias by Kristen Welker, the new host of NBC's *Meet the Press*, who the RNC had picked to moderate an upcoming primary debate. The RNC was organizing the debates because of widespread regret over the free-for-all forums during the 2016 primary, which Republicans came to view as too numerous and badly moderated. McDaniel decided that this time her staff would set the qualification criteria and choose the media partners. As a result, she became the punching bag for everyone's complaints about the process.

The donors wanted the RNC to cancel the debate with Welker and partner with conservative outlets instead. One suggestion for a moderator was an editor at *The Washington Free Beacon*, a right-wing website that Singer funded. McDaniel politely declined, telling the donors she was trying to introduce the party to new voters. She left stunned, asking her staff if that was really what she'd come for.

Trump had reason to be acting so relaxed and confident at the golf club. Not only was he dominating the primary polls, his lawyers and advisers assured him that he was not facing criminal charges imminently, if ever. Trump started joking that there was still time to order a special set of golden handcuffs. Much of his optimism came by way of his lawyer, Boris Epshteyn.

Epshteyn wore three-piece suits and drove a Bentley because he liked the large B on the hood. "B for Boris," he told people. He ate at the Palm steakhouse in Washington for lunch almost every day and bragged about having his caricature on the wall. Since graduating from Georgetown, where he met Eric Trump, he had never tried a criminal case (though he had appeared as a defendant, pleading guilty to disorderly conduct after a late-night fracas at a Scottsdale bar in 2021). Epshteyn had a hand in both the legal and political sides of Trump's operation, and he indulged Trump's impulses to fight prosecutors at every turn. Trump liked Epshteyn, viewing him as unfailingly loyal.

Wiles, on the other hand, constantly complained about Epshteyn, and she wasn't alone. Another of Trump's attorneys, Christopher Kise, repeatedly told others how misguided and uninformed he thought Epshteyn's approach was. Kise, a well-respected former Florida solicitor general, was the kind of heavy hitter who handled complex, high-profile, high-stakes cases. He had a long-standing relationship with Wiles and joined Trump's team in September 2022. To justify leaving his cushy Big Law job, Kise insisted on getting paid three million dollars up front.

Once he was on the team, he recommended trying to settle the classified documents case. He said there was a path to work with the government to avoid prosecution. "Take the temperature down," Kise argued. Epshteyn disagreed and badmouthed Kise to Trump. He wanted to keep fighting the government and never admit anything. The lawyers clashed for an entire weekend, until Trump sided with Epshteyn.

Epshteyn's ace was his unflinching focus on protecting his standing with the only person who mattered. While other staffers focused on doing their jobs and staying out of Trump's way, Epshteyn would rush to call Trump with the latest breaking news. If there was nothing new, he'd recycle old information. "He's the good news fairy," another adviser said. "Just a shameless suck-up." One Epshteyn associate remembered a lunch when Epshteyn called Trump twice in two hours to congratulate him on public statements that Trump had just released. Trump was not oblivious to the ploy. Once, when Epshteyn called him in early 2023, Trump held the phone up to other advisers at his golf club, put Epshteyn on mute, and said, "I could be hauled away in a police car for twenty-three felonies, and Boris would call and say, 'Everything's great!'"

By March, the Manhattan district attorney had invited Trump to testify before a grand jury in the hush money case, a possible sign that the investigation was nearing its conclusion. In Atlanta, the DA investigating interference in Georgia's 2020 presidential election results said a charging decision could come within weeks. The federal special counsel, Jack Smith, had interviewed Trump allies and advisers several times. Nevertheless, Epshteyn said Trump was not going to be indicted anytime soon. He was not alone in his thinking. Several of Trump's lawyers were preparing to take some time off, expecting a few quiet weeks ahead. Instead, on the afternoon of Thursday, March 30, they were informed that Trump had been indicted in the hush money case in New York. The arraignment would be on the following Tuesday.

Trump would often ask out loud what his parents might think about his being indicted. He would quip that they didn't teach indictments at the Wharton School of Finance. Trump had had many brushes with the law before. In the 1970s, federal prosecutors accused Trump, his father, and the family's real estate business of discriminating against Black and Puerto Rican tenants, leading to a settlement with no admission of guilt. In the '80s, he worked closely with an FBI informant to expand his casinos and real estate holdings, and New Jersey authorities examined possible mob ties before granting Trump a casino license. The '90s and 2000s brought more state and federal scrutiny surrounding his Atlantic City casinos, and in 2013, the New York attorney general sued his for-profit business school for fraud, leading to a $25 million settlement. As president, he faced two impeachments, a special counsel probe, and multiple congressional investigations.

Being indicted was different. Trump was at turns shocked and deflated, then angry and irritated. At his club, members came up to express their support, and he responded by showing off his upcoming book (a collection of letters to and from celebrities and world leaders).

Trump desperately needed a lawyer, so he turned to Epshteyn. Epshteyn recommended his own lawyer, Todd Blanche, who had also represented Paul Manafort.

The assignment was intriguing to Blanche, a forty-eight-year-old marathon runner who worked at the white-shoe firm Cadwalader, Wickersham & Taft. Just as he had done with Manafort, Blanche approached his firm's executive committee about taking on the new client. The partners had been fine with Manafort, but they voted against Trump. Sorry, he couldn't do it, they wrote. Trump was too toxic.

Blanche responded to the executive committee's denial within a few minutes. He quit. The firm's leaders were stunned. They wanted him to stay for a few months to transition his other cases, but Blanche said he was going to be appearing in court with Trump in three days. That expedited his departure. Some of Blanche's friends told him they, too, were shocked and angry that he would work for Trump. He told them it was hard to turn down an opportunity to represent a former president of the United States.

Blanche soon learned how representing Trump would challenge his calm demeanor. Trump would regularly tell him he needed to be more aggressive and gave him pointers from other lawyers with fewer qualifications (often Mar-a-Lago members). When the judge set a trial date for March 2024, Blanche thought it was a win—far off in the future. But Trump berated him with obscenities and thought about getting a new lawyer. Blanche eventually calmed him down.

Epshteyn hadn't been designated to accompany Trump into the courtroom for the arraignment, but he maneuvered his way inside anyway, appearing at Trump's side in photos and courtroom sketches beamed around the world. Trump's other advisers stood outside, gobsmacked by Epshteyn's nerve. On the flight back to Mar-a-Lago, Epshteyn asked someone to bring him a Diet Coke, and LaCivita snapped. He grabbed a can and tossed it at Epshteyn: "Here's your fucking Diet Coke!"

Trump spent part of the plane ride sitting alone, stewing about the indignity he'd just suffered. He was trying to project strength and defiance publicly, but he was personally humiliated. "Can you fucking believe they indicted me?" he kept asking. He seethed that some aides didn't seem to care as much as he thought they should.

The plane landed in West Palm Beach, and the passengers motorcaded to Mar-a-Lago for another ballroom speech, an affair that one attendee dubbed the world's first "arraignment reveal party." Trump's aides processed before him down the center aisle like bridesmaids, underscoring the absence of the candidate's wife. Eighteen years earlier, the ballroom's inaugural event had been Trump and Melania's wedding reception; now, she was missing from his side as he faced charges arising from cheating on her with a porn star shortly after the birth of their son.

After the speech, Trump ate a late dinner and stayed up until about 2:00 a.m. deejaying for a small group of aides and guests. When Trump played "Justice for All," a mash-up of him reciting the Pledge of Allegiance and the National Anthem sung by inmates held at the DC jail on charges connected to the January 6 riot, everyone stood up and put their hands over their hearts. He was tying their fates together as victims of government persecution, giving life to his campaign motto, "They're not after me, they're after you, I just happen to be standing in the way." The criminal jeopardy that pushed Trump to run in the first place would now increasingly dominate his campaign, since winning back the presidency was his surest path to staying out of prison.

Trump woke up the next day around 6:00 a.m. and started calling associates to ask about the news coverage of his arraignment. His aides were struck by the outpouring of support from Republicans, collecting statements from six governors, twenty-six senators, House Speaker Kevin McCarthy, sixty-three other House Republicans, and ten state attorneys general. The Trump campaign quickly fielded polls showing that Trump's support in the Republican primary was topping 50 percent and growing. Armed with that data, his aides lobbied Capitol Hill, arguing that Trump would be the nominee and Republicans should endorse him sooner rather than later. He would remember who was with him and when. A burst of congressmen and senators jumped on board, citing the indictment as a tipping point and talking about Trump as the inevitable nominee. Even other presidential hopefuls rushed to Trump's defense. "I was a little surprised," Trump later said in an interview for this book. "I was impressed because they were campaigning against me. And every single one of them just about came out and said, 'This case is ridiculous.'"

The sole exception was Ron DeSantis, who initially responded to the news of Trump's indictment with a cutesy dig at the tawdry details underlying the case. "I don't know what goes into paying hush money to a porn star to secure silence over some type of alleged affair," DeSantis said. "I can't speak to that." DeSantis and his team were flooded with blowback, which caught them by surprise. He quickly reversed course, suggesting that if Trump refused to surrender to New York State authorities, he, as the governor of Florida, would refuse to cooperate in extraditing him. "We should have known it was over right then," a top DeSantis adviser said later. His campaign had not even officially started yet.

DeSantis's official presidential launch was originally supposed to take place in May, on a pitcher's mound. As a kid, DeSantis had been a promising young hitter and outfielder, playing in the Little League World Series and going on to captain the baseball team at Yale. But DeSantis had another idea. He sometimes spent hours a day scrolling through Twitter, and he was obsessed with right-wing influencers and thought they could propel him to the Republican nomination. DeSantis told advisers he wanted to announce his campaign on a live audio broadcast on Twitter's "Spaces" feature with the site's new owner, Elon Musk. Some of his advisers believed it was a mistake: The classic approach was a classic for a reason. But DeSantis thought the move would show how his campaign was different, and he would not be dissuaded.

On the night of the announcement, May 24, 2023, the technology did not work. DeSantis could not get a word in until twenty-five minutes after the event was supposed to start. "Nobody knew what the fuck was going on," donor Dan Eberhart remembered. He called his brother to ask if he could hear either. "No one knew what to do." Eberhart asked DeSantis advisers what he should tell reporters, and they told him to say

DeSantis was so popular he had crashed the website. Eberhart chuckled to himself and thought he might have backed the wrong candidate. "That was the moment I knew the campaign was in trouble," he said. It was day one, and DeSantis had struck out.

The Trump team watched the debacle with glee. "They can't even get this right," Wiles said to others.

As the DeSantis campaign struggled to get off the ground, Trump's aides had their hands full with new subpoenas, long sittings in front of grand juries, and even agents knocking on their doors. Wiles spent several uncomfortable days testifying as prosecutors asked which classified documents Trump had shown her. LaCivita joked that he was the only one around Trump who was "subpoena free in '23."

After the New York hush money case came the first federal indictment, accusing Trump of mishandling classified documents and trying to stop the government from recovering them. His team worried about the case because prosecutors had extensive evidence, much of it provided by his own advisers. Trump turned the arraignment, in Miami in June, into a campaign spectacle with a protest/MAGA street festival outside the courthouse (organized by Laura Loomer, so the campaign could say it wasn't involved), an unannounced stop at the iconic Cuban restaurant Versailles, and a prime-time speech at Bedminster.

Smith indicted Trump again in August, on charges connected to his efforts to overturn the 2020 election. The arraignment in Washington was Trump's first return to the capital since leaving office, and the campaign and the Secret Service were furious with the DC police for declining to close off the interstate between the airport and the courthouse, leading to a stomach-churning motorcade ride through traffic. The motorcade exited the highway near a soup kitchen, and Trump winced at the sight of graffiti and homeless people, followed by mostly silent spectators recording on their phones. He was so dismayed by the experience that he only briefly addressed reporters at the airport and took no questions. The campaign discussed visiting the Capitol or the DC jail, where some January 6 defendants were held, but the timing and security arrangements didn't work out.

Two weeks later came the fourth and final indictment, in Atlanta. The district attorney, Fani Willis, charged Trump and eighteen codefendants—including former White House Chief of Staff Mark Meadows and lawyers Rudy Giuliani, Sidney Powell, Jenna Ellis, and John Eastman—using the state's convoluted racketeering law to accuse them of conspiring to overturn the 2020 election.

As the Trump indictments dominated the news, the DeSantis campaign's daily media surveys often showed Trump getting twenty-five or fifty times more coverage. "Nothing we do is breaking through," Nick Iarossi, a Tallahassee lobbyist and the DeSantis campaign's finance co-chairman, told others. "We're losing the earned media war." Campaign aides began to joke that maybe DeSantis should try getting arrested. DeSantis himself lamented the campaign's listlessness in a conversation with Iarossi and Mike McClellan, a college friend and the finance co-chair. What was the bumper sticker? What was the message? What was the reason for voters to pick us other than we aren't Trump?

To put together a majority or even a plurality, DeSantis needed to appeal to moderate Republicans who didn't like Trump on one end, far-right Republicans who thought Trump didn't go far enough on the other, and still peel off some solid Trump supporters in between. DeSantis wanted to emphasize policy, contrasting Trump's shortcomings with his accomplishments. But that story didn't connect with most Republicans, who viewed Trump as the most successful president of their lifetime, and it stood no chance against the visceral bond that many Republicans still felt for him, especially with the string of indictments.

DeSantis replaced his first campaign manager with the chief of staff from his governor's office, James Uthmeier, who had no campaign experience. Uthmeier reviewed the campaign's research into how to attack Trump. Watching the focus groups was surreal. Voters would watch videos of Trump himself saying something they didn't like and just say they didn't believe it. The campaign decided that DeSantis would not proactively attack Trump and only address him if asked directly.

The DeSantis campaign wasn't alone in grasping in vain for ways to dent Trump. One allied effort found that voters' affinity for Trump was so strong they would contradict their own stated opinions to justify supporting him: Voters might agree with a position in the abstract, but when the moderators identified Trump with the opposite position, those same voters would switch sides to realign with him. Test ads that contrasted Trump's position with another candidate's position backfired because voters viewed it as an attack on Trump. Trump's opponents were so desperate that nothing was off-limits; one DeSantis-aligned operative sent mail pieces to Christian conservatives in Iowa purporting to praise Trump as a supporter of gay marriage and trans rights. Even if they could find the right line of attack, some Republican strategists and ad makers told donors they wouldn't work on anti-Trump efforts because the Trump campaign would retaliate by blacklisting them from congressional clients.

As DeSantis stumbled that summer, his Florida archrival, Senator Rick Scott, reconsidered his earlier decision not to join the presidential primary. He, too, commissioned research looking for Trump's weaknesses. In one focus group, when Trump supporters were shown the facts about his shortcomings on building a border wall, one woman explained that Trump must have done that on purpose, in order to funnel the migrants through gaps where they could be apprehended more readily. Scott decided to stay out of the race.

There was one crack that spooked Trump's camp. In a September interview on *Meet the Press*, Trump criticized DeSantis for signing a ban on abortions after six weeks of pregnancy, calling it "a terrible mistake." Iowa had an identical law, and the state's popular Republican governor who signed it, Kim Reynolds, called Trump out for it. A *Des Moines Register* poll found a majority of likely caucus goers said they disagreed with Trump's comments and that abortion was important to their vote. News reports said a pro-DeSantis outside group was preparing to launch an ad campaign on the issue, but the abortion attack ads never came. The DeSantis campaign's research showed attacking Trump on the six-week abortion ban probably wouldn't work.

By August, the primary field expanded to include former UN Ambassador Nikki Haley, businessman Vivek Ramaswamy, former Arkansas Governor Asa Hutchinson, Senator Tim Scott of South Carolina, former Vice President Mike Pence, North Dakota Governor Doug Burgum, former New Jersey Governor Chris Christie, former Texas Congressman Will Hurd, and Miami Mayor Francis Suarez. Hurd and Suarez didn't meet the polling and donations threshold to make the first debate and would soon drop out. As was customary, the RNC scheduled the first debate to coincide with a site visit to the convention venue in Milwaukee.

Trump said he didn't want to debate before Labor Day, thinking fewer people would watch. When the RNC set the date for August 23, Trump said he wouldn't come. McDaniel flew to New Jersey and begged him to attend. "If you don't debate, Biden won't agree to debate you," she said. He still said no.

"Why would I debate?" he explained his decision to donors, according to an audio recording. "They're not dummies, they're good with their mouth. That's why they're politicians. Why would I subject myself to being ridiculed, shouted at, and screamed at. People are demanding an intelligent president, not a stupid president."

Skipping the debate was a gamble. Trump went over the decision with his top advisers again and again. Aides discussed the possibility of scheduling his Fulton County booking on the same night, to draw attention away from his rivals. But they ended up choosing the following day. Trump wanted to leave himself the option of attending the debate after all. Up until the night before, he polled his advisers on whether he was making the right call. He did not want to look afraid of anyone, and there was a chance the other candidates could gang up on him when he wasn't there to defend himself.

As it turned out, Trump was barely mentioned during the first full hour of the debate. Finally, the moderators addressed "the elephant *not* in the room." They asked for a show of hands: "If former president Trump is convicted in a court of law, would you still support him as your party's choice?"

Ramaswamy's hand shot up first, like an overeager teacher's pet. Haley followed. Then Tim Scott and Doug Burgum. DeSantis looked around, saw the others, and joined. So did Pence.

Next to Pence, Chris Christie shook his head. The former New Jersey governor believed the only way to beat someone was to beat them. He felt some personal responsibility for having endorsed Trump in 2016, a decision he came to regret; this Trump was different from the person he used to know—his sense of humor and irony replaced by bitterness and anger. Christie had heard, over the years, every one of the other candidates (except Ramaswamy) say privately they thought Trump was reprehensible. But he was the only one in this field willing to directly attack Trump. Christie walked offstage shaking his head "over the fact that these folks would absolutely prostitute themselves that way," he later said in an interview for this book. "That's the day the primary ended."

"This is over," McDaniel privately told senior members of her team as the candidates left the stage. Trump was going to be the nominee.

The next day, Trump flew to Atlanta to turn himself in at the Fulton County Jail. All eighteen codefendants had already done so, producing a procession of awkward mug shots. Trump's aides shared a meme of the mug shots styled like Halloween costumes, or photoshopped their own portraits onto the Fulton County Jail's backdrop. But Trump's own mug shot was no joke. He was determined to get it right and practiced on the flight down. "You only get one shot," he told advisers. "You don't get to take it again."

A phalanx of white-helmeted motorcycle cops led the motorcade from the airport through historic Black Atlanta. Trump's advisers looked out at the crowds gathered to watch from sidewalks and balconies. Some heckled, but some cheered. Wiles later told others it was the most surreal experience she'd ever had in politics. The crowd's display bolstered the Trump team's confidence in polls showing he had a real opportunity to sand down the Democrats' overwhelming advantage with Black voters. Outside the jail, Loomer had assembled another crowd of supporters, but Trump didn't see them because the motorcade took a different route.

The jail, known in Atlanta by its address on Rice Street, consisted of two asterisk-shaped cell-block towers surrounded by razor wire and a low-slung windowless administrative building. It looked less like a real-world corrections facility than a horror film set, the kind of place people seldom left alive. Seven inmates had died there so far that year, often with little public information to account for the circumstances. The sheriff called the conditions "a humanitarian crisis" after the discovery of one dead inmate, covered in bedbugs and lice, prompted a federal investigation. Unidentifiable stains covered the walls inside. The concrete was crumbling, leaving hunks of debris that the prisoners collected and sharpened into shanks. Toilets overflowed. The air-conditioning broke.

Obviously a man who lived most of his life in a gold- and marble-decked triplex fifty-six stories above Fifth Avenue had never been anywhere like this. Trump entered with just his lawyer and a few Secret Service agents, while his staff waited outside in the motorcade. He was focused on his mug shot. The jail didn't make it easy: The photograph was taken from above, at an awkward angle, at only a moment's notice.

The photo came out with Trump's signature scowl. He and his advisers thought he nailed it.

Sleepwalking

Joe Biden decided to run for reelection by not deciding. He told aides: I'm running until I tell you I'm not. And he never told them he wasn't. There was no decision memo, outlining the case for and against. Some aides worried that if they told Biden that he should not run, they would be accused by the president and his closest advisers of disloyalty. So no one ever said anything. The closest any of them came was calling to his attention the difficulties he would face as a candidate.

In April 2023, the president and the first lady sat in the White House Treaty Room with Bob Bauer, his lawyer. Bauer brought a presentation outlining the legal challenges that lay ahead for the president's family, specifically his son Hunter and his brother James. Anyone who had ever worked for Biden knew his family's travails were his kryptonite; when he ran for president in 2020 and Hunter's business dealings emerged as a flashpoint in the campaign, Biden confided in aides that if he had to lose the race over Hunter, that would be okay. Jeff Zients, the new White House chief of staff, had asked Bauer to review the status of the ongoing challenges the family faced. They wanted the Bidens to know Hunter's legal troubles were not going away and would intersect with much of the presidential campaign. The Department of Justice was continuing its investigations into Hunter. Republicans in Congress were investigating his overseas business dealings for what would later turn into an impeachment inquiry. Hunter was also involved in a child-support case over a child he fathered with an Arkansas woman, and ethical questions lingered about the sales of his paintings, which a New York gallerist was listing for $75,000 to $500,000 apiece—prices that critics said the works would never fetch without the artist's surname. The White House helped set up a system in which the dealer would conceal the buyers' identities.

With Hunter's paintings as his main source of income, the family was growing concerned about how he could continue to afford high-powered Washington lawyers like Abbe Lowell, who was defending him in both criminal and congressional investigations. At one point, the family asked senior White House aides to consider whether the president could help his son raise money for his legal bills. The question became more urgent amid concerns that Lowell might drop Hunter as a client if the bills weren't paid. Hunter found out the Democratic National Committee was paying President Biden's legal fees arising from the classified documents investigation, taken over by a special counsel, Robert Hur. Hunter asked why the DNC could not pay his legal expenses too. Lawyers ultimately decided the president should not be involved in fundraising for Hunter, and the DNC could not justify picking up the tab for the president's son.

Hunter's legal troubles were not the only concerns haunting some Biden aides. Zients and Anita Dunn had serious reservations about the octogenarian's ability to win, but they largely kept those concerns to themselves. As the reelection campaign took shape, Dunn would oversee the communications and press operation, reassembling the army of loyal lieutenants who both worshipped and feared her. The chief strategist, it went without saying, would again be Mike Donilon. Described as Biden's alter ego and conscience, Donilon started working for Biden in 1981, and Biden grew to trust him reflexively, particularly on messaging and advertising. A creature of Washington, Donilon shunned the spotlight, appearing at society events only because his wife, Trish, loved them. He showed no interest in managing anyone or anything. Aides joked that if Donilon was the White House chief of staff, he would cancel all meetings and ban email.

The final piece of the campaign—the operational side—would be handled by Jen O'Malley Dillon. The relationship between Dunn and O'Malley Dillon had frayed in the early days of Biden's presidency, and the two argued about the right approach to the reelection. Dunn thought O'Malley Dillon should leave her White House position to run the campaign, formalizing her work building an operation from the ground up. But O'Malley Dillon resisted because she did not want to uproot her family from Washington or spend more time away from her three small children. She had agreed to work in the White House after Biden won but made it clear she did not want to run the reelect, figuring she would leave for the campaign only in the final stretch. Also, power in Bidenworld depended on proximity to the boss.

After O'Malley Dillon's refusal, Biden's senior team set out looking for someone else who would serve as a campaign manager in name only. The leadership group, which was almost exclusively white, male, and over sixty, converged on two top candidates. The first, Julie Chavez Rodriguez, was a top White House staffer and granddaughter of labor legend Cesar Chavez. Chavez Rodriguez was well liked among the staff and especially by Biden's closest allies. She brought deep ties to elected officials throughout the country and had experience on several campaigns, although she had never actually run one—normally a prerequisite for a presidential campaign. But that could be overlooked because she would not be substantially fulfilling the duties of a traditional campaign manager.

The second finalist was Quentin Fulks, a Black Georgian in his early thirties who had just managed Senator Raphael Warnock's successful reelection. Fulks had never worked for Biden and had no relationship with any of Biden's senior team, which to some aides was a benefit. Ultimately, O'Malley Dillon wanted someone she knew and trusted to carry out the vision set by her and the senior team. Chavez Rodriguez got the top job, and Fulks, after some convincing, became the number two.

To launch Biden's reelection, the leadership team decided against staging a large public event or rally. Instead, the announcement would be the same as in 2019, a slickly produced video shared on social media, intended to activate the small-dollar donors who Biden needed to fund a campaign against Donald Trump. Filming was scheduled for April 16, and Biden's longtime campaign videographer and his producing partner were hired for the task. The crew scripted and plotted the footage, along with the other visual elements needed to illustrate Biden's words, and planned to record with the president at his vacation home in Rehoboth Beach. But as the date approached, the campaign lawyers flagged a problem. Payment for the filming of the video would formally trigger a fifteen-day countdown to announce the campaign, in accordance with campaign finance regulations. O'Malley Dillon wasn't sure they were ready; the campaign organization was still taking shape.

Aides asked the lawyers for options. What if they didn't pay the video team until later? Didn't matter. What if they filmed different versions of the video, including one where Biden declared he would not seek reelection? The lawyers still said no. One alternative the lawyers presented was to film a wide range of footage that could be used for other political purposes. But the political officials considered that too costly and time-consuming. Biden would have to officially file his paperwork for the

2024 presidential election. Aides checked the president's calendar, but it was too complicated to reschedule. The official launch became another decision made by default.

Two days before the shoot, on April 14, thousands of people lined up at security checkpoints, waiting for hours in cold, spitting rain. They were undeterred, even joyous. They danced. They waved flags. They sang. At last, Marine One clattered overhead, and the crowd roared—a rave reception like the one that usually greeted Trump. But for once it was Biden being greeted by twenty-seven thousand people packed onto both shores of a riverbank, and he strolled onto the stage like a rock star, strobe lights flashing around him, to the crashing strains of the Dropkick Murphys.

It was the largest and most jubilant crowd Biden had ever assembled as president—a dream setting to launch his reelection campaign. The only problem was that Biden could not be elected there. He was in Ireland, not the United States, concluding an ancestral romp accompanied by his sister, Valerie, and Hunter. The speech was the grand finale, and as soon as he walked offstage, Biden started his journey home, where no crowd would be waiting for him. Most Americans, including the majority of his party, did not want him to run again. His announcement would be in the dining room of his Delaware vacation home, with just a handful of aides.

At the last minute, the video crew learned about a change to the script. Donilon had completely rewritten it. The new script centered on January 6, opening with images of Trump's supporters attacking the Capitol. Those images were unshakable for Donilon and Biden alike. They often lunched together in the private dining room off the Oval Office, reminding themselves that it was where Trump sat watching the riot on TV, doing nothing to stop it. In Donilon's hands, the core message of Biden's campaign would be protecting freedom and democracy. The script made scant mention of the economy, only that Republicans would seek to cut taxes for the wealthy.

Biden sped through hair and makeup and entered his dining room early as the video crew was setting up. He dressed in his casual presidential look—dark blazer with American flag lapel pin, open-collared blue dress shirt, no tie. He was preoccupied by the latest mass shooting (four dead at a sixteenth birthday party in Dadeville, Alabama) and he showed little interest in filming. He wanted to get it over with. He read off a teleprompter for a handful of takes.

A little more than a week after the shoot, on April 25, four years to the day since he launched his 2020 campaign, the video went live. Overlaid with moody Instagram filters and available in a format designed for iPhone viewing, it crosscut between scenes of rioters at the Capitol, abortion-rights protesters outside the Supreme Court, and the White House. Biden appeared for only a few seconds. The signs of age—crepey skin, liver spots, deep forehead wrinkles, and thin, combed-over white hair—showed through despite extensive cosmetic work. That day, he made two public appearances—at the North America's Building Trades Unions Legislative Conference and the Korean War Memorial with the president of South Korea—but only one oblique, passing reference to his newly launched campaign. He told the union workers, "It's time to finish the job."

I n June, just over a month after the announcement, Biden traveled to Colorado Springs to deliver the commencement address at the Air Force Academy. Dunn happened to be traveling with the president that day. After his speech she was already en route to the motorcade when she got a call from Annie Tomasini, an aide who was almost always at Biden's side and managed his life like a surrogate daughter. She told Dunn the president had fallen.

"Where did he fall?" Dunn asked.

"On the stage," Tomasini responded. "He tripped over a sandbag."

The video was devastating for the octogenarian who was already trying to overcome fears he was too old for the job. "I got sandbagged," Biden said to Jeffrey Katzenberg, the billionaire movie producer who became a cochair of the campaign to help with fundraising, and a few other high-dollar donors who met him back at the White House.

"Personally, I'm thrilled that happened," Katzenberg replied, according to someone who overheard the conversation. Biden appeared surprised, and Katzenberg explained the fall would prompt staff to ensure it never happened again. Seventeen months before Election Day, the fall was a blip; if it happened closer, it would be a disaster.

Senior White House officials spent the next several weeks working to update protocols for how Biden moved around and walked on and off stages, looking for ways to limit obstacles. The president started using a shorter staircase to board Air Force One, instead of the grand eighteen-foot movable staircase. He started wearing sneakers more often while traveling. Aides enveloped him when he walked across the South Lawn to board Marine One, to obscure his ataxic gait. He cut back on the nighttime dinners on foreign trips when other heads of state would socialize. Some White House aides worried about the first lady or vice president overshadowing him with their own international travel.

The officials who planned events at the White House tried to avoid any surprises or unpredictable situations. If the president was going to speak, he would go to the podium, deliver remarks from a teleprompter, and leave. There was no room for creativity or spontaneity. Everyone could see the president was aging. He sometimes failed to recognize former staff at functions. Still, current aides insisted his decline was strictly physical, and even then they acknowledged it only by trying to Bubble Wrap the president and avoid any more catastrophes. Staff limited direct access to the president, keeping meetings with him small.

For months, Katzenberg had encouraged the president and his team to lean into age, citing the successful examples of Harrison Ford starring in another *Indiana Jones* sequel and Mick Jagger performing on a world tour. At the same time, Katzenberg implored Biden and his aides to prioritize his health—particularly his sleep, exercise, and nutrition. Biden needed eight hours of sleep, and when he fell short of that, staff could tell he wasn't on top of his game. Katzenberg also encouraged Biden to cut back on travel and unnecessary appearances to conserve energy. Staff could also see when he wasn't regularly meeting with his physical therapist, noticing his gait would stiffen significantly. Katzenberg worried Biden's raspy voice exacerbated concerns about his age. He repeatedly urged Biden and his aides to have the president see an ENT doctor and a voice coach to help him improve. His suggestion went unheeded.

Katzenberg had more success raising money and allaying high-dollar donors' fears about the president's fitness for the job. He did so by inviting them to meet with Biden in intimate settings, either at the White House or on the road. During the sessions, usually with only a handful of people, donors could ask the president questions on any topic. Donors often left satisfied with the president's ability to converse on a wide range of topics, which helped pad the campaign's coffers after years of isolation for Biden during the pandemic and the early part of his presidency.

That summer, Kamala Harris had dinner at her official residence at the Naval Observatory with two of Biden's longtime confidants, and she questioned them about the campaign strategy. She was

particularly anxious about third-party candidates, a cast of fringe char-
acters including Cornel West and Jill Stein, as well as a hypothetical
candidate from the centrist group "No Labels." The environmental and
health activist Robert F. Kennedy Jr. was also challenging Biden in the
primary, with the foreseeable threat of going independent. "Why are we
not shutting these third parties down?" Harris asked. She was also concerned that Biden seemed too tepid in attacking Trump. "Why are we
not moving more aggressively?" she asked. Biden's confidants were surprised that Harris expressed her concerns to them and not the president.

Obama had the same concern and took it straight to Biden. Despite
their complicated relationship, the presidents remained in touch, so it
was not unusual when Obama swung by the White House in June for a
private lunch in the residence. For a while it genuinely felt like two old
friends catching up. They discussed their families and summer vacation
plans. Biden planned to take his family to Sunnylands, the former home
of publisher Walter Annenberg, in California, which Obama had visited
multiple times during his presidency.*

But Obama was also there to deliver a message: Trump was going to
be incredibly difficult to defeat for a second time, and he was worried
about Biden's candidacy and lack of urgency. Trump had an intensely
loyal following, Obama told Biden, not to mention a robust Trump-
friendly conservative media ecosystem. (The Democrats had no equiva-
lent.) The country, Obama reminded his former vice president, remained
deeply divided, and tens of millions of people would support Trump no
matter what. He also warned Biden not to overschedule himself as he
mounted his reelection campaign. Obama pledged to do anything he
could to help, and indeed got started before he left by filming videos to
help Biden with online fundraising. In one clip, Obama reminded

*The Biden vacation was ultimately scrapped because of concerns about extreme heat.

Democrats he had "won a couple of these" elections, causing some of Biden's aides to roll their eyes. There was a lot of overlap among aides to Obama and Biden, but to Biden loyalists, Obama was a prick. They thought he and his inner circle had constantly disrespected and mistreated Biden, despite his loyal service as vice president. They felt vindicated when, for the first time during Biden's presidency, Obama publicly returned to the White House and began by saying "Thank you, Vice President Biden." Obama was quick to claim he was joking, but to Biden's stalwarts it was merely the latest example of Obama's arrogance.*

The Biden campaign opened its headquarters in the president's hometown of Wilmington, Delaware, chosen at his insistence despite concerns about the impact on recruitment that led his last campaign to pick Philadelphia instead. Still, the power center remained in the White House. Chavez Rodriguez did not have the final say on anything important. No one in Wilmington had a direct line to the president. The campaign staff wrote memos to the senior advisers in Washington, who discussed them with the president, in meetings that only sometimes included senior campaign officials. As they feared, even though Biden was the only national campaign for Democrats to work on, officials still struggled to attract top talent, both because people did not want to move to Delaware and Biden did not personally inspire many people.

The stress of the job was taking a toll on Chavez Rodriguez, who was widely respected in the White House, but became more volatile in Wilmington. She yelled at staff at all levels, even those who she did not know well.† She sometimes embarrassed specific staff members in group

---

*An additional strain on the Obama–Biden relationship was the fraught relation between their spouses. Michelle Obama was close friends with Hunter Biden's ex-wife, Kathleen Buhle, because their daughters had attended Sidwell Friends School together, and she resented how the Bidens ostracized Buhle after the ugly divorce. A spokeswoman for Jill Biden said the former first lady has consistently maintained a warm friendship with Michelle Obama.

† Chavez Rodriguez denied yelling at staff, saying she sometimes got frustrated but did not yell.

meetings. Staff filed complaints about her behavior with the campaign's human resources department, and word got back to the White House that staff were growing increasingly despondent in Wilmington. The staff began to feel aimless, and were worried about losing valuable time to build out the campaign in the battleground states. They needed to work to win back voters drifting away from Biden.

The president's most pressing problem was the economy. The reopening from the pandemic created pent-up demand from consumers, combined with supply-chain bottlenecks. Inflation was a global phenomenon, but Biden had pushed for a $1.9 trillion relief package that Republicans, and even some Democrats, like Larry Summers, now blamed for overheating the economy. In September 2022, consumer prices rose 8.2 percent over the last year, far outpacing the average of 2 percent annual gains from before the pandemic. The White House settled on calling the price spikes "transitory," a term few Americans recognized. Biden would argue he had seventeen Nobel Prize–winning economists who argued the president's signature economic legislation would ease inflation in the long term. Senator Joe Manchin of West Virginia, who resisted that bill because of his concerns about inflation, told Biden, "You've got seventeen educated idiots."

On paper, all the economic indicators pointed Biden's way, and he felt he should be rewarded for his stewardship. The United States was poised to avoid the recession many economists predicted, wages were up, and employers were adding jobs. But Americans were still feeling the effects of postpandemic inflation, and even though it had slowed, prices remained elevated. Republicans derisively referred to the president's economic policy as "Bidenomics."

Biden and his team thought the public had the wrong impression about the economy, and they could set it straight. Their attitude was, if we don't tell the positive story of the economic recovery, no one will. They set out to appropriate the name "Bidenomics" and build his reelection campaign's economic argument around it. He toured the country, bragging about his record, even as polls showed Americans remained broadly dissatisfied with the economy. Some Democrats worried he sounded tone-deaf. Pollsters wanted the president to take a softer tack and do a better job acknowledging that many Americans were still struggling. To the extent that voters did recognize accomplishments by the Biden administration, they tended not to give the president credit for them because they saw him as out of it. In research conducted by the DNC, voters named Biden's age as a top concern and said they didn't view him as in control.

One time in the Situation Room, House Speaker Mike Johnson was alone with Biden for about twenty minutes. Biden ribbed him, "You're in line to the presidency. And I'm real old." They shared a laugh. Biden started telling stories from his time in the Senate but trailed off. Other times when Johnson asked the White House for a meeting with the president, aides would instead offer senior officials or cabinet members. During one of the only large meetings he attended with Biden, Johnson told others the president was reading notes off a laminated page.

In July 2023, a plea bargain for Hunter Biden collapsed, all but ensuring the president's son would stand trial in the thick of a presidential campaign. Hunter's lawyers had negotiated with prosecutors for him to plead guilty to two misdemeanors for failing to pay taxes in 2017 and 2018, and to avoid prosecution on the gun crimes by enrolling in a diversionary program for nonviolent offenders. Both sides had already agreed to these terms when they showed up at a court hearing, expecting a formality that would end with Hunter reading a statement to news cameras about putting this painful chapter behind him. But the judge started poking holes in the agreement, revealing that the two sides did not have the same understanding of its implications. Hunter's lawyers thought the deal protected him from any additional charges related to a broader Justice Department investigation into his foreign business deal-ings. Prosecutors disagreed, telling the judge that the investigation was ongoing and that the deal did not preclude additional charges.

Biden had no public events that day, as some aides worried about ex-posing him to the press while the hearing unfolded. When the plea deal collapsed, aides were relieved that Biden had no scheduled appearances, so he didn't get any questions about it.

By September, some of Biden's closest aides started to have private conversations about the state of his candidacy and looming challenges, specifically Hunter's legal troubles, Biden's classified documents investi-gation, and the Republicans' impeachment threats. Most of Biden's aides were uniformly subservient, often shying away from direct con-frontation or wading into topics that upset him. That made it all the more extraordinary that a select few of his closest advisers wanted to have one last conversation with the president about his campaign.

The aides planned to encourage Biden to consider how much of his time those problems would take up and the toll they would take on him personally. They would ask him to reflect on his responsibilities as a president, candidate, and father. The filing deadlines for appearing on primary ballots meant that it would soon be too late to turn back from running. The time to decide was now.

But the aides never found the chance to have the conversation with Biden, and no one the president trusted ever told him not to run. Those internal discussions were largely cut short by an October surprise that came a full year early.

On October 7, 2023, Hamas militants broke through Israel's fence on the border with the Gaza Strip, killing more than 1,200 peo-ple and taking roughly 250 hostages. Biden immediately embraced Israel, planned a trip to the region, and promised unwavering support. Yet Israel's response—an unrelenting military campaign, killing tens of thousands of Palestinians, many of them women and children—splintered the Democratic Party coalition Biden needed to win, as young people and Arab Americans, especially in Michigan, started to defect. Senator Bernie Sanders later warned the president the war in Gaza was going to be his Vietnam moment.

The war in the Middle East made Biden's lawyers reconsider his appointment the next day with Robert Hur, the special counsel investigating his handling of classified records. Hur offered to postpone it, and some lawyers and staff thought that might be a good idea. But Biden insisted they go ahead; he wanted to get it over with.

Most of Biden's preparation for the interview with Hur focused on reviewing documents that were more than a decade old. The lawyers gave the president the same advice any client typically receives before a deposition: Answer only the question being asked. No extraneous information. This client, however, was not practiced in depositions and struggled to internalize that advice. And unlike other clients who clear their schedules to prepare for high-stakes legal encounters, Biden didn't have that option. His final prep session was also scaled back because of the crisis in the Middle East.

The president and the special counsel got off to a chummy start. Hur noted that some of his questions would be about events that occurred years ago, asking the president to give his "best recollection." Biden replied, "I'm a young man, so it's not a problem." As the interview proceeded, the joke got less and less funny.

At times, Biden played the storyteller. He went deep into his mental archive, digressing far and wide with colorful details, such as a long-ago legal client who'd "lost part of his penis and one of his testicles" at age twenty-three. When discussing the FBI's extensive search of his house,

Biden winked, "I just hope you didn't find any risqué pictures of my wife in a bathing suit. Which you probably did. She's beautiful." He also recounted disagreements with Obama on Afghanistan, conversations with his wife about his future presidential library, and his administration's foreign policy accomplishments.

As the interview stretched for five hours across two days, Biden appeared forgetful at times. Hur was particularly struck by Biden's inability to identify a fax machine, needing his lawyer to remind him what the device was called—twice. Dates also proved challenging. He asked for clarity on when he became vice president, when he stopped being vice president, and when he announced he was running for president. Discussing events in 2017 and 2018, Biden, trying to situate himself, asked, "What month did Beau die? Oh God, May 30." One of his lawyers interjected that Beau died in 2015. "Was it 2015 that he died?" Biden asked. That exchange was fateful. Shortly afterward, Hur suggested they take a break. Biden refused. "Let me just keep going to get it done," he said.

Biden's inner circle thought the interview went fine. Some aides thought the president's memory could pose a problem; others said it was just Biden being Biden and there was no reason to worry. Biden's lawyers were strictly focused on protecting the president from a criminal case that Hur could charge. They were not focused on the political liability of Biden appearing forgetful.

Hur was more circumspect. After the first day of the interview, he wondered if Biden was playing him or if he really didn't remember anything. He had Biden on tape telling his ghostwriter he "just found all the classified stuff downstairs." The ghostwriter later admitted to deleting additional tapes when he found out Hur had been appointed to investigate Biden. The evidence could have formed the basis for charging Biden with mishandling classified documents and the ghostwriter with obstruction. Biden's scatterbrained interview with Hur might have been the one thing to spare him from getting indicted.*

As the holiday season approached, Biden's approval rating was hovering in the high thirties, nearly the lowest of his presidency, and polls showed him trailing in most of the battleground states. Voters kept telling pollsters and journalists that they did not want to have to choose between him and Trump. Senate Majority Leader Chuck Schumer privately told people he thought Biden would lose, and Elissa Slotkin, the Michigan congresswoman running for that state's open Senate seat, told allies she might not be able to win her race with Biden at the top of the ticket. That would ensure Republican control of the upper chamber.

The night before leaving Washington to spend Thanksgiving on Nantucket, Biden gathered his top political advisers in the White House residence. "Why is my approval rating so low?" he barked.

Donilon replied with his usual explanation: that voters were still unaware of his accomplishments and inflation remained stubbornly high. He promised Biden's numbers would rise as economic conditions improved and the campaign continued to tout his record. "We're on the right track," he said. "We just have to keep working on it."

Biden wanted more ads—always his first proposed solution to any polling problem. Donilon said they were working on it, even though they had already spent $25 million on a fall advertising campaign, unusually early in the cycle. Some advisers thought that spending had been short-sighted, that the money could have been spent on building out operations in the battleground states, or saved for later, when more voters were thinking about the election.

---

*Department of Justice guidance states that a sitting president could not be charged with a crime, but Hur could have recommended charges that would have been brought after Biden left office.

Biden also turned to O'Malley Dillon. "How many offices do we have open around the country? Members tell me all the time we don't have offices in their district." O'Malley Dillon ticked off the places where offices were opening.

Most of Biden's political meetings followed a version of this script, with similar questions and answers. Some of his closest aides felt that he was assessing the reelection with benchmarks from one of his early Senate campaigns from the 1970s or '80s. To Biden, the case was simple: my administration is doling out billions of dollars to communities across the country—or as Senator Joe Biden would say, "I brought home the pork." New bridges and roads were being built. COVID was a distant afterthought. Companies were breaking ground on new semiconductor factories. It might have worked for a Senate campaign. But not for the presidency.

Ron Klain, Biden's first White House chief of staff until February 2023, was worried that Biden was too focused on international conflicts in Ukraine and Israel. To many Americans these were faraway problems.

"I think you're running for president of Europe, not president of the United States," Klain told Biden during one phone call.

"I'm doing what I have to do," the president responded.

Klain urged him to put forward a new agenda. He said voters don't care about what you have done, they want to know what you're going to do in the future. Biden responded that he wanted to be careful about making promises that he wasn't sure he could keep. He already had a great record, he said. That should be enough.

Capitulation

L eading up to the Iowa caucuses on January 15, 2024, a blizzard blanketed the state in a foot of snow, with winds up to fifty miles an hour and temperatures as low as minus fifteen degrees. Nikki Haley had trailed far behind in the state until the first debate, when her strong performance prompted a flood of calls from newfound supporters and wannabe volunteers to her bare-bones Iowa office. Haley focused her attacks on DeSantis, and DeSantis turned his fire on her, squabbling for second place while Trump expanded his lead. Some donors discussed trying to back-channel a truce between DeSantis and Haley, but the idea never went anywhere because it was too late: Haley had the momentum but none of the infrastructure that it took to turn out supporters to seventeen hundred precincts in the bitter cold; DeSantis had the infrastructure but his polls were trending steadily downward. The Florida governor remained in denial, telling an adviser the night before the caucuses that all the surveys showing Trump 30 points ahead were wrong, and he was going to beat Trump 35 to 34.

Trump arrived at his Des Moines hotel not wearing a tie or makeup, and not expecting to see reporters and fans waiting for him in the lobby.

"That's a lot of cold weather!" he said, smoothing back his hair. His campaign canceled most of the final weekend's rallies because of the freeze, but his supporters still lined up for hours outside to see him. Chris LaCivita didn't pack appropriately and hurriedly bought an extra-large North Face, accidentally picking up a women's jacket, leading to endless taunts from his colleagues. Trump and his staff spent most of the weekend holed up in the Hotel Fort Des Moines or other downtown restaurants connected by a maze of indoor skywalks. Their food and bar tabs were often picked up by a group of Florida volunteers who came to phone bank wearing matching bedazzled Trump beanies and American flag jackets, calling themselves the "Ladies Who Lunch." "If you write anything bad about the president, I'll kill you," their leader, Lauren Pizza, told a reporter at the hotel restaurant. She quickly added, "Don't write that!"

On caucus night, Trump summoned LaCivita to his room. LaCivita was wearing his favorite tie, red with a white stripe, made by Italo Ferretti, a brand he'd gotten into on Trump's recommendation. Trump would gently tease LaCivita about his clothes, critiquing the wrinkles around the midsection of his dress shirt, then correctly guess his size and send him three new elegantly wrapped Brooks Brothers shirts with French cuffs.

LaCivita entered the room and saw that Trump had the same red-and-white-striped tie around his neck. "I guess I'm not wearing this one," Trump said, and took it off to pick a different one. It became LaCivita's lucky tie for all the important nights of the campaign.

Trump won Iowa with an outright majority above 50 percent, leaving DeSantis and Haley 30 points behind. The New Hampshire primary was a week away, and DeSantis publicly insisted he was pushing forward, even though his polling in New Hampshire was even worse. For days DeSantis's team went through the motions of scheduling events while he and his top advisers discussed exiting the race. Word spread in Florida that DeSantis had ensconced himself in the governor's mansion and would be dropping out soon. Trump saw a tweet from Susie Wiles replying to a report that the DeSantis campaign cleared its website of upcoming events. "Bye, bye," she posted. She almost never tweeted (her previous post was an accidental exclamation of her own name). Trump asked if it was really her. She confirmed, and they shared a laugh.

In Tallahassee, DeSantis recorded and released a video in which he withdrew from the race and endorsed Trump. An adviser, Phil Cox, gave LaCivita a heads-up just before the video went live. LaCivita promptly offered the Florida governor a plane to come to New Hampshire to campaign with Trump. Doug Burgum, Vivek Ramaswamy, and Tim Scott, who'd all dropped out and endorsed Trump, would be there too. DeSantis declined. He was still stinging from Trump's insults and wasn't ready to see him yet.* He told advisers that he feared Trump could not win a general election.

The Iowa caucuses convinced Senate Republican leader Mitch McConnell that Trump was going to be the nominee again. Trump had few harsher critics left in the party than McConnell, who tried to avoid uttering Trump's name after January 6. Trump repeatedly mocked McConnell's age and appearance and his wife's ethnicity. (His wife, Elaine Chao, had served as Trump's transportation secretary.) The two men had not spoken in more than three years. Even so, McConnell cared most about winning. He recognized that Trump controlled the party, and he didn't want to cause a rift with Senate candidates or make his relationship with Trump into a story.

McConnell dispatched a top aide, Josh Holmes, to speak with LaCivita. The two operatives had known each other for more than a decade.

---

*A DeSantis adviser denied he was still stinging.

Holmes asked LaCivita to open a line of communication, and they began talking almost every day, relaying messages back and forth between their bosses, who still had no desire to speak directly.

As a result, the former president agreed to endorse Senate primary candidates whom McConnell favored, and the Senate leader agreed to endorse Trump in early March—a validation that Trump's team hoped would show the rest of the Republican Party that the primary was over. If McConnell was endorsing Trump, could anyone hold out?

The last holdout was Nikki Haley. In New Hampshire, she had a plausible path to a historic upset. The state's primary was open to independents, who viewed Trump less favorably than registered Republicans. In the past, independents made up as much as 42 percent of the turnout; Haley would have to push that even higher to get within striking distance of Trump.

Juicing independents was the same strategy that Chris Christie was pursuing, and he realized that he and Haley were now splitting that vote and spoiling any chance of beating Trump. Christie thought he should be the one to stay in, because he took a firmer stance against Trump, and he doubted his supporters would come around to Haley, whose only knock on Trump was to say "chaos follows him," as if Trump had no role in causing the chaos.

But Haley picked up the endorsement of New Hampshire's Republican governor, Chris Sununu, one of the party's few other prominent anti-Trump voices. Christie was furious that Sununu chose Haley over him (without even the courtesy of a heads-up) but when one last round of advertising failed to move up his numbers, Christie decided to drop out rather than give Haley and Sununu a scapegoat. In the final moments of his campaign, he predicted backstage on a hot mic that Haley "is gonna get smoked." Christie's son was listening at home and called him screaming, "Hot mic! Hot mic! Hot mic!" His adviser Maria Comella also received a panicked call from Christie's daughter. Christie looked mortified, but later stood by his prediction.

The Trump campaign tried to intimidate Haley by flying in a slew of elected Republicans from her home state of South Carolina, which was next up on the primary calendar—an unmistakable message that she should not risk the humiliation of getting clobbered in the state where she once served as governor. James Blair—the Wiles disciple she'd recruited to the campaign from the super PAC—came to New Hampshire boasting that the campaign would smear Haley so badly she would regret daring to stay in the race. Once she was out of the picture, Blair said the campaign would take over the RNC and clean house. (He had unsuccessfully sought to become the RNC political director in 2022.) "We'll put on the RNC like a skin," he said, grinning. "Then we'll start raising real money."

As for Biden, Blair said the campaign planned to emphasize Hunter Biden's legal problems in order to cancel out the charges against Trump. They planned to exploit Israel's war in Gaza to fracture the Democratic coalition: "We haven't even started pouring gas on that fire." And they would pressure Biden to debate, confident of having the advantage either way. "If he won't, it proves he's incompetent," Blair said. "If he does, he displays his incompetence."

Trump caught another break with the implosion of one of his criminal cases. The Atlanta DA, Fani Willis, saber-rattled about putting Trump on trial for months, spanning Election Day and Inauguration Day. Her case became harder to doubt as several of Trump's codefendants—lawyers Sidney Powell, Kenneth Chesebro, and Jenna Ellis, and bail bondsman Scott Hall—pleaded guilty. But metro Atlanta courthouse gossip focused on Willis's choice of a deputy. Nathan Wade had never worked on a felony prosecution before, much less one so high stakes, high profile, and complex, and he was billing $250 an hour; his compensation had already surpassed more than $500,000 dollars. Suspicions that Wade was underqualified and overpaid made their way to the attorneys for Trump's codefendants. One of them, Ashleigh Merchant, who represented former campaign aide Mike Roman, learned from Wade's former law partner that he and Willis were in a romantic relationship.

Merchant revealed her allegations in a January court filing that instantly became a media sensation. The evidence, though, was incomplete, and many lawyers, including Trump's, were skeptical that Willis could have been so reckless. That didn't deter Trump. He'd already baselessly accused her of having an affair with a gang member. He told his attorney, Steven Sadow, to congratulate Merchant, and Trump helped the allegations explode across right-wing media. Substantiating the affair and trying to use it as a reason to disqualify Willis from the case would be a long-drawn-out process in court. But politically, the damage was done.

On the day of the New Hampshire primary, January 23, 2024, Trump visited a polling place in Londonderry, and a reporter asked him how he planned to reconcile with Haley's supporters. He waved off the question: "I'm not sure we need too many." In a similar spirit of impunity, a couple of Trump staffers spotted a reporter on the phone nearby and started pelting him with snowballs. The rest of the team was in Nashua, at a Sheraton designed like a Tudor castle, where the watch party would be. The hotel was the nicest around, but that didn't stop LaCivita from complaining that his room's closet was "in the shitter!" and the hotel's bar closed early. LaCivita, who does not usually smoke, bummed a cigarette and had his picture taken holding it in front of a No Smoking sign out front.

In the evening, the Sheraton ballroom began to fill up with the Republicans Trump had invited, as well as some he hadn't—such as disgraced fabulist congressman George Santos, who arrived in a black trench coat. Backstage, Trump exploded at the first batch of exit polls showing a surprisingly tight race. He started berating his staff—Why was the margin so close? He even cursed about donors present, singling out casino magnate Steve Wynn, who had yet to open his checkbook for Trump's bid. "He hasn't given a fucking dime," Trump said. Wynn always had advice but had not yet cut a check.

The former president really lost his temper when the televisions showed Haley taking the stage to speak. She said she wasn't dropping out, "this race is far from over." Trump was furious that she had beaten him to the cameras, hogging the best broadcast time and making him wait to deliver his own remarks, as if she were the one declaring victory that night instead of him. "Can you fucking believe this?" he asked before walking out to speak.

Trump's rage energized Haley's team. This was the one-on-one, head-to-head showdown that Haley had always wanted. A crowded field helped him by dividing the opposition. Haley thought she could be the last woman standing. She was polished and poised, whereas Trump couldn't control himself. She could win over rooms. She liked to remind people that she'd never lost an election, and she didn't intend to start now. She didn't flinch when someone from the Trump campaign put a birdcage outside her Des Moines hotel room, a symbol of the former president's demeaning nickname for her.

Most analysts joined Trump's campaign in puzzling at how Haley could keep going after losing New Hampshire by 11 points. She insisted she still had a path. Most of the upcoming primary contests allowed independents to participate as well, keeping alive her hope of pulling off upsets. Asked in late February to explain why Haley was still running, Sununu answered earnestly, "To be president."

It didn't feel like a dying campaign. She still drew crowds. She still met inspired young girls who gave her beaded friendship bracelets like Taylor Swift fans. She kept running for them. She was not beating Trump head-to-head as she hoped, but she was still pulling about 40 percent of voters despite a mathematically vanishing path to the nomination. The polls continued to show that most Americans didn't want a Trump–Biden rematch. Haley kept saying, "The first party to retire its eighty-year-old candidate is going to be the party that wins this election."

Paul Singer's donor network invited the Trump and Haley campaigns to deliver their competing pitches in a private room at the Four Seasons in Palm Beach. Wiles presented a slideshow with data on the Republican electorate in key states. Her goal was to overwhelm the billionaires with numbers and show them how Trump's current campaign was different from the past: They were prepared. Wiles impressed the crowd with a long presentation on delegate math—how the campaign had changed the nominating rules in early states to Trump's advantage, and he was all but guaranteed to win.

Singer asked what Trump was looking for in a vice president. Wiles avoided specifics, but said Haley had less of a chance every day she stayed in the race. Another donor pressed Wiles on tariffs, saying how they would hurt the economy. "Would Trump really put sixty percent tariffs if he got back into office?" the donor asked. Wiles threw up her arms and said Trump was being provocative to have a negotiating position. She wasn't pitching policy. She was pitching inevitability. Wiles impressed the donors, who'd long seen Trump's operation as dysfunctional. They believed an adult was finally in charge. After the meeting, several of the donors told Trump fundraiser Meredith O'Rourke they'd start writing checks.

Haley's top aide, Betsy Ankney, followed with a different kind of pitch. While waiting to go on, she'd read a new report saying Trump had spent more than $50 million on legal bills. She used the news to make a blunt case about Trump's weaknesses: He would keep shedding voters he needed to win, and the GOP would keep losing general elections with him as its standard-bearer. She reminded the donors, many of whom she knew personally, that Trump was changing the party in ways they didn't like, and Haley was closer to their traditional conservative positions on fiscal and foreign policy.

"It's an uphill battle," Ankney acknowledged. "The odds are against us." But she was equally blunt about the stakes. "If we don't get this right," she said, "it won't change." Haley lost South Carolina by twenty points, and Trump made sure to declare victory within minutes of the polls closing. She lost every state on Super Tuesday except Vermont, and dropped out the next day.

At the start of February, Trump summoned RNC chair Ronna McDaniel to Mar-a-Lago for a meeting. "I think it's time for a change," he said on the phone.

McDaniel had been Trump's personal pick to lead the party's central committee. He credited her with helping him win her home state of Michigan in 2016, and she'd even agreed to stop using her maiden name, Romney (Mitt is her uncle), at Trump's request. She loyally defended him for years, even using party cash to pay his legal fees. She joined him on calls to pressure local election officials into delaying certification of the 2020 results, offering the RNC's help with legal representation. On the day after the January 6 attack on the Capitol, she put him on speakerphone in a meeting with RNC members, letting him hear them shout, "We love you!"

But their relationship cooled after the 2020 election because the RNC wouldn't back some of Trump's lawyers' wildest fraud claims. In a November 2021 meeting with reporters, McDaniel maintained there were some "problems" with the election that needed to be examined, but she acknowledged Biden won. Trump sent her a copy of the resulting article with a handwritten note: "Thanks a lot, Ronna."

McDaniel was skilled at tending to her committee members and holding together the party's precarious coalition. At the start of 2023, she ran for an unprecedented fourth term as chair, partly out of fear of who might take over otherwise. Trump supported her at the time. But as the year went on and the primary heated up, he repeatedly demanded that McDaniel cancel the debates. Trump would call her names and swear at her, people familiar with their calls said. "You brought this on yourself," he said before posting an online attack on her. "They're really mad at you," he told her when the RNC announced another debate. He did not say who "they" were, but he was definitely one of them.

Trump wanted McDaniel to endorse him. When she said she had to stay neutral, he reminded her that he picked her. "You're neutral like I'm neutral," he said. McDaniel told him the RNC's neutrality meant it could not keep covering his legal bills as a candidate, but he didn't believe her. "You absolutely can," he said. On several occasions he told her to cancel the entire primary. "I can't," she would say. "I can't legally do that."

Trump's staff fed him damaging reports that the RNC was falling behind in fundraising. LaCivita was openly gunning for McDaniel, saying he would soon be taking over the RNC. Wiles had been McDaniel's biggest advocate in Trump's circle, but even she was growing annoyed and stopped defending McDaniel. In Iowa, Trump quietly met with

Michael Whatley, the North Carolina GOP chairman he was considering to take McDaniel's job.

McDaniel told advisers she feared her days were numbered. Yet Trump kept sending mixed signals. "Honey, you're doing great. Why don't you come work for the campaign?" he told her in early 2024, just weeks before inviting her to Mar-a-Lago to talk about her future.

When they met at the club in February, Trump and McDaniel had a largely pleasant two-hour interaction and drafted a statement. They agreed to decide her future after the South Carolina primary. She hadn't resigned, and he hadn't asked her to, but over the next few weeks, McDaniel would hear that his team was discussing replacements and had private meetings with other candidates.

By that point, she was ready to go. It didn't matter anymore that she was Trump's chosen chair and had served him loyally for years. His team was already preparing to move into the party headquarters on Capitol Hill. Whatever happened going forward, they would own it. She didn't want to be responsible if Trump lost. It was his party now.

Part Two

REMATCH

7

A Poor Memory

As Trump began to turn his attention to the general election, Biden kept hearing complaints from lawmakers that his campaign lacked a presence in their districts. He'd seen the polls showing Trump remained a slight favorite. His campaign staff in Wilmington was growing despondent. Biden even admitted to one aide, "I have a leadership problem on the campaign." So when the president received a call from Barack Obama to wish him a happy eighty-first birthday, on November 20, 2023, he invited him back to the White House for another lunch.

Obama brought concerns of his own. He remained slightly incredulous that Biden was running for a second term, but he focused on structural problems with Biden's operation. At the lunch in December, he told the president that splitting the leadership between Wilmington and Washington didn't suit a modern presidential campaign, which needed to make decisions quickly and grow exponentially. Biden could not have all the campaign's decision-makers located a hundred miles from the headquarters. Obama reminded Biden that for his own reelection campaign in 2012, he sent two of his top White House aides, David

Axelrod and Jim Messina, to Chicago to run the operation. He encouraged Biden to speak with David Plouffe, Obama's 2008 campaign manager, about campaign structure and strategy.

After the lunch, Obama did not leave the White House right away. He stopped to visit with Biden's senior staff, many of whom used to work for him, and shared his account of what he and Biden had discussed. Obama was more blunt with the staff. "Your campaign is a mess," he told them.

In Wilmington, senior aides were losing patience with their nominal boss, Julie Chavez Rodriguez, for her inability to make decisions. Three top officials—Quentin Fulks, principal deputy campaign manager, Rob Flaherty, deputy campaign manager, and Michael Tyler, communications director—decided they needed to go to the White House and ask for adult supervision. They wanted O'Malley Dillon to run the campaign full time. No meeting ever took place, but the message was conveyed.

The standstill was not entirely Chavez Rodriguez's fault. She lacked authority by design. O'Malley Dillon insisted on signing off on all major decisions. Mike Donilon and Anita Dunn controlled their own silos. Donilon oversaw the campaign's overall message and paid media strategy, producing ads without answering to or even consulting most other top officials. Donilon saw no value in other pollsters and excluded them. During the entire campaign, Biden met with the pollsters exactly once, shortly after the campaign launch. The only approval Donilon sought was that of Biden, who demanded to review every ad released by his campaign.

The pollsters and the communications team would often see the ads at the same time as the general public, once they appeared online or on TV. Sometimes the results shocked them. One ad centered on Biden's upbringing in Scranton, Pennsylvania, and the values the community instilled in him. To tell that story, the video highlighted Biden's first cousin and his childhood friend, who both appeared with gray hair, pale skin, and frail voices. *Who thought this was a good idea*, one adviser thought when he saw it. *Are we trying to remind people how old he is?*

The communications team remained in Dunn's purview. She controlled hiring and remained deeply involved in daily messaging. Since Donilon, Dunn, and O'Malley Dillon each reported directly to the president, the senior officials under them felt pulled in several directions. Some took the step of scheduling individual weekly check-ins with each of them, hoping to stay on top of what the campaign was doing.

After lunch with Obama, Biden commanded O'Malley Dillon: Fix my campaign. She still did not want to move to Wilmington, so she explored whether she could shift more of her work to campaign activities, shedding some, if not all, of her official scheduling and operational responsibilities. White House lawyers said no. The federal law known as the Hatch Act, which walled off politics from official business (though often ineffectively), meant she could not work in the White House on mostly campaign tasks. She would have to leave the White House.

In January, Biden announced O'Malley Dillon would be moving to Wilmington to become the campaign chair, and Mike Donilon would become chief strategist. Donilon would not join O'Malley Dillon in Wilmington though. He stayed in Washington and kept his prime parking spot on West Executive Avenue, right near the West Wing, because he met with Biden so frequently, often for lunch. For Hatch Act purposes, the Democratic National Committee opened an office for him a few blocks away from the White House.

The leadership changes came just as the perfunctory Democratic primary was getting under way. Biden's only competition was Marianne Williamson, the spiritual self-help author who also ran in the 2020 Democratic primaries, and Representative Dean Phillips, a little-known

House backbencher whose longshot bid was premised on concerns about Biden's age. Phillips didn't want to take on the primary challenge himself; he tried to recruit prominent Democratic governors like Gretchen Whitmer and J. B. Pritzker, but they would not meet with him.

New Hampshire, bound by state law to hold the nation's first primary, went ahead with a January 23 contest, but since the primary wasn't sanctioned by the Democratic National Committee, Biden didn't put his name on the ballot. His supporters organized a write-in campaign, and Biden won with just shy of 65 percent of the vote. Phillips finished in second with just under 20 percent, and Williamson garnered 4 percent. Less than two weeks later, on February 3, came South Carolina, which Biden was certain to win, but he couldn't afford anything short of total domination after overhauling the calendar to put the state first. Biden cruised to victory in South Carolina with 96 percent of the vote.

The results helped Biden loyalists, chiefly Steve Ricchetti, brush off the Democratic hand-wringing as all coming from the same group of people who were always underestimating and second-guessing the president. Ricchetti argued to Biden doubters that the president was not just winning primaries, he was also succeeding in governing. He highlighted the president's role—and sometimes his own—in winning the negotiations with Republicans to lift the debt ceiling and avoid a government shutdown, leading Republicans to topple their own House Speaker, Kevin McCarthy. "We are doing a good job in the presidency," he said, often citing a survey of historians ranking Biden as the fourteenth-best president.

Around the same time as the South Carolina primary, the office of Special Counsel Robert Hur informed Biden's legal team that the investigators' report was complete, after about thirteen months of work. The president's lawyers would have the opportunity to review the report before public release. They were told to report to a building in Washington. They could not bring any devices. They would have four days to read the report and then one day to raise any concerns with Hur, particularly as it related to presidential privilege or clear-cut factual errors. They were given strict instructions that they could not discuss the report with anyone other than their client, the president. Hur never told Garland or senior Justice Department officials about his conclusions in the report; they found out when he submitted it.

Partway through the second day of the review, Hur called Dick Sauber, one of the White House lawyers, and said it was over. The news website *Axios* had reported that Biden's team didn't expect charges but worried the report would "include embarrassing details—possibly with photos—on how Biden stored documents." Hur's team assumed the Biden legal team had leaked the information to *Axios*. White House officials argued to the special counsel that the article was just speculation about what the report might include—to prove their point, they said the reporter had reached out about the story before the privilege review began. They believed the timing was coincidental. But Hur did not relent.

Even with their review cut short, Biden's lawyers had seen enough to know they had problems. The report detailed multiple instances of Biden appearing forgetful or confused, including, most troublingly, about the years when he served as vice president and the death of his beloved son Beau. Finally, as part of his explanation for why he wouldn't prosecute Biden, Hur wrote that it would be hard to win a jury trial because the president would portray himself as "a sympathetic, well-meaning, elderly man with a poor memory." It wouldn't matter for headlines and cable chyrons that Hur was technically describing how Biden's defense team would present his case, not his mental acuity directly. The phrase was devastating for a president running for a reelection campaign, especially one already facing widespread concern, including among his own supporters, about his ability to serve another four years.

What the uproar overshadowed, though, was how close Hur came to recommending criminal prosecution of Biden.

On February 5, Sauber and Bob Bauer sent Hur a five-page letter contesting several parts of the report, beginning with the description of Biden's memory. They were less concerned about Biden's words in the transcript than how Hur characterized them in the report. They argued that the special counsel had gone rogue, speculating and editorializing beyond "the bounds of your expertise and remit." The lawyers briefed Biden on the report and their protests to Hur. After that meeting, Bauer and his colleagues returned to the White House counsel's office on the second floor, and Bauer exploded. He said it was outrageous that this investigation was even happening. It was outrageous that Garland was letting it happen. It was outrageous that the special counsel was ignoring their response.

Two days after the letter to Hur, Ed Siskel, the White House counsel, and Bauer escalated their objections, going over Hur's head and writing a letter directly to Garland. They argued that parts of Hur's report "violate Department of Justice policy and practice by pejoratively characterizing uncharged conduct" (the same fault attributed to then-FBI director James Comey in 2016, when he publicly excoriated Hillary Clinton's private email server while declining to charge her). The next day, Bradley Weinsheimer, the highest-ranking career official at the Department of Justice, responded. He said the letters to Hur and Garland were repetitive, and he disagreed with their complaints. Case closed.

On the morning of February 8, more than a year after Garland tapped Hur as the special counsel, the Department of Justice summoned its press corps for a procedure known as a lock-in. The reporters would be able to read the Hur report under embargo and prepare stories. White House lawyers got wind of the plans and freaked out. If the press was getting a heads-up, why wasn't the White House? Siskel called Matt Klapper, Garland's chief of staff. He was furious. The White House had been waiting to see the final report and learn whether any of the changes they had requested were made. They also wanted to be able to share it more widely within the building. Klapper explained the reporters were under an embargo, and they were following standard department procedure.

As the report went public, Biden was appearing at an annual retreat for House Democrats, at the Lansdowne Resort in Leesburg, Virginia. Before taking the stage, Biden huddled with congressional leaders backstage. When one lawmaker asked Biden how he was doing, the president erupted. "How the fuck could I forget the day my son died?" he said. "Of course I remember everything."

The president then spoke publicly for about fifteen minutes. All he said about the special counsel's report was that it closed the investigation without charges, and he emphasized the clear differences between his and Donald Trump's cases. After the press was ushered out, Biden participated in a question-and-answer session moderated by Congressman Pete Aguilar, the chair of the House Democratic Caucus. But the lawmakers who were called on had been preselected. Biden could read the prepared questions and answers on extremism, immigration, and student loan forgiveness out of a binder he had open in front of him. The president had used this setup before, but at the previous year's retreat, Biden was so loquacious his aides couldn't get him to wrap up. This year's performance was shorter and did nothing to dissuade lawmakers that Hur was right about Biden's age and memory.

Biden and his team wanted another chance to show he was in command. They convened a press conference at the White House that night. In the Diplomatic Reception Room, Biden was surgical in citing page numbers to point out inconsistencies in the report, feisty in defending his acuity, and outraged at the suggestion that he forgot when his son died. "I'm well-meaning, and I'm an elderly man—and I know what the hell I'm doing," he told reporters. The press conference grew increasingly chaotic as reporters shouted over one another trying to get the president to answer. But Biden mostly held his own, staying focused on the report.

He closed his briefing book and started toward the exit. His aides exhaled. But then Biden paused and turned back to face the shouting reporters.

"A question on Israel, sir," one of them said, asking for an update on the hostage negotiations.

Biden returned to the lectern and reopened his briefing book. "I'm of the view, as you know, that the conduct of the response in Gaza—in the Gaza Strip has been over the top," he said. "I think that—as you know, initially, the president of Mexico, El-Sisi, did not want to open up the gate to allow humanitarian material to get in. I talked to him. I convinced him to open the gate."

He blew it. Abdel Fatah El-Sisi is the president of Egypt, not Mexico. It didn't help that the night before Biden twice mistakenly referred to the late German Chancellor Helmut Kohl, who left office in 1998 and died in 2017, when describing a conversation he had with Angela Merkel in 2021. The whole press conference became another fiasco.

Now the failures were compounding. A few days before the Hur report came out, CBS announced that Biden would skip a televised interview to air just before the Super Bowl, a presidential tradition since 2009. Trump had declined the interview in 2018, and Biden had skipped it in 2023, when the host network was Fox News. This time, White House officials defended the decision by saying Americans wanted to see football, not politics. But to many Democrats, turning down an audience of tens of millions while trailing in a reelection campaign was another worrying sign that Biden might not be up for the job. To make matters worse, Biden did fewer interviews than any of his predecessors and refused to sit down with any major newspapers. When Biden did hold press conferences, his aides handpicked reporters and often went to great lengths to figure out beforehand what questions or topics they would ask; reporters who didn't share that information were often not called on.

At the end of February, the president received his annual physical at Walter Reed, after which his doctor declared Biden "continues to be fit for duty." The exam, however, did not include a cognitive test. Weeks earlier, some of Biden's closest aides discussed whether they should have the president take one. Aides saw how Biden's mannerisms—digressing during his speeches, mixing up details, rambling—had been exacerbated by age and were perceived by voters. There was a joke among senior staff about how many hours he had actually spent with Chinese President Xi Jinping because he often provided vastly different accounts. Sometimes it was thirty-six hours. Other times it was seventy hours. Or maybe it was ninety-some hours.

Aides did not worry about Biden failing the cognitive test, but some feared it would do nothing to silence Biden's critics and could open the door to more questions. His doctors did not identify a specific medical reason to administer the test, so taking it anyway could cause people to wonder. Aides may also have faced resistance from Kevin O'Connor, the president's longtime physician, who made it clear he would not take political considerations into the exam room.

Kamala Harris had another concern: shrinking support from Black and Latino voters. She invited campaign leaders to her residence for a pair of summits, one for each group. The session on Black voters came on a Saturday in January. Around her dining-room table, Harris interrogated her staff about Trump's appeal with Black men, asking her aides to share their opinions. Fulks, the principal deputy campaign manager, told the vice president that many Black men saw Trump as a strong leader, in contrast to Democrats as weak. He said the party needed to focus more on economic mobility for Black men. The group also discussed how the campaign needed to do a better job reminding people of Trump's history of racism—the advertisement he placed calling for bringing back the death penalty, implicitly targeting the Central Park Five (the young Black and Latino men who were wrongfully convicted of assaulting and raping a white woman jogging in Central Park in 1989); the 1973 Department of Justice lawsuit brought against his family business for allegedly discriminating against Black people; and his role in spreading the birtherism conspiracy theory about Obama's citizenship. Harris said she wanted to do more Black radio and speak directly to the community. The summit led to a series of events in battleground states specifically focused on the administration's economic policies and investments, often in front of Black audiences, styled as her "economic opportunity tour."

The discussion on Latinos, on a Saturday in late February, plotted ways to improve the campaign's messaging and outreach. Harris expressed concerns about polls showing Biden losing support among a group that backed him by nearly 30 points in 2020. Democrats were also worried that Spanish-language media, especially the largest network, Univision, was taking a more open posture toward Trump after years of sparring with him.

"Where are we right now with Latino voters in every battleground state, and where do we need to be on Election Day?" Harris asked.

Matt Barreto, a political science professor at the University of California Los Angeles and a pollster for the campaign focused on Latino voters, told her the campaign was off by more than 10 points, and they needed to invest in state-level polling of Latinos to better understand the scope of their problems.

"I guess we still have a ways to go," Harris said.

Barreto noted that Latino voters skewed younger than other demographic groups, and overwhelmingly thought Biden was too old. He added that Harris could be an effective surrogate given her track record with Latino voters when running in statewide races in California. He encouraged Harris to campaign more in Latino communities, especially in Arizona and Nevada.

When Barreto noted that the median age of Latino voters was under thirty, Harris asked about the impact of the war in Gaza on Latinos, knowing the conflict was hurting Democrats' standing with younger and more progressive voters. Barreto told her that his research showed the war did not rank as a top voting issue for Latinos or most Democrats more broadly—inflation, among other issues, was much more important. But Barreto said the conflict was presenting an enthusiasm problem for Biden and Harris, particularly among young people, and he worried it could result in depressed turnout. He told Harris that the campaign needed a more empathetic message about the widespread suffering in Gaza. Harris agreed. For months, she had been privately telling her aides the same thing, expressing concerns about the plight of Palestinians and Biden's handling of the issue. Shortly after that meeting, she delivered a major speech on Israel, echoing Biden's call for Hamas to accept a ceasefire and going slightly further than he had in describing the situation in Gaza as a "humanitarian catastrophe" and urging Israel to allow in more aid.

Left-wing discomfort with Biden's unwavering support for Israel wasn't just an electoral problem—it was also an operational one. Political campaigns are largely staffed by young people, willing to work long hours for little pay and often relocate to states they are not from. Young people were not inspired by Biden, and the war in Gaza further put them off his candidacy. O'Malley Dillon conceded privately that the war was hurting their ability to hire organizers around the country.

Nowhere was that danger more acute than in Michigan, home to one of the country's largest Muslim communities, and about 200,000 registered voters who were Muslim. Trump won the state by about 10,000 votes in 2016, and Biden flipped it back in 2020 by about 154,000 votes. Protesters were becoming a common feature of Biden's events, forcing the White House to take extra steps to conceal the location of where the president would speak and often hold events by invite only. When Biden made his first campaign trip to Michigan in early February ahead of the state's primary, he had no interaction with the Arab American community, and his motorcade traveled on side streets to avoid protests. Organizers started encouraging voters to register their objection to Biden's Israel policy by voting against him in the primary, choosing an option on the ballot called "uncommitted." Organizers initially set their sights on 10,000 votes, equal to Trump's 2016 margin, and ultimately notched 101,000. Debbie Dingell, the state's outspoken congresswoman known for warning Democrats ahead of Trump's 2016 victory, repeatedly told Biden officials their problems went beyond the robust Arab American community. Dingell could not believe how many Arab Americans told her they were open to voting for Trump. But she also said Biden was struggling with Black men in Detroit and union workers throughout the state. She pleaded for the campaign to invest in the state. She told others that Biden's aides were not listening.

Before Harris met that month with Democratic governors from around the country to discuss the campaign, Rahm Emanuel, the pugilistic former Obama chief of staff and Biden's ambassador to Japan, called Minnesota Governor Tim Walz, whom he had a close relationship with from Congress. He wanted Walz to use the audience with Harris to deliver a stern warning about Biden's prospects. Don't keep up the facade, he said. Walz didn't act on the advice.

Biden's team looked to his State of the Union address, on March 7, as a chance to reset the race. He still had never held a formal campaign launch, and the joint session of Congress would provide him with his largest TV audience until the convention. The scathing report from the special counsel raised the stakes too. Days before the speech, *The New York Times* published a poll with Siena College that put Biden trailing Trump by 5 points, with 47 percent disapproving of Biden's job as president, the highest level of his presidency so far.

The president and his aides knew he needed to deliver a flawless performance to tamp down concerns about his fitness. Biden had outperformed expectations in previous addresses, earning plaudits for his ability to spar on the fly with Republicans during his 2023 speech. The Friday before the 2024 address, Biden withdrew to Camp David to spend four nights working on his remarks. Biden battled a stutter in childhood and still struggled with public speaking; he was better at working a rope line or consoling a grieving mother. Before every speech, aides would set aside time in his schedule for prep, but he would spend that time nitpicking over specific words and facts. When Ron Klain was his chief of staff, he would often say to Biden, "The speech is good. Let's practice." Biden's typical response: "I'm just not happy with the text yet, Ron. I'm going to work on it more." To get around Biden's tendency to neglect rehearsing his delivery, aides enlisted Steven Spielberg, the Academy Award–winning director. Spielberg started working with Biden over the preceding year, and when he was involved, aides credited him with improving Biden's public performances.

In the State of the Union, aides wanted Biden to lay out an agenda for a second term while also sharpening the contrast with Trump—a delicate balance for an official rather than political speech. They presented him with different options to open the speech, and to no one's surprise he picked Donilon's version: a sweeping opening invoking the 1940s, when Hitler was on the march in Europe and freedom and democracy were under threat. Biden never spoke Trump's name. Instead, he pointedly said "my predecessor" thirteen times.

Biden's plea for the cause of freedom at home was supposed to center on the overturning of *Roe v. Wade*. His prepared text called for him to introduce Kate Cox, one of the first lady's guests, by explaining, "Because Texas law banned abortion, Kate and her husband had to leave the state to get the care she needed." Instead, Biden said, "Texas law banned her ability to act." It was not a slipup. He would sometimes tell aides outright: "I'm not going to say abortion." Advisers lamented that it was hard to make abortion rights a core part of the president's campaign when he refused to say the word.

Other than that, advisers were pleased with Biden's performance. He made no major gaffes. He stood up to heckling from far-right Georgia Congresswoman Marjorie Taylor Greene. White House aides concluded the speech was a success when Republicans started criticizing Biden after the speech for being "jacked-up" and "overcaffeinated."

Biden followed up the State of the Union with a swing through battleground states. The fresh energy gave some staffers the feeling, for the first time, that they could actually win. But Biden's numbers remained stubbornly low. Neither the devastation of the Hur report nor the success of the State of the Union did much to alter the head-to-head with Trump. Biden trailed by a few points in most public polls, and nothing seemed to change. Biden's pollsters told senior campaign officials the president's challenge remained that the public's impressions of both candidates were firmly established and hard to shift. They did not have much data of their own to draw on, because they polled less frequently than typical for a presidential campaign.

Campaign officials expected the race would be decided by an even smaller margin in the key battleground states than in 2020. For that reason, they needed a more aggressive strategy to deal with Robert F. Kennedy Jr. After the DNC decided not to hold primary debates and moved South Carolina ahead of Iowa and New Hampshire, Kennedy spurned the party that his family was synonymous with and launched an independent bid for president. He was polling in the low double digits.

The DNC built its first-ever team dedicated to counter third-party and independent candidates, focused on digging up opposition research and legal challenges to keep them off the ballot. Biden got involved too. The White House invited more than four dozen members of the Kennedy family—RFK Jr. not included—for the St. Patrick's Day celebration, and Biden posed for a photo with the clan in front of the bust of RFK Sr. that Biden placed in the Oval Office. The next month, most of RFK Jr.'s siblings endorsed Biden at a rally in Philadelphia. Biden, a proud Irish Catholic who long idolized the Kennedys, told aides it was one of his best days of the campaign.

Whatever glimmer of hope Biden and his staff were feeling after the State of the Union, grassroots supporters did not share it. According to internal documents, in April, the campaign raised $25 million from small donors—$19 million short of their goal. Officials cut their targets for the next two months. In May, they hoped to raise $35 million, down from their original goal of $53.3 million. In June, they cut their goal by 41 percent, to $40 million.

Around the same time, the Biden campaign commissioned a fresh round of polling in the battleground states. The pollsters developed their survey questions in collaboration with the campaign's state leadership teams, seeking input on what to ask. The results came back showing Biden behind across the decisive states, and the pollsters shared the data with top campaign officials in Wilmington. Soon after, the state leadership teams asked what happened to the polls, hoping to see the data.

The top campaign officials asked the pollsters to brief the state leadership teams on the results, but to leave out the top-line horse race. The pollsters balked. How could they discuss the underlying findings without presenting the overall results? O'Malley Dillon and others worried about upsetting the staff, but the pollsters argued that taking the numbers out of the presentation would upset them even more. They also pointed out that the state teams were working hand-in-hand with Senate and gubernatorial campaigns, giving them access to similar high-quality poll results. At the pollsters' insistence, Wilmington reversed course and the pollsters presented the full results. The state staffers were unfazed. It was no secret to them that Biden was behind.

Seeing from the outside how the campaign was falling behind in fundraising, grassroots programming, and digital presence, a group of alumni from the Obama campaign looked for a diplomatic way to offer free assistance. The group pitched a program for bringing in experienced campaign professionals earlier than the usual push in the final stretch. They proposed specific projects they thought they could help with, including small-dollar fundraising, online organization, expanding the campaign's website, and working with digital teams in battleground states. Flaherty, the deputy campaign manager, showed interest in the project and said he would follow up to discuss further. The effort never got off the ground.

Since the State of the Union did not provide the reset Biden needed, his advisers turned to the only other event that could redefine the campaign and prove to the public that Biden was up to the task. Traditionally, debates were held after Labor Day, in the height of the fall campaign season. For 2024, the Commission on Presidential Debates, the bipartisan commission that organized the forums since 1988, planned face-offs on September 16 in Texas, October 1 in Virginia, and October 9 in Utah. Biden's team didn't understand the decision to hold the debates in noncompetitive states, and they opposed the commission's standard format of having live audiences that could distract or interrupt the candidates.

In the spring, Anita Dunn approached Biden's other senior advisers about ditching the commission and negotiating directly with the Trump campaign and the TV networks to set up an early debate. The Trump campaign was already talking about spurning the commission, both because of long-standing Republican grumbling about biased moderators, and because Trump was taunting Biden to debate him anytime, anywhere. Dunn thought scheduling an earlier debate could work to Biden's advantage. The campaign could negotiate rules to suit him, such as having no live audience and muting microphones to restrain Trump's interruptions. Plus the Biden campaign needed money, and a strong debate would surely be a fundraising boon.

In April, the senior advisers brought their recommendation for an early debate to Biden. "By holding the first debate in the spring, you will be able to reach the widest audience possible before we are deep in the summer months with the conventions, Olympics, and family vacations taking precedence," they wrote in a memo. "In addition, the earlier you are able to debate the better, so that the American people can see you standing next to Trump and showing the strength of your leadership, compared to Trump's weakness and chaos." There was one other potential upside of an early debate that went unstated in the memo but was on the minds of some aides: If the president had a bad night, he would have time to recover.

Some of Biden's top campaign officials, including Quentin Fulks, and the president's allies thought the president should never have agreed to debate Trump. In 2020, Trump had ignored the commission's requirement to test for COVID before the first face-off, and he was hospitalized with the virus a few days later, meaning he had almost certainly exposed Biden. Some aides argued there was no point in debating a flagrant liar. Others conceded they didn't think Biden was up to the task. In May, Biden attended a small fundraiser in Chicago, where he read off a teleprompter and didn't take any questions. One donor, alarmed by the appearance, called a senior White House official and advised that Biden not debate Trump. He encouraged the White House to find an excuse to get him out of it, fearing it would not go well. His advice was not heeded, in part because some of Biden's top aides, including Mike Donilon, were adamant that Biden needed to debate. As Donilon told anyone who broached the subject, he thought Biden had no option. He had to debate, and he thought he would do well.

The president signed off on an early debate, and they quickly struck a date with the Trump campaign and CNN for June 27. The senior advisers highlighted this potential date as "ideal" because it would come almost two weeks after his final overseas trip before the November election. To start preparing well ahead of time, the advisers recommended he start weekly prep sessions with Bruce Reed as well as practicing through press and radio interviews and a network town hall. The town hall never happened. Aides struggled to schedule one because the TV networks said town halls with Biden got poor ratings.

A Takeover

With Ronna McDaniel out of the way, Chris LaCivita was excited to introduce the RNC to the new regime. Michael Whatley and Lara Trump were titularly in charge, but Trump tasked LaCivita with running the organization day to day. He wanted the RNC to work in lockstep with the campaign. No turf wars. No dissent. His first step was to tear the place up.

LaCivita showed up to his first day of work at the party headquarters on Capitol Hill on a Monday in March, ready to make heads roll. Just as soon as he could get inside the building. He realized he didn't have access. Someone had to come let him in.

LaCivita wanted to meet with Elliott Echols, the RNC's political director. A mild-mannered Georgia operative, Echols actually liked Trump, which was more than some RNC staffers could say. Some friends warned Echols that his job was in danger, but he expected LaCivita would at least let him make his pitch. He brought binders full of detailed plans for every battleground state: eighty-eight staffers across twelve offices to knock on 3 million doors and make 2.4 million phone calls in Pennsylvania; sixty-two staffers across seven offices to make 558,000 voter contacts in Arizona. Each state had a detailed analysis on why Trump lost in 2020 and how Republicans could improve.

Echols never got the chance to open the binders before LaCivita fired him. It took forty-five seconds. It was nothing personal, LaCivita said, sitting with the RNC's HR director. Echols wouldn't need to address his staff. They would figure out he was gone. He could clean out his office quickly or have his things shipped to him.

The new political director would be James Blair, Susie Wiles's enforcer, whose smoldering intensity and vaguely militaristic bearing at first frightened other Trump staff. A burst of articles came out questioning whether gutting the RNC eight months before the election would hurt Trump, and Blair yelled at the staff for not defending the RNC. One aide replied that the communications team would be happy to push back if they could have some information about what was going on. Blair said there was no need. He would deal with the press himself. "I'm going to beat these reporters into retardation!" he yelled.

"Could you beat me into retardation first?" the aide responded.

Blair started interviewing RNC staff who were hoping to keep their jobs, and he asked them, did they believe the 2020 election was stolen? From a certain point of view, it was a sensible question for people signing up to work for a nominee who made it the whole premise of his candidacy. But the suggestion of an ideological litmus test, one that put loyalty above empirical reality, unnerved some staffers.

The firings continued as the day went on. The staff began sending each other a guillotine GIF. LaCivita appeared to barely know some of the people he fired. "You're from Nevada?" he asked Keith Schipper, a communications official who he summarily fired in a two-minute meeting. "Maybe we could find you something out there."

The only thing that slowed down LaCivita's purge was a warning from an RNC official that he would trigger a mass layoff notice under DC labor laws. He fumed but stopped for the day.

LaCivita reassured some rattled RNC employees that he often led with his bark and didn't usually bite. He startled staffers with his colorful vocabulary, regularly yelling about "retards" and "fucking idiots" and "people who need their fucking heads examined" as he walked in and out of offices, according to people who heard him. He demanded to cut off the severance of a former employee whom he suspected of spreading gossip. "Don't give him another fucking penny," LaCivita said. After spending months harping on the old RNC for spending too much money, he received a luxury apartment in Washington's Navy Yard neighborhood and a $20,000 monthly consulting fee from the RNC— on top of his monthly $30,000 from the campaign. He also paid an aide at an annual rate of almost $450,000.

One of his first big clashes was with Danielle Alvarez, a senior communications aide who spoke her mind and was close to Wiles. LaCivita attacked her on an email thread over a news story that he caused, and then criticized her in another meeting. Alvarez sent Wiles an email saying she could not effectively do her job in this climate. Wiles begged her to stay and said she would try to improve the situation.

The turmoil at the RNC took Wiles by surprise. She knew there would be cuts, but she did not expect this much chaos, she later told others. Two days after the firings, she showed up at the headquarters wearing all black leather, instead of her usual pastel suits. The staff were upset and clamoring for answers. LaCivita was holed up in a palatial office upstairs. She waited in a shared kitchen space eating a salad with demoralized staff. Finally she went into LaCivita's office, and the grandmother who rarely swore had one question for him: "What the hell are you doing?"

"Well," he said, "we call it a takeover." He was doing what he thought needed to be done. The hard right was clamoring for a head on a platter, and it was Ronna McDaniel's that he was serving. He wanted to send a message. He knew it was going to be messy. He wanted it to be.

Wiles posted up at the RNC, taking phone calls and complaining about the mess she now had to fix. Some of the fired staff would be re-hired. LaCivita fired one staffer, John Seravalli, thinking he was someone else. He agreed to hire him back and gave him a raise. He renegotiated a consulting fee for Boris Epshteyn, thinking he had achieved a reduction, but it was actually an increase.

LaCivita also scrapped McDaniel's signature programs, community centers for minority outreach and a turnout drive called "Bank Your Vote." Donors and senators called to object that the money and time they'd invested in those programs was being squandered, and Wiles had to calm them down. Staff who'd been ordered to take down the "Bank Your Vote" website were then told to get it back online within fifteen minutes. The community centers were not closed, but new ones weren't opened.

It was the first, and turned out to be only, major rift between Trump's co–campaign managers. "Don't ever do anything like that again," she told LaCivita over dinner.

"Yes, ma'am," he replied.

Wiles brought in another longtime lieutenant, Tim Saler, to handle the campaign's voter data. He and Blair analyzed Trump's performance in 2016 and 2020 and made a startling discovery. The conventional wisdom had been that Trump lost in 2020 because of his erosion among women, particularly suburbanites horrified by his handling of the coronavirus pandemic and tired of his taunts and insults. But Saler and Blair concluded Trump's problem in 2020 was that he slipped among men. Trump's challenge, as they saw it, was not with the women who voted for Romney in 2012 and Clinton in 2016; it was with their husbands, who voted for Trump in 2016 and Biden in 2020. "The paramount main thing is restoring our numbers with White men back to 2016 levels," Blair and Saler wrote in a memo. "It is clear that matching or exceeding our 2016 strength with men of all demographics is a major opportunity for us and key to our success."*

Saler and Blair thought chasing swing voters backfired by wasting time and money on people who ended up turning out for Democrats. They went back into the RNC's files to see who the Republicans had targeted in 2020, and found that a third of them voted for Biden. They thought the campaign's money would be better spent motivating infrequent voters who, if they showed up, would definitely vote for Trump. Instead of chasing demographics who were moving away from Trump, Saler and Blair thought the campaign should try to hold its ground with those groups while running up the score with voters who were already trending Trump's way. Instead of focusing on suburban women or other groups Trump struggled with, why not focus on rural white men and other groups who Trump had already performed well with?

Pollster Tony Fabrizio refined the analysis by identifying 11 percent of the electorate that could tip the race to Trump. Compared to the overall electorate, the group skewed young, male, and nonwhite, and they tended not to follow politics closely or receive their news from traditional media. Saler modeled each of these voters individually, estimating what issue motivated them most, and planned to target them directly with digital ads or mail. Mail was especially important for about a million voters whose phone numbers weren't available, so it was the only way to contact them.†

---

*The memo delicately referenced the 2020 defeat as "our reported raw vote shortage."

†The campaign sent postcards asking them to reply with their phone number so they could start contacting them in other ways.

Blair viewed the RNC's preexisting program as an off-the-shelf template that pumped money into staff and offices without thought to the conditions of this race. The campaign's strategy and tactics had to suit the candidate. A generic, interchangeable turnout program was a bad turnout program. Blair and Wiles did not want to devote all the campaign's money to hiring thousands of staffers in hundreds of offices like Trump's 2020 campaign had done or like the Biden campaign was doing now.

Instead, the Trump campaign would set up a nationwide version of the grassroots network that won Trump the Iowa caucuses, taking advantage of organic enthusiasm among Trump's supporters and existing relationships with neighbors to mobilize infrequent voters. The system, dubbed Trump Force 47, bore some resemblance to a multilevel marketing scheme. The campaign would recruit volunteers in battleground areas and assign them each twenty-five neighbors who, based on demographics and consumer data, looked like Trump supporters but didn't reliably vote. Volunteers who completed their mission by converting ten of those twenty-five neighbors received a new list of fifty. Those who recruited twenty-five out of fifty received their next-level challenge: forty-seven out of a list of one hundred. Blair's confidence in the strength of this system and the accuracy of the campaign's data targeting withstood months of grousing from local-level Republican Party officials that they saw none of the usual signs of office openings and door knocking.

The gamble on a bare-bones ground game soon got a boost from an unexpected source. The Federal Election Commission, which regulates campaigns and outside groups like super PACs, decided to loosen the restrictions on coordinating between the two. Ironically, the request for the policy change came from Marc Elias, a Democratic elections lawyer whose prolific litigating and ubiquitous social media presence made him an object of right-wing loathing and envy. But the Republicans would be quicker to take advantage of the new flexibility. The RNC's new chief counsel, an experienced election lawyer named Charlie Spies, devised an arrangement for the campaign to outsource expensive ground-game programs to allied super PACs that could fund them with unlimited donations.

Spies took the job on the assurance that Trump knew he had a record that was less than pure MAGA. His past clients included campaigns or super PACs for Mitt Romney, Jeb Bush, and Ron DeSantis, and he was on the record saying that many allegations of fraud in the 2020 election weren't true. As word of Spies's role got around, some other Trump allies were aghast, believing the RNC was supposed to be getting rid of "RINOs" and secret Trump haters, not hiring them. One Mar-a-Lago member came up to Trump's table at the club with a folder of Spies's past criticisms. Others worked Trump at fundraising photo lines to tell him how disloyal Spies had been in the past. Trump told Wiles to fire him, but Spies wasn't fired right away. Wiles told others she was trying to fix the situation.

In the late spring, LaCivita, Wiles, Blair, and Spies convened a meeting of super PACs to start collaborating on turnout efforts. LaCivita told the groups they weren't going to be just a part of the ground game. They were the ground game. The groups signed data-sharing agreements with the campaign and took its cues on where to go, who to talk to, and what to say. Each of the groups—including campus activist Charlie Kirk's Turning Point Action, Trump White House alumna Brooke Rollins's America First Works, and JD Vance ally Christopher Buskirk's Turnout for America—had its own theories of how to reach the right voters in the right places, as well as their own donors to please and vendors to pay. The new ability to coordinate with the campaign gave the groups additional credibility with their donors, while the campaign kept strategic control.

The next day, Trump attended an RNC fundraiser in Florida, where some donors told him that Spies was still working for him. He again told his team to fire Spies. LaCivita called Spies into a conference room and told him he couldn't stay. They would release a statement attributing his sudden departure to "conflicts" with other clients. Wiles later expressed regret for the whole episode, but Spies's arrangement for coordinating turnout operations with super PACs survived.

The most important allied group turned out to be a super PAC called America PAC, funded by Elon Musk. The world's richest man started supporting Trump notwithstanding some reservations about him. During an early 2024 meeting at billionaire Nelson Peltz's house, Musk encouraged donors to support Trump even if they did not want to be seen giving publicly. He said he understood wanting to keep money away from the official campaign for fear that it would end up covering Trump's legal bills. Forming his own super PAC let him control the spending, and he encouraged others to contribute.

Musk presented the election as a binary choice and warned that the party and the country would end if record numbers of unauthorized immigrants poured across the southern border. He would regularly call other donors or Ronna McDaniel to talk about illegal immigration or point out things he'd seen on his social media website. He would also call Wiles about election fraud allegations he'd heard and argued the campaign needed to do more to protect the vote. He told others he disliked the Biden administration's regulatory agenda and resented the Democrats for not inviting him to the White House.

During this period, Musk and Trump were not in regular contact. When Trump received a news alert that Musk was rebranding Twitter as X, Trump called him and asked, "Why in the world would you do that? Everybody knows what Twitter is."

Trump was getting conflicting advice on how to handle the issue that had dragged down Republicans in the 2022 midterms: abortion. His own position had long been a moving target, from suggesting women who undergo the procedure should be punished to maintaining exceptions for rape, incest, and health, and vowing to appoint Supreme Court justices who would overturn *Roe v. Wade*. As soon as they actually did, Trump instantly recognized the political implications. LaCivita was with Trump in his office when he received the news alert and congratulated him. "You just did what Ronald Reagan couldn't do." Trump replied, "Oh shit. This is going to be a problem." After the 2022 midterms, Trump told another antiabortion activist, "I have to find a way out of this issue. It's killing us."

In 2024, abortion referendums would be on the ballot in key states such as Arizona and Nevada. Some advisers, especially Kellyanne Conway and Senator Lindsey Graham, encouraged Trump to come out in support of a national minimum ban at around fifteen or sixteen weeks. Graham argued that it would not be acceptable to take a state-by-state position on abortion, which he viewed as a moral issue, likening it to civil rights in the 1950s and '60s. Conway, who was working for Susan B. Anthony Pro-Life America at the time, argued that Trump would have to own stricter state policies if he didn't articulate his position. Antiabortion groups lobbied Trump with polling showing support for a fifteen-week ban, but LaCivita challenged them to survey whether people preferred a federal or state-by-state policy. Trump would get mad when Marjorie Dannenfelser, SBA's president, made statements gently criticizing him. "Do they know what I've done for them?" he said to his advisers. He asked one movement leader, if he agreed to take their position, would they spend hundreds of millions on ads supporting him to match what the Democrats would spend attacking him for it? "You aren't doing enough," Trump said.

Trump's advisers consistently tried to steer him away from getting dragged into a debate over the number of weeks. They thought his more moderate stance on abortion hadn't hurt him in Iowa, whose caucus goers skewed more Christian and conservative than the general electorate. Ralph Reed, an evangelical leader who often spoke with Trump on the phone, told Trump that voters gave him latitude they wouldn't give to other politicians, and he did not believe Trump needed to support a ban with a specific number of weeks as long as he reiterated he was pro-life.

At the start of April, the Florida Supreme Court upheld the state's six-week abortion ban that DeSantis signed but allowed voters to decide the policy on the ballot in November. A Florida voter himself, Trump would have to take a position. At the instigation of speechwriter Vince Haley, the staff put together a presentation showing the existing abortion policies in the "Blue Wall" states of Pennsylvania, Michigan, and Wisconsin. Wiles delivered the presentation to Trump on a flight to a campaign stop in Grand Rapids, Michigan, along with Blair, LaCivita, Haley, and Jason Miller.

The presentation was titled "How a National Abortion Policy Will Cost Trump the Election." The advisers argued that if Trump supported a national ban, he would be campaigning on a stricter rule than was currently in effect in the Midwest battlegrounds—twenty-two weeks in Wisconsin, twenty-four in Michigan, twenty-four in Pennsylvania. Endorsing a ban at "ANY" number of weeks, the presentation said, would invite Democratic attacks of "Trump restricting a woman's right to choose."

"Only electoral math matters," the presentation said. "Bottom line: Declaring any number of weeks would play directly into Joe Biden's hands on his simplest path to electoral victory."

Trump decided to come out in support of leaving the question to the states—no federal ban. He would announce the position in a video the following week.

The video was not easy to make. When he entered Mar-a-Lago's library bar and received the script, he did not like it. "This is shit. This is not what I want to say," he said, even though the writers believed they were following his instructions. For hours, the team rewrote the text. Trump left to give a speech in another room. The video crew sat waiting in the bar.

Trump returned and said, "I'm just going to do my own thing." For seven minutes, he talked about abortion on camera. Wiles sat nearby and worried that antiabortion activists would criticize him for it, which they did as soon as the video was released. But the voters who Blair and Saler were targeting proved receptive to Trump's position. There were thousands of voters who reflexively thought they aligned with the Democrats on abortion, but when told that Trump was committed to leaving abortion restrictions to states and vetoing a federal ban, they said they agreed with him more.

The other big problem from the midterms that Trump advisers were determined to address in 2024 was the widespread Republican distrust of early voting and mail-in ballots—fueled, of course, by Trump's lies about the 2020 election. The campaign reviewed polls showing that more than half of Trump's supporters wanted to vote only in person on Election Day.

Trump would sometimes agree to tell voters to cast their ballots by mail or early—only to quickly reverse himself and start attacking those voting methods again, or going off about how the election was stolen. He wanted the RNC to push for all states to use paper ballots only.

Trump's team tried everything they could think of to get him to stop. Wiles and Blair wrote detailed memos showing how early and mail-in voting could help Trump win. Blair presented data arguing that if Republicans had returned mail ballots at the same rate they voted in person, they would have won at least some of the major Senate and governors' races they lost in 2022. Advisers explained that voters who cast ballots early let the campaign check them off their list and focus resources on the remainders.

Wiles asked friends and allies to help make the case to Trump. Sean Hannity lobbied him. Even election deniers such as Steve Bannon joined the push. Brian Ballard, the Florida lobbyist, reminded Trump that he'd won Florida in 2020 while supporting mail-in ballots. Conway told Trump that he wouldn't like seeing news stories in the weeks before the election saying Democrats were ahead in early voting. She also enlisted Melania Trump to agree to vote early. "If the lion roars, the entire kingdom will follow," Conway told Trump at a Mar-a-Lago meeting.

Lindsey Graham tried an analogy he thought Trump would understand. "What if you played golf and you get six clubs and the other guy gets fourteen?" he said. "You're at a disadvantage. Use all the clubs."

One Saturday night in early 2024, Trump was talking with Rob Gleason, the former chairman of Pennsylvania's Republican Party. Trump started going on again about how much he didn't like early and mail-in voting, and Gleason asked him to think of it this way: When a Trump supporter gets a mail ballot, he argued, they were so excited to vote for him they wanted to do so right away. Why wouldn't he want them to have that chance to show their enthusiasm for him?

Trump patched Wiles into the call. "Why didn't you tell me this is what people want to do?" he said. "The minute they get their ballot, they want to vote for me."

Wiles laughed. Of course this was how to convince him.

Years earlier, Danielle Alvarez had pitched a proposal called "Too Big to Rig." She argued that Trump won Florida despite allowing mail-in voting because Republicans turned out in such huge force that they offset any possible fraud. "We need to get our voters out in numbers big enough to flood the system and erase any doubt," Alvarez had written. Now she and Wiles decided to introduce the slogan to Trump.

He smiled when he saw it and started using it. It began appearing on signs at rallies and in campaign ads. Advisers began writing supportive language about early and mail-in voting into Trump's speeches, which he would sometimes actually deliver. Other times, staff would try to take out words and phrases that they feared would trigger him to go off script and start railing against the 2020 election or mail-in voting. Trump agreed to tape another video supporting "Too Big to Rig." When Ballard told Trump how beneficial he thought the video would be, Trump responded, "It's still fucked up. I'll say what I've got to say, but it's still fucked up."

Criminal

C an you believe it?"

Trump was at a high-dollar fundraiser at Mar-a-Lago on Friday, February 16, just after the final judgment came down in his New York civil fraud trial. Even though the civil trial had no threat of carceral punishment, it was deeply personal to Trump because of its effect on his life's work, and he had insisted on voluntarily attending the trial in person, over the advice of some aides.

The judge, Arthur Engoron, had already ruled that Trump and his companies committed fraud by presenting high valuations to lenders while claiming lower ones to tax authorities. The one question was how much Trump would have to pay. The penalty announced that day was a staggering $355 million, plus $99 million in interest.

The amount enraged Trump. "It's so much that people won't even buy it," he told donors at the fundraiser that evening. The judgment came on top of an $83.3 million penalty for defaming the writer E. Jean Carroll, who accused him of sexually abusing her decades earlier, meaning Trump suddenly owed more than half a billion dollars.

Even a billionaire does not keep that kind of cash on hand. And bond companies were not in the habit of making sureties of that size with the risk of trying to collect on a once and possibly future president.

The deadline to put up the money coincided with a hearing to decide when to schedule Trump's New York criminal trial. He was charged with falsifying business records to cover up hush money payments before the 2016 election to Stormy Daniels, a porn star who accused Trump of a sexual encounter ten years earlier.* The scandal had already led to jail time for Trump's former fixer, Michael Cohen, and a nonprosecution agreement with the *National Enquirer*, the supermarket tabloid that bought stories in order to suppress bad publicity about Trump. Federal prosecutors named Trump as a coconspirator in the scheme but declined to charge him. The Manhattan DA picked up the thread and indicted Trump under state law.

No one knew what was going to happen that Monday, March 25, as Trump reported to court in Lower Manhattan. The state attorney general, Letitia James, was preparing to enforce the civil judgment by impounding Trump's assets—nothing so dramatic as showing up at Trump Tower with a giant padlock, but filing a court motion to the same effect.

The criminal courthouse physically resembled something between a run-down public middle school and a jail. Every morning buses brought shackled defendants from Rikers Island. The whole place disgusted Trump, especially the bathrooms, which had no mirrors, and the dingy holding room where he and his lawyers and staff waited outside the courtroom. His personal aide, Walt Nauta, cleaned the area where he sat.†

Trump glowered as he took his seat in the courtroom. Todd Blanche, the mild-mannered lawyer, had one strategy for this and all of Trump's cases: delay. It was not a novel approach for defense attorneys, but

---

*Trump denied the encounter.

†A Trump spokesman denied that Nauta cleaned his seat.

Blanche and his partners pursued it with special zeal. They looked for every opportunity for motions, even ones that would fail, as long as they would soak up time. Everything had to be a fight.

This hearing was Blanche's last chance to postpone the trial. He argued that the defense team had just received some hundred thousand records from the earlier federal investigation and needed time to review them in case they affected the state case. The judge, Juan Merchan, tried to pin Blanche down on how long he would need. Blanche resisted specifying. "Every document is important," Blanche said. "Every single one." He stressed the significance of giving the defense a fair chance to see the files, or else the prosecutors might be suspected of hiding material that could be exculpatory.

Merchan took offense at that suggestion. "You are literally accusing the Manhattan DA's office and the people assigned to this case of prosecutorial misconduct, and of trying to make me complicit," the judge said. In his view, Blanche's team was responsible for the delay. If he thought the federal files were so important, why had he waited until January to ask for them? He could have subpoenaed them months earlier. "This has been frankly going on for months," Merchan said. "It's really odd that we're even here and that we've taken this time."

With that, he called for a break. It was not hard to predict how he would rule when they returned. Ordinarily, defense attorneys would take pains to avoid antagonizing the judge. But this would be no ordinary trial.

As soon as Trump stormed out of the courtroom for the recess, he learned that a New York appeals court agreed to reduce his bond to $175 million and give him another ten days to pay. Suddenly he was all smiles and thumbs-up. Then he returned to the courtroom and faced Merchan again. The judge set the trial to begin in three weeks, on April 15. Trump frowned and shook his head.

He wanted a news conference. His campaign team scrambled to assemble the press corps in the lobby of 40 Wall Street, the crown jewel of his commercial real estate portfolio. Foreign tourists visiting the Stock Exchange and the Charging Bull sculpture crowded up against a police barricade set up outside.

"Criminal!" someone shouted as Trump stepped out of his limo. He saw an overflow line of cameras waiting outside and wanted to bring them in. Inside the shiny marble lobby he was disappointed to see only a small huddle of reporters. But the Secret Service balked at screening more late entries.

Trump toggled between trashing Merchan and praising the appeals court. He said he had plenty of cash to secure a bond, but would prefer to use it on his campaign. A reporter correctly noted that Trump hadn't put his own money into his campaign since 2016. "It's none of your business," he snapped.

By the time he left, some supporters had found their way to the crowd outside. A "Fuck Joe Biden!" chant echoed down the chasm of Wall Street skyscrapers.

"Keep fighting for us!" a man shouted as Trump returned to his limo, to ride to his New Jersey golf club.

He raised his head back out of the open car door. "I will," he said.

Trump and his core campaign team dreaded the trial. As much as they publicly argued that it was juicing his fundraising and consolidating his support, they honestly had no idea how it would play in the general election. Having to appear in court nearly every day for weeks caused a scheduling nightmare, and it ruined Trump's mood. He ranted about how many lawyers he had, how much money they cost, and how often he had to meet with them. Wiles advised aides to use extra caution around him on court days, and some advisers learned to stay away from any conversation that touched on his legal problems.

To improve Trump's spirit and keep the campaign moving, aides scheduled a series of fundraisers and foreign leader visits. They had to make the most of being stuck in New York for weeks.

On the second day of the trial, his campaign arranged a surprise visit to a Harlem bodega where a crowd feted Trump with cheers. That night he returned to his Manhattan apartment to have dinner with lobbyist Brian Ballard, co-campaign manager Chris LaCivita, and health-care executives. Trump spoke extensively about a documentary he'd just finished about the Civil War. He wanted to give the group a tour of the New York apartment. He frequently liked to turn the lights off in the apartment so visitors could admire the shimmering view of Manhattan in the dark.

At the dinner, Ballard made an impassioned case for Trump to choose Senator Marco Rubio of Florida as his running mate. Trump listed several other contenders, then asked LaCivita, "What do you think?" LaCivita initially demurred. "My favorite is whoever you pick, sir," he said. Trump pressed him, and LaCivita said he was a fan of Senator JD Vance of Ohio, whose name had not yet come up that night.

Then Trump offered another idea. "What do you think about Kennedy?" he said, meaning RFK Jr. "Can you imagine it, a Trump-Kennedy bumper sticker?"

At another dinner, Trump entertained two lobbyists from Reynolds American, who wanted him to oppose a looming Biden administration ban on menthol-flavored cigarettes. The tobacco lobbyists brought extensive materials to make their case, not to mention campaign checks. Personally Trump had never liked smoking. But he told them he liked their pitch better than that of oil CEOs he'd recently met with. "They badmouth their own products because of global warming," Trump said.

"Fuck that. We need oil. What the fuck? That's your business. You're basically shooting yourself in the foot."

Trump had become an audacious fundraiser. Sometimes he was polite: "I really appreciate if you'd help." Other times he was more blunt: "Have you guys done anything yet? Are you going to do anything?" He told nursing home representatives they were "going to get fucked" by Biden administration regulations on staffing, served them well-done steak, and asked for millions more than they'd originally planned to give.

He could be even more explicit when he talked numbers. In April, he'd startled oil executives and his own staff by asking their companies to give him $1 billion because he would be good for their industry. He'd complained at another dinner, at billionaire investor John Paulson's house, that donors could not legally give more than about $1 million combined to his campaign and various GOP committees.

In the years since the Supreme Court blew a hole in campaign finance rules with the 2010 *Citizens United* decision, it became common for candidates to speak at super PAC events, where donors could write unlimited checks. Still, the candidate was technically not supposed to explicitly solicit super PAC donations. It remained illegal for candidates to ask for contributions above federal limits. But Trump, at the same time he was standing trial for charges arising from alleged campaign finance violations, showed little regard for such technicalities. Since the Federal Election Commission routinely deadlocked on enforcement questions, and the Justice Department lacked the time or will to bring a case before the election, any violations were almost certain to remain technicalities.

"A million dollars is not a lot," he told donors at an exclusive roundtable at New York's Pierre Hotel. "You're worth five, six billion. We got much richer than that." He told a story about aides telling him to have lunch with someone who'd given $1 million, and he'd say, "You got to make it twenty-five million." Then he'd tell the donor, "I'd be really happy at twenty-five, but I'd be much happier at fifty." And the donor would reply, "What about thirty-five?" Trump concluded, "A lot of it is you have to have the courage to ask."

At the Pierre fundraiser, Trump also offered a special peek into his negotiations with foreign leaders. In public, Trump would routinely claim that he deterred Russian President Vladimir Putin from invading Ukraine and Chinese President Xi Jinping from attacking Taiwan by telling them something shocking. What exactly he never specified. But for the donors he elaborated. "I was with Putin and I told him, 'Vladimir, if you do it, we're going to bomb the shit out of Moscow,'" Trump revealed, according to an audio recording. "'If you go into Taiwan, I'm going to bomb the shit out of Beijing.' He thought I was crazy . . . He didn't believe me either, except ten percent. And ten percent is all you need."

He promised to cut taxes for the wealthy, asking for a show of hands on who used a particular tax break he promised to restore. (He joked that his friend Steve Witkoff bought a private jet he didn't even want just to take advantage of the write-off.) He leaned on Jewish donors with vows to support Israel's war in Gaza. "Any student that protests, I throw them out of the country," he said of pro-Palestinian demonstrators.

During the Q & A, a donor lobbied Trump to choose Nikki Haley as his running mate. "You need every vote you can get," the donor said, according to the recording. "It's not about whether you like her or don't like her, you have to make a determination of any candidate: How many votes can they bring and put on the table for you?"

Trump replied that he'd heard that case before, and he wasn't moved by it. "She's a very disloyal person," he said. "She actually didn't do that well except she stayed long. . . . She got Democrat votes, all Democrat votes that are going to vote for the Democrat."

Trump saw some of the donors shaking their heads. "You have to have your self-respect," he insisted. "She stayed in too long and she was too nasty. . . . She should've gotten out. She didn't have a chance. . . . All those people are going to come to us anyway. Remember, who are they going to vote for?"

Every morning Trump would ride to the courthouse from his tower down the FDR Drive and grumble about the graffiti and rusted steel. The city had declined, he told his staff, asking why the mayor wasn't doing anything to clean it up. Then he'd start telling stories about his developments in the area, such as the skating rink in Central Park and the golf course in Westchester. "It's terrible what has gone on in New York," Trump lamented to his entourage.

Jury selection was an iconic New York tableau, like pulling everyone off a rush-hour subway car and interviewing them one by one. There were women in sweatpants and men in silk cravats. There was a woman who worked at Bloomingdale's, previously held "a performance job," and liked to "go to the club." Another prospective juror described his interests as "the four C's": cameras, computers, cop work, and charity. He was dismissed after bringing up Trump's ad calling for the death penalty after the Central Park Five arrests.

Merchan tried to protect the jurors' identities, but Trump's team of expensive jury consultants was able to see their names, look up their social media accounts, and unearth disqualifying posts. The judge warned Trump not to threaten the jurors or witnesses. Such gag orders were routine for criminal defendants; the judge overseeing his DC election-interference trial had imposed one too, as had Judge Engoron in the civil fraud trial.

Some advisers encouraged Trump to say what he wanted, gag order be damned, call it his First Amendment right as a presidential candidate, and dare the judge to punish him. But Trump didn't go for it. He was the one who would have to spend the night in jail.

The posts that got him into trouble had to do with the judges' families and were spurred by the blogger Laura Loomer. Trump promoted screenshots that Loomer said were anti-Trump tweets by Engoron's wife; the posts were not from her account. Loomer also publicized Merchan's daughter's work with a digital consulting firm serving Democratic politicians. Trump tried to use the connection to disqualify Merchan from the case, but an ethics panel concluded the judge did not need to recuse himself.

Once, Blanche rushed to Trump Tower and demanded an aide delete a Truth Social post that had violated the gag order in the civil fraud trial. The aide said the post could not be deleted without Trump's permission, and he was occupied with an interview. "I'll tell him it was me," Blanche said. When Trump finished, Blanche told him he'd violated the gag order and Blanche had ordered the post deleted. To Blanche's surprise, Trump took the news calmly and said he understood. He was later fined for the post. At other times, Trump would call Blanche to ask him if he could post something incendiary. Maybe it wasn't a good idea, Blanche would say, but Trump could do it if he wanted. Trump took to calling Merchan "conflicted" as a way of alluding to his daughter without violating the gag order. After the initial set of fines, Trump went right up to the line but did not cross it again.

Trump did not try to hide his disdain for the process. He hated the trial. It brought up personal indiscretions he did not want to relive, such as the *Access Hollywood* tape, his alleged affairs with Daniels and other women, and Cohen's turn against him. "He thought it was embarrassing for him," a friend who talked to him said. Trump's audible muttering during Daniels's testimony earned another rebuke from the judge.

He was an unusually active defendant. He would regularly tell

Blanche or attorney Susan Necheles to ask a certain question or bring up certain evidence. He repeatedly wanted Blanche to call for dismissing the case. He complained nonstop about how unfair the judge was. He applauded Blanche in the holding room after his cross-examination of Michael Cohen, and he said he liked how ferocious Blanche's law partner, Emil Bove, was when he questioned former *National Enquirer* executive David Pecker. Sometimes he would tell his lawyers they were doing a "fantastic" job. Other times he would berate his defense team, harshly critiquing Blanche and Bove. At times his political staff would clear the room because Trump was getting so heated, or they stayed and winced silently. When the lawyers would leave, Trump would call other lawyers to complain about them.

He told his lawyers they should have prevented the testimony of Karen McDougal, the *Playboy* model who sold the story of her affair with Trump to the *Enquirer*. He was furious that Daniels described their liaison in graphic detail. "This is ridiculous!" he yelled at his lawyers. "Why didn't you object more?" After her testimony, Blanche moved for a mistrial, arguing that her story had unfairly prejudiced the jury. Merchan replied that Trump's lawyers should have objected more while she was on the stand, just like Trump had told them to.

"I used to have Roy Cohn and Jay Goldberg!" he shouted.* "Is this the best money can buy?"

Some of Trump's advisers feared Blanche would walk away. But he told others he respected Trump's anger with the process, because it enraged him too. Blanche never considered quitting, partially because he had nowhere to go. He was largely persona non grata in the elite New York legal circles where he'd made his career. For better or worse, he was Trump's lawyer now.

---

*Cohn was a ruthless former counsel to Senator Joseph McCarthy who mentored a young Trump. Goldberg represented Trump in his divorces.

If there was one lawyer who could usually calm Trump down, it was Boris Epshteyn. Some other advisers had opposed letting Epshteyn come to the trial since he had just been indicted himself, as part of the scheme to overturn Arizona's 2020 presidential election results. But it turned out to be one of the few times that other advisers were grateful to have Epshteyn around.

Another constant source of frustration for Trump was the lack of protesters outside the courthouse. He blamed police for restricting access to the area. "It's locked down. It looks like Fort Knox," he told donors during the trial. "There's not a civilian within five blocks. It's all police." Toward the end of the trial, a few fans showed up with chants and flags. A pickup truck with Trump flags and an image of Biden hogtied on the tailgate circled the block. A man who posted a 2,831-word manifesto about a global financial conspiracy lit himself on fire. But Trump never saw the outpouring of outrage he expected.

He was heartened by some friendly court staff. One court employee wrote Trump a letter saying how unfair she thought the trial was. (She later resigned.) Others smiled or shook his hand as he traversed the bowels of the building. Aides would arrange for friends and lawmakers to ride with Trump in the motorcade or sit in the courtroom. At turns his entourage included House Speaker Mike Johnson, running-mate hopefuls Doug Burgum, Vivek Ramaswamy, and Tim Scott, Senators Rick Scott and Tommy Tuberville, and several state attorneys general. Few people could soothe Trump like Witkoff, who started traveling with him frequently. "I honestly felt it was rigged every day I was there," Witkoff said of the trial. "He felt that too."

His campaign team saw every aspect of the trial as maximally calibrated to disrupt his candidacy. Court was in session four days a week, with a break on Wednesday. Judge Merchan always scheduled his trials this way, but Trump's aides were convinced the rhythm was designed to thwart him from having three-day weekends to campaign.

He took advantage of the time in New York to chase a fantasy that he could win his home state. The head of the New York Young Republican Club, Gavin Wax, piqued Trump's interest in holding a rally in the South Bronx. Wax told him it would set the stage for a landslide. Trump loved the idea, and Wax helped the campaign draw a crowd to Crotona Park. "You may never see me again," Trump joked to donors beforehand.

It did not look like your typical Trump rally. The red caps and profane apparel were the same, but, for a change, the people wearing them were not almost entirely white. Democrats could reassure themselves that the Bronx did not matter, New York was a safe blue state. But the rally gave human form to polls showing Trump was gaining with Black and Latino voters, especially men.

Toward the end, Trump invited on stage two rappers, Sheff G and Sleepy Hallow, and the former president admired the former's jeweled grills. "I want to find out where you did—I got to get my teeth like that," he said. "I want that to happen to me." There was no mention of the charges the rappers were facing—conspiracy to commit murder and weapons possession, part of a gang warfare prosecution. But the association was not accidental. Trump and his aides believed the former president gained cred with Black men because he had a mug shot—and they didn't care who called them racist for saying so. Backstage at the rally, Trump was thrilled. "Can you believe we got this crowd in the Bronx?" he asked aides.

Trump would do local TV interviews some mornings from Trump Tower before leaving. Every day, he'd ask his staff if he should talk to the press in the hallway outside the courtroom, and he usually did. His advisers tracked how much media coverage he was getting, and Trump saw that as a win, even if the coverage was not often positive. "Nobody is talking about Biden," he said.

After twenty-two days in court, the trial broke for jury deliberations. Trump was not allowed to leave the courthouse while the jury met, since police worried that a delay returning could invite mischief. He had to sit around and wait. On the second day of deliberations, he returned to the courtroom expecting the judge to send them home for the day. He and Blanche were all smiles, whispering and bantering. Judge Merchan stepped out briefly, then returned, announcing he'd received a note from the jury. "'We the jury have a verdict,'" he read.

Everyone froze. A quick verdict usually means guilty. Trump crossed his arms and knitted his brows. He continued to whisper with Blanche, but no longer cheerfully. Blanche had tried to lower Trump's expectations, telling him he hoped for a mistrial at best. Trump had started saying out loud he believed he was going to be convicted. Now he stared solemnly ahead while they waited. A tense half hour passed.

Finally the jury entered the courtroom. "Mr. Foreperson," Judge Merchan said, "without telling me the verdict, has the jury, in fact, reached a verdict?"

"Yes," the foreman said. "They have."

"Take the verdict, please," the judge instructed the clerk.

"Have the members of the jury agreed upon a verdict?" the clerk asked.

"Yes, we have."

"How say you to the first count of the indictment, charging Donald J. Trump with the crime of falsifying business records in the first degree, guilty or not guilty?"

"Guilty."

"How say you to count two?"

"Guilty."

Thirty-two more times he repeated, "Guilty." Guilty on all counts. Trump stared straight ahead blankly. Merchan thanked the jurors for their service and instructed them to leave the courtroom. Trump adjusted his tie and stood as they filed past him. They did not look at him, and he did not look at them.

Blanche immediately asked the judge to reject the verdict. "Your motion is denied," Merchan said.

Trump looked flushed as he walked down the center aisle for the last time and stormed out of the courtroom. Reporters were waiting outside in the hallway. "This was a rigged trial by a conflicted judge who was corrupt," he seethed. "The real verdict is gonna be November fifth by the people."

He was in shock. He hugged his son Eric, an unusual occurrence. He was pleased that most Republicans continued to defend him, but the possibility of a carceral sentence suddenly became real. He still faced other trials on classified documents and attempting to overturn the 2020 election. His advisers increasingly saw winning in November as his only way to stay out of prison.

On the day of the verdict, LaCivita saw a tweet from Larry Hogan, the Republican governor of Maryland who was running for Senate, promising to make a real race in the reliably blue state. Hogan had always kept his distance from Trump, and in anticipation of the verdict he'd posted: "Regardless of the result, I urge all Americans to respect the verdict and the legal process. At this dangerously divided moment in our history, all leaders—regardless of party—must not pour fuel on the fire with more toxic partisanship. We must reaffirm what has made this nation great: the rule of law."

LaCivita lashed out. "You just ended your campaign," he wrote. But when LaCivita saw Trump later at his Virginia golf club, the former president delivered a surprising message. "Go easy on Larry," Trump said. "We need the seat."

The sentencing was scheduled for July 11, a week before the Republican convention. Trump's campaign started seriously considering how Trump might give an acceptance speech from jail. On a campaign leadership call, Lara Trump said a speech from Rikers Island would be attention grabbing and work in Trump's favor. "He'd be the ultimate political prisoner."

The Block

The month of June 2024 was going to be momentous for Joe Biden's presidency. He would first travel to France to commemorate the eightieth anniversary of D-Day, and planned to go to the Aisne-Marne American Cemetery outside of Paris, in an implicit but clear rebuke to his predecessor who'd infamously refused to visit. Biden would return to DC, only to fly back to Europe a few days later to attend the Group of Seven summit in Italy. He would then travel directly to Los Angeles to attend a star-studded fundraiser with Barack Obama, George Clooney, and Julia Roberts. With his advisers fretting over their dwindling cash advantage over Trump, Biden hoped the fundraiser would help pad his campaign's monthly haul. The president's busy month would conclude with the first presidential debate. Polls showed Biden trailing Trump by about a point, a measly 1 point improvement in the national polling average after the president's campaign pumped $50 million into ads that spring.

But there was another matter at the top of the president's mind. As Biden confided to a close friend, "The only thing I care about is that my son is not convicted."

On June 3, Hunter Biden reported to the J. Caleb Boggs Federal Building, the Wilmington courthouse named after the senator Joe Biden defeated in 1972. The president's son faced three felony counts for lying on a federal firearms application and possessing a gun while abusing drugs. Beyond the danger to Hunter's liberty, the trial was sure to publicly embarrass the Biden family, airing the family's sordid secrets from the painful years after Beau Biden died of brain cancer. Much of the American public was unaware of the depths of turmoil within the Biden family—affairs, addiction, alcoholism—and now it would all spill out in a federal courtroom five months before the election. In order to prove Hunter Biden was abusing drugs when he purchased the gun, prosecutors planned to call three star witnesses: his ex-girlfriend, whom he met when she was a stripper; his ex-wife, the mother of three of his daughters; and his brother's widow, with whom he started a romantic relationship after Beau's death. The government also planned to use the audiobook of Hunter's memoir, narrated in his own voice, to demonstrate his drug use.

Republicans continued to make Hunter Biden a centerpiece of their attacks on the president. When Biden's top aides reviewed word clouds put together by outside pollsters to see what issues were animating voters and what they thought about the president, Hunter Biden's name almost always appeared. But inside the White House, Hunter Biden was largely a forbidden subject. The president felt deep guilt about his only surviving son's struggles and largely refused to talk about his family woes—only doing so with his lawyers or closest advisers.

The near-total ban on discussing Hunter infuriated some aides, who thought the White House needed to plan for how to respond to the attacks and the trials. Anita Dunn, who led communications related to investigations from congressional Republicans, often pushed for more internal transparency around the family. One White House ally warned her to stop talking about Hunter Biden, or at least be careful who was around her when she did, because Jill Biden's top aide and enforcer, Anthony Bernal, was telling others that Dunn was being disloyal.*

Bernal was a mercurial figure in the Biden orbit. His title, senior adviser to the first lady, belied his influence and his involvement in decisions that expanded far beyond the East Wing. He fell in with the Biden family in 2008, when he was assigned to be the scheduler for the spouse of Obama's running mate. He quickly bonded with Jill Biden and never left her side, becoming unflinchingly loyal to her and using his proximity to her to exert power wherever he decided. It was often unclear if the opinion he was expressing was his own or the first lady's. Sometimes, when donors or voters asked her questions, Bernal would jump in to answer. Aides said he could be unnecessarily harsh, routinely making people cry with blistering criticism. He brushed off complaints about his comments, saying he just expected excellence.† And despite Joe Biden's warning to staff on his first day in office that he would "fire you on the spot" if they disrespect others, Bernal seemingly did that multiple times a day without incident.

The warning about Bernal did not change Dunn's attitude. She told colleagues she felt she had a responsibility to protect the president, and she remained shocked that there was no open discussion about the tawdry criminal trial unfolding roughly a hundred miles from the White House. If aides mentioned it at all, it was only in passing: *and the trial*, they would say—without dwelling on the reality that the president's son was on trial for federal crimes in an election year.

For Biden, the trial was devastating. As a father, his biggest fear was Hunter relapsing and losing him again. The president was convinced that Republicans' goal in attacking Hunter was to break him psychologically

---

*Bernal said he did not remember saying that and did not think Dunn was disloyal.

† Some who worked closely with Bernal said he was very good at anticipating problems, predicting the news cycle, and staging public events. He also, they said, could be very generous to colleagues.

so that he would return to drugs and alcohol. That belief undergirded Biden's entire approach to handling his son's challenges, and he feared the trial—which made Hunter, his granddaughters, and the entire family relive those terrible years—would ruin the stability and peace Hunter found in his sobriety.

Before the trial began, Joe Biden spoke to Abbe Lowell, Hunter's lawyer. "Is there something you need at trial that I can be a witness to?" Biden asked. The president was not the only one asking. The first lady, the president's brother, and Hunter's daughter Naomi Biden Neal all said they would testify. Lowell and his team considered each of the offers, including the president's. But they determined the president did not provide any testimony that other family members couldn't testify to, and they couldn't justify the complications of bringing the sitting president into the courtroom.

Biden wished he could have attended the trial; he went to Wilmington a few times, but he never entered the courtroom. In his absence, the first lady showed up almost every day. Most senior aides in the West Wing had no idea the first lady planned to attend the trial until she arrived, accompanied by Bernal and other aides, family, and friends. The first day of the trial happened to fall on Jill Biden's seventy-third birthday. Hunter Biden greeted her: "Happy birthday. I got you a special event."

As the prosecutors put on their case, they presented photographs of Hunter with drug paraphernalia, sometimes shirtless or partly censored for nudity. They displayed text messages between Hunter Biden and his drug dealers, while his ex-lovers, one by one, confirmed his regular use of cocaine and crack. Ashley Biden cried, but Jill showed no emotion, embodying her own instruction to her staff, "Never let them see you sweat." Jill Biden attended the first three days, flew to France to join her husband at the D-Day commemoration, then left after less than twenty-four hours to return to Wilmington for the fifth day of the trial. The costs of the flights were in part covered by the Democratic National Committee.

The trial was not televised or live streamed, so Joe Biden followed along mostly through updates from family members and his own lawyers. They thought the trial was going well and were optimistic about a hung jury. Then the defense called Naomi, Hunter's eldest daughter. She wanted to testify, hoping to help her father by providing a sympathetic account of him as someone who was in recovery and sober after years of struggles. On cross-examination, however, prosecutors showed text messages between Naomi and her father from around the time he bought the gun. The messages showed erratic and inconsistent communication between the two, including a text Naomi sent to her father in October 2018, the same month he bought the gun, saying, "I'm really sorry, dad, I can't take this." Naomi told prosecutors she did "not recall" sending the texts. Family members and allies were outraged at the legal team, believing they'd done a disservice to Naomi by failing to prepare her for all the text messages submitted in evidence. Hunter and his lawyers told others that Naomi had been fully prepared but said the prosecution misled her on the stand. Everyone agreed it was the lowest point of the trial.*

Jill Biden flew to France that weekend for a state dinner in Paris, and was back in the courtroom on Monday for closing arguments and the start of jury deliberations. The jury deliberated for only three hours and five minutes, usually the sign of a conviction.† The verdict came on Tuesday morning just after eleven: guilty on all counts. It happened so

---

*Lowell said the president and the first lady never expressed outrage to him, and the president called him after opening and closing arguments and expressed gratitude for his work defending Hunter.

† One anonymous juror told news organizations that the jury was initially split 6–6.

quickly that the first lady did not make it back inside the courtroom in time to hear.

Shortly after the verdict, Hunter returned to his room at the Hotel Du Pont, the venue where Biden held his election night celebration party when he won his first Senate race in 1972. The younger Biden, though obviously disappointed in the outcome, was in surprisingly good spirits when he connected with his father on the phone. "I'm really good," he told his dad. "I can't really describe it. It's like being able to go to your own funeral," referring to his being surrounded by loved ones.

Joe Biden was at the White House when the verdict came in. Annie Tomasini delivered the news. In a few hours he was scheduled to speak at the Washington Hilton, and his aides worried about him appearing publicly. "You don't have to do this," Anita Dunn told him. "You can go home to Wilmington. Everyone will understand." Kamala Harris offered to speak in his place. But Biden refused. "I want to do it," he said.

Watching the speech, you would not have known his son had just received a guilty sentence. The president spoke for nearly twenty minutes, receiving rapturous applause as he called for stronger gun safety legislation. But right after the speech, instead of returning to the White House, Biden's motorcade took him to Joint Base Andrews. He changed his schedule to fly home to Wilmington. Hunter, his wife, Melissa Cohen Biden, and their young son met the president on the tarmac of Delaware's New Castle Air National Guard Base. Hunter was headed home to California, so the three of them only embraced and chatted briefly before going their separate ways.

While Hunter was reassuring his friends and family that he was okay, Biden's closest confidants grew increasingly concerned about the president. The trial and the verdict came just before a critical time in his campaign, when he needed to prove his vigor and vitality to make inroads with voters who were drifting away from him. Some of those who were closest to Biden feared he might not be able to muster the stamina necessary to do so. They worried about the toll Hunter's ordeal had taken on his father—how it had suddenly aged him and reinforced the deep guilt he felt for not being able to protect his son.

The next day, accompanied by three of Hunter's children, Biden headed to Italy for two days for the G7 summit. Much of Biden's focus for the two-day trip was on bolstering support for Ukraine, demonstrating that the Western allies would continue to support the prolonged war against Russia despite political turbulence throughout the coalition. Biden and Ukrainian President Volodymyr Zelensky planned to hold a joint press conference to sign a ten-year security agreement. But in the hours before, some of Biden's aides suggested scrapping the news conference. Though never explicitly stated, the clear concern was that the president was too tired and would perform poorly. Other aides warned that canceling would cause more of an uproar than whatever mistake Biden might make onstage. They won out.

In the shuffle, Biden ended up at the lectern without all his notes in the usual place. Some aides furtively orchestrated the mishap because they thought Biden would do better by speaking extemporaneously about a subject he knew well. They thought his performance that evening vindicated their intervention: Biden stayed on message when addressing Hunter's guilty verdict for the first time, reiterating his support for him while promising not to pardon him or commute his sentence; he also showed command of the nuances of how the United States was assisting Ukraine. The president, however, was furious. "This cannot happen," he barked at staff after he walked off the stage.

Air Force One returned to the States, stopping to refuel at Joint Base Andrews, before continuing on to Los Angeles for the fundraiser. Some of Biden's aides, much younger than the president, were themselves exhausted by the back-to-back European trips, and they worried about the toll it was taking on the president. Some wondered why he had to go to LA at this time.

The president's schedule, known inside the White House as "the block," is a complex puzzle, involving scores of people across many government departments. Each day of his life is assigned to an individual scheduler to manage, but the decision-making power rests with the deputy chief of staff. The Office of Scheduling and Advance regularly circulates a rough outline of the next fourteen or twenty-one days and a looser outline of the next two months. As a result, most White House officials didn't fully realize what the month of June would look like for Biden until late April or May, and almost immediately some started to raise questions. They discussed having Biden stay in Europe instead of returning to the United States between the France and Italy trips, but they decided an extended continental sojourn would look bad just months before Election Day. Neither the D-Day commemoration nor the G7 summit could be moved or skipped. That left the question of flying directly from Italy to California.

The Los Angeles fundraiser was scheduled for the only date the campaign could find when both George Clooney and Julia Roberts could attend in person. It also didn't hurt that the fundraiser was being held the night before Father's Day, allowing the president to spend the holiday with Hunter, who lived in Los Angeles. The fundraiser was a priority because the campaign was nervous about money—in fact, the campaign was in such a cash crunch ahead of the debate that it was beginning to discuss potential cost-cutting measures if fundraising did not increase. Some of those included pulling out of specific states, especially if Biden's numbers weren't improving there. At the same time, Biden demanded that the campaign open more offices because Obama had told him his campaign didn't have enough of a presence on the ground. Campaign leaders had a weekly tracker to make sure they were hitting targets on field offices, even after the campaign overhauled its organizing strategy to rely less on the brick-and-mortar approach. Most staffers viewed office openings as an unhelpful performance metric.

The need for money meant the fundraiser had to go forward, and the attitude became: We just have to do it. Initially, Biden was supposed to continue on to Chicago for more fundraising, but aides finally drew the line there. "Each one of these decisions by itself maybe is okay," one aide later said. "Put them all together, and the month of June ended up being a very rough month on the president. It would have been if he had been forty-one and not eighty-one."

Air Force One touched down at Los Angeles International Airport at 5:04 a.m. Pacific time, and the president arrived at his hotel just after 6:00 a.m. Less than twelve hours later, at 5:15 p.m., Biden was at the Peacock Theater, where he first spent hours in a photo line with scores of elected officials and top donors. After the whole event had been built around their availability, Clooney and Roberts never appeared onstage with the president. Clooney's relationship with the White House had taken a rocky turn earlier in the month. His wife, Amal, had worked on the International Criminal Court's decision to issue arrest warrants for top Israeli and Hamas leaders. Biden had criticized the decision, and Clooney complained about it directly to Steve Ricchetti, one of Biden's top aides.

Clooney and Roberts were only part of the celebrity-filled preprogram, as they both had to leave to catch flights for other work commitments. The event also featured appearances by Barbra Streisand, Jack Black, Jason Bateman, and Kathryn Hahn. Biden finally took the stage with Obama and Jimmy Kimmel just before 8:00. Kimmel opened by rattling off a list of Biden's accomplishments before asking the president which one he was most proud of. Biden stuttered. He meandered. Sitting next to two men who were decades his junior, he looked even older than eighty-one.

Many people in the audience were aghast. "It felt like Kimmel and Obama were talking and Biden just was sort of looking off into space, and he just seemed like not with it, like out of it," said Jon Favreau, a former Obama speechwriter turned liberal podcaster who attended the event. A video of Obama appearing to guide Biden off the stage went viral, fueling suspicions about the president's disorientation; but Biden aides said the reality was that the event was running overtime and Obama was eager to leave without Biden stopping to greet more people. Financially, the event was a success: The campaign raised more than $30 million, and Favreau remembered hoping Biden's performance was the result of being tired from his hectic travel schedule. Favreau figured he would find out for sure whether that night was a one-off when Biden faced Trump for the debate twelve days later, on June 27. "Either he'll be great at the debate, and we'll know he was just tired," he said, "or it'll be like this at the debate, and then the whole world will know."

Five days after the LA fundraiser, on the evening of June 20, Biden arrived at Camp David. The next morning, he started debate prep in the presidential cabin, known as the Aspen Lodge, with Bruce Reed, Mike Donilon, and Ron Klain. Klain had overseen debate preparations for every Democratic presidential candidate since 2004. It was not ideal, he'd later acknowledge, that he had not started working with Biden until less than a week before the matchup in Atlanta. The sessions should have begun earlier, especially because Biden was rusty. Klain told colleagues he was reminded of their preparations for the first Democratic primary debate in 2019, when Biden struggled to parry attacks, especially from Kamala Harris.

Sitting at the dining-room table with his aides, Biden reviewed note cards spanning different policy areas, then practiced delivering answers from memory. Klain would respond as he imagined Trump would. When pressed on economic issues, Biden often repeated the same points: "I created sixteen million jobs." Klain wasn't satisfied. "That's just not going to get this done," he said.

Biden also knew it wasn't going well. "I haven't done this in a long time," he told Klain. "I'm not at the top of my game. I need to practice more."

But Biden also conceded something else: "I'm tired."

By Sunday night, additional staff had arrived at Camp David, and they had planned to have a staff dinner and begin prep with more aides. But the night was called off. The president was too tired.

It was clear throughout the debate camp that Biden was sick. He was coughing. His voice was weak. He said he had a cold, but to take extra precautions, doctors tested him for COVID and the flu. Both tests were negative. Still, everyone agreed Biden needed to get more rest. Aides ripped up the schedule, abandoning plans to have Biden participate in two full ninety-minute mock debates, knowing that it was most important Biden displayed vigor on the debate stage. They tried to limit how much talking he was doing, worried about how his raspy voice would sound to voters anxious about his age. Americans had rarely seen him in unscripted forums—in part because he rarely did them, but also because Americans rarely watched him do anything at all—and public concerns about his age and mental acuity were only growing.

In one of the airplane hangars at Camp David, Biden's staff set up a replica debate stage, complete with studio lights, a moderator's table, and two lecterns. But Biden never held even one full-length mock debate. He participated in one that ran more than an hour, in which his lawyer Bob Bauer played the part of Trump, and Dunn and White House communications director Ben LaBolt played the moderators, CNN's Dana Bash and Jake Tapper. Biden largely held his own, but he struggled to land any attacks on Trump. Biden had always had trouble responding quickly when someone spoke directly at him, an impediment some aides attributed to his childhood stutter. As he grew older, aides said Biden's stutter resurfaced more frequently—though Biden denied he still had a stutter—and his auditory processing skills seemed to worsen. It was clear in the mock sessions that Biden was not as quick on his feet and was unable to swiftly counterpunch.

In those sessions, Biden leaned on input from Steven Spielberg, reprising his coaching after the success of the State of the Union in March. In a Zoom meeting, the Oscar-winning director recommended that Biden make facial expressions when Trump spoke, especially when he would say something particularly outrageous. Biden seized on the advice "like a life raft," one aide said. But Klain had reservations.

"Mr. President, that's not going to work," he said. "People are going to think you're just befuddled."

Biden disagreed. "People are going to see me reacting this way and they're going to know what Trump's saying is crazy."

"I don't think that's a great idea," Klain responded.

Spielberg insisted. "I think if the president is expressive, it shows his engagement," he said. Biden sided with Spielberg, who had been working with the president for more than a year at that point.

By Wednesday, the night before the debate, most aides left Camp David, either to meet Biden at Joint Base Andrews the next day or to watch the debate from Washington. Staffers knew debate prep wasn't a smashing success, but they tried to stay optimistic—telling allies that Biden would do fine. Privately, they had more concerns.

"This is going to be really touch and go in Atlanta," Klain told Donilon and Reed.

ad

"We're F——ed"

Leading up to the debate, Trump called Steve Bannon, who was preparing to report to prison for four months. Bannon had been convicted of contempt of Congress for defying a subpoena in the January 6 investigation. When Trump called, Bannon was broadcasting his *War Room* talk show, interviewing Senate candidate Kari Lake. "Hey, Mr. President," he said, "I'm live on TV, can I call you back?"

"Love *War Room*," Trump said. "Call me back."

When he did, he asked Trump, "Why are you doing this debate?" Trump said he was going to blow Biden out of the water. But Bannon warned him the debate would lead to one of two things. Either Biden would show up, hold his ground, not get blown out of the water, and tighten the race; or—worse, in Bannon's view—Trump would beat Biden so badly the Democrats would replace him. Trump disagreed. His advisers had told him Biden could not be removed. Bannon reminded him that Biden wasn't officially the nominee, and the ballots wouldn't be printed until September. "He's not on the ballot, the printed ballot," Bannon told Trump. "If you beat this guy like you know you can, they're gonna remove him."

In the past, Trump had often not taken debate prep seriously. He did not want to do traditional rehearsals with someone playing the opponent. He especially did not want it *reported* that he was doing debate prep. Susie Wiles looked for a way to help him get ready without frustrating him. The staff gave him occasional "refreshers" on his record in the White House, hoping he would enjoy reading about his own accomplishments or seeing former White House officials. They also brought in allies such as Senators Eric Schmitt, JD Vance, and Marco Rubio, former trade ambassador Robert Lighthizer, and former acting Immigration and Customs Enforcement Director Tom Homan. These "policy sessions" were quick, to suit Trump's attention span. He would get excited while talking with Homan about the border or Vance about Ukraine. Advisers hoped he would absorb new information from those conversations and remember things he'd done in his first term. Trump did sometimes seem to focus.

"I want to debate this Biden guy. I'm dying to do it," Trump told donors at a private fundraiser. He scoffed at Biden's challenging him to a round of golf instead: "He's never going to play me."

Often on Trump Force One, a big-screen TV plays UFC matches, or Pavarotti, James Brown, and Sinéad O'Connor are blasting so loudly from the speakers that the staff flee the cabin. But on June 27, during the short trip to Atlanta for the debate, Trump was not his usual rambunctious self. He sat at his table talking to advisers quietly. He knew his first debate against Biden, in 2020, hadn't gone well. He'd come in too hot, talked over Biden, come across as mean and out of control— traits that many voters liked least about him. He blamed it on the coronavirus (which he'd denied having at the time). This time he was determined to nail it.

When he arrived at CNN, Trump went into the waiting room, sitting in a big chair with notes. "He was absolutely still for an extended period of time, talking to no one," a longtime adviser said. "I have never seen him do anything like that."

Biden departed from Camp David on Marine One, the presidential helicopter, in the early afternoon and picked up Air Force One at Joint Base Andrews en route to Atlanta. During the flight, Klain and Reed joined the president in his cabin for some last-minute practice. Before they landed, Klain suggested they go straight to CNN studios for a full walk-through of the debate stage. But Biden said no. He wanted to go to the hotel and relax. He spent much of the next four hours in his suite at the Hyatt Regency, engaged in some final Q&A with Klain, Donilon, and Reed.

Biden did not enter the Beast until 8:27 p.m. He arrived at the CNN studios less than thirty minutes before the start of the debate. Having declined a typical walk-through, Biden agreed to walk out and look at the debate stage, briefly.

Just offstage, Biden's closest aides winced as the president started answering the first question about the economy and voters who felt they were worse off under his presidency. Biden was ready for this one. He had practiced a specific response over and over. Aides had prepared him to blame inflation on Trump's mishandling of the pandemic, then pivot to his administration's efforts to bring down costs, citing data showing inflation cooling and the economy growing. Finally, Biden was supposed to warn the American people about the danger to the economy if Trump were reelected—something along the lines of: "If you put him in charge, he'll screw it up again."

Biden started slowly. "We've got to take a look at what I was left when I became president, what Mr. Trump left me," he said. "We had an economy that was in free fall. The pandemic was so badly handled, many people were dying. All he said was, 'It's not that serious. Just inject a little bleach in your arm. You'll be all right.'" He then talked about rebuilding the economy. "We created fifteen thousand new jobs. We brought on—in a position where we have eight hundred thousand new manufacturing jobs," he said, completely messing up the numbers. He meant to say *sixteen million* jobs—a mistake that was all the more glaring to his staff because he had resorted to citing that number so often during debate prep. He went on to blame corporate greed for inflation and mentioned his upbringing in Scranton.

Biden's aides thought he blew it. He'd missed the chance to pin the blame squarely on Trump. Trump pounced, blaming the virus, not his handling of it, for ruining the economy and Biden for stunting economic growth. When Jake Tapper gave Biden a chance to respond, he voluntarily changed the topic to one of the biggest debacles of his presidency: the withdrawal from Afghanistan, which involved the deaths of thirteen U.S. service members in a suicide bombing at the Kabul airport and had irreparably shattered the public perception of competence that Biden tried to project in contrast to Trump's chaos. Trump pounced again, calling that attack "the most embarrassing day in the history of our country's life."

For a moment, Biden's aides reassured themselves. He usually got off to a rough start. But hope quickly evaporated. For the second question, Tapper asked Biden about the national debt, and in less than a minute, the president mixed up multiple facts—saying trillionaires instead of billionaires and millions instead of billions. He struggled to complete his sentences. He eventually trailed off while making an unintelligible point about health-care policy, tripping over his words until he finally stopped, seemed to sigh, and concluded, "We finally beat Medicare." He meant Big Pharma, but that was lost on most everyone watching.

Back in the hold room, Klain stood up and announced: "We're fucked."

The Trump campaign staff, family, and allies were watching from a volleyball arena on the Georgia Tech campus. A massive projector was set up against one wall. Catered rubber chicken with green beans and platters of McDonald's were served. The group fell silent as the debate started and Biden began answering the first question.

"The sound is off!" spokeswoman Danielle Alvarez shouted. She and her fellow communications aide, Brian Hughes, started panicking that the feed was malfunctioning. Then they realized the TV was working fine. The problem was Biden. The group started gasping. Alvarez and Hughes gripped each other's arms and whispered to each other.

"Oh my god, it's happening!" she said.

"It's happening!" he replied.

Before the debate, Trump campaign advisers believed Biden would perform relatively well and feared Trump would go off script or forget to mention some of his accomplishments. But Biden's wipeout was so obvious that they quickly began developing new talking points, using a printer that Alvarez had in the room. Trump's team had questioned Biden's mental acuity for years, but they did not expect him to perform like this.

The group whooped and hollered when Trump suggested Biden didn't even know what he just said. Rubio told jokes about Biden and slapped the table. On abortion, which should have been the Democrats' strongest topic, Biden confusingly pivoted to discussing women murdered by immigrants and raped by "brothers and sisters." Biden even got drawn into a squabble with Trump over golf handicaps.

Near the end of the debate, Alvarez addressed the surrogates heading to the spin room. "President Trump just delivered a knockout debate performance," she said. She urged the surrogates not to fall into the trap of calling for Biden to withdraw. "Biden is their nominee," she said. Everyone agreed to say that. "The conclusion here is not only President Trump is the best debater but the best president and the best golfer," she said. The room laughed.

Governors, members of Congress, and other surrogates began lining up to bolt 150 yards to the spin room as soon as the debate ended. Some jogged there. This was going to be fun.

The scale of the disaster was equally apparent to Biden's campaign staff at their headquarters in Wilmington. They started looking at each other, silently asking in unison, *WTF?* One aide thought to himself that maybe everything the Republicans had been saying for months was right, and he'd been complicit in a massive cover-up. Staffers started rethinking their interactions with the president, wondering if they had overlooked something, or suddenly seeing past small slips in a new way. But everyone agreed they had never seen anything like this.

The staff in the war room knew they had to organize a huge response. Aides immediately identified the urgency of drumming up support from top Democrats like Obama, Nancy Pelosi, and Chuck Schumer. It took twenty-five minutes for senior staff to authorize aides to tell reporters that the president had a cold—something they had previously not disclosed because they didn't think it was bad enough.

As the debate continued, Biden's staff believed the president recovered. Dunn watched from her home in Washington so she could monitor the panels of voters who used dials to record their real-time reactions. She was reassured. Biden struggled for sure, but the voters also did not like Trump. The Biden campaign quickly latched onto their spin for the night: Biden started slow, but he finished strong. To anxious allies, they distributed talking points that argued the fundamentals of the race remained unchanged. The focus groups reported that Biden did not perform well, but they hated Trump even more. As Klain tried to help mitigate the political fallout, he found allies didn't want to hear it. He recalled their reaction being, "They think he had a stroke in the middle of the health-care answer."

As soon as the debate ended and Trump returned to the hold room, he asked the head of his security detail to bring in Wiles. Melania Trump had not come with him, and offstage he was alone again.

"How do you think it went?" he asked Wiles. "Did I do okay?"

"Better than okay," she said.

Earlier he'd wanted to crash the spin room but he quickly agreed to skip it. Instead he went to a larger room with other advisers who cheered as he entered. They told him the reason Biden had looked so bad was that Trump had done so well, hitting all the points they'd prepared, exactly what they'd hoped for. Trump couldn't believe Biden was so out of it. He wouldn't stop talking about it. "I couldn't look at him," Trump said. The word he used most was "sad."

Jill Biden went into the studio and helped her husband down the steps of the stage. Klain was among the first staff members to see the president after the debate.

"That did not go very well, sir," Klain told him.

"Yeah," Biden said, "I know."

He was frustrated but had little time to dwell on it. He still had several stops on his schedule. First, he had to head back to the Hyatt Regency to greet supporters who had gathered to watch the debate in one of the hotel's ballrooms.

"You have to go into the post-debate rally and really punch 'em out," Klain said. "Use all the stuff you didn't use in the debate in the rally."

At the party, a DJ drowned out the live feed of cable news commentators trashing Biden's performance with music. Handpicked supporters and some campaign staff who had traveled to Atlanta to meet with donors chanted "Four more years" when Joe and Jill Biden took the stage. The first lady spoke first, trying to spin the unspinnable: "Joe, you did such a great job," she said. "You answered every question. You knew all the facts." Then Biden spoke for less than two minutes without mentioning his performance or any of the material from his debate prep that he had forgotten onstage.

His first comment on the debate came at a nearby Waffle House, where he stopped to pick up food for staff, and reporters got close enough to press him, despite his handlers' best efforts. "I thought I did well," Biden said, adding that it was challenging to debate a liar. As for his illness, he said he only had a sore throat. Biden was quickly whisked away to the Dobbins Air Reserve Base outside Atlanta, where Air Force One waited to take him to North Carolina. On the plane, Donilon started rewriting a speech the president would deliver the next day. They needed somehow to address what had just unfolded in those ninety minutes.

Kamala Harris watched the debate from a ballroom in the basement of the Fairmont Century Plaza, a five-star hotel in Los Angeles where her staff always stayed when she went home. She was booked to do a round of television interviews immediately afterward, in an interview room her team set up just down the hall. Across interviews with CNN, MSNBC, and ABC, she argued that Biden had a slow start but a strong finish. "Let us not decide the outcome of who's going to be president of the United States based on a ninety-minute debate," she said on ABC. "Let's measure that decision against the last three and a half years." Her defense of Biden's abysmal appearance, even as some started to whisper about replacing Biden on the ticket, earned her plaudits in Bidenworld. She could have backed out of the interviews or hedged. Instead, she backed Biden fully.

Biden arrived just before 2:00 a.m. at the Raleigh-Durham airport, where about two hundred supporters were waiting on the tarmac, along with a DJ and a marching band. Biden worked the rope line and Anthony Bernal danced to Diana Ross. But not everyone was in a mood to celebrate.

"It wasn't your best night," Durham Mayor Leonardo Williams told the president when he landed. Candidly, he thought the president had sucked.

"When you get knocked down, you get back up," Biden responded. "That's what we do."

Democrats across the country weren't so sure. Even some of Biden's allies thought the president could not survive. Others immediately started looking for scapegoats. Some raged about the debate prep. They argued Biden's aides had pumped him with too many facts and figures and he got lost in the details, a suggestion those responsible for the prep scoffed at. Biden kept demanding more details, like always, and they were trying to wean him off the specifics. In the debate they watched, too much information was not Biden's problem.

In Wilmington, staffers were deluged with pleas for Biden to drop out. Family members, friends, and even high school teachers sent messages. What was there to say in response? Some privately agreed with the messages, but they were still being paid to elect Biden, so they kept it to themselves. Others were furious, embarrassed that for years they had defended Biden to their friends and family. Those who worked in the White House or on the campaign and had few, if any, interactions with the president felt they, too, had been lied to by his inner circle. They wondered, if those people knew he had declined this much, why did they let him run? Nearly everyone was filled with sorrow and fear.

When some of Biden's former staffers found out about the lack of a full walk-through, they were astonished. More time in the studio might have fixed, or at least ameliorated, some of Biden's most glaring performance problems. The audio might have been better tuned to his voice, he would have had a better idea which camera to look at, and his makeup could have looked better. He wouldn't have looked so confused! He wouldn't have looked like a ghost! He wouldn't have sounded so raspy! But they also knew a walk-through wouldn't have prevented the full-scale collapse.

The next morning, Jen O'Malley Dillon and her deputies joined some of Biden's biggest donors at the Ritz-Carlton hotel in Atlanta for a scheduled breakfast briefing. They hadn't been expecting to have to defend that performance. O'Malley Dillon opened the meeting and sought to soothe the nerves, reminding donors that Obama had face-planted in the first debate of his reelection campaign. She acknowledged that Biden had struggled, but said all their data suggested the race was unchanged. The team bragged about their online fundraising metrics from the night before and emphasized all the crazy things Trump said about abortion (he falsely accused Democrats of supporting infanticide), January 6 (he blamed Nancy Pelosi for the insurrection), and "Black jobs" (he said undocumented immigrants were taking "Black jobs" and "Hispanic jobs" as he criticized Biden's handling of immigration). The pitch worked, at least for a while, on some donors, who left feeling somewhat reassured.

Klain departed North Carolina early Friday morning, and when he returned to Washington, he called Jeff Zients. Klain was disturbed that Biden was planning to spend the weekend at Camp David.

"We have an emergency," Klain told his successor as chief of staff, who ran the White House more deferentially and was not as politically minded. "We have a crisis on Capitol Hill, and the crisis is going to accelerate." He urged Zients to bring the Congressional Progressive Caucus, the liberal group of lawmakers who were some of Biden's most ardent supporters, to the White House on Monday. Klain wanted Biden to stand with the caucus and announce a far-ranging second-term agenda that addressed childcare, workers' rights, elder care, and paid family leave.

Many campaign staffers and Biden allies supported Klain's push for a more forceful response from the White House. But Zients and other aides disagreed with Klain's prioritizing the progressives. "He's going to Camp David with his family," Zients insisted.

"I have no fucking clue why he's going to Camp David this weekend," Klain said. "He needs to be working the phones, day and night."

The morning after the debate, Mike Donilon was eating eggs and bacon alone in the lobby restaurant of the Westin Raleigh-Durham Airport. He was in no mood to engage with the discussions convulsing the Democratic Party, immediately dismissing the notion that the president would drop out. He was adamant that Trump was the one who had disqualified himself in the debate with his answers about American democracy and the January 6 attack. "Lots of people have bad nights in debates. They don't generally lead to people losing their minds," Donilon said in an interview for this book. "Here's one fact which I know people hate it when I say it: There was only one person who has ever beaten Donald Trump. Ever."

Donilon's outlook got a boost from Biden's reception a few hours later at the North Carolina State Fairgrounds. The crowd was raucous as Biden took the stage, and in interviews many brushed off the president's debate performance. "It's a battle in the war, and you shouldn't make decisions off one battle," Ross Dragon, a fifty-year-old from Raleigh, said. "If you look at his policies, the things that he's passed, you can't argue against that, so you have to make something up. If age is an issue then Trump shouldn't be on the stage either."

In his own remarks, Biden skewered Trump for lying and debuted the new Donilon message to counter the age concerns. "I don't walk as easy as I used to," he said. "I don't speak as smoothly as I used to." As if to drive home the point, the official White House transcript continued: "I don't deba—debate as well as I used to. But I know what I do know: I know how to tell the truth." He concluded defiantly, "And I know, like millions of Americans know: When you get knocked down, you get back up."

By midafternoon on Friday, Barack Obama, who did not watch the debate live, posted on social media in support of Biden. "Bad debate nights happen," he wrote, in part. "Trust me, I know." Biden's aides were disappointed. They felt Obama's statement was too tepid. When Obama spoke with Biden in the days after the debate, he offered Biden his support as a sounding board and private counselor to help navigate the turbulence of the debate aftermath. "You need to think about what's best here," Obama told Biden, according to a Biden aide briefed on the conversation. Obama never told Biden to drop out, but he emphasized the serious problem he was facing. It was the only time they spoke.

By Friday evening, the calls for Biden to drop out were growing louder. The *New York Times* editorial board—never a big fan of Biden—called on the president to abandon his campaign. Biden's campaign publicly brushed off the editorial, reminding their supporters that the *Times* editorial board dismissed Biden in 2020, issuing a double endorsement of Elizabeth Warren and Amy Klobuchar in the Democratic primary. "The last time Joe Biden lost the *New York Times* editorial board's endorsement it turned out pretty well for him," former congressman and cochair of the campaign, Cedric Richmond, a close Biden ally, told the press. But it wasn't just Biden antagonists. Thomas Friedman, who Biden deeply respected and often summoned to the Oval Office to discuss foreign policy, also wrote that Biden should withdraw. Even Joe

Scarborough, who Biden watched almost religiously on *Morning Joe* on MSNBC, suggested the president should consider dropping out. But Biden still had some prominent backers. Reid Hoffman, the billionaire cofounder of LinkedIn and a major Democratic donor, emailed his network that Friday evening to say he was sticking with Biden. He acknowledged the debate "certainly delivered a blow to the mood among donors and organizers," but he maintained Biden could still win the race and he was "doubling down on my bet that America will choose Biden's decency, care, and proven success over Trump's violence, lies, and chaos."

Steve Ricchetti was ardently fighting back at any discussion of replacing the president. As his phone blew up with frantic messages from distraught Democrats, he repeated his go-to line: Biden controlled the delegates, he said, and no one could push him out. But that wasn't fully true. Some campaign lawyers started to quietly explore what would happen if Biden were to drop out. The delegates were pledged to support Biden, but they were not bound to do so. They were able to exercise discretion. Aides disagreed about how loyal the delegates were. Some thought they might abandon the president on the convention floor. Others argued that they had carefully selected faithful Biden supporters, and delegates were telling staff they remained behind Biden. The problem was the delegates who were ignoring the campaign's calls.

Deputy campaign manager Rob Flaherty emailed supporters making the case for Biden, touting his record as president and his performance in the events after the debate. "At the end of the day, we'd switch to candidates who would, according to polls, be less likely to win than Joe Biden—the only person ever to defeat Donald Trump," he wrote, attaching a screenshot of polls that showed Biden faring similarly against Trump to a host of Democrats, including Harris, Pete Buttigieg, Gavin Newsom, Gretchen Whitmer, and Josh Shapiro. The polling graphic pleased no one. Biden allies objected to the suggestion he could be replaced. His opponents noted that the graphic actually showed other candidates running statistically even with the president, with more room to grow.

On Saturday, Klain finally spoke with Biden directly. "We have a big problem on our hands," he told the president, urging him to rally the progressive wing of the party behind him. Some in the party—particularly the donors—were already gone, and it was no use trying to win them back, he said. Some Democrats urged the president to do an interview or a press conference to prove he was still capable, but Klain took a pessimistic view of that approach. "It's just a bar they're going to keep moving every day because they want you out," he said. The progressives, Klain told Biden, wanted the president to stay in the race and were his best allies in the fight.

Biden signaled his support for Klain's approach, but others in the White House disagreed. They wanted to show regular order, not chaos. Biden would meet with the governors next week and they would attest to his ability to serve. The week after he would command the world stage at the NATO Summit in Washington, where he would hold a press conference, reasserting his capacity to lead and govern. The attitude among some senior White House officials became *steady as she goes*. Even a drop in poll numbers would not shake them. Senior Biden officials argued that any change in survey numbers would be media driven, not a real reflection of voters' attitudes. As usual, the Biden view was: It's not the president's fault. The media is the problem.

As Biden departed for a fundraising swing through the Hamptons, he polled his coterie of traveling aides on what the outside world was saying. His aides gave an overly generous picture of the landscape, seemingly tiptoeing around the reality that the Democratic Party was beginning to tear itself apart. Some who heard the conversation freaked out, worrying that Biden was getting only a sanitized version of things. Still, no one said anything.

Shortly after landing, Biden got an earful. He attended a small, closed-door meeting at the home of Avram Glazer, where Biden faced his first postdebate reckoning with fewer than a dozen high-dollar supporters. The donors challenged him on his performance. One donor told Biden that they were close in age, and he conceded he was not as smart or sharp as he once was. He told Biden to convince him that he was still capable of performing the job for another four years. That set the tone for the meeting, as other donors piled on. They asked why he was so bad and how he was going to beat Trump. Biden was never asked point-blank about staying in the race, but he offered largely the same explanation he gave in public. It was a bad night, the race was unchanged, and he vowed to do better.

Just around the corner, Biden arrived at the $137 million home of Barry and Lizanne Rosenstein. On the way, Biden's motorcade passed a small group of people holding signs that read: PLEASE DROP OUT FOR U.S., THANK YOU NEXT, STEP DOWN FOR DEMOCRACY, and WE LOVE YOU BUT IT'S TIME. At the Rosenstein compound, as donors waited for the event to start, some of them pressed Biden's top aides about the debate. Even in private, aides aggressively played down the significance of the debate, spinning their longtime friends and supporters that everyone was overreacting. When cornered about Biden dropping out, Biden's aides gave the same answer: "It's either us or her," meaning Kamala Harris, "and we are currently better."

When the Bidens finally took the stage, hours late, the first lady spoke first, delivering a vociferous defense of her husband: "Joe isn't just the right person for the job," she said. "He's the only person for the job." For decades, Jill Biden had played the role of protective spouse, encouraging the president to eat vegetables, keeping him on time, and questioning staffers when she felt they erred. In January 2022, after the president held a nearly two-hour-long news conference at the White House, the first lady dropped by a postmortem meeting he was holding with his aides in the Treaty Room. She wanted to know why they allowed the press conference to go on for so long and who was responsible for ending it. A Biden aide apologized to her.

Now, with her husband in the fight of his political life, Jill was making clear: The Democratic Party had to stick with Joe. But even as the president tried to make the case for himself, he stumbled. "I didn't have a great night," he said, before arguing, without evidence, that the polls showed positive movement for his campaign in converting more undecided voters than Trump. He then confused Italy for France twice, telling the story of how Trump refused to go to the cemetery in France and called the American soldiers who were laid to rest there "suckers." Many of the donors at the event were appalled. The debate did not seem to be an anomaly.

Biden's final event of the night was another fundraiser at Governor Phil Murphy's lavish compound on the banks of the Navesink River in suburban New Jersey. In front of about fifty people in a tent, holding a microphone and reading from a teleprompter, Biden was very difficult to understand. He mumbled and meandered, as the press corps strained to transcribe his words. Afterward, Biden joined Murphy and his wife, along with a few other major donors, for a dinner inside. Donilon sat at the table and reassured the donors that the debate did not change anything. Voters, he said, care about democracy and abortion, and that would continue to be the case. But most of the conversation largely centered on policy, not politics, and Biden's participation was uneven. He would often begin engaging on a topic before abruptly changing the subject. "They're serving, we should eat now" was a common redirect. Or he would trail off and say, "I guess that's all I was going to say about that."

The fundraising swing ended in New Jersey, and Biden finally headed to Camp David, the rustic presidential retreat in Catoctin Mountain Park that the president loved. He would spend the weekend with his family, the people who had been central to navigating every crisis in Biden's political career. The president was not entertaining the idea of dropping out of the race; he was taking stock of how bad things really were. He knew the chattering class—in the op-ed pages and on cable news—were saying it was terrible. He was trying to figure out a way forward.

At Camp David, Biden saw his son. Hunter had watched the debate from his home in Los Angeles, and his reaction had been *What the fuck?* He thought it was out of character for his father. He was worried about his well-being. Hunter had never seen him so run-down before.

"I love you," Hunter told his father when he arrived. "Get some sleep."

The elation among Trump's team turned to anxiety as Democrats called for Biden to drop out. On returning to Mar-a-Lago, they began calling members of Congress, allies, and lobbyists to gather intelligence. Would Biden really quit? They had prepared an entire campaign against him, spent millions attacking him, and believed he was fatally wounded after the debate. If he dropped out, they'd have to rethink everything. "What can we do to keep him in the race?" LaCivita asked.

The campaign was not entirely unprepared. An internal memo in May had outlined scenarios such as Biden stepping aside, facing an internal rebellion, or an "act of God," mostly concerned with the Democratic Party's rules that could allow for a revolt at the convention. Now it was time for more serious contingency planning. The first step was to take stock of the RNC's research library on Kamala Harris: what it already had and what was missing. There was a trove of video footage to

start combing through, looking for contradictions or policy pronouncements that had aged poorly. Wiles began discussing what a hypothetical
bid against Harris would look like with the campaign's pollsters and
advisers. But they still believed Biden would stay in, and they told
Trump so.

Trump could not imagine Biden allowing the party to boot him.
"How could he let them do that?" he asked one ally. He began saying
how easy it would be to beat Biden now. He reacted dismissively to other
suggestions.

"Good news, bad news," Lindsey Graham recalled telling him. "You
did great. Bad news. He's not going to be your opponent."

"You're wrong," Trump replied.

As the Democrats descended into internal warfare, Trump was for
once content to cede the spotlight. He was happy to stay out of their
way. He started working Harris into his stump speeches, just in case.
But with public polls showing Harris faring no better against him than
Biden, Trump could profess not to care whom he ran against. He was so
confident that he told one group of visitors to Mar-a-Lago shortly after
the debate, "All I have to do is stay alive."

The Drumbeat

Biden's weekend at Camp David had been on the block for weeks. Back in March, he had attended a star-studded fundraiser at Radio City Music Hall with former Presidents Barack Obama and Bill Clinton. In a ploy to raise more money, donors could pay for a photo with the three presidents, taken by the famed photographer Annie Leibovitz. During the event, Leibovitz suggested to Hunter Biden that she take a portrait of the extended Biden clan. But because some of the president's granddaughters weren't there, Hunter invited her to come to Camp David ahead of the Fourth of July, when the whole family would be together.

The only important decisions the family members were focused on that morning were how to color coordinate their outfits for the photos. After breakfast, they gathered near the Hickory Lodge, a mess hall converted into a rec center. Leibovitz surprised the family with her efficiency, leaving plenty of time to enjoy the afternoon by the pool. The president sat out on the deck, making calls to staff and allies, discussing what steps to take in the coming days to demonstrate he was still capable of running for president.

The afternoon by the pool was not a family crisis meeting, not by any stretch. The Bidens knew as well as anyone the debate had been a disaster. Hunter's concerns about his father's well-being had softened in the days since the debate. He thought his father was fine, just exhausted. For a family that had weathered tragedy, addiction, and defeat, this debate debacle was just another challenge to overcome. No one discussed the idea of the president dropping out—it was not even a consideration. The ideas for next steps included sitting for a TV interview or participating in a press conference. The president was also focused on Hurricane Beryl, bearing down on the Gulf Coast, and he was eager to get back on the campaign trail.

Outside the gates of Camp David, reports of the family summit fueled anxious Democrats' fantasies that some form of reckoning or intervention was under way. The Democratic polling group OpenLabs released a presentation on the fallout from the debate, and the data was ugly. Sixty-nine percent of voters were very or somewhat concerned about the impact of Biden's age on his ability to do the job of president. Forty percent of voters who'd supported Biden in 2020 believed he should drop out of the race, up from 25 percent in May. OpenLabs found Biden trailing in every battleground state, while Trump was making inroads in states usually considered safely blue, such as Virginia, Maine, Minnesota, and New Mexico.

The next morning, on July 1, the Supreme Court announced its long-awaited decision on Trump's bid to thwart his prosecution for trying to overturn the 2020 election. His lawyers argued that presidents enjoyed absolute immunity. The justices didn't go quite that far, but they recognized broad immunity for official acts. The immediate practical effect was to send the January 6 case back to the trial court to work out whether Trump's actions were official (and therefore immune) or not, a question that would inevitably get appealed back up to the Supreme Court. There was no way the trial would happen before the election. The decision even gave Trump a foothold to put off his New York sentencing date. Top Justice Department officials were stunned by how far the justices went, as were Trump's own lawyers. Todd Blanche had predicted a narrower ruling. Trump told his lawyers he was surprised the court had given him such a "big" win and a 6–3 vote.

The Supreme Court's decision also addressed the disputed constitutional question of the president's control over the Justice Department. Since Watergate, the department had exercised a measure of independence from political influence on law enforcement decisions. The Supreme Court set that aside, saying explicitly, for the first time, that the president had "exclusive authority over the investigative and prosecutorial functions of the Justice Department and its officials." Jack Smith's lawyers, and the liberal justices in dissent, warned that this decision would do worse than let Trump get away with trying to overturn the 2020 election; it would embolden him to act with impunity in a second term.

At the White House, senior staff and lawyers immediately began to discuss their response. Biden and his aides had long taken the approach of not commenting directly on Trump's legal cases; they didn't want to lend any credence to Trump's accusations that the president was behind the prosecutions. But Biden wanted to respond to the Supreme Court decision, believing it to be historically consequential and impossible to ignore.

Jeff Zients convened a video call with Mike Donilon, White House counsel Ed Siskel, communications director Ben LaBolt, and Ian Sams, a spokesman for the counsel's office. Annie Tomasini was with the president at Camp David, and Jill Biden's aide Anthony Bernal was there too, though the Camp David contingent kept their camera off. Anita Dunn was not on the call because she did not show up for work that day, telling colleagues she was ill. In fact, she was frustrated by press reports that the Bidens were blaming her and her husband for the poor debate performance.*

Donilon, who came on the call late, had already written a statement, so the discussion centered on whether the White House would release it in writing or whether Biden would deliver remarks on camera. Donilon's draft directly addressed Trump, but Siskel recommended some caution. Biden decided he wanted to return to the White House to speak, and the staff on the call began to work out details about when and where. "This is a terrible decision," he said, according to one person's recollection. "It's historic."

Suddenly an unidentified voice piped up from Biden's screen and recommended an Oval Office address. At first, some aides had no idea who was speaking. It soon became clear the voice belonged to Hunter Biden, who the White House staff had not known was on the call. Siskel expressed some concern about the appearance of using the Oval Office.

Hunter snapped back: "This is one of the most consequential decisions the Supreme Court has ever made." He said his father had every right to use the powerful imagery of the Oval Office to deliver that message. They later settled on the Cross Hall, the long hallway on the first floor of the White House. After the call ended, Siskel told colleagues Hunter's presence was inappropriate.

Biden returned to the White House that evening and immediately went to the Red Room to prepare for the speech. Hunter joined him and suggested the president not take questions from the press. Biden put on bronzer, spoke for less than five minutes, and took no questions.

Earlier that afternoon, Democratic governors from around the country gathered on a conference call. They told each other they wanted to hear directly from the president about how he was going to move forward

---

*Allies of Dunn were quick to point out that she did not lead debate preparations. Hunter Biden denied blaming staff.

and alleviate Democrats' fears. For an hour, the governors lamented the low profile Biden had kept since the debate and their desire for him to do more events in public to reassure people of his fitness for the job. Minnesota Governor Tim Walz, the chair of the Democratic Governors Association, who organized the call, said he would work on setting up a meeting with Biden.

On Tuesday, July 2, Biden had his first defection in Congress. Lloyd Doggett, a Texas congressman since 1995 with a limited national profile, released a statement calling for Biden to drop out. The president ignored it, and maintained his business-as-usual facade. He visited the DC Emergency Operations Center for a briefing on extreme weather forecasts and delivered routine remarks, ignoring reporters' shouted questions on Doggett.

That evening, he attended a fundraiser in McLean, Virginia, at the home of Congressman Don Beyer. For most of the campaign, Biden only ever spoke with the assistance of a teleprompter, even for small, private audiences. The presence of the machine made for extremely awkward interactions in intimate settings, and irked donors who had paid thousands of dollars for a personal view of the president, not expecting a canned speech they could see on TV. He once read from a teleprompter in front of thirty people in the open kitchen of a Palo Alto mansion. Donors complained for months about the president's reliance on the machine. Aides defended the teleprompter as a tool to keep the famously garrulous president on schedule. But it also limited him from saying anything he shouldn't—with varying degrees of success. At Beyer's house, the campaign was eager to prove Biden could speak off the cuff. There was no teleprompter to be found. The president blamed his poor debate performance on a heavy travel schedule and said he "almost fell asleep onstage." He spoke for about six minutes.

On Wednesday, July 3, Congressman Raúl Grijalva of Arizona became the second Democratic lawmaker to call for Biden to step aside. That same day, many of the Democratic governors traveled to Washington for the meeting Walz had arranged. Those who couldn't attend in person joined by Zoom. In the Roosevelt Room, Walz began by expressing support for Biden and asking for an open discussion; everyone should air their feelings. Biden reaffirmed his commitment to stay in the race and asked for questions.

Governor J. B. Pritzker of Illinois, who everyone in the meeting understood was both the host of the upcoming convention in Chicago and one of the first people who'd want to run if Biden didn't, asked the president what he saw as his path forward. Biden said he needed to get out there, run an effective campaign, and talk to voters about issues that mattered. Governor Michelle Lujan Grisham of New Mexico warned that Biden might lose her state, which he'd won by nearly 11 points in 2020. She said he needed to have a strategy to address economic issues and Latino voters. Governor Janet Mills of Maine, another state that should be safely blue, told the president that voters did not think he was up for running. There was a lot of back-and-forth, and Biden didn't articulate a clear plan. Governor Josh Green of Hawaii, an emergency room physician by training, asked Biden about his health. The president said he was fine and had received a checkup from his doctor after the debate. "It's just my brain," he joked. Not everyone found it funny.

Biden also acknowledged he needed more sleep and said he told his staff that he should not participate in events that start after 8:00 p.m. But his message was clear: He was staying in the race. Many of the governors thought Biden's response was pathetic, and some were shocked by it. The president of the United States said he needed more sleep and couldn't do events after 8:00 p.m. Really? Biden's proposed solution seemed to only exacerbate, not solve, the problem. Vice President Kamala Harris concluded the meeting by underscoring the stakes. "This is about saving our fucking democracy," she said.

After the meeting ended, three of the governors—Walz, Wes Moore of Maryland, and Kathy Hochul of New York—came out to face the press. Hochul said the governors "pledged our support" to Biden, which hadn't actually happened. Many of the governors were deeply skeptical that Biden could continue his campaign, and they were furious with Hochul for suggesting otherwise.

As part of Biden's efforts to reassure Democrats he could do his job, he held a pair of radio interviews, with Black hosts in Pennsylvania and Wisconsin. The interviews were largely uneventful—until Biden, seeming to jumble serving as Obama's vice president and choosing Harris as his, said he was "proud to be, as I said, the first vice president, first Black woman, to serve with a Black president." It got worse. Some observers noticed that the hosts asked several nearly identical questions; they later admitted to receiving the suggested questions from the Biden campaign, prompting one of the hosts to resign from her radio station. No one was reassured. A third congressional Democrat called for Biden to drop out.

On Independence Day, Biden held the annual picnic for active-duty military service members and their families on the South Lawn, and Harris joined him for a fireworks show. On the rope line, a supporter yelled, "Keep up the fight." Biden replied, "You got me, man. I'm not going anywhere."

Senator Mark Warner of Virginia approached colleagues about holding a meeting to talk about next steps. Warner thought Biden needed to drop out. He'd had the jarring experience of the president twice calling him "John," the name of his deceased predecessor. Warner said he was willing to spoil his political future over pressing the issue, but he couldn't go it alone. There was some discussion about a group of senators going over to the White House to tell Biden the hard truth. But as soon as the discussions were reported in *The Washington Post*, the interest from his colleagues dried up. Even worse, some senators who privately told colleagues they thought Biden had to go issued supportive statements about the president.

Still, some senators started sharing stories about past experiences they had with the president that they found troubling. Senator Michael Bennet of Colorado had attended a White House event in June where he'd noticed Biden stumbling over words and rarely modulating his voice while reading from a teleprompter; the president seemed to struggle to engage with the text or with the people around him. Bennet returned from the event to share his concern with his staff, but he didn't tell his Senate colleagues about it until now.

In the days after the debate, Senator Chris Coons of Delaware pressed Biden's aides for a phone call with the president. He was horrified by Biden's performance, and he wanted to figure out what had happened. Was it just one bad night or was there something else going on? Coons, who held Biden's old Senate seat, was a longtime ally and staunch supporter. His colleagues assumed that closeness meant he often spent time with Biden. In reality, Coons traveled on Air Force One only once (near the end of Biden's presidency) and sometimes struggled to get Biden on the phone. This was one of those times. Nearly every old friend tried to reach Biden. The presidency is often isolating, but Democrats said Biden was harder to reach than any of his predecessors. His staff kept him in a bubble.

Coons finally reached Biden a week after the debate. He pressed the president to demonstrate that he could do better than he had in the debate. "You need to do an unscripted town hall," Coons said. "You need to do an interview that isn't friendly. You need to do something that can put these constant questions to rest."

"We're working on it," Biden replied.

On the afternoon of July 5, he would do both a public campaign event and a television interview: a visit to Madison, Wisconsin, and a sit-down with ABC's George Stephanopoulos. The campaign hoped a strong showing would change the narrative and stem the Democratic defections. His top aides were adamant that Biden's problem was a creation of the media and donors, since their research showed that voters who watched the debate thought Trump did worse. The media narrative, they argued, was convincing people who didn't watch the debate that Biden failed. At Sherman Middle School in Madison, Biden was greeted by signs that read SAVE YOUR LEGACY DROP OUT and BE A HERO ONE MORE TIME. On the other side of the middle school, protesters shouted, "Biden Biden you can't hide, we won't vote for genocide." But inside, the crowd was boisterous, and Biden was defiant. "They're trying to push me out of the race," he said of his critics. "Well, let me say this as clear as I can: I'm staying in the race!" He said he was not too old to create jobs, put the first Black woman on the Supreme Court, or defeat Trump.

Biden walked into the Stephanopoulos interview heartened by the rally. He repeated his talking points, calling the debate an anomaly, "a bad night," as he said five times. Stephanopoulos asked the president the question on every professional Democrat's mind. What would it take to convince him to step aside? An intervention from Chuck Schumer, Hakeem Jeffries, and Nancy Pelosi? Biden just laughed. "They're not gonna do that," he said. "If the Lord Almighty came down and said, 'Joe, get outta the race,' I'd get outta the race. The Lord Almighty's not comin' down."

What scared Democratic pollsters the most was Biden's insistence that he was not losing. "All the pollsters I talk to tell me it's a toss-up," he said. "And when I'm behind, there's only one poll I'm really far behind." Steve Ricchetti had been privately touting a postdebate poll from NBC that showed Biden down one point nationally, but if he was trailing by one nationally, he was down much more in the battleground states.

Stephanopoulos pressed him: "Mr. President, I've never seen a president [with] thirty-six percent approval get reelected."

"Well, I don't believe that's my approval rating," Biden said. "That's not what our polls show."

Biden's pollsters were in disbelief. *Is this guy seeing the polls I'm seeing*, they asked each other. They feared Biden was not getting a complete picture of the race. They also worried other Democrats would accuse them of lying to the president—even though some of them had met the president only once, nearly a year ago. They had not spoken to him since the debate.

Just after the interview aired, another House Democrat called for Biden to quit. The president wasn't fazed. "You were wrong about 2020," he told reporters as he boarded Air Force One to leave Wisconsin. "You were wrong about 2022 that we were going to get wiped out. Remember the 'red wave'?" His aides understood that one interview wouldn't be enough. The party kept setting up more hurdles that he would have to clear.

The next evening, Saturday, July 6, Biden called Representative Alexandria Ocasio-Cortez from his home in Wilmington. Biden and Ocasio-Cortez were not natural allies, but they'd talked over the years. He'd called to thank her in February after she defended him on CNN. Now she began by emphasizing that he needed to take care of himself, and making sure he was getting some sleep. Ocasio-Cortez reiterated her support for Biden staying in the race and suggested he could rally voters around a forward-looking, working-class agenda. She recommended proposing specific policies to reduce the cost of housing, protect Social Security, and fight corporate greed. Biden said they were working on some new policies, specifically a forthcoming proposal on reforming the Supreme Court. Other progressives were stunned that Ocasio-Cortez, along with Bernie Sanders—two of the party's most high-profile, disruptive left-wing lawmakers—were sticking with the octogenarian president. Ocasio-Cortez and Sanders saw Biden as an ally in supporting their progressive policy priorities, after he worked closely with them on legislation in the first two years of his term. But other Democrats knew that wouldn't get them anything if Biden couldn't win.

Biden returned to the campaign trail on Sunday, attending a Black church service in Philadelphia. The pastor said the Lord had changed the president's schedule "because God knew President Biden needs some love." He visited a campaign field office, then headed to Harrisburg for a labor event and a coffee with Pennsylvania Governor Josh Shapiro. Shapiro told Biden he needed to get out more to reassure voters that he can defeat Donald Trump. Biden remained defiant. He was on the trail today and would be again. He was not dropping out.

By Monday morning, July 8, the tally of House Democrats calling for Biden to drop out was up to ten, and Biden and his top aides wanted to put an end to it. They viewed the defections, mostly from backbenchers, as distracting. They knew lawmakers were returning to Washington that night from their July 4 recess, and reporters would be waiting in the Capitol hallways to get more Democrats on the record. Biden had to go on the offensive.

He sent a two-page letter to congressional Democrats, saying he was "firmly committed to staying in this race, to running this race to the end, and to beating Donald Trump." He acknowledged lawmakers' concerns and said he would not be running again if he wasn't convinced he was the best person to defeat Trump. He concluded: "The question of how to move forward has been well-aired for over a week now. And it's time for it to end."

Shortly after sending the letter, he called into MSNBC's *Morning Joe* and dared those who wanted him to step aside to challenge him at the convention. Some of his own staff questioned why he didn't appear on camera. The interview was hastily scheduled, so there was not enough time to set up an on-camera appearance, but it also allowed the president to read off prepared talking points, which he did for portions of the interview.

Biden's letter landed on Capitol Hill with a thud and aggravated the frustration pulsing through the party. Many Democrats felt it did nothing to reassure them of his fitness for the job and was dismissive of their concerns. Instead of assuming they would back him, they thought he should show up and make the case in person. "It was not a constructive letter. Dealing with Congress, that's just not the approach to take," Nancy Pelosi, the former Speaker still serving in her California seat, later said in an interview for this book. "What we thought would come next would be the president putting to rest some of the concerns that arose, that he would be in the public domain making presentations to dispel some of this."

That same day, campaign officials scheduled a meeting for the president, vice president, first lady, and second gentleman with their campaign pollsters—the first time since the start of the campaign that the pollsters would have an audience with the principals. They were instructed to present what the data showed. The meeting was initially scheduled for 2:00 p.m. It got pushed to 4:00. Then 7:00. Then 8:00. It never happened.

Later that evening, Biden joined a conference call with his top campaign donors and fundraisers and took four questions. They were softballs, and the president repeated the same message: He was staying in, and he would beat Trump. Some campaign aides were annoyed that the donors didn't ask tougher questions, since they had spent the past several days pummeling the staff in private. In the days since the debate, many top donors and bundlers had given up. Biden officials kept hearing the same message: "Don't call me until there's a new candidate." Some aides started leaking details of the fundraising drop-off to the media, trying to send distress signals. The campaign's finances were wobbling before the debate, and aides feared they might not be able to cover operating costs if Biden stayed in the race and fundraising did not pick up.

At Future Forward, the main super PAC supporting Biden, donors who had previously pledged millions of dollars now said those commitments were on hold, and if Biden stayed in the race, they would never release the funds. Other donors were less definitive but wanted to wait and see how the race shook out. They were going to hold back funds until they had more clarity. Then there were the Biden loyalists, who were furious that the super PAC was not jumping in to defend Biden with TV and digital ads. But the group's research found the ads wouldn't work. Voters did not want to see a glossy, curated version of Biden—they wanted to see him unscripted and unfiltered, to prove the debate was an aberration.

On Tuesday, July 9, at 9:00 a.m., House Democrats reported to the Democratic Congressional Campaign Committee's offices near the Capitol for a caucus meeting. The meeting ran long as lawmakers discussed what would happen if Biden dropped out. Would there be an open primary? How would it work?

Some Democrats were sensitive about undermining Biden that week, while he was hosting America's closest allies at a NATO summit in Washington. Biden's aides thought he was at his best in foreign policy and global leadership, and the summit could be an opportunity to tout his work to repair alliances and support Ukraine's fight against Russia. On the summit's opening day, Biden delivered a stirring speech, mostly free of verbal stumbles. Nervous Democrats were eager to see how he would perform at the press conference at the summit's conclusion. But one lawmaker, Mikie Sherrill of New Jersey, had already seen enough, becoming the eleventh Democrat calling for Biden to withdraw.

The next day, Pelosi appeared on the president's favorite news show in the 7:30 a.m. block. She brought with her Sviatlana Tsikhanouskaya, the leader of the democratic opposition of Belarus, to promote a new op-ed they coauthored on NATO, timed to the summit in Washington. But Pelosi surely knew the focus of her appearance on *Morning Joe* would be the state of Biden's candidacy. Mika Brzezinski briefly mentioned the op-ed and then immediately asked Pelosi about Biden. Pelosi praised his record and his speech at NATO. But she was noncommittal on whether he had her support to remain at the top of the ticket. "It's up to the president to decide if he is going to run," she said. "We're all encouraging him to make that decision. Because time is running short."

"He has said he has made the decision," Jonathan Lemire, who was interviewing her, pointed out. "Do *you* want him to run?"

"I want him to do whatever he decides to do," Pelosi said. For anyone watching, it sounded like she was asking Biden to reach a different decision than the one he'd said he already made.

The campaign staff in Wilmington got the hint. At the senior staff's morning call at 9:00 a.m., Adrienne Elrod, a top communications official known for her bubbly demeanor, said, "If you didn't watch *Morning Joe*, Speaker Emerita Nancy Pelosi was on, and she didn't quite call for us to drop out, but she came very, very close." That was the end of the call.

Privately, Pelosi was less cryptic. Ever since the debate, her phone had been blowing up with concerned lawmakers, union leaders, donors, and activists. She insisted she never placed any calls herself. But people saw her as a helpful ally in their effort to convince Biden to drop out and made sure to provide her with polling to support that. She came to agree with the assessment that with Biden in the race, Democrats had no chance of winning the House. When people asked her for her opinion, that's what she told them.

Shortly after she appeared on *Morning Joe*, Pelosi arrived at the White House for an undisclosed meeting with Biden. She grew frustrated as the president continued to insist the polling showed no real change since the debate. She saw it differently. At one point, Biden asked an aide to put Donilon on the phone. He didn't believe what Pelosi was saying about the polls. Pelosi was adamant that the polls showed Biden would lose. Donilon disagreed. For Biden, Pelosi's criticism stung the most. He expected it from Obama and the donors. But Pelosi was different. He genuinely considered her a close friend. He felt betrayed.

Later that day, George Clooney published an op-ed in *The New York Times* calling for the president to bow out. Clooney had given Ricchetti a heads-up a few days earlier, prompting a blitz to try to talk Clooney out of it. Jeffrey Katzenberg, his longtime collaborator who had organized the LA fundraiser, pleaded with him. Some Biden aides mused that Obama, who was close to Clooney, must have been involved, if only by not weighing in against the op-ed. It was true that Obama knew what Clooney was working on and didn't try to stop him. But he also did not encourage it or review the text. He didn't have to. Clooney was distraught by the debate performance and wanted to take a stand. The op-ed was devastating not only because of Clooney's star power but because he said the Biden he saw at the fundraiser three weeks earlier was just as bad as he'd been at the debate. It was not just one bad night.

Obama shared his own concerns with others. He'd noticed Biden appeared exhausted at the Radio City fundraiser in April. He told the president's staff they needed to closely manage his schedule. But he was careful not to be too loud about his views, lest it backfire. He had already made clear he didn't think Biden should run twice—in 2015 and 2019—and he knew Biden and his closest advisers resented him for it. But in the days after the debate, Obama concluded Biden did not have a path forward; he talked with Pelosi, Schumer, and Jeffries, trying to help them navigate the moment.

That same evening of July 10, Ricchetti, a former lobbyist who handled many of Biden's relationships on Capitol Hill and was now trying to keep lawmakers from abandoning the president, spoke with Congressman Pete Aguilar of California, the third-ranking House Democrat. Aguilar told Ricchetti that Biden staying in the race was going to cost Democrats the House and Senate in addition to the White House. Aguilar was being flooded by colleagues concerned that the polling numbers—and their political fate—were getting worse by the day. Ricchetti continued to cite old surveys showing Biden had a chance to win.

"Do you realize how bad it is?" Aguilar asked. "Has anyone told the president how bad it is?" Ricchetti said they knew *some* people felt that way. Aguilar interrupted: "Steve, has anyone walked into the Oval and told him we could lose everything?" Ricchetti said no. He insisted many members of Congress still supported the president. Over the course of the nearly one-hour call, the two men raised their voices as they sparred over the full scope of Biden's problems on Capitol Hill. "You've given me a lot to think about," Ricchetti concluded.

Biden spent Thursday, July 11, at the NATO summit, meeting with world leaders and holding a bilateral meeting with Ukrainian President Zelensky. "Mr. President, is your decision final?" a reporter asked. "I support Ukraine to the end," he replied, ignoring the question. Later in the day, Biden introduced Zelensky as "President Putin," before correcting himself.

Meanwhile, Biden's senior campaign aides were trying to stave off the spreading crisis in the Senate. Senator Peter Welch of Vermont published an op-ed in *The Washington Post* the day before, calling for Biden to withdraw. Senate Majority Leader Chuck Schumer had been fielding complaints from his caucus members and trying to hold them back from going public amid the growing calls for the president to drop out. Schumer was familiar with Biden's Irish stubbornness and feared public calls for him to step aside would only harden his resolve to stay in the race. He wanted Biden's team to hear the senators' concerns for themselves and have the chance to make their best case for the president's continued candidacy.

The campaign resisted and initially denied Schumer's request for a meeting with Senate Democrats. Schumer blew up. He told them they had a responsibility to hear from senators directly. He also let them know he had been holding back senators from calling for Biden's withdrawal, but if they did not hold the meeting, he wouldn't continue to do so. Schumer won.

At 12:30 p.m., nearly every Democratic senator (with the exception of Senators Jon Tester of Montana and Sherrod Brown of Ohio, two of the most endangered members up for reelection in November) gathered in a large conference room at the Democratic Senatorial Campaign Committee's offices near the Capitol. The Biden campaign sent Donilon, Ricchetti, and Jen O'Malley Dillon, and they began with a presentation that sought to make the case for Biden's path forward.

Ricchetti pointed out that Bill Clinton was at a 32 percent approval rating at the same point in the cycle. Other candidates had recovered from bad debates. O'Malley Dillon gave an overview of the campaign infrastructure, discussing hiring and offices and the campaign's success in elevating Project 2025, a detailed written agenda organized by right-wing think tanks, as a catchword for unpopular policies that Trump would pursue. Donilon acknowledged that Biden was doing better with older voters than traditional Democratic candidates, while underperforming with younger voters and voters of color. Donilon argued that this was a favorable position because older voters were harder to persuade.

Many of the senators were appalled by the presentation. They felt it was condescending, and the aides avoided the one topic they were most concerned about: the president's health.

The DSCC chairman, Gary Peters of Michigan, spoke first. He asked how the campaign was planning to improve support among Black, Latino, and young voters. Donilon said younger voters tend to decide late but he was confident they would break for Biden. The answer did not satisfy the senators.

There was an awkward silence, then Senator Jeff Merkley of Oregon spoke up. He said the senators were all there as people who knew and loved Biden but recognized he was not able to lead the party and win the campaign. That was what they were hearing from everyone contacting them, and Merkley said most of the senators in the room shared the judgment that Biden should step down.

Jack Reed of Rhode Island said two independent neurologists should evaluate Biden and release their findings. Bernie Sanders of Vermont said the president needed a new agenda for working-class people and to change his position on Gaza. Brian Schatz of Hawaii said the president's policies were not the problem—it was his age, and he needed to abandon his bid. Dick Durbin of Illinois jokingly suggested putting Biden in a muscle shirt and filming him chopping wood, like Ronald Reagan.

In all seriousness, Sheldon Whitehouse of Rhode Island said the senators were in danger of burning their credibility if they were asked to deny the obvious about Biden's condition. Joe Manchin of West Virginia compared the situation to when a family has to take the car keys away from Grandpa. He said it was cruel that staffers were allowing Biden to stay in the race. Chris Coons took offense to Manchin's analogy and scolded his colleagues for disrespecting the president.

John Fetterman of Pennsylvania started screaming, saying he'd had a dismal debate after suffering a stroke and still won. He asked everyone who supported Biden to raise their hand. Only Coons and Tammy Duckworth of Illinois, who was a campaign cochair, joined him. Ricchetti and Donilon looked shocked.

Alex Padilla of California recited the Serenity Prayer: "God grant me the serenity to accept the things I cannot change, the courage to change the things I can, and the wisdom to know the difference." Catherine Cortez Masto of Nevada asked a simple question: What is the option if not Biden? The response: There was no alternative.

The senators begged the advisers to share their concerns with Biden, worried they were blocking bad news from reaching the president. As the meeting ended, Schumer pulled the Biden aides aside and asked if they would convey the discussion to the president. They said yes. Their car ride back to the White House was quiet.

That night, Biden held his long-awaited press conference. He showed command of foreign policy, providing detailed answers on China and the conflict in the Middle East. But still, he rambled through answers and largely failed to make the case for his continued candidacy. It didn't help that he answered a question about Harris by saying he "wouldn't have picked Vice President Trump to be vice president" if he didn't think she was qualified to be president. Harris, who continued to fundraise, campaign, and defend the president, later told reporters that Biden did an "outstanding job" at the press conference and described him as a "master of the issues."

Afterward, back at the White House, Biden greeted House Democratic Leader Hakeem Jeffries. Jeffries told Biden that if he stayed in the race, Democrats feared they would not be able to take control of the House. By the end of the night, eight more House Democrats had called for the president to drop out.

The president started Friday, July 12, with more calls to lawmakers, making his case to members of the Congressional Hispanic Caucus and the Congressional Asian Pacific American Caucus. He then flew to Detroit to unveil the new hundred-day plan he'd been previewing, adopting some of Sanders' suggestions, including expanding Social Security benefits and eliminating medical debt. From the moment Biden took the stage, the crowd was electric, chanting, "Don't go, Joe," "Don't you quit," and "Four more years."

"What's Joe Biden going to do?" he said. "Is he going to stay in the race? Is he going to drop out? I am running, and we're going to win," he said to loud applause. "I'm not going to change that." He cited a national survey from Marist that showed him leading Trump, 50–48. He reminded voters he was the only one who had ever defeated Trump. And he was going to do it again.

He genuinely believed it. He was not going anywhere. He flew directly from Detroit to Dover Air Force Base and motorcaded to his beach house for the weekend. The drumbeat of Democratic defections in the House was up to twenty-six.

July 13, 2024

I t was the Saturday before Donald Trump would officially accept the Republican nomination at the GOP convention in Milwaukee, and he still had not picked his running mate. He was down to Senators Marco Rubio and JD Vance. (Despite the allure of a Trump-Kennedy bumper sticker, Trump told aides he ultimately viewed RFK Jr. as "too crazy" to share the ticket.) Rupert Murdoch had been pushing a third finalist, Governor Doug Burgum of North Dakota, but Trump's advisers argued he was too unknown and untested nationally, and Burgum annoyed Trump with efforts to bond by talking business during plane trips.

Some aides, including Susie Wiles, pleaded with Trump to put the runners-up out of their misery. Advisers hoped Trump was joking when he said he was going to announce his running mate at the convention. He liked the suspense. He enjoyed keeping everyone guessing, and he loved the prospect of a grand reveal in a live, made-for-TV moment. He was also enjoying watching the Democrats melt down over Biden's debate performance, and he didn't want to interrupt them or draw any attention away.

That morning, he was nearing a decision but still wanted to kick the tires one last time. He had just met with Rubio the night before. The meeting went well, but they just didn't have the right chemistry, he said afterward. He wanted to meet once more with Vance. He sent his friend Steve Witkoff's private plane to Covington, Kentucky, just over the border from Cincinnati, to fetch the Ohio senator and bring him to Mar-a-Lago.

They met in Trump's office above the ballroom for more than an hour. No meal, not even coffee. There were no new twists to discuss; in previous meetings they had already gone over Vance's Silicon Valley career, his past criticisms of Trump, and his legislative record. This was "a rapport check," in the words of one adviser. "It was really trying to feel like he could have a close relationship with that person. Like, can I hang out with him?" It was uneventful, no drama. Chitchat about the news of the day, the convention, whatever was on Trump's mind.

Much of Trump's team was already in Milwaukee for the convention; only twelve staffers were around to accompany Trump to a rally that night in western Pennsylvania. Some Vance allies thought that rally, so close to the Ohio border, would be his debut as running mate. But Trump did not invite Vance to come with him, or give him any kind of answer. He returned to Ohio still in limbo.

After Vance left, Trump told advisers, "I think I'm gonna go with him." But he kept taking calls from Rubio backers, such as Sean Hannity, Kellyanne Conway, Brian Ballard, and Senator Lindsey Graham. Trump spoke with José "Pepe" Fanjul, a Cuban American sugar billionaire and major Republican donor in Florida, to inquire about Rubio's loyalty. Other senators, donors, and Mar-a-Lago members weighed in with their own suggestions. Trump grinned as he took the calls.

Wiles asked Trump again to make his decision. But he still wanted to save it for Milwaukee. "I don't want to announce my VP at a farm on a

Saturday night," he said. Then he boarded his plane for a town called Butler.

Joe Biden woke up that morning at his vacation home in Rehoboth Beach, Delaware. Purchased for $2.7 million in 2017, the house has two signs on the front: "Beau's Gift" and "Forever Jill." Biden promised he would buy the house for his wife using money from the book deal he signed after serving as vice president. It was her favorite place, and she often escaped there, even without him. This was the site of Biden's political last stand.

His morning began with a bit of official business: calling into the USS *Dwight D. Eisenhower* to thank the personnel on board for their service as they returned home from a nine-month deployment. By the afternoon, he had moved on to trying to save his presidency. He had a Zoom meeting with the nearly hundred-member Congressional Progressive Caucus, which was established in part by Bernie Sanders in the early 1990s, and represented the most left-wing members of Congress. In 2020, the caucus had largely supported Sanders's presidential campaign and had been some of Biden's most vocal critics. But Biden and the progressives had grown close while working together on legislation.

The meeting began cordially, with Biden emphasizing that he wanted the group's support on a new initiative he teased. "I'm going to need your help on the Supreme Court," he said, "because I'm about to come out—I don't want to prematurely announce it—but I'm about to come out with a major initiative on limiting the court and what we do and within—I've been working with constitutional scholars for the last three months, and I need some help."

But as lawmakers started to push the president and raised some concerns about his campaign, he quickly became more defensive. Some lawmakers said voters had never heard about the administration's accomplishments. Biden said lawmakers should do a better job of communicating about and campaigning on his progressive victories. Representative Delia Ramirez of Illinois asked the president about the ongoing Israeli bombardment of Gaza, pointing out that Israeli Prime Minister Benjamin Netanyahu did not seem to be listening to him. Many of the caucus's members had been some of the most vocal critics of Biden's staunch support of Israel even as tens of thousands of Palestinians were dying. They wanted Biden to take a tougher stance on Israel, and some argued for imposing an arms embargo.

The president took umbrage at the criticism. He said he was on calls nonstop trying to end the fighting and free the hostages. He said Netanyahu hoped Trump would be reelected and was an impediment to any ceasefire deal. Biden lamented that he was taking heat from many directions while he was doing the most of anyone. Finally, he asked Ramirez what she thought he should do, and she said she had a few suggestions. He told her to send him an email. Some members saw Biden as genuinely interested in feedback; others saw it as Biden being dismissive. How does one email the president of the United States? *Should I email dearmrpresident@gmail.com?* Ramirez thought. She also asked Biden to prevent Netanyahu from delivering a speech to Congress in the coming weeks. Biden said he had no authority over who speaks on the House floor.

At one point in the meeting, an aide passed the president a note, which he read out loud: "'Stay positive,'" he read. "'You are sounding defensive.'" The caucus's chairwoman, Pramila Jayapal, tried to defuse the tension, reminding the president that a significant number of her members supported him and hoped he continued. "We were trying to put forward some of the concerns, so I hope you don't feel like we're, you know, trying to silence those positive voices," she said. "But obviously we're trying to rally everybody around a unified nominee." Some members walked away from the call feeling that Biden's basic argument was that he was the real progressive and they only cared about Gaza.

Biden's next audience, coming right after, should have been friendlier: a group of moderates known as the New Democrat Coalition. But many of these lawmakers came from battleground districts and were growing anxious about the unpopular president dragging them down. In the week leading up to the meeting, Congressman Jason Crow, an Army veteran from Colorado who became famous for protecting his colleagues in the House chamber on January 6, was struggling with what to say to Biden. He deeply respected the president but saw no data to support the idea that Biden could win his race and was considering calling for him to drop out. Crow held off after conferring with the New Dems chair, Congresswoman Annie Kuster, a close friend. Kuster told him the White House had finally agreed to a Zoom meeting with the coalition, but it would last only thirty minutes and the president would take only a few questions. There was another catch: The White House insisted that the questions could not come from anyone who had publicly called for Biden to withdraw. Kuster said she wanted Crow to ask one of the questions on behalf of Democrats with national security backgrounds. Crow decided to hold off on a statement and spent the next two days workshopping his question.

For the first twenty minutes of the Zoom call, Biden defended his record and made the case for his candidacy. He mumbled and rambled, sometimes incoherently. The lawmakers' group chats and Signal chains started lighting up. "This is worse than the debate," one alarmed lawmaker texted colleagues.

Finally, it was time for Crow to ask his question. "'National security is a major issue in this campaign,'" he read from a note he'd written on his phone. "'Americans want a commander in chief who can project strength, vigor, and inspire confidence at home and abroad. They need to feel that you have the helm when they go to bed each night,'" Crow said. "'Despite your many successes and the dangers of Trump, we are seeing overwhelming evidence in our districts that many voters are losing confidence you can do this in a second term. It's not fair, but it's true.'"

"I don't want to hear that crap," Biden exploded. "First of all, I think you're dead wrong about national security. You saw what happened recently in terms of the meeting we had with NATO. I put NATO together. Name me a foreign leader who thinks I'm not the most effective leader in the world on foreign policy. Tell me, tell me who the hell that is. . . . Tell me who enlarged NATO. Tell me who did the Pacific basin."

Then he got personal. "Tell me who did something that you've never done with your Bronze Star," he snapped directly at Crow, a decorated Army Ranger. "And you're—like my son"—Beau had won the same honor—"and, you know—proud of your leadership—but guess what?—Well, what's happening? We got Korea and Japan working together. . . . Find me a world leader who's an ally of ours who doesn't think I'm the most effective president they've ever met."

"It's not breaking through, Mr. President," Crow replied.

Biden said that was the fault of Crow and other Democrats, arguing they were not doing enough to sell his agenda to their constituents. "You know it, talk about it," he said. "Talk about how I built NATO. Talk about how I enlarged NATO. Talk about how I put together what's happening in Asia. Talk about what's going on in the Middle East. Talk about it."

The yelling was loud enough that Biden's next appointment, Senate Majority Leader Chuck Schumer, could hear the commotion from another room in the beach house.

Crow tried to end on a respectful note. "I do want to be for you, Mr. President," he said. "And that's why we're all on this Zoom trying to figure out the path forward. I think that's why we asked the question in that spirit."

But the interaction wasn't salvageable. Crow and his colleagues couldn't believe what had just unfolded. Crow thought to himself, *What the fuck just happened*, and expected Biden or at least a top White House aide to quickly follow up with an apology. He never received one. He fixed himself an old-fashioned as his group chats continued to buzz about the meeting.

Schumer's meeting was not on the president's public schedule, and many of Biden's aides—even some who were traveling with him to Rehoboth Beach that weekend—didn't know about it. Schumer had long held concerns about Biden's ability to win reelection. He panicked when Ron Klain, whom Schumer trusted, left the White House, worried that he would be less involved in the president's operation. Schumer thought Biden had long odds to defeat Trump even before he collapsed in the debate. He wasn't concerned himself about the president's mental acuity, but he believed Republicans had succeeded in creating the perception that Biden was too old for the job by capitalizing on the president's physical stumbles. The debate only reinforced that view. Schumer released a tepid statement of support, far from a full-throated endorsement. His Senate Democratic caucus was irate and believed the president would take them down with him.

As the days went on, Schumer lost patience with Biden's political advisers too, believing they were hiding the truth about the dire state of the polling. He knew better because some of Biden's top pollsters worked for him too. He also came to believe that Biden's aides did not brief him on their meeting with the Senate Democrats. So Schumer had called Jeff Zients, Biden's chief of staff, to deliver an ultimatum: Let me see Biden or I'm going to publicly request a meeting. A meeting was quickly scheduled.

Schumer arrived that Saturday with three main points. First, the vast majority of the Senate Democratic caucus wanted Biden to drop out. Schumer told Biden that if they held a secret ballot, maybe five of the fifty-one senators would want him to stay in the race. Biden seemed surprised, and Schumer's fears that the president was not fully briefed on the meeting with the senators were confirmed.

"I know my caucus," Schumer told him.

Second, he appealed to Biden's legacy. You have an incredible record of accomplishments, Schumer told him, and if Trump wins, it will all be reversed. He warned Biden that he would be remembered for helping to elect Trump.

His final point was blunt: Your pollsters don't believe you can win. They put it at 5 percent, Schumer said. "I don't believe you are getting all the information," he said. "Or the information you are getting is inaccurate."

Schumer didn't bring paper printouts of the polls, but he didn't have to. The senator, who still carried a flip phone and knew every senator's cell-phone number by heart, was exceptionally talented at memorizing information. He had all the poll numbers in his head.

Biden listened. He didn't lash out like he did at the members of Congress. He absorbed the information and asked for time. Give me a week, he said.

The meeting had to end for Biden to attend Mass. Before Schumer left, Biden asked him a question: "What do you think about Kamala?" he said. "Do you think she could win?"

Schumer said he didn't know, but he was sure she had a better shot than he did. He was sure that Biden couldn't win. "If I were you, I wouldn't run, and I'm urging you not to run," he said.

The two of them then walked to the small elevator in the president's home, and Biden grabbed Schumer by the shoulders. "You've got bigger balls than anyone I've ever met," Biden said.

The two men hugged. Schumer returned to Washington, and Biden got ready to leave for church.

That afternoon, in the town of Bethel Park, Pennsylvania, ten miles south of Pittsburgh, a twenty-year-old man named Thomas Matthew Crooks asked his father for his AR-15. He said he was going to the gun range, as he'd done the day before, and many other times. Crooks had taken the day off work, telling his boss at a nursing home that he had "something to do."

That was all he said. He didn't tell anyone why. He didn't leave a manifesto or a social media trail. He was quiet, did well in school, and won a math science prize. His final project in honors American History was on the JFK assassination.

He searched online for the upcoming Republican and Democratic conventions. He learned Trump would be coming to Butler, about ninety minutes north. He'd filled out the form on the campaign's website to register to attend. He broke down his rifle to fit into a black SwissGear backpack, packed a drone and improvised bombs in the trunk of his car, and set out for Butler. On the way, Crooks bought fifty rounds of ammunition.

Traffic lined up for miles approaching the Butler Farm Show fairgrounds. Some people camped out overnight to make sure they got in. Others crawled in their cars for hours, passing a Trump–Pence sign with Pence taped over, a dead deer on the side of the road, and a sign touting road improvements funded by Biden's bipartisan infrastructure bill. A man in a homemade T-shirt reading JAN 6 SURVIVOR shouted "Let's Go Brandon!" into a megaphone.

By the thousands, people parked and paraded past the row of tents and trucks hawking MAGA caps and camo bucket hats, visors with orange Trump hair, Trump flags, and fresh T-shirts with all the latest memes. They filed through an airport-style Secret Service checkpoint and streamed into the fairgrounds until the entire grassy bowl was a sea of red hats under a cloudless blue sky.

Crooks stayed outside the security screening. He flew a drone over the site, surveying the grandstand about two hundred yards away. The red-carpeted stage and bunting-adorned bleachers were set up in front of two red barns, under a giant thirty-by-sixty-foot American flag strung up between two cranes.

Inside the fairgrounds, the crowd was restless. Trump was running an hour late. The bathroom lines took twenty minutes. The concession stands took thirty. People ran out of water. There was no shade, and many were packed in too tightly to sit. Trump's event staff on site were sweating through their suit jackets. Paramedics treated five hundred people for heat exhaustion, and eight had to be hospitalized. The county Republican chair, Jim Hulings, called 911 three times for EMTs to come to the VIP section, where he sat up front. He would remember wondering why he never noticed any surveillance drones. The Secret Service's equipment wasn't working that day.

"Fuck this DJ!" someone jeered at the playlist repeating itself between speeches. While Senate candidate Dave McCormick spoke, the giant American flag overhead became twisted in the wind. Some people thought it looked like an angel.

Crooks walked past a row of vendors toward a factory complex just outside the perimeter. He took a seat on a low concrete wall. Other people around were seeking shade in the ninety-five-degree heat or trying to get a good view of the stage. They came with friends and family and picnics and lawn chairs, wearing MAGA caps and Trump shirts. Crooks, in a gray T-shirt and light shorts, with long brown hair and glasses, kept to himself, scrolling on his phone or looking at the factory building. He noticed a sniper stationed in one of the windows. He put his phone in his pocket, took out a range finder, and pointed it at the stage to measure the distance. The previous week, he had researched online, "how far was oswald from kennedy."

The sniper Crooks had spotted on the second floor of the factory building was Sergeant Greg Nicol, from neighboring Beaver County. Nicol had likewise noticed the young man with long hair lurking around the building, acting suspiciously, and he moved around the floor to keep track of him. He got a photo and circulated it to a group of local snipers. "I did see him with a rangefinder looking towards stage," Nicol texted at 5:38. "I lost sight of him." The officers who got Nicol's text shared the information with Secret Service agents, but the report of a suspicious person never reached the agents in charge of the rally or in Trump's detail. They were tuned to different radio frequencies. Several police officers started searching around the factory complex.

Nicol spotted the long-haired young man again a few minutes after 6:00 p.m., now at a picnic table with a backpack. He saw him pick up the bag and take off running. The suspect disappeared between the buildings of the factory complex. Nicol reported the sighting over his radio. "He has a backpack," Nicol said.

Some rally goers started to notice someone crawling on the roof of the factory buildings, and several called the police or tried to find officers in the crowd. A patrolman saw the man on the roof from a hundred yards away and headed toward the building but lost sight of him. "Someone's on the roof," he radioed to officers in the area.

A Butler police detective heard the call and decided to leave his post directing traffic and go to the factory complex. He parked his patrol car next to a state trooper and they started discussing the report of a suspicious man on the roof when the detective saw him. Another patrolman helped raise the detective onto the roof. As the detective tried lifting himself over the ledge, like climbing out of a pool with only his arms, he looked left and locked eyes with the long-haired young man. He had a backpack and extra bullet magazines. The man looked surprised, like "What are you doing up here?" Then he turned to point his rifle at the detective.

The detective slipped off the roof and fell to the ground. He yelled into his radio, "He's got a gun!"

At last, the loudspeakers blared: "Ladies and gentlemen, the next president of the United States, President Donald J. Trump!" The crowd screamed and raised their cell phones to record as two Secret Service agents walked out past a row of flags and then Trump appeared, a MAGA hat shading his eyes, white dress shirt open at the collar, no tie. Trump clapped his hands, fist-bumped, and pointed to his fans, to the tune of Lee Greenwood's "God Bless the U.S.A." He mouthed "Thank you" as he climbed a few stairs to read from the lectern.

Trump always loved to marvel at his masses of supporters, but today they really did stretch as far as he could see. "This is a big crowd!" he said. "This is a big, big, beautiful crowd."

He was just getting warmed up. "You don't mind if I go off tele-prompter, do you?" he teased. The crowd cheered obligingly. Trump called out for McCormick to come up onstage, but the Senate candidate wasn't ready, so Trump changed course.

"Do you guys have access to that chart that I love so much?" he asked his tech team. At his command, a graph appeared on two giant screens on either side of the stage. "Wow!" he exclaimed. "They're getting better with time."

The chart showed government data on apprehensions at the border. It was misleadingly labeled to suggest the collapse in border crossings because of the coronavirus pandemic was the result of Trump's policies. "Look what happened to our country," he said. "Take a look what happened—"

A popping noise rang out, with a kickback, like an enormous keyboard click. The time was 6:11 p.m. The people in the bleachers gasped and froze. Trump felt a sting on his right ear, like the world's largest mosquito. There was another pop as he raised his hand to touch his ear, then held it in front of his eyes. Blood. People screamed and Trump sank into the stage and his Secret Service detail tackled him. *"GET-DOWN-GET-DOWN-GET-DOWN-GET-DOWN!"*

Biden arrived at St. Edmond's Catholic Church in Rehoboth Beach at 5:43 p.m. At 6:05 p.m., Schumer released a terse statement that stunned many of Biden aides: "I sat with President Biden this afternoon in Delaware; we had a good meeting," he said. They had no idea the meeting happened, and they were alarmed by the tenor of the statement. Schumer did not express continued support for Biden. Reporters lit up the phones of White House and Schumer aides trying to get more details.

Minutes later, White House officials learned about the shots fired in Pennsylvania and scrambled to figure out who was with the president at church and how to inform him of what was happening. Annie Tomasini, one of the president's top aides, contacted the Secret Service. In the church before Biden left, Jacob Spreyer, his body man, quickly told the president about the shooting—but their information was still limited. It all happened so quickly. *My God*, Biden thought when he first heard.

Biden returned home, where his staff briefed him more fully. The president and his aides quickly decided three things: He needed to appear on camera to address the nation, he needed to speak to Trump, and he had to return to Washington that night. The president joined additional briefings throughout the evening and the next day with his homeland security team. In one conference, Biden kicked things off with a choice of words that struck some as inopportune. He asked for updates by saying, "Fire away."

Backstage in the holding tent, Susie Wiles had just finished a briefing from the campaign's brand-new Pennsylvania state director, Ashley Walukevich, when she heard the gunshots. She recognized them instantly. Strangely, no one else in the tent seemed to realize. She saw speechwriter Ross Worthington walking to the side of the tent to see what was going on.

"Get down!" Wiles yelled. Those were gunshots, she told them. "Get down!" she repeated. Some of the aides took cover under a table that Trump used to sign souvenirs and put on his hairspray.

The shooting stopped. Wiles rushed to the side of the tent to see if she could tell what happened. She caught a glimpse of Trump just as he was standing up. She saw the blood. She saw him struggling with the agents, looking for his shoes, raising his fist. She couldn't tell where he was hit, but she thought he was going to be okay.

Suddenly one of the advance men ran over to her with her tote bag and ushered her to the motorcade so hard he almost knocked her over. Steven Cheung, one of Trump's spokesmen, fell behind so Wiles told the advance man to help him instead. Wiles usually rode with Chris LaCivita and Dan Scavino, but LaCivita wasn't there that day; he and many other aides who usually traveled with Trump were already in Milwaukee for the RNC or were taking the weekend off before the busy week. Cheung got in with her instead. Wiles didn't see Scavino in the car either. She looked back and saw him some forty feet behind, picking something up off the ground. She rolled down her window and shouted, "Get in the car!" Only when he got inside and the motorcade started rolling did Wiles notice what Scavino had stopped to retrieve: the red MAGA cap that Trump had been wearing, stained with his blood.

They had no idea where they were going. Trump was in another car, and they couldn't reach him. LaCivita called. He was with his daughter, a spokeswoman for the Michigan GOP, in his Milwaukee hotel, when she'd knocked on his door and said, "Dad, the president's been shot."

Cheung received a call from Danielle Alvarez, the communications adviser. She and another spokesman, Brian Hughes, had been on the phone talking about convention news stories when Hughes saw a chyron on TV and interrupted, "I think the president has been shot." Alvarez was running late to the airport and started screaming, "What is happening?" She called Wiles but she didn't pick up. Cheung told her, "I've got Susie and we're okay," and hung up.

The motorcade left the fairgrounds through what looked like a horse trail, and there were popping sounds again to the right of the car. Some of the aides thought for a second they were getting shot at again, but this time the sounds were from fireworks.

In the car, Wiles called the head of Trump's Secret Service detail, Sean Curran. He told her Trump was breathing. He was okay. They were going to the hospital.

Before every trip, the Secret Service scouts out an area hospital, just in case. Almost four years earlier, when Trump campaigned at the Butler regional airport in October 2020, the agency had established an emergency plan with Butler Memorial Hospital. The medical center went into lockdown and diverted patients to other facilities to prepare for Trump's arrival.

People froze in the ER as black SUVs pulled up with red and blue lights flashing, and assault officers unloaded with helmets and long rifles, followed by suited Secret Service agents with handguns drawn. "Oh thank God, he's walking!" the people in ER cried as Trump emerged on his own two feet; he'd refused to take a stretcher. He didn't want the visual.

"Thank you, Jesus, he's walking," a man in the ER exclaimed.

By the time Wiles's car arrived, doctors and nurses were running around the ER. She saw Trump's body man, Walt Nauta, exit the hospital, leaving her with Cheung and Scavino standing behind a water cooler to stay out of everyone's way. Trump's children were calling Scavino for information, but he didn't have any. Cheung's phone was blowing up. Wiles started praying. Had she been mistaken to conclude that Trump was okay? Maybe it was worse than she thought.

A doctor came up to her and asked, "Are you Susie?"

"Yes," she said.

"He's ready to see you," the doctor said. She didn't say if Trump was okay.

Wiles, Cheung, and Scavino walked into his hospital room, guarded by the Secret Service. Trump was sitting up in bed, still wearing his suit. A bandage covered his ear. There was blood everywhere. "It was bleeding like a bitch," he later said in an interview for this book. "They thought I had four or five bullets in me because there was so much blood." His aides realized he was okay because he started making jokes.

The agents were discussing where to go next. Trump said he wanted to return to Florida. But Melania called and wanted him to come to Bedminster, where she was staying. She argued with Curran for a while, and eventually she won. Curran told Wiles to go take care of it.

Wiles went into the next room to call the club manager and tell him to evacuate. But we have people staying overnight, he protested. People are eating dinner. People are still on the golf course.

You don't understand, she told him. The president had been shot. He needed to clear everyone out of the club immediately.

Back in Trump's room, he told the doctor he wanted a CAT scan. The doctor asked why, and Trump said he felt like he needed it. He went down the hall with a squad of Secret Service agents to get the scan. Someone from the White House called Wiles, trying to connect Biden, but she said Trump wasn't available to talk now.

Trump asked to see the film from the scan. The doctor said that wasn't done anymore, and offered him a written report. "I want the film," he repeated. She left to get it, and while she was gone, one of the aides asked him why.

"It's like an IQ test," Trump said. "They tell you that your brain is good, so I just want to have that."

Wiles put the film in a manila envelope in her bag. Nauta returned with a new pair of sneakers and a golf shirt from a local store. Trump said he didn't want those clothes, he would wear his suit. Wiles said he couldn't wear that suit with blood everywhere. He argued with the staff and eventually changed. (He later got the suit dry-cleaned.) He inspected the hat that Scavino had saved.

Trump kept talking about the shooting. He couldn't believe it. He seemed to want to relive it over and over. The doctor told him he was so lucky, they should go buy a lottery ticket.

He talked to his children on the phone. He talked to Melania several times. He spoke to Dave McCormick, who was only moments away from being onstage with Trump when the shooting started, and joked that he could have been on the news too. (McCormick was glad he wasn't.)

Wiles noticed that Trump had an IV in his arm, and she knew they would eventually have to get it out. She asked the doctor if she would come on the plane with them to Bedminster. The doctor agreed. Trump asked his aides to summon Ronny Jackson, his former White House physician who now served in Congress, to come in the morning, so the doctor from Butler would be able to return home.

Finally, Trump and his staff left the hospital for the airport. But they had to wait there for the Secret Service to sweep the plane again, and for Bedminster to get evacuated and secured for his arrival. They waited so long they had pizza delivered. There were TVs in the room playing wall-to-wall coverage of the shooting.

Trump was flooded with calls and messages expressing relief, sending strength, and wishing him well—some from unusual sources. Sylvester Stallone called. Trump heard from two of the richest men in the world, Mark Zuckerberg and Jeff Bezos. Both men, who'd been frequent targets of Trump's criticisms, now told him how courageous he'd appeared when he'd raised his fist and shouted "FIGHT!" Bezos said Trump's instincts showed who he was, and he wanted them to have a friendship. Wiles marveled that before, some of these people wouldn't give him the time of day. Trump loved it. He was having a great time. At one point he saw Wiles crying and told her, "Straighten up. Stop that."

Wiles reconnected with the White House, and Trump spoke with Biden. The exchange was awkward after their tense debate just two weeks earlier. The call was brief. But Trump described it as "very nice, actually." He said he'd turned his head at just the right time, leaving out that he had done so to point to a chart attacking Biden's immigration policies.

Finally, Trump spoke to Robert F. Kennedy Jr. Trump had seen how Kennedy's opposition to vaccines had lit up corners of Trump's own movement, and he thought his famous family name could lend a bipartisan halo, especially in this moment of calling for unity after a tragedy. He invited Kennedy to visit him in Milwaukee in the coming week.

The motorcade arrived at the Bedminster gates, and Trump retired to his residence. The rest of the staff went to a nearby Marriott to process what they had seen and try to sleep. They had to report back in the morning, to head to the convention.

14

Unity

Over the years, Susie Wiles had occasionally talked to Trump about her relationship with God. He never seemed particularly interested. After the shooting, Trump kept saying to Wiles that he didn't understand how he'd just happened to turn his head at the instant the bullet passed. "I'm not supposed to be here," he said over and over. Wiles told him he knew better. She said he was spared. Trump didn't seem to know what she meant. "You do know this is God," she said. He looked at her and said nothing. But by the next day, he had found a new way to describe the event. He would say, "If anyone ever doubted there was a God, that proved there was."

For months, as Trump confronted indictment after indictment after indictment after indictment, only to see his polling improve, interviewers kept asking him what his enemies would try next. "Why wouldn't they try and kill you, honestly?" Tucker Carlson had prodded. His fans at Mar-a-Lago kept coming up to him and warning him, he had to be careful not to pick a "deep state" plant as his running mate or else they would take him out. "God saved me," he started saying. "I'm not supposed to be here."

Trump briefly considered taking some recovery time at Bedminster before traveling to Milwaukee later that week for his acceptance speech, but he decided to go on Sunday as scheduled. Initially, Trump had planned to avoid overnighting in Milwaukee altogether, preferring to stay at his own hotel tower in Chicago. That is, until he was quoted calling Milwaukee a "horrible city" to a room of congressional Republicans. Republicans privately urged Trump to make nice with the convention's host city, especially in a swing state, but he told them he was just telling the truth. Ultimately, he decided to stay in Milwaukee.

Leading up to the convention, the campaign was determined to avoid a messy floor flight over the party platform. The issue they knew would be the most contentious was abortion. The existing platform, last updated before the Supreme Court overturned *Roe v. Wade*, called for a constitutional amendment banning the procedure. That was one thing when it was purely aspirational; quite another in the post-*Roe* world. Christian conservative groups such as Susan B. Anthony Pro-Life America would object to weakening that plank of the platform. But a constitutional amendment was clearly at odds with the position Trump had taken of leaving abortion restrictions to the states. Chris LaCivita handled the standoff with his usual couth when he was overheard saying of SBA's leader, "Is Marjorie Dannenfelser being nominated for president of the fucking United States? I don't think so."

Throughout the primaries, the campaign had screened delegates both for their loyalty to Trump and their willingness to support his position on abortion. A team led by Clayton Henson flew to every state convention to shape the delegations. Trump's team consulted with an array of religious and social leaders, holding meetings and asking for input. Ralph Reed, the evangelical leader, sent the Trump staff a clip of Ronald Reagan arguing that a constitutional amendment banning abortion wasn't needed because the Fourteenth Amendment already protected the right to life. Reed recommended putting that in the platform. Trump's advisers began to see Reed as helpful, unlike some of the other antiabortion advocates.

For months, the members of the Platform Committee debated and drafted thousands of words. But they later learned it was all an exercise in futility. Trump told Vince Haley, a top aide, what he wanted. He didn't want a long manifesto like the 2016 RNC platform, which ran for nearly sixty pages. And he was determined to leave his mark on the party's official positions. "I don't care what you have to do to get it done, but get it done," he told his top advisers.

Just before the convention, Trump personally edited the platform with a Sharpie, turning ten key points into twenty core promises in all caps. The entire platform fit on sixteen pages. It included Trump's signature campaign proposals such as tariffs and no tax on tips, as well as some new positions, such as supporting cryptocurrency.

Trump had once called crypto "a scam" "based on thin air." But in early 2024, his former campaign chairman turned felon Paul Manafort and others presented Trump with a pitch on cryptocurrency. Industry executives wanted to have a fundraiser for him in Nashville that summer, where he could raise $15 million. Others wanted to hold events at Mar-a-Lago. Trump still did not understand cryptocurrency, but he was open to hearing from tech leaders frustrated with the regulatory reach of the Biden administration.

Trump's draft went to the Platform Committee the next day. LaCivita told the young staffers from his home state who were assigned to managing the committee, a group he called the "Virginia Degenerates," to be brutally efficient in passing the platform. They nixed subcommittee discussions. They collected phones so people could not post pictures or share information. The draft was never shared electronically, not even with senior staff. If no one knew what was in the platform, they couldn't mobilize against it.

As aides distributed the draft on paper, they called each committee member's name individually. For those they knew they could count on, the staff announced their names calmly. But for those they suspected of making trouble, they shouted the names, to put everyone on notice.

Senator Marsha Blackburn of Tennessee ran the meeting tightly. Trump called in to address the members, revealing that he had personally written and edited the draft. "I want you to know that this platform has my absolute blessing, worked on it long and hard," he said, according to a recording. "This is something that hopefully you'll pass, you'll pass it quickly, and want to show unity in our party as opposed to the disaster that's going on with the Democrats." He insisted they were stuck with Biden. "He's not leaving. And as people understand, when you have delegate votes, which he has, there's not a lot they can do."

Trump went on for fifteen minutes with his usual riffs about crime and immigration, until Blackburn interrupted to thank him and move ahead with the business of the meeting.

James Blair saw some members rise to propose an amendment that he knew would be about abortion. Further, he knew considering one amendment would open the door to entertaining endless quibbling. He and a few other campaign advisers checked their whip count and knew they had the votes to adopt the platform as written. Blair signaled to Michigan GOP chairman Pete Hoekstra, who stood and made a motion to adopt the platform without any amendments. Hoekstra had recently taken over a state party in total dysfunction from ideological infighting, so he especially appreciated the importance of not getting bogged down in nitpicking phrases and paragraphs. The motion passed.

Trump's platform included Reed's suggestion of endorsing an interpretation of the Fourteenth Amendment that protected unborn life as a justification for state abortion restrictions. It also expressed opposition to "Late Term Abortion," without specifying how many weeks, or whether at the federal or state level. While most media coverage focused on how the platform was toned down on abortion, antiabortion activists took it as a green light for a national ban. "We got all we needed," a Republican involved in the process said. "And he got what he needed."

Some conservative groups were frustrated with the new platform and convened calls on whether to voice their displeasure, according to Marc Short, Mike Pence's former chief of staff. But most of the groups declined to say anything publicly for fear of angering Trump. "It was a dramatic departure from where our party and movement have been for decades," Short said. "It was very lonely to be speaking about that."

In Milwaukee, Trump holed up in the Pfister Hotel, a few blocks from the site where, in 1912, Teddy Roosevelt survived a gunshot thanks to a glasses case and a copy of his campaign speech in his chest pocket. The Secret Service blocked off the entire sixteenth floor for Trump, and he spent much of the week there, meeting with a select few visitors and working on his new acceptance speech.

A speech had already been written by Haley and Stephen Miller, but after the assassination attempt, Trump wanted to tear it up and start over. He wanted to take this opportunity to strike a new tone. The speech could be a unique chance for him, the most famous, most polarizing man in the world, to reintroduce himself to the American people. He would appeal for unity. On his terms, of course. He said the Democrats could start by dismissing the prosecutions. One friend joked that Trump saw unity as "You agree with me, and we are unified."

One of the first visitors to his Milwaukee suite was Kimberly Cheatle, the director of the Secret Service, who came to apologize for the security lapses in Butler. Trump asked her polite questions about the shooting and his protection, and she said everything his detail had requested in Pennsylvania had been provided. Wiles was upset because the Secret Service had repeatedly turned down other requests from the campaign for more resources.

Trump's team and the Secret Service had clashed for months over convention logistics, specifically how close to the arena protesters could gather. One aide even threatened Secret Service officials to abruptly move the convention to a different city if they did not agree to the campaign's demands. As the week went on, Trump grew angrier in conversations with friends, casting doubt on whether the Secret Service could protect him.

Cheatle held a tense briefing with lawmakers about the Butler shooting and then went to visit local law enforcement partners in the convention arena. Trump aides were stunned to see her show up in a VIP box. One adviser flagged her location to several Republican senators, who went to confront her. The senators chased her out of the box, screaming questions she wouldn't answer, until she ducked into a bathroom. Aides recorded video and posted it online. Five days later, Cheatle resigned.

Trump also took his meeting with Robert F. Kennedy Jr. The former president and his staff were electrified by the possibility of winning the former Democrat's endorsement, and believed it was critical to winning the White House. They thought Kennedy got a crowd response a little like Trump himself in 2016, especially with young mothers who were not natural MAGA types, and believed campaigning with a Kennedy would reinforce the ways in which Trump was redefining the political landscape and building a new, unconventional coalition. RFK arrived with his daughter-in-law and campaign manager, Amaryllis Fox Kennedy. When they walked into Trump's suite, Ronny Jackson had just finished rebandaging Trump's ear, and the nominee was dressed unusually casually. RFK talked to Trump about what interested him—vaccines, safe soil, sustainable farming, saturated fat. Trump seemed bored. He wanted an endorsement.

The first meeting ended inconclusively, and Kennedy came back another day, this time with his wife, Cheryl Hines, whose crossed arms and legs conveyed she did not want to be there. The two had snuck into the building through an underground parking garage to avoid being seen. Amaryllis was pressing for a deal. Kennedy would offer his endorsement in exchange for a major administration job, and potentially a speaking slot at the convention. There was even talk of putting a proposal in writing.

Wiles said she did not want an explicit trade. Trump would welcome RFK's endorsement, and he would be happy for him to be part of the campaign. But he would not promise him something in return. Kennedy left without any commitments, but his security team stayed in town just in case he got a speaking slot.

The campaign was also in talks with Elon Musk about a speaking slot, and a draft schedule listed him as a keynote speaker early in the week. But Musk never committed.

Another floor of the Pfister was blocked off for the VP nominee, his family, and advisers. But since Trump had still not informed his running mate of his selection by the time JD Vance and Marco Rubio arrived in Milwaukee, they both had to check in somewhere else. Trump was still enjoying the suspense. His aides were afraid he would surprise them all with the news of his pick in a public appearance.

Lindsey Graham had continued lobbying for Rubio aboard Trump's plane to Milwaukee. He argued that Rubio would vacate a Senate seat for Trump to fill, which appealed to Eric Trump because his wife, Lara, wanted the job. Wiles was peeved that Graham was still pushing for Rubio after she'd spent a month working to make everyone comfortable with Vance. "It's not gonna happen," she said, as she got up and went into the office at the front of the plane.

Trump thought Vance could help him in Pennsylvania, which both parties viewed as pivotal to deciding the election. On a personal level, he liked Vance's Ivy League credentials and his looks. Vance won over LaCivita with their shared Marines service and Wiles with his ability to faithfully deliver the campaign's talking points in interviews ranging from pro-Trump media to *Meet the Press*. Vance's advisers were determined to win the veepstakes by showing he was a team player, never returning the sniping from the other contenders' camps. His biggest champion was Trump's eldest son, Don Jr., who was impressed by *Hillbilly Elegy*, the 2016 memoir that made Vance famous, and by how Vance articulated his opposition to U.S. involvement in the war in Ukraine. A mutual friend, political adviser Andy Surabian, helped connect Don Jr. and Vance, and the two hit it off.

Vance's relationship with Trump had deepened since they first met at Mar-a-Lago in February 2021. Less than a month after Trump left the White House in disgrace, Vance was not his likeliest visitor, as someone who was on the record in 2016 calling him "dangerous," "reprehensible," and "unacceptable." At that meeting, Trump confronted Vance about his past criticisms, and Vance stunned him by apologizing. He said he'd bought into the media's lies and had gotten Trump wrong.

Vance made clear that he'd since changed his view. By his own account, the reversal arose from the reception to his book, the way he saw liberal elites using him as a whisperer for the Trump phenomenon they didn't understand. He didn't want to be a part of that. He recalled meeting a business executive in 2018 who complained to Vance that Trump's immigration restrictions led to higher wages, implying Americans didn't want to work. He told Vance something like, "You understand this as well as anybody. These people just need to get off their asses, come to work, and do their job."* In Vance's telling, the executive's comment repulsed him. Vance took exception to the assumption that he would sympathize with the boss more than with his workers. It situated him on the side of the elites, looking down on left-behind Americans. He recalled realizing, "I have to get off this train, or I'm going to wake up in ten years and really hate everything that I've become." He left his bougie Bay Area lifestyle, moved back to Ohio, and ran for Senate as a next-generation MAGA rising star.

The day after winning his Senate seat, in November 2022, Vance told Trump's team he would support him for president. It wasn't an obvious or easy position at the time, when DeSantis was still looking like the future of the GOP and plenty of other senators were keeping their options open in the primary. Trump was keeping close track of who endorsed him when and how effusively, and Vance's immediate support, formalized in a January 2023 *Wall Street Journal* op-ed, counted for a lot.

For Trump, the only thing better than an original loyalist was a convert. A critic-turned-defender was the ultimate testament to his power. It proved they needed him. Just ask Lindsey Graham or Kevin McCarthy. Vance also vowed that he would not disappoint Trump like his previous running mate: If he had been vice president on January 6, 2021, he said he would not have agreed to certify Joe Biden as the winner of the Electoral College.

The formal vet on Vance had begun in February, when Wiles tasked the campaign's lawyers, Stan Brand and Stanley Woodward, with

---

*Such sentiment was, in fact, consistent with a plain reading of *Hillbilly Elegy*, which was widely criticized for victim-blaming and overgeneralizing in holding the Appalachian poor responsible for their own misery.

scouring public records, archived web pages, and hundreds of news articles to catalog every conceivable political liability that might attach to Vance. The lawyers compiled a 271-page dossier with all of Vance's past comments, topped with a warning that his selection could fuel press coverage resurfacing those critiques and questioning his integrity. None of that struck Trump or his advisers as disqualifying. It was routine for campaigns to commission such assessments of their own vulnerabilities. These stockpiles of damaging information were among the most sensitive and closely held of a campaign's files, and they were among the known targets of Russian hackers who penetrated the Democratic National Committee and the Clinton campaign in 2016. Now it was the Trump campaign's turn to learn they were in danger of a similar hack-and-leak operation.

The trouble started, ironically, with Roger Stone, one of the biggest cheerleaders of the WikiLeaks disclosures that damaged Democrats in 2016. Stone had no idea how an old, idle Hotmail account became compromised, but once hackers got into it, they used it to email Trump staffers. Microsoft alerted Stone to the intrusion, and he called James Blair to warn him not to open any links from him. Blair avoided the phishing message, but Wiles opened an email from Stone, which gave the hackers access to her emails, including the Vance vet. Others, including a campaign lawyer, were hacked too.

Microsoft discovered the breach and alerted the Trump campaign. The culprit appeared to be Iran, whose government made no secret of wanting revenge on Trump and other officials in his administration who were involved in the January 2020 strike that killed their General Qasem Soleimani. The campaign had even received a warning from Biden administration national security officials that Iran wanted to kill Trump—apparently unrelated to the Butler shooting, but nevertheless contributing to Trump's team's mistrust and frustration.

The campaign overhauled its email systems and hired new specialists to improve cybersecurity. Aides debated whether to inform the FBI that the campaign was the apparent victim of a cybercrime, and ultimately decided against it. Wiles and his other advisers did not trust the Biden Justice Department to investigate, and feared the FBI would want to inspect the campaign's email servers. The RNC similarly did not tell the FBI that Chinese hackers had stolen some three hundred thousand emails, apparently looking for information about the party's platform on Taiwan.

Vance spent the first day of the RNC waiting in his hotel room for his phone to ring. Yet when Trump called, he missed it, and the former president got his voicemail. Vance called back as soon as he saw. "JD," Trump said, "you just missed a very important phone call. Now I'm gonna have to pick somebody else." Vance later said he felt like he was about to have a heart attack.

At that moment, Vance's seven-year-old son, Ewan, came up to him and tried to tell him something about Pokémon cards. Vance had to put Trump on mute to tell his son, "Shut the hell up for thirty seconds about Pikachu, this is the most important phone call of my life." Trump overheard the boy and asked Vance to put him on the phone. The former president started reading Ewan the statement he was about to put out naming Vance his running mate. Trump asked Ewan what he thought, and he said it sounded good.

On the same day, Rubio and Burgum learned that neither of them had been chosen—from staff, not Trump himself. Though it wasn't the real reason, Rubio's boosters attempted to save face by blaming his and Trump's shared residency in Florida, which would create a potential problem in the Electoral College under the Twelfth Amendment.

Trump began portraying Vance to donors as a decision about preserving his legacy and keeping the Republican Party in his image. He told a group of Florida Republicans that Vance was a "star," but the choice was as tough as picking a winner on *The Apprentice*.

While Trump was naming his running mate, the judge overseeing the classified documents prosecution threw out the charges. The documents case had been viewed by Justice Department officials, Trump's own team, and many legal analysts as the most straightforward, maybe even a slam dunk. Even Republican lawmakers would privately concede that Trump's conduct deserved to be prosecuted when FBI officials briefed them on the case, telling officials they could not believe he took so many sensitive papers and refused to give them back. The case was not affected by the Supreme Court's immunity ruling because it involved his conduct after leaving office. Many of his current advisers had to testify before the grand jury, and they feared having to take the stand under oath in open court.

Trump's team knew they'd gotten lucky when the case was assigned to Judge Aileen Cannon, a young Trump appointee in Florida. They expected her to slow-walk the case, pushing off a trial until after the election. But they did not expect her to grant their motion to dismiss the charges altogether. Cannon accepted the lawyers' argument that Smith's appointment was unconstitutional. Smith would appeal, but the trial clearly wouldn't happen by November.

Trump's lawyers had been preparing for more hearings and months of haggling over classified materials in a secure facility in Florida. They had no idea a dismissal was coming. Todd Blanche called Trump to tell him. "Do you think it's because of the assassination attempt?" he asked. Blanche said it couldn't have been because the ninety-three-page decision had clearly taken time to write. Trump called the judge "amazing" and invited Blanche and Emil Bove to the convention. They booked flights that afternoon and arrived in Milwaukee within twenty-four hours to celebrate with Trump's other advisers.

How could he lose now? The prosecutions were collapsing. Biden's support was still in free fall. Trump seemed poised to gain sympathy from the assassination attempt. Republicans did not have to stretch to imagine a landslide. The campaign was seriously studying expanding the battleground map to include Virginia, Minnesota, New Hampshire, and New Jersey. Inside the Trade Hotel, where staff stayed, next to the convention arena, Trump allies and advisers were discussing who might get cabinet posts and top administration jobs. LaCivita had a cigar lounge built in the parking garage outside the arena, also serving game meats and red wine.

Trump called Vance before his speech, telling him he'd be great and he was proud of him. Vance thanked him and added, "No takebacks. Even if I screw this speech up, we're stuck together."

Trump made a grand entrance into the arena that first night, and he looked unusually moved by the roaring cheers that greeted him. He let his signature tough-guy scowl slip, showing a hint of mist in his narrowed eyes. His very presence, after the assassination attempt, bestowed a rare solemnity. Just his being there those nights was something special. The bandage on his ear inspired convention delegates to wear paper flaps in solidarity; his call to "FIGHT" became the week's defining chant. Throughout the convention, the programming showcased the party he remade, from a new platform that upended Reagan-era orthodoxy on trade and abortion, to the presentation of a hip-hop parody extolling America First, "Trump Trump Baby."

Trump sat in a VIP box surrounded by his family and his new running mate, delighting in the parade of tributes—especially the speeches by his vanquished primary challengers, Nikki Haley and Ron DeSantis. Getting DeSantis to appear was the result of sensitive negotiations, including some bluffing. Several of DeSantis's advisers, concerned about his prospects for 2028, insisted that he repair his relationship with Trump and show his support during this campaign. Without DeSantis's approval, they started reaching out to Trump's team to set up a meeting. Trump agreed, leaving DeSantis's advisers scrambling to convince their boss to go, especially now that Trump was expecting him. Trump's friend Steve Witkoff cajoled DeSantis over four and a half hours of golf. But DeSantis continued to resist, up until the night before.

At the end of April, the former rivals sat for three hours over bacon and eggs. The first hour was tense, with Trump telling DeSantis he never should have run against him. DeSantis didn't apologize but made clear he wanted to help him now. The tone improved by the second hour, and they finished with a handshake. After that, DeSantis agreed to hold a fundraiser for Trump in May, and the former president called in and thanked him—only to turn around and mock him in front of his donors. "You should have hit me earlier, Ron," Trump said. "You might have had a chance."*

DeSantis decided he would not ask for a speaking slot at the convention, but when he was offered one, he took it. Unlike Haley and everyone else, the Florida governor did not speak in praise of Trump as much as he delivered a standard stump speech.

Some of the prime-time speakers struck the donors watching from the club boxes as unlike those at any Republican convention they'd ever seen before. Reality TV star Amber Rose appeared with a shaved blond head and the words "Bash Slash" tattooed in Gothic cursive on her forehead. Teamsters president Sean O'Brien, there as part of Trump's outreach to workers, acknowledged the strangeness of having a labor leader address the party more commonly aligned with management. He made

_____

*A DeSantis adviser denied that he resisted meeting Trump, that the meeting started out tense, and that Trump mocked him at the fundraiser.

some donors cringe by calling some corporate practices criminal or "economic terrorism" and singling out companies including Amazon, Uber, Lyft, and Walmart. Those were common refrains at Democratic conventions, but previously unthinkable at an RNC, where hundreds of corporate chieftains packed the arena's highest tier. Some donors scoffed or walked out. But convention planners, working with Trump, had wanted a different message that would appeal to Black men, Latino voters, and young people who did not usually vote. Justin Sayfie, a longtime top Florida lobbyist sitting in a luxury box, who'd attended GOP conventions since 1992, said he'd never seen a similar scene. "We weren't just trying to shore up our base, but we were going after voters of color, union voters, and we were making an aggressive play for Democratic voters," he said. "I thought it was brilliant."

On the convention's final night, Trump's aides watched from a wood-paneled luxury box. As the convention held an invocation, everyone closed their eyes except LaCivita, who kept talking and laughing. Lindsey Graham gently reminded him to be quiet and reverent. "I think they're praying," Graham said. LaCivita laughed and then stopped speaking.

Speaker after speaker described the near miss in Butler as an act of divine intervention. "At that moment, that was a transformation," Tucker Carlson said from the stage. "This was no longer a man. . . . He was no longer just a political party's nominee, or a former president, or a future president. This was the leader of a nation." The group in the VIP box spent much of the evening oblivious to the proceedings on the floor, instead gossiping among themselves. Former Treasury Secretary Steven Mnuchin showed Graham the election predictions in online betting markets. Graham predicted that Biden would drop out in three days and speculated about who Kamala Harris should pick for her running mate, suggesting Senator Mark Kelly of Arizona was the best choice. He said choosing a moderate governor would be formidable too. Some of Trump's aides said they most feared Josh Shapiro of Pennsylvania.

The group in the box began paying attention for Hulk Hogan, the retired professional wrestler who roared and ripped his shirt. Evangelical leader Franklin Graham spoke next, leading Lindsey Graham to bellow: "Only Trump could bring Hulk Hogan and Franklin Graham to the stage on the same night! Next is the Dalai Lama!"

The entire arena fell completely silent for Trump as he recounted the assassination attempt for the first time in public, still wearing an ear bandage. Some guests in the VIP box grew emotional. But about twenty minutes in, Trump reverted to his standard rally material. As the speech went on and on, people became restless and lost focus. The feeling on the floor, as the speech veered off course, was that after what he'd been through, he'd earned himself a good ramble. Delegates didn't leave early like supporters did at the typical rally, but some donors in the VIP boxes did. Trump spoke for ninety minutes, breaking his own record from 2016 for the longest acceptance speech ever. Many of his advisers saw it as a missed opportunity. "It could have been a little bit shorter," one aide said, laughing. "A lot of that wasn't on the teleprompter."

The speech ended, as was customary, with the release of thousands of red, white, and blue balloons. As they drifted down to the delegates, some people started popping them in celebration. Several campaign staffers who had been at the Butler rally noticeably flinched or froze. The pops sounded like the gunshots.

Lord Almighty

Some of Biden's advisers thought the assassination attempt could finally be the reset they needed. Republicans (and many Democrats) believed the shooting was game over, propelling Trump to an easy victory in November: the former president looked like a badass, with his fist in the air and blood streaming down his face; he was getting well-wishes from people across the spectrum; and he was raising gobs of money. But Biden's team thought the shooting could work in *his* favor instead, by giving him the opportunity to appear presidential, speaking loftily about the values and virtues of American democracy. He delivered an Oval Office address the day after, urging Americans to lower the temperature and condemn all forms of political violence. For twenty-four hours after the July 13 shooting, no lawmaker called for Biden to drop out. In an interview with NBC's Lester Holt two days later, Biden made clear his mind had not changed. The polling showed "a lot of different things, but there's no wide gap between us," he said, again at odds with the views of his own pollsters.

On Wednesday, July 17, the campaign's pollsters finally had their first audience with the president's full senior team since the debate. Jen

O'Malley Dillon called the three pollsters—Geoff Garin, Jef Pollock, and Molly Murphy—for a quick huddle before the meeting. She told them to give their honest read of the race. Don't sugarcoat it. Don't overly dramatize it. Give a clear-eyed assessment of where things stand. The pollsters did not prepare a slideshow, but coordinated a list of bullet points that they wanted to convey.

They logged onto Zoom at 10:30 a.m. along with O'Malley Dillon, Jeff Zients, Mike Donilon, Anita Dunn, and Steve Ricchetti. The pollsters were never given access to internal campaign analytics after the debate, so they focused on public polling. Citing data from RealClear-Politics, an aggregator of public polls, the pollsters walked the group through each of the battleground states. Biden trailed Trump in all of them, though more significantly in the Sun Belt states than in the Blue Wall. More troubling was that reliably Democratic states, including Virginia, Minnesota, and New Mexico, now appeared to be competitive. Given scant public polling of those states, the pollsters relied on data from other clients' private polling to bolster their case.

Murphy then explained the president's demographic challenges, citing the erosion of support among Black voters and young voters. She concluded by noting the difficulties Biden faced with the current makeup of the electorate. Trump was retaining a higher share of people who voted for him in 2020 than Biden. Trump also had a 9-point advantage with people who did not vote in 2020 but were expected to this time. It was hard, she said, to imagine a scenario in which Biden could make sizable gains without some sort of fundamental shift in how voters perceived the president or Trump. Pollock talked about turnout and said the universe of voters still remained unclear, but research showed Trump supporters remained more enthusiastic about their candidate than Biden voters about the president.

Garin was even grimmer. He discussed the long list of obstacles

Biden faced, particularly views of his age and fitness. Garin said there were messages that could move voters back into Biden's camp, but Biden was not in position to deliver them. The problem was the messenger. The pollsters' research found that voters were moved by hearing about the danger Trump posed to the country and steps the Biden administration had taken to lower costs. But Biden had taken too long to prioritize inflation and spent too much time touting his economic record. Voters who couldn't afford groceries weren't interested in hearing how strong the economy was or how many jobs had been created.

The pollsters tried to be as polite as possible but their conclusion was damning: Their research found Biden was just not able to persuade voters that he was up for the job. The president had no path to victory.

After the pollsters finished, Donilon said he looked forward to seeing their presentation. He liked to review polling on hard copies. But his response confused the pollsters. They thought they had just given him their presentation. They had just laid out the data and told Biden's senior team that their campaign was moribund, and Biden's chief strategist seemed to be shrugging it off. The pollsters left convinced Biden was staying in the race.

Two days later, when Garin checked in with Ricchetti, he lit into Garin, telling him the presentation was out of line. It was not their job to tell them there was no path to victory. The pollsters, Ricchetti said, were supposed to provide the path to win.

As the RNC went forward in Milwaukee, Biden was in Las Vegas, in search of that path himself, courting the key constituencies of Black and Latino voters. Family and aides said Biden always had a stunning ability to compartmentalize and focus on the next task. His every day was governed by the schedule printed on a card in his breast pocket.

Such tunnel vision was how he continued his duties as vice president even when he (but not the public) knew his son Beau was dying from brain cancer.

His first public event in Vegas was the 115th NAACP National Convention, where guest after guest in a photo line implored him to stay in the race. He walked onto the stage to chants of "Four more years." Biden heard what the talking heads said on cable news, but he also heard these chants and saw these supporters everywhere he went. Hunter Biden, who had come from his home in Los Angeles to be with his father for part of the Vegas trip, thought the NAACP speech was a home run. "That was great, Dad," he told his father after he walked off the stage.

The next day, Jeffrey Katzenberg drove from Los Angeles for a last-minute meeting to pitch Biden on how to revive his campaign. Biden walked into the small hotel conference room around 10:00 a.m., and he looked and sounded terrible. His nose was running, his eyes were watery, and he was coughing. He said he woke up not feeling well and was going to see the doctor after Katzenberg left.

Katzenberg walked Biden through his proposal for an aggressive media campaign to restore voters' confidence in his ability to do the job. Katzenberg reassured the president he could execute the plan, but they needed to act quickly; time was running out. Biden asked what he should start saying as part of the aggressive push. Katzenberg acknowledged he didn't know. The message was the missing piece of his plan. They still needed to figure that part out.

Soon after, a White House aide called Katzenberg to let him know that the president tested positive for COVID. When an aide called Hunter Biden, his first thought was *Fuck*. It was, in his mind, the worst nonfatal thing that could happen to an eighty-one-year-old president trying to prove he was not a doddering, incapacitated old man. Biden would have to cut his trip short and quarantine at his vacation home in Rehoboth Beach.

Leaving Las Vegas, Biden had trouble getting out of the Beast, needing assistance from a Secret Service agent, before slowly walking up the stairs of Air Force One. The thumbs-up he gave to reporters who asked how he was feeling belied his true condition. He looked even worse when he deplaned at Dover Air Force Base. It took him longer to descend the steps of the plane than it had to climb them a few hours earlier, and he took nearly twenty-three seconds to settle into his limousine.

He finally made it to his home shortly after midnight, and climbed into bed in a spare room on a separate floor from Jill. The next day, the White House distributed a letter from the president's doctor that described Biden "experiencing mild upper respiratory symptoms." But the president was hit hard by COVID and spent a good amount of Thursday sleeping.

In Wilmington, some staff were thinking about resigning. Some started venting to the press. Many believed Biden needed to go, but feared saying that publicly and had no avenue to share their concerns with the president directly. Staffers believed Biden would see the information if it came from *Morning Joe*, which Biden watched most mornings while riding his Peloton. Scarborough was speaking with a number of Biden officials who did not see a path forward. Adrienne Elrod, a Biden campaign adviser who was close to Scarborough and Mika Brzezinski and had been a regular on their program before joining the campaign, called Scarborough and discussed the polling and concerns inside the campaign, particularly fears that the president was not fully aware of how dire the situation was. Campaign officials blamed Donilon and Ricchetti for hiding the facts from the president and preventing others from sharing a different outlook with him directly. On Thursday's program, Scarborough channeled those frustrations when he said on the air, "The anger that I hear is not at Joe Biden. The anger I hear are the people who are keeping him in a bubble."

The next morning, on Friday, O'Malley Dillon went on *Morning Joe* and said the president was "absolutely" still in the race, though she acknowledged "some slippage" in support since the debate.

In Rehoboth, Biden started to feel better on Friday and started making calls to family and allies. In the evening, he spoke on the phone with Ron Klain, who told the president to "stay in" the race. "That's my intention," Biden said. "That's what I'm going to do."

On Saturday, Biden spoke on the phone with Chris Coons and asked how he was doing with Senate Democrats. "It's getting harder and harder," Coons said. Coons said he wanted to share a message from someone they both knew in Delaware, a union leader who used to join them on Amtrak rides between Washington and Wilmington. The union man expressed his love for Biden alongside his belief that the president needed to step aside for the good of the country. "I just want you to realize that people who've known you for years, who don't want anything, who've always believed in you, see that it's time to step aside," Coons said.

There was a long silence. Then Biden asked, "Are you one of them?"

"With all due respect," Coons replied, "yes." He went on, "I was one of the first ones on this plane. I will be among the last off this plane. But I owe it to you to tell you that the view through the windshield is the ground, and we are heading in a very bad direction. I will support you no matter what you do."

Biden called Ricchetti. "I need you and Mike at the house," he said. Ricchetti and Donilon had stayed loyal to the end. Cynical Democrats argued that was because they had the most at stake. Ricchetti believed

226

he would be the chief of staff in Biden's second term, the position he desperately wanted and believed he should have already had. Donilon stood to make millions of dollars by the end of the campaign, since overseeing campaign ads meant he got a cut of the media buys. Both advisers denied their own interests had any bearing on their counsel to the president.

The three of them all wore masks and met for several hours on the screen porch of Biden's house. Biden asked for the latest update on the political fallout and the polling. Ricchetti reviewed the latest batch of lawmakers who called for the president to step aside: since the shooting, sixteen additional members of Congress, including Senators Sherrod Brown, Martin Heinrich, and Jon Tester. They discussed the brutal meeting with the senators at the Democratic Senatorial Campaign Committee office. Still, Ricchetti emphasized to Biden that many of his allies, notably much of the Congressional Black Caucus, wanted him to stay in the race.

Donilon shared the latest internal polling, which showed Biden had lost ground nationally and even more so in battleground states. But Donilon reassured Biden he could still win. He told Biden he was not hemorrhaging support in the way people were saying. (Donilon's interpretation of polls never completely aligned with conventional wisdom.) Still, he cautioned, it would be ugly, pitting him against most of the Democratic Party. Staying in the race would mean a drawn-out fight culminating at the Democratic National Convention. Organizers were already expecting massive pro-Palestinian protests, and nervous Democrats were anticipating comparisons to the disastrous 1968 convention, also held in Chicago.

At one point, the conversation turned to Kamala Harris. "Can she win?" Biden asked. Donilon said she could.

Throughout the meeting, Jill Biden along with two other top aides, Annie Tomasini and Anthony Bernal, shuffled in and out, often summoned by Biden who wanted them to hear things. Hunter Biden, who was in Los Angeles, joined by phone for part of the conversation too. As dinnertime neared, Biden made clear he agreed with the assessment of his top aides that he faced a grim picture. He feared tearing apart the party. He decided he would step aside and wanted to figure out how to exit the race. He asked Donilon to write a statement and Ricchetti to work through the logistics of ending his campaign and notifying key advisers and stakeholders. Donilon and Ricchetti left Biden's house and returned to their hotel, the Bellmoor Inn and Spa.

They came back a few hours later to review the draft statement. They also went over the timing and logistics. Biden read the statement and made some edits. It was too late to announce his decision that night. He would do it in the morning.

Hunter Biden made clear to his father that he supported whatever decision he made. But he did tell him, "I sure would love having you back." What Hunter meant was that the presidency, beyond all the pressure and stress, took all his father's time, and he wanted more time to spend with him. After years of being a favorite topic on Fox News and subject to relentless investigations, Hunter often told others that he had more of an interest in his father abandoning his campaign than anyone. Hunter would come to believe that catching COVID—which forced his father to take a break from the constant barrage of decisions and events that engross the commander in chief—created the space for Biden to reflect for the first time, to see how, even if he could win, the party was tearing itself apart. Maybe the illness was like a message from God.

Biden and his aides reconvened in the morning to execute on his plan to drop out of the race. First he had some official business. He joined a call with his two top national security advisers, Jake Sullivan and Jon

Finer. It was scheduled for only about five minutes, to prepare to speak with the Slovenian prime minister about a prisoner swap to free *Wall Street Journal* reporter Evan Gershkovich from Russia. But the call went on for about twenty minutes, as Biden inquired about Ukraine, China, and Venezuela. He appeared nostalgic, seemingly reminding himself of the immense amount of information at his fingertips as president. He gave no indication to Sullivan or Finer that one of his next calls would be to Kamala Harris.

Part Three

SHAKEUP

Unburdened

On Sunday, July 21, at 11:00 a.m., Kamala Harris's brother-in-law, Tony West, summoned the vice president's closest advisers for a secret meeting. Since the debate, Harris had remained adamant that Joe Biden was the nominee, and she would not entertain discussions about any alternative scenarios. Her aides obliged—at least in front of her. Out of her earshot, there were conversations to plan for the what-if. Staffers thought it would be malpractice if they did not at least start thinking through what might happen if Biden dropped out. A few weeks after the debate, Sheila Nix, Kamala Harris's campaign chief of staff, wrote "To Do" on top of a piece of paper and started keeping a running list of people to call if Biden decided to leave the race.

At the vice president's official residence in Washington, Harris was in the kitchen making pancakes for her great-nieces, Amara and Leela, while Nix joined West's secret meeting in the pool house out back. With Nix and West around a coffee table were Lorraine Voles, Harris's White House chief of staff; Brian Fallon, her top communications adviser on the campaign; and Josh Hsu, her former counsel in the White House. Minyon Moore, a longtime confidante, joined by Zoom from Chicago, where she was chairing the Democratic National Convention. West told the group that he wanted to prepare in case Biden decided to drop out. He framed the discussion as "Let's assume, as a hypothetical, he drops out tomorrow."

Fallon said there was no way that would happen. West acknowledged that was unlikely, but his point was to map out the steps Harris would take *if* it happened. Who were the first people they would call? What would they need to do on the political front? What about fundraising? What would her first statement be? Before they got into those questions, they traded gossip. What were people hearing about Biden's thinking? Who else was calling for him to drop out?

If Biden quit, the Harris advisers agreed the vice president would need to work for the delegates so that voters wouldn't feel like the nomination was handed to her. That led them to discuss the rules of delegate selection, and they decided to consult David Huynh, a senior adviser on Harris's 2020 presidential campaign who remained close to the Harris orbit and was nicknamed "Delegate Dave" for his expertise.

Around 1:00 p.m., West's son-in-law, Nikolas Ajagu, came running to the pool house, banging on the door. He said Harris needed Tony. He found her on the phone in her office on the second floor, still in her gym clothes from a morning workout on the elliptical. Biden was on the line.

"Are you sure?" Harris asked the president. "Don't let them pressure you. Don't let them push you out."

Biden said he was sure. The situation was untenable. He was going to announce that day that he was abandoning his reelection bid. He'd give a speech at a later time endorsing Harris to be the new Democratic nominee.

Harris thought the lag time was a problem. If he didn't endorse her immediately, the press and public would view it as a lack of confidence in her. Then, if he endorsed her later, it would be viewed as bowing to pressure. Other challengers would jump into the race. Steve Ricchetti and Mike Donilon, who were in the room with Biden, said they understood and would call back shortly.

Once Biden decided to drop out, he never considered any option other than endorsing his vice president. He knew that rejecting her would reflect poorly on him. Representative Jim Clyburn of South Carolina told him that day that not endorsing Harris would be admitting he'd made a mistake in selecting her as his vice president. A few minutes after their first call ended, Biden called Harris back and said he would not change his statement announcing his withdrawal, but he would follow up with another statement endorsing her soon after.

As soon as she hung up with Biden, Harris tried to call her husband, Doug Emhoff, who was across the country at their home in Los Angeles. She couldn't reach him. Emhoff had gone out to a SoulCycle in West Hollywood, and he didn't have his phone with him inside the spin class.

Biden and the first lady had already called Jen O'Malley Dillon to tell her his decision. The campaign manager cried as the president, in a calm and steady voice, explained it was the right choice for the party and the country; they needed to defeat Trump.

O'Malley Dillon called one of her deputies, Rob Flaherty, but he didn't pick up. He was walking in Wilmington's Alapocas Run State Park with his wife, Carla Frank, who oversaw the campaign's surrogate operation. The two were talking about the state of the campaign and speculating about what might happen if Biden did drop out. About midway into their hike, Frank started to scale a rock wall, and Flaherty looked down at his phone. He saw the missed call from O'Malley Dillon, swore, and called her back.

"In forty-five minutes, we're going to post a letter and it says that he's going to drop out," she told him. "You can't tell anybody. Can you get to a computer?"

"I can get there in thirty minutes."

"I need you there faster."

Flaherty oversaw the campaign's digital efforts but did not have access to the social media accounts. He never actually posted from them. O'Malley Dillon asked if he had someone he trusted who could hit publish. Flaherty did. His name was Parker Butler, a twenty-four-year-old social media whiz. O'Malley Dillon approved, and Flaherty called Butler.

"Are you near a computer?" he said. "I'm going to send you a letter in about thirty minutes. I need you to post it in forty-five minutes on Twitter and Instagram and whatever." He didn't tell him what the letter would say.

While relaying the instructions to Butler, Flaherty was also trying to figure out how to get out of the woods. Frank found a road eight minutes away, and the pair sprinted up a hill and called an Uber. Flaherty also needed help converting the letter into a PDF for it to be posted online. He started a group chat with some other members of his team, telling them they had to prepare for an urgent post. Since he couldn't reveal what it really was, he told them to expect another medical update about Biden's COVID.

Flaherty was in the Uber when he received the letter and passed it to Butler, around 1:35. Around the same time, senior White House and campaign staff received an invite for a Zoom, at 1:45. As the staff logged on, Butler hit send on the letter. Biden, with his camera off, told his team that he had decided not to run for reelection. Among those finding out for the first time was Anita Dunn, who'd been one of the campaign's top officials. Biden said a letter would be shared with the public shortly. It was already online.

Back at the vice president's residence in Washington, Harris had no time to shower or change out of her workout clothes. Other aides rushed to the house: Kirsten Allen, her White House communications director; Erin Wilson, her White House deputy chief of staff; Steven Kelly, one of her speechwriters; and Lawrence Jackson, her official White House photographer. There was no celebration. All talk was operational. One of their first tasks was to craft a statement. Kelly worked on an initial draft with Adam Frankel, a speechwriter who'd worked with Harris for years. They wanted to signal to the American people—and to other potential wannabe candidates—that she planned to earn the nomination. Harris wanted the statement to be issued from the Wilmington headquarters, to send a signal that she was taking over the campaign. When aides gave her a draft to proofread, it had Biden's campaign logo on the top. They took it off. She didn't have her own campaign logo, so the announcement would have to go out without one.

Biden's endorsement went live at 2:13. Six minutes later, the campaign posted a follow-up message with a link to donate to her campaign—even though campaign lawyers had yet to file paperwork with the Federal Election Commission to change the name of the fundraising entity from Biden for President. The campaign also wasn't ready to prompt the donors to volunteer or help in other ways, a missed opportunity to capture valuable supporter data and energy.

At 4:00, the Biden for President email account sent Harris's statement saying she was honored to have Biden's endorsement and would work "to earn and win this nomination." She had already started. Prominent Democrats including former President Barack Obama and Speaker Emerita Nancy Pelosi thought a public process to choose a new nominee would be better for the party and for Harris. They imagined a miniature primary with town halls or debates leading up to an open convention. Harris's team thought that idea was ludicrous. The convention started in four weeks. Early voting started within two months. The election would be over in 107 days. Harris's team approached the process like a congressional leadership race: There was a defined universe of delegates, and Harris would seek to win the majority of them. Go out and whip the votes.

Names started to fly around the dining room of whom she should call. Allen urged organization. "We need to document this," she said. "We need a system to keep track of the calls that she's making."

Hsu started making a list and passed it off to Opal Vadhan, Harris's personal aide. Harris focused on the Democratic leaders while her staff worked on the nuts and bolts of lobbying delegates. They identified members of each delegation to serve as whips for their state.

Among Harris's first calls was to her sister, Maya, for which she and West left the dining room for a private space in the mansion's turret. Harris also called her pastor, Amos C. Brown, and the two prayed together.

She reached Bill and Hillary Clinton, who quickly endorsed her. Harris aides noted the Clintons' loyalty to the party. They supported Biden until the moment he decided to withdraw, and then quickly backed Harris, in contrast to other prominent Democrats who pushed for Biden to drop out and were slow to endorse Harris—chief among them Obama. When Harris reached him, he told her it was important for her to earn the nomination. Obama signaled he was supportive, but he also said he was not going to endorse her yet. He reiterated his belief that he felt he was best positioned to unify the party at the end of the process, whatever that looked like. But in private, he made clear he thought other Democrats would be stronger candidates.

Some of Harris's early calls were to other governors who she viewed as potential rivals for the nomination—Michigan Governor Gretchen Whitmer, Illinois Governor J. B. Pritzker, and Pennsylvania Governor Josh Shapiro. The governors, who had close relationships, started to talk among themselves about what to do. Should they endorse Harris? Or what should they say when she called? When Harris talked to Shapiro, he asked her what the process was for securing the nomination. Harris told him this *was* the process—she was working to win the support of the delegates to the convention. Shapiro got on board and endorsed her at 6:12.

Whitmer, who had already ruled out running when it was still hypothetical, initially demurred when Harris asked for her support. Pritzker, too, declined to endorse Harris immediately, telling her he needed to check if he had to stay neutral because his state was hosting the convention—an explanation that Harris's aides found laughable. Some of Pritkzer's aides called other Democrats, trashing Harris and suggesting the Illinois governor was going to challenge her.

Harris never connected with her longtime California frenemy, Governor Gavin Newsom. She called, but he missed it. The two had known each other for decades and shared the same consultants. He was San Francisco's mayor when she was the city's district attorney. They'd both long harbored presidential ambitions, and some Harris aides believed Newsom wanted to jump in the race despite public pronouncements to the contrary. But he endorsed later that evening.

Pelosi kept Harris on the phone for a long time, going on about process and fairness. They had drama from San Francisco politics, and other Democrats observed that Pelosi didn't appear to like other powerful women, noting she wasn't a fan of Hillary Clinton until she lost in 2016. Harris's staff could tell Pelosi was not interested in endorsing her and they wanted her to make that clear and move on. Harris had other calls to make.

Despite some holdouts, Harris was racking up endorsements, giving her and her team growing confidence that they would secure the nomination quickly. She ended up making more than a hundred calls that day. The chairs of the state Democratic parties had already met and decided to stick with Biden if he stayed in the race, or if he dropped out, immediately support Harris.

West, who spent much of the day seated directly beside Harris at the long dining-room table, started working on setting up the new campaign. He called Eric Holder, the former attorney general who used to be his boss, to see if he could oversee the vetting process for Harris's running mate—usually a monthslong process that would now have to occur in a matter of weeks. He also started reaching out to donors, especially those in Silicon Valley circles who swore off donations to Biden after the debate, hoping to bring people back into the fold.

Harris's staff started scrambling to figure out her schedule. She initially had no public events planned for the next day, but her staff thought she needed to be in front of cameras. Her aides agreed her first trip should be to Wilmington to meet with and reassure the campaign staff.

Harris spoke with O'Malley Dillon on Sunday and asked her to stay in her role on the campaign. But O'Malley Dillon said she wanted to sit down with Harris before committing. They decided to meet the next day. O'Malley Dillon wanted assurances that if she stayed she would be in charge and have direct access to the candidate. Harris would agree, remembering how her 2019 campaign had suffered from unclear lines of authority.

Some staff suggested Harris go to nearby Philadelphia for a brief stop at a small business. But one of Biden's aides nixed that idea, suggesting that a stop in a city where Biden had long-standing ties would be pouring salt in the president's wounds. They obliged.

Even before Harris arrived in Wilmington, staff started working to turn over the entire campaign to reflect the new candidate—a Black woman in her late fifties instead of an eighty-one-year-old white man. They had to overhaul the website design and order new merchandise. They needed to transfer the official fundraising committee from Biden to Harris—and quickly, so they could capitalize on the rush of excitement and pad their dwindling coffers. They collected $81 million in the first twenty-four hours. The Democratic National Committee scrambled to figure out who controlled access to KamalaHarris.com, which for years just redirected to Biden's website. Campaign staffers also had to learn how to write for the vice president. No more Irish poetry, aviators, malarkey, and ice cream. The new memes promoted Harris phrases that internet fans had already transformed from repetitive and strange to quirky and fun—falling from coconut trees and being unburdened by what has been.

At 8:29, British pop star Charli XCX, who became a cultural icon that summer for her new hit album, *Brat*, posted on X: "kamala IS brat." The Gen-Z contingent that ran the campaign's social media accounts immediately pounced, rebranding the @KamalaHQ_X account with the album's distinctive lime green color. Later that night, the campaign finalized new scripts for organizers and volunteers who would hit the doors the next day to talk to voters. They created a new logo and ordered lawn signs. The state party chairs put out their endorsement at 9:12, making it that much harder for any other Democrat to challenge Harris. By the next day, Pelosi, Pritzker, and Whitmer would endorse Harris, and the Associated Press would declare her the new presumptive Democratic nominee. Obama's team proposed producing a video showing Barack and Michelle calling Harris to officially endorse her; it would take days to schedule, so their endorsement wouldn't come until later that week.

Around 10:00 p.m. on Sunday, Harris gathered her staff and finally had a moment to reflect. She told them they had a huge mountain to climb, and that it would be difficult. But, she added, they had a duty to deliver for the country. Before everyone left, staff recommended they memorialize the moment with a group photo. Harris, with her hair pulled back into a tight ponytail, and still in her Howard sweatshirt and workout clothes, beamed in the center, surrounded by some of her family and closest aides. With one hand she held a notebook and with the other hugged one of her great-nieces, who'd come downstairs barefoot because they were already in bed. The staff around her smiled and embraced. They thought they were making history.

Cruel Summer

Trump was anxious when he saw Biden's post announcing his withdrawal. He wasn't exactly afraid he was going to lose, but he wanted to know what it meant to run against Harris instead. He believed he'd already won the race against Biden. Susie Wiles told him it was all okay: By the time the race was over, Harris would be easier to beat.

"Why do you think that?" he asked. Wiles said Biden had residual goodwill that Harris did not. There would be a honeymoon, she cautioned, but it wouldn't last.

"You don't know that," he said. He became sullen and furious. The entire campaign had been premised on beating the incumbent. He'd spent a $100 million. He'd taken Biden out. Now they needed a new message, a new strategy, new everything.

The team convened a series of frantic calls to reorient the campaign. They had considered this scenario for weeks, and had begun preparing some materials against Harris. But suddenly it was real. Chris LaCivita compared the feeling to facing a team with a terrible record, expecting them to forfeit, and then seeing them show up and make you play the game.

Over dinner in Bedminster with a longtime friend, Trump said his campaign was "stalled." Because of tightened security after the assassination attempt, he couldn't campaign outside, which capped his audiences and made it harder to find venues where he could appear. He complained about the Secret Service snipers surrounding his properties.

"I have to win two races," he said. "It's not fair. I thought it was over."

Trump confided that he was thinking of shaking up his team. The friend asked why, and Trump said his advisers had told him Biden would never drop out. He blamed them for convincing him to agree to an early debate. "They said he wasn't leaving," Trump said.

The friend cautioned Trump that firing staff would generate bad press and distract from the campaign. He advised staying the course. Trump moved on to describing how much he hated Harris. He hated all his opponents, he said, but he had "zero" respect for her.

On the last day of July, Trump flew to Chicago to address the National Association of Black Journalists. He wanted to show the Democrats he was not afraid and he was serious about reaching out to Black Americans, especially while Harris was ducking media interviews. His mere presence plunged the host organization into turmoil, with some members objecting to platforming him.

Trump said ahead of the appearance that he might question Harris's race. He'd recently seen a photo of Harris (born to a Jamaican father and an Indian mother) in traditional Indian dress. Advisers including Wiles and James Blair argued against challenging Harris's identity. But Trump wanted to do it because he wanted to cast her as a fraud, someone who would shape-shift and pander.

Just before he took the stage at the NABJ conference, his aides learned that the interviewers, three prominent Black journalists, planned to fact-check him in real time. Trump's aides said he wouldn't accept that. It was either no fact-checking or no interview. The audience waited out the standoff for more than an hour.* Several aides huddled with Ken Lemon, the NABJ president, and others called in by phone to urge the organization to drop the fact-checks. At one point, Lemon said the Trump team told him the interviewers could fact-check as long as they did not announce that they were. Finally Lemon said he would walk out and tell the audience that Trump was standing them up over the fact-checking issue. Only then did Trump take the stage.

One of the interviewers, Rachel Scott of ABC, confronted Trump with what some congressional Republicans were saying about Harris—that she was a "DEI hire," meaning they were accusing her of becoming vice president only because of her race. Trump pretended not to understand the term DEI, despite making it a common campaign theme. Scott pressed him more directly. "Sir, do you believe that Vice President Kamala Harris is only on the ticket because she is a Black woman?"

"I think it's maybe a little bit different," he answered slyly. "She was always of Indian heritage and she was only promoting Indian heritage. I didn't know she was Black until a number of years ago, when she happened to turn Black, and now she wants to be known as Black. So I don't know. Is she Indian or is she Black?"

Scott pointed out that Harris attended a historically Black college, and Trump brushed back at her, calling her "nasty" (a word he frequently used for women who stood up to him).

The audience began to jeer and laugh at some of Trump's answers. "It was a very revealing moment," Lemon reflected later. "We were shocked at what some of the answers were."

Back on his plane, Trump erupted at his small traveling team of

*A Trump spokesperson said the delay was due to technical audio issues. There were audio issues, but they were fixed long before he took the stage.

advisers. "What the fuck was that?" he said. "That was an ambush." He repeatedly asked who approved the event, even though he'd been the one who wanted to go. He said he believed that Harris would be there, which his team knew wasn't true. Most of his senior advisers—LaCivita, Wiles, and Tony Fabrizio—had skipped the event. They got on a phone call to decide what to do, as Trump's remark exploded across headlines.

The advisers decided to roll with it. They found old headlines describing Harris as the "first Indian-American US Senator," and flashed them across the big screens at an arena filling up with Trump's supporters for his next stop in Harrisburg, Pennsylvania. Trump would continue to complain about the NABJ event for weeks.

Trump was feeling sorry for himself. For four years everyone had been saying Harris was a disastrous vice president—suddenly, she could do no wrong. Trump's advisers fully expected Harris to quickly consolidate the Democratic base, bring home all the Democratic voters who should already have been supporting Biden, and get fawning media coverage. Still, Fabrizio told others he had never seen such a surge of enthusiasm for a candidate. The polls tightened. The election was slipping away. How was this even possible?

Trump's advisers tried to cheer him up. "Look at it this way," LaCivita said. "You'll be the first presidential nominee in American history to defeat two opponents in one year."

Trump couldn't accept it. He couldn't understand. "How could he let that happen?" he said of Biden. Other times he'd say, "I beat him. I've got to beat her too. This is bullshit."

Trump was getting constant phone calls from concerned friends. They saw a campaign in trouble, and they reinforced putting the blame on Wiles and LaCivita. Many worried it was too late in the race to make changes. Then again, Trump had replaced his campaign manager in July 2020. And in August 2016. Some alumni of Trump's earlier campaigns pined for a return of Steve Bannon. Bannon said he wasn't interested, and as of July he was confined to the Federal Correctional Institution in Danbury, Connecticut.

On August 2, Kellyanne Conway and Lara Trump went to see the former president at Bedminster to discuss the campaign's direction. Conway was hearing from lawmakers and donors who worried Trump's campaign was sputtering. She insisted she wasn't interviewing for a job.

"You beat a woman before, you can beat a woman again," she said to begin the meeting. "You took Hillary seriously and you had respect for her. I don't think you respect Kamala Harris."

"I don't respect how she got there," Trump said.

Conway said he had to move on. Harris was the nominee. "You've got to treat her like a worthy opponent."

Privately, Conway had expressed some doubts about LaCivita and others on the campaign's staff. But when Trump asked for her opinion that day, she did not go there.

Trump kept telling Wiles and LaCivita their jobs were safe, but LaCivita grew frustrated with the outside sniping. He warned critics to be careful coming after him and posted a message on social media "to all my fans": a photo of Tony Soprano raising his middle finger. He told Trump, "It's hard to fight the enemy in front when people behind you are trying to put a bullet in the back of your head."

The day after Conway's visit to Bedminster, Trump had a rally in Atlanta. On the flight down, Trump told LaCivita he wanted to rip into Georgia's popular governor, Brian Kemp, whose wife had told a local TV reporter that she planned to write in Kemp's name for president instead of voting for Trump. "Should I say it?" Trump asked LaCivita. LaCivita would regret that he didn't push back hard enough. At the rally, Trump went on an extended tirade against Kemp and his wife.

Kemp had not been invited to the event, and state and local officials flooded his phone saying Trump shouldn't have attacked him and was putting the must-win state in jeopardy. The governor had spent years annoyed that Trump kept sniping at him, all because he wouldn't overturn the 2020 election results. Many times he'd considered fighting back but decided not to waste his time. "I don't have a problem with the president," he would say. Kemp wanted to avoid a feud that he viewed as damaging to himself, Trump, and Republicans everywhere. He envisioned a different kind of GOP than Trump, but he understood reality. He'd planned to mobilize his massive and sophisticated get-out-the-vote operation to help Trump win Georgia, for the sake of party unity. But now that Trump had attacked his wife onstage, Kemp's advisers said that plan was off.

The task of brokering a truce with Kemp fell again to Trump's personal peacemaker. Steve Witkoff flew to the governor's mansion in Atlanta and met with the couple. He said he understood why Kemp was frustrated with Trump. But Trump needed Kemp to win Georgia. Could the two make amends? They didn't have to be best friends.

Lindsey Graham pulled Kemp aside at a Republican fundraiser and acknowledged that Trump had been unfair to him. It was uncalled for, Graham said. But a détente would benefit both of them. "It's in your interest to have a good relationship with him, and it's definitely in his interest to have a good relationship with you," Graham said. "He just doesn't know it yet." Kemp said he agreed—he didn't want to fight. Graham offered to get Kemp on Sean Hannity's show and make sure Trump was watching. Kemp would just have to say on air that he supported Trump, and Trump would respond with a conciliatory Truth Social post.

Trump was also lashing out at other people whose help he needed. He sent a hostile message to Miriam Adelson, the megadonor who was bankrolling a powerful super PAC, because he learned she was going to employ operatives he believed were not loyal to him. Adelson was taken aback. They'd known each other for years, and she, with her late husband, Sheldon, had been one of Trump's most generous benefactors. Witkoff and JD Vance called to do damage control. Later, Adelson would print out the angry note and bring it to a dinner with Trump, passing it to him with a smile and asking if he wanted to make any revisions. He would cross out some of the text.

On his way to a fundraiser in Montana on August 9, Trump's plane encountered a mechanical problem and had to make an unscheduled landing at an unfamiliar airport. Enraged, he used the time to call and scream at a *New York Times* reporter, threatening to sue the newspaper for correctly reporting that he'd misremembered a long-ago emergency helicopter landing. (At first people thought he was confusing former San Francisco Mayor Willie Brown with former California Governor Jerry Brown. It turned out he was mixing up Willie Brown with a different Black municipal politician from California.)

His flight the next day to a fundraiser in Aspen rocked with severe turbulence. Some passengers called it the worst flight they'd ever taken. Trump groused that his friends weren't seeing any campaign ads. LaCivita explained that the ads weren't running nationally, only in battleground states; Trump's rich friends in Florida and New York weren't supposed to see them. Trump still demanded to know where all the money was going if people weren't seeing the ads.

LaCivita offered an idea to calm him down: "Let's write something."

He spent the next hour taking Trump's dictation of thirty-word scripts for fifteen-second spots, simple stuff like, "President Trump is going to end all taxes on Social Security benefits and end all taxes on tips." LaCivita gave the scripts to the campaign's ad maker, John Brabender, and told him, "Produce these. The boss wrote them. They're good." They were on the air a few days later.

Trump remained in a bad mood at the Aspen fundraiser. He didn't put on his usual makeup, appearing old and tired. Casino developer Steve Wynn urged Trump to focus on crime and immigration. "We have to go after the persuadable independents," Wynn told the former president, in front of the other donors. Trump sat silently and grew annoyed.

Adding to his malaise was the fact that it was August. Trump didn't want to work that hard in August. For rich New Yorkers, August is not a month for hard work. He wanted to play golf in August. Instead, he was spending August doing daily campaign stops in places like Howell, Michigan, and York, Pennsylvania.

"I'm still here," he would tell aides before taking the stage. "We're gonna have a great rally, as long as they don't shoot me again."

Stick to the issues, his advisers told him. They gave him a policy theme for each speech. "These people don't want a policy speech," he huffed backstage in Pennsylvania. "They want a show."

Fabrizio's data showed that Democrats were most vulnerable, and Trump was strongest, on inflation and the economy. But Trump often wanted to talk about other things, especially immigration. Stephen Miller became a frequent companion on the campaign trail, channeling what Trump wanted to say. His rallies started featuring images of a knife-wielding assailant stalking a woman in a dark alley captioned "No one is safe with Kamala's open border," and a huddle of turbaned men burning an American flag labeled "Meet your new neighbors if Kamala wins."

Speak shorter, his advisers told him. Maybe an hour instead of ninety minutes. But Trump didn't want to shortchange his fans. "They've waited all day," he told an ally. He bragged about how long he could talk without taking a sip of water. Trump began polling his rally crowds on whether he should stick to the script or improvise, talk about policy or personal insults. He sarcastically called his advisers "my geniuses" and "joked" about firing them.

During a fundraiser in the Hamptons, Trump repeatedly referred to his "disciplined campaign," a sarcastic dig at his advisers taking credit in news stories and sounding like they were managing him. "What about the candidate?" he asked.

At another fundraiser on the Jersey shore, multiple donors expressed concern that Trump's momentum was slipping away. Harris was gaining. Trump was losing focus. The staff was growing weary. Something had to change.

On a visit to rural Pennsylvania, Trump saw David Urban, a longtime ally from the state. Urban believed Harris was going to have a hard time winning over blue-collar voters in places like Scranton, where Biden had been popular in 2020. "We could win this race," Urban told Trump as they walked toward the stage. "But it's all up to you."

Amid his frustrations with his top campaign officials, Trump increasingly turned to Corey Lewandowski, his original campaign manager from 2016. Lewandowski was a hard-charging, foul-mouthed New Hampshire operative with a high and tight haircut reminiscent of his time at the police academy. In 2021, Trump's team publicly cut ties with Lewandowski after he was accused of harassing a donor's wife.*

*A misdemeanor battery charge was dismissed when Lewandowski agreed to take an impulse-control course, perform fifty hours of community service, and "stay out of trouble" for one year, according to court records. He issued an apology with no admission of guilt.

But now Trump wanted Lewandowski back, and Lewandowski was eager to come in off the sidelines. Lewandowski's motto was "Let Trump be Trump"—especially appealing to a candidate who hated feeling like he was being managed, and was feeling that way now. He liked the idea of putting Lewandowski on TV to defend him, something his current co-campaign managers didn't do.

Wiles and LaCivita had apprehensions about Lewandowski's involvement, but LaCivita thought he could charm him. They talked and agreed on a few concrete tasks for Lewandowski to focus on, such as TV interviews and his home state of New Hampshire. LaCivita thought he could live with that, and told Wiles it would be fine. They announced Lewandowski's hire on August 15 alongside several other additions to the team, so the campaign could portray it as an expansion rather than a shake-up. But Lewandowski suggested to others that he was going to be in charge.

That day, Trump held a news conference at Bedminster. His aides purchased groceries to illustrate inflation, displayed on a table outside his clubhouse. Aides gave him a binder of statistics for him to read, along with detailed remarks about the economy.

"Should I read this?" he asked before walking out. He did not think it would command attention or get ratings like he wanted. "I don't want to read this," he said. He deemed it "boring."

Communications adviser Danielle Alvarez told him he could move onto other topics and take questions, but could he first read the economic remarks as given? Reluctantly, he agreed.

He walked to the podium and told the press he was reading remarks his aides wanted him to read, and that he did not agree with them that the economy was the most important topic. He spoke for forty minutes before acknowledging the grocery displays. "Wow," he said, pretending to admire the setup. "What a nice job. . . . I haven't seen Cheerios in a long time." Flies circled the meat and milk spoiling in the August sun.

Lewandowski started showing up early at the campaign headquarters in West Palm Beach and took over a conference room on the sixth floor. He began interviewing staff one by one, saying he was auditing everyone's job and all spending to make recommendations to Trump on how to course correct. He called field staffers seeking their views on the campaign leadership, saying he was acting at the request of the president. He said Trump authorized him to audit the campaign's finances, demanding to review every contract. He found an ally in the campaign's CFO, Sean Dollman, whom he had known for almost a decade.

Dollman had disagreed with Wiles about some spending decisions and privately raised concerns about some contracts with top campaign officials. He believed LaCivita and others were making potentially millions of dollars on commissions for placing advertisements. He also argued privately that the campaign was spending too much money sending mail to the homes of potential voters and should be spending more on digital advertising. Lewandowski asked Dollman to give him the campaign financials, and Dollman obliged, after consulting with a member of the Trump family.

LaCivita was furious when he found out. A senior colleague on the campaign told Dollman he would be fired. The campaign's top lawyer, David Warrington, called Dollman into a conference and questioned him about what information he provided Lewandowski and why. Lewandowski had not signed a nondisclosure agreement with the campaign, and officials feared he could release the information publicly. Dollman managed to keep his job, but he never had real influence again.

Lewandowski knew Trump hated the idea of others profiting from his name. The candidate also disliked campaign spending on mail, preferring TV ads and rallies. Lewandowski began preparing a report to show Trump.

Wiles realized that she was under siege when employees kept calling to tell her about Lewandowski's questions and commands. Another longtime Trump ally who started working with Lewandowski, Bob Paduchik, asked James Blair to send him data on the campaign's political efforts for him to analyze and make improvements. Blair declined, saying he worked for Wiles and LaCivita, and they had not instructed him to share proprietary information. When LaCivita realized that Paduchik, who he'd considered a longtime friend, was helping Lewandowski, LaCivita told Paduchik he was dead to him.

Trump's 2024 campaign had been different because the senior staff always presented a united front to the boss. Lewandowski destroyed that cohesion. So soon after envisioning a landslide at the convention, the campaign was on the verge of falling apart. Trump was in a funk. "We have to get him out of this," Wiles told others.

Honeymoon

Kamala Harris's most urgent decision as the presumptive Democratic nominee was choosing her running mate. Being a vice president herself, Harris knew what she wanted: a governing partner who understood their place. Not the decision-maker. Not the center of attention. She also desperately wanted to inform her choice with polling: who would help her most electorally to beat Trump.

Her VP search began on the day Biden dropped out, when Tony West asked Eric Holder to run the vetting. Holder and Dana Remus, Biden's former White House counsel and a top campaign lawyer, enlisted dozens of lawyers from their firm, Covington & Burling, to help vet the candidates. Soon after, Harris's top aides started batting around ideas of potential running mates.

There were the obvious ones: Pennsylvania Governor Josh Shapiro, North Carolina Governor Roy Cooper, and Arizona Senator Mark Kelly. Other names that quickly emerged included Kentucky Governor Andy Beshear, Transportation Secretary Pete Buttigieg, Illinois Governor J. B. Pritzker, and Michigan Governor Gretchen Whitmer. Sheila Nix encouraged the team to consider Minnesota Governor Tim Walz, who was not immediately on everyone's radar. West seemed surprised but encouraged her to share more. Nix said Walz had solid experience as a governor, but he also brought his own brand of enthusiasm and support, particularly among younger voters. That was enough to put him into the vetting process.

Almost immediately, Cooper and Whitmer declined to move forward in the process. Cooper withdrew from consideration partially because of a quirk in the North Carolina state constitution that put the lieutenant governor in charge whenever the governor leaves the state. Cooper's lieutenant governor was Mark Robinson, a Republican who'd made racist, anti-Semitic, and sexually offensive comments and was currently running for governor, and Cooper was worried about what Robinson might do in his absence. As for Whitmer, she just wasn't interested in the job. The lawyers ultimately vetted nine candidates.

There was no time for drawn-out auditions, and limited, if any, opportunities to schedule joint campaign events where Harris could test out chemistry. Each of the candidates tried to showcase their strengths on their own, mostly through cable TV interviews, fundraisers, and surrogate appearances in battleground states.

The field narrowed to six finalists: Shapiro, Walz, Kelly, Buttigieg, Beshear, and Pritzker. They each had a Zoom interview on Friday, August 2, with a panel of West, Nevada Senator Catherine Cortez Masto, former Louisiana Congressman Cedric Richmond, and former Labor Secretary Marty Walsh. The next day, the group of advisers met with Harris at her official residence to discuss the six finalists. They started with some good news: Harris could win with any of the candidates, and she should not feel constrained in making her decision.

Each member of the panel was assigned one of the finalists to make an affirmative case for Harris to pick them before opening it up for discussion. Walsh presented Walz, West did Shapiro, Cortez Masto talked about Kelly, and Richmond discussed Buttigieg. The group did not spend much time discussing Beshear and Pritzker.

On paper, many Democrats thought Shapiro was the obvious choice. The Trump campaign, too, feared him the most. Chris LaCivita was so concerned about Shapiro that he began pitching opposition research, hoping to knock him out. He was the popular governor of Pennsylvania, which both campaigns viewed as the most important battleground state. He was young, fifty-one, and cut a moderate profile—a helpful counterbalance to the perception of Harris as a radical California liberal that the Trump campaign was eager to hammer home. Shapiro was a compelling speaker in the mold of Barack Obama—maybe too much like Obama, in the view of some Democrats, to the point of parody. Obama himself was a fan of Shapiro, who was one of the earliest supporters of the former president's 2008 campaign. They'd kept in touch. Some aides worried that Harris's and Shapiro's backgrounds were too similar—two lawyers who'd served as state attorneys general.

Much of the progressive wing of the Democratic Party declared war on Shapiro, largely because of his support of Israel. Some Shapiro allies saw the criticism as deeply unfair and borderline anti-Semitic, since the governor was an observant Jew, but his positions on the Palestinian conflict broadly aligned with the Biden administration and the other vice presidential contenders. The lawyers vetting Shapiro did flag some comments they viewed as more incendiary, particularly as it related to pro-Palestinian protests on college campuses after the October 7 attacks. One that caught their attention was his commentary on CNN from April: "We have to query whether or not we would tolerate this, if this were people dressed up in KKK outfits or KKK regalia, making comments about people who are African American in our communities."

Kelly also looked like he could be a compelling choice. An astronaut who represented a battleground state on the U.S.–Mexico border, Kelly was an immigration hawk who Democrats hoped could help neutralize Trump's advantage on the issue. He also had a compelling personal story; he was married to former Congresswoman Gabby Giffords, who was gravely injured in a shooting while serving in Congress and went on to make an inspiring recovery and become an advocate for gun safety. His challenge was that he was bland. He didn't have a particularly strong connection with Harris, and he was not viewed as a great campaigner. As one adviser put it: "so boring."

Walz's biography—Midwesterner, veteran, former high school teacher and football coach, and red-district congressman—seemed to offer cross-over appeal to independents. He had a background as a moderate, but progressives adopted him as their own, touting that he signed legislation for free school meals in Minnesota and had agreed to be the faculty sponsor for the gay-straight alliance club at the high school where he worked in the 1990s. Pelosi privately pushed for him too, because she'd worked with him in Congress. The pitch for Walz was straightforward: He could appeal to white voters across the Blue Wall states (Wisconsin, Michigan, and Pennsylvania) and hopefully help Harris with male voters. He'd never lost an election.

Harris's panel made clear that Walz was the favorite. Harris decided to invite three of the finalists to her residence for interviews the next day: Walz, Shapiro, and Kelly. When staffers asked the candidates' what they would want to drink, Shapiro and Kelly just asked for water. Walz requested a Diet Mountain Dew.

The interview with Shapiro revealed the two were not a perfect match. He came across as overly ambitious, pushing Harris to define what his role would be. He also conceded it would not be natural for him to serve as someone's number two, leaving Harris with a bad impression.

By contrast, Walz was deferential, showing no interest in himself, only how he could support Harris. He flatly denied any interest in running for president and said he would do anything Harris needed. He went so far as to proactively volunteer reasons why she might not want to pick him. In his interview that Friday, he said he had never used a teleprompter before. On Sunday, he told Harris, "I would understand if you went with someone else because I'm really nervous about the debate, and I don't think I'll do well." Still, the vetting team did not fully appreciate his tendency to misspeak, his folksiness sometimes tipping into factual imprecision.

On Sunday night, Shapiro called Harris's aides and expressed some further reservations. He said he wasn't sure he was ready to leave his job as Pennsylvania governor. Harris was perplexed when she was briefed on the call. Aides remarked on how differently Walz and Shapiro presented in the interviews. Shapiro seemed to want Harris to be invested in his success as much as he was in hers, and he didn't say he wasn't interested in potentially running for president in the future.

Still, she struggled with her decision. She clearly had a stronger rapport with Walz and viewed him as a better number two. But she also knew that was irrelevant if she didn't defeat Trump, and the road to the White House ran through Shapiro's state.

What she really wanted was polling to help guide her decision. But there was no clear-cut answer. The research did not conclusively show one candidate helped more than the other, and it didn't prove Shapiro would carry a meaningful advantage for Harris in Pennsylvania. The vice president pressed her team, but Jen O'Malley Dillon kept saying there was no answer in the polling. There was no empirical evidence that Shapiro would deliver Pennsylvania and with it the White House.

Harris wanted to sleep on the decision. In the absence of a mathematically "correct" answer, Harris went with her gut. Walz was the better fit. She also thought he'd be a better governing partner. By Monday night, Harris told her family and some staff that she would pick Walz. The staff was unanimously behind him too.

When Harris called Walz to tell him, he missed the call. She called back and on both ends aides recorded the conversation to release on social media. "Would you be my running mate?" she said with a grin.

Almost immediately, Liz Allen, a veteran of the Obama White House and Biden campaign, and Kate Berner, a longtime Biden communications aide, showed up at Walz's house. Allen told the governor that he should pack for five days. He was going on a swing of rallies throughout the battleground states with Harris. Allen helped the governor select his ties, and then they headed off to the airport, where Walz boarded his first private plane (not counting the State of Minnesota's small prop plane for use by the governor). Finding the plane had been a hassle—campaigns usually spend months working through contracts to find a private plane suitable to fly around presidential and vice presidential candidates. When they arrived in Philadelphia, Walz practiced his speech using a teleprompter, and Allen and Gwen Walz, the governor's wife, steamed the governor's suit in the visiting team's locker room of Temple University. They didn't have a personal aide to do that yet.

Walz had none of the support operation that Harris's campaign took for granted with a sitting vice president. The Secret Service had to stand up an entire new protective detail for Walz and his family. Allen had to figure out who was going to come on his flights, something the Air Force handled for Harris. Walz needed someone to print out his briefing books.

The new Democratic ticket set out on a tour across the battleground states, drawing crowds that Biden only dreamed of and Trump would envy: more than twelve thousand apiece in Philadelphia, Eau Claire, Wisconsin, and Las Vegas, and more than fifteen thousand in Detroit and Glendale, Arizona. Democrats raved about Harris's appearances on the stump, surprising some of her former staff who saw her stumble through the early years of her vice presidency. Most people didn't know she had been practicing—and improving—for more than a year. As students were returning to campuses in fall 2023, Harris had toured colleges around the country with a message centered around issues animating young voters, including abortion, gun safety, climate change, and voting rights. At the start of 2024, she focused on reproductive rights, beginning her tour on the fifty-first anniversary of *Roe v. Wade*. Then, in the spring, she traveled across the country on her "economic opportunity" tour. Harris aides reminded surprised Democrats that she had been putting in the work while no one was paying attention.

The good vibes on the campaign trail didn't stand up to hard data analysis at campaign headquarters. In a meeting soon after Biden's withdrawal, the analytics team led by Becca Siegel and Meg Schwenzfeier gave a presentation explaining that the surge of enthusiasm came from disaffected Democrats—base voters whom they should have already been winning. They would not be enough for a majority. The campaign pollsters, no longer excluded as they'd been during what staffers came to call the "before times," warned that Trump's favorability numbers had also crept up. Democrats had long been frustrated by what they called the Trump amnesia effect: research showed voters had rosy memories of Trump's presidency, associating his time in office with a booming economy, forgetting the insults, impeachments, firings, and fights, and not blaming him for his handling of the coronavirus pandemic. Much like Trump's Republican rivals during the primary, Harris's advisers debated and struggled with how to talk about him.

As for Harris, the campaign's research showed that voters felt they did not know her. The pollsters tested what would happen when she was introduced as a former prosecutor, and voters responded favorably. The team discussed potential downsides of emphasizing that part of her background, with some aides recalling the progressive backlash Harris received during her 2019 presidential campaign for her record as a law enforcement official (she was derisively called "Kamala the Cop"). But in the years since, as crime spiked during the pandemic and Trump was convicted of felonies, research suggested Harris should lean into her prosecutorial experience.

The staff had to grapple with many more unanswered questions. What was Harris's core message? What would the paid media strategy look like? What should be the balance between ads telling her biography, articulating policy positions, and attacking Trump? How much should they emphasize her background as a prosecutor versus her middle-class upbringing? How could they show she was ready to be commander in chief? How could she differentiate herself from Biden, or should she? Most campaigns would wrestle with those sorts of questions more than a year before Election Day. The Harris campaign had less than four months, raising the stakes of those choices, with no time for trial and error.

Biden's shadow proved to be a persistent problem for Harris. She felt deep loyalty to him and was part of his administration, but by most metrics, Americans were deeply dissatisfied with his job performance. In July, a *New York Times*–Siena College poll found 69 percent of Americans thought the country was on the wrong track, compared to 22 percent who thought it was on the right track—and in few areas was that more apparent than the economy. Persistent inflation, experienced most acutely at the grocery store and gas pump, had been dragging down Biden's approval rating for years. The cause of the inflation was a source of debate among economists—some said Biden overheated the economy with his $1.9 trillion stimulus package, while Biden defenders pointed to pent-up demand and supply-chain bottlenecks coming out of the pandemic. Some Harris loyalists observed that Harris had trouble breaking with Biden on the economy because her policy team was staffed by some of Biden's top economic advisers (namely Brian Deese and Gene Sperling) who had crafted the stimulus package.

For Harris, one obvious place to break with Biden was on Gaza. She genuinely disagreed with the president's approach, and some Democrats saw it as a clear political liability, especially with the core Democratic constituency of young voters. Others disagreed and thought more Americans agreed with Biden's staunch support for Israel. Either way, as the sitting vice president, Harris felt she could not publicly separate herself on a sensitive national security issue. It would undermine the president's leverage in negotiating with Israel and Hamas, especially as the U.S. tried to free hostages in Gaza.

There was no time to build a new campaign customized to the new candidate, nor to correct the existing operational problems held over from the "before times." For weeks, staffers still used joebiden.com email accounts. The headquarters was still decorated with Biden-themed wallpaper. The headquarters was still in Wilmington! Some departments crossed out Biden's name on signs and wrote Harris's name on top. O'Malley Dillon sometimes said "the boss" when she meant Biden, fueling suspicions among longtime Harris aides about her loyalty.

Biden's closest aides were gone: Mike Donilon returned to the White House; Anita Dunn left the White House for Future Forward, the main super PAC supporting the campaign; and Steve Ricchetti, Jeff Zients, Bruce Reed, Annie Tomasini, and Anthony Bernal turned their attention to Biden's final months in office. In their place, Harris, West, and O'Malley Dillon built a new leadership team, like a board of directors, stacked with veterans of Barack Obama's political orbit: David Plouffe, Mitch Stewart, Stephanie Cutter,* and David Binder.†

---

*Cutter had been working with Harris for more than a year at this point, helping her with message and interview prep.

† Binder joined the campaign before Biden withdrew.

O'Malley Dillon assured the staff that she was mapping out a new structure, and several Harris aides who'd been with her on and off since 2019—Megan Jones, Sergio Gonzales, Jalisa Washington-Price, and Shelby Cole—expected a staff-wide memo outlining new roles for them. But the memo never came. None of the other senior or midlevel staffers were leaving their jobs, making no room to promote Harris's aides. Instead, they watched people who'd spent years disparaging Harris now running her presidential campaign. They found it sickening.

The vice president picked up on the rocky transition, telling her close aides they needed to be more involved in approving text that was published in her voice. She worried that what was being written didn't sound authentic to her. She dispatched Ian Sams, who worked on her 2019 campaign, from the White House to take over the campaign's press operation and appear on cable TV. Harris wanted more people out there defending her.

The campaign also had to adapt to Harris's routine. She hated to be late. Biden would almost never start or end an appearance on time, but the vice president did not want people waiting long for her; she thought it was disrespectful. Harris would work out nearly every morning on an elliptical machine that was brought into her hotel suite. She usually watched *Good Morning America* on ABC while working out. Sometimes, she would tune into *Morning Joe*. She would then get her hair and makeup done, during which she almost always spoke to Minyon Moore. She would have roughly an hour of reading time, to review briefing materials and other memos. She also held calls with her top communications advisers to ensure she was briefed on the latest news developments. She always had a standing call with O'Malley Dillon, Lorraine Voles, and Nix, who became known as the "Holy Trinity." The standing call became the venue for staff to have Harris sign off on decisions, as in "Have the Holy Trinity bring it up on the call."

During a leadership retreat shortly after Harris became the nominee, Plouffe said the campaign didn't have time to be cautious or cut corners. They needed to take risks, and when they made a decision, they needed to go all in. "If you think we need to spend twelve dollars, spend twenty dollars," he said. "We don't just need to do things well. We need to do them exceptionally." He advocated for Harris to agree to participate in a debate hosted on Fox News, an idea he continued to push in the coming weeks, arguing Harris needed to show voters she was bold and unafraid. Plouffe's sense of urgency was refreshing to many holdovers from the Biden campaign, who thought the "before times" inner circle often moved at half speed.

But Harris did not sit for her first interview until August 29, more than a month after she became the nominee. The delay fed a Republican narrative that she was unable to face tough questions. It also prevented Walz, who rose to viral fame on cable TV, from doing his own interviews. He couldn't do one before Harris did. Some advisers would later acknowledge that waiting so long for interviews was a mistake; voters continued to feel like they didn't know Harris, and Trump was being allowed to define her instead.

In Chicago, staffers were working to overhaul the entire program at the Democratic National Convention. Planning for Biden's coronation had been challenging. At most conventions, ambitious politicians are desperate for speaking slots to raise their national profiles, and Democrats usually have no trouble attracting big-name talents to perform. Not this time. Confronting the challenge of convincing Americans that Biden should serve another term, organizers planned a program around negative messaging about Trump. Biden would give an acceptance speech on the final night and unlikely anything else—especially nothing impromptu. At a planning meeting back in May at the White House, Harris suggested showcasing Biden's accomplishments through an original song by *Hamilton* creator Lin-Manuel Miranda. Younger aides could not help but hear the idea as a little too cringe, for an artist whose appreciation peaked in 2016. Jill Biden objected because she said Miranda was too closely associated with Obama.

When Biden dropped out, the floodgates opened for Harris. Politicians and celebrities rushed to support her and campaign on her behalf. Rumors started spreading that Beyoncé would make a surprise appearance at the convention (wrongly carried by some news outlets). The program became younger and more energetic and more diverse. Instead of just running negative programming about Trump, Democrats could now draw a contrast between Harris and Trump. They also had to introduce Harris to the nation.

An appearance by Harris on the first night surprised everyone, even her husband, who giddily told people around him in the VIP box that he had no idea she would walk out onstage. Emhoff actually had been told that she would appear, but he forgot in the heat of the moment. One night during the convention, an aide approached Emhoff to tell him that the production team said he wasn't smiling enough. He said he'd just received a call from his wife backstage who said he was laughing and talking too much. Pay attention to the program, she said, reminding him the cameras were fixated on him. Emhoff was chagrined and marveled that Harris was focusing on him when she had more important things to handle.

The convention largely went off without major drama—with the exception of how to address the war in Gaza. Convention organizers invited the parents of an American hostage held in Gaza to speak, and many in the party's left wing demanded a speaking slot for someone of Palestinian descent. Some of Harris's top aides did not want a Palestinian speaker onstage, a view bolstered by the national security apparatus at the White House who worried about how the speech could undermine Biden's diplomatic efforts. Others thought the storyline was more damaging than the reality, and some even suggested having a taped speech to minimize risks. Jaime Harrison, the party chairman, sent a message to campaign leadership, expressing concern that rejecting a Palestinian speaker would hurt Harris politically. He was told the vice president would address the conflict. Ultimately, the Palestinian cause went unrepresented on the main stage, as protests rang out in the convention hall and outside the arena.

The first night was set aside for Biden, as a send-off for the president before he headed to a vacation near Santa Barbara, California. Chris Coons, Jill Biden, and Ashley Biden were all scheduled to speak, and the president would be the evening's prime-time headliner. But the program started to run long. Shawn Fain, the president of the United Automobile Workers, had a five-minute speaking block, but after finishing the five-minute speech on the teleprompter, he continued reading off his phone for another five minutes. Representative Jasmine Crockett of Texas and Senator Elizabeth Warren of Massachusetts both received long ovations, delaying the program further. Cutter, who was the executive producer of the convention, went backstage, warning speakers to stick to their time and speak through the applause. She looked for places in the program to trim a minute here and there. The clock kept ticking. Eventually, she had to cut a performance by James Taylor, several speakers, and a video about Biden.

The president would end up not taking the stage until 11:25 p.m. Eastern time, after many viewers had gone to bed. Ricchetti complained to anyone who would listen that it was a huge mistake to push the president out of prime-time. Biden ended his speech after midnight, flew to California, and had no role in the rest of the convention.

"Kick His A——"

A little more than two weeks after the DNC ended, Trump got on his plane on Saturday, September 7, in a foul mood. He was heading to a rally in Wisconsin, and Susie Wiles saw on the schedule that Trump had just had a meeting with Corey Lewandowski. In the air, Trump told Wiles to meet with Lewandowski in the office at the front of the plane.

Lewandowski started telling her the findings of his audit—all the things he thought the campaign was doing wrong. He suggested the campaign's spending decisions were driven by making money for advisers and consultants rather than winning the election, that everyone's commissions were too high. She told him he was wrong. But he said he would be in charge now. She couldn't hire or spend any money without his approval.

Wiles had already had her integrity challenged once (by Ron DeSantis), and she wouldn't go through it again. She had spent three and a half years of her life working for Trump, through four indictments, a primary campaign, and an assassination attempt. Now they were in striking distance, and someone was trying to knock her out. Wiles told others that in four years of working for Trump, these were the worst weeks by far.

As soon as the plane landed, Wiles called Chris LaCivita to tell him what had happened. LaCivita agreed they couldn't live with Lewandowski's ultimatum. But they couldn't deal with it now either. Trump was debating Harris on Tuesday.

Trump had initially refused to debate Harris on September 10 on ABC, arguing he'd made that deal with the Biden campaign, which no longer existed. After weeks of playing games, he finally agreed. He still would not prepare by doing mock debates with lecterns and people playing Harris and the moderators. He insisted he did not need to practice. His rallies were his prep. But he would sit around conference tables with some of the same advisers from before the first debate—Jason Miller, Stephen Miller, Vince Haley, Ross Worthington, Matt Gaetz—now with the addition of Tulsi Gabbard, the former Hawaii Democrat who ran for president in 2020 and left the party in 2022. Trump valued her experience debating Harris in the Democratic primary.

The prep did not go as well for this debate. Trump would lose interest and get frustrated. Some of the sessions were canceled. "He didn't want to be there," said a person present. "He didn't want to do it."

Trump's team expected Harris to try to provoke him about his legal cases, portraying him as the felon and her as the prosecutor, or criticize his handling of the COVID-19 pandemic and his failure to deliver an infrastructure deal like Biden and Harris had. They sought to accustom him to hearing those attacks so that he wouldn't overreact. They briefed him on her past support for Medicare for All and banning fracking, hoping to lure her into making a mistake off script. Trump promised his advisers he wouldn't be overly aggressive like in his first 2020 debate with Biden.

The Harris campaign made a big show of pushing to change the rules so that the microphones would stay on the whole time instead of being muted while the other candidate talked. Aides thought Harris's best chance for a viral breakthrough moment was in a spontaneous direct confrontation with Trump, rather than in the open-ended answers where she tended to sound canned and vague. But Trump's team wouldn't budge, and the Democrats realized they weren't going to achieve the change, so they acted like it was a huge loss for them as a way of lowering expectations for the vice president. The campaign worried that the bar was set too high for her because of her background as a prosecutor and her starring role in Senate hearings grilling Trump officials during his first term.

Harris started preparing for a debate in late spring, at that point expecting a vice presidential face-off. Without a known opponent, she and her aides gathered in sessions that largely focused on honing her message on a range of topics. To oversee the prep, Harris brought back Karen Dunn, a powerhouse Washington lawyer who'd also run her 2020 prep and agreed to do so again despite simultaneously representing Google in a monumental antitrust trial. Dunn was assisted by Rohini Kosoglu, Harris's former domestic policy adviser who co-led the prep four years ago. Dunn also brought in Sean Clegg, a California strategist who'd advised Harris's 2020 presidential campaign. They met regularly at the official vice presidential residence and sometimes at Howard University, Harris's alma mater, where she'd also studied for the 2020 VP debate.

When Trump narrowed down his list of vice presidential finalists to Vance, Rubio, and Burgum, Harris's aides decided that Philippe Reines, who played Trump in Hillary Clinton's 2016 debate prep, would play Vance or Burgum and Congressman Robert Garcia of California would play Rubio. Reines got the job after Trump picked Vance, and kept it to play Trump. Reines showed up with binders of transcripts of Trump speeches and pictures of Trump's hand gestures. His performances were mesmerizing—he blew the staff away.

Several staffers who worked closely with Harris caught COVID at the DNC, so the campaign instituted strict testing for anyone attending the debate prep sessions. Dunn, Kosoglu, and Clegg would bring Harris material on the most likely topics, and she would give feedback on how she wanted to revise or reorder the arguments. The hardest subject was the economy—what to say in two minutes about the administration's record. The team kept trying different variations, pausing, and coming back to it.

For the final five days before the debate, Harris advisers always planned to set up a prep "camp" in a battleground state, to allow for surprise drop-ins at area businesses. They chose Pittsburgh in order to be in Pennsylvania but not too close to the bubble forming around the debate venue at Philadelphia's National Constitution Center.

On the flight to Pittsburgh, the Harris debate team realized they happened to be on the same plane as Mike Pence. At first he seemed guarded. He said nothing when a Harris aide asked him if he wanted to say hi to Harris. The aide joked that he would take that as an endorsement. As they left the jet bridge, the aides tried again, more seriously, asking the former vice president for any tips or advice. Finally Pence reflected on his own experience debating Harris in 2020. "She was very good on the attack," he said, "less so defending her record." One of the aides thought his tone communicated, "Go get 'im."

The team set up on the seventeenth floor of the Omni William Penn Hotel, which the advance team named "Camp Pioneer," after Harris's Secret Service code name. The team showed Harris clips of Trump's 2016 debates, illustrating that he did not speak as sharply and cogently as he used to. Dunn brought hard copies of all the materials, passed them out, and collected them at the end of the day, so nothing could leak.

In the main ballroom, the campaign advance team built an exact replica of the ABC News debate set for practice debates, getting the news outlet to share the specifications of the room being built at the National Constitution Center. They had monitors showing a split screen of the two candidates, and they kept the room cold to simulate the studio. Communications aides Kirsten Allen and Colin Diersing played the moderators. Reines would wear a navy-blue suit and red tie to imitate Trump, with platform shoes to boost his height by a few inches. For the mock debates, he would also put on bronzer to simulate Trump's iconic complexion.

Harris wanted to use the debate to get under Trump's skin, to provoke him and make him lash out in ways that would showcase the most disliked parts of his personality. She planned to needle him about drawing smaller crowds, something she could work into answers to multiple possible questions. She received encouragement for the approach in a call with Hillary Clinton, with whom she'd developed a closer relationship over occasional dinners together.

The mock debates started each night around the time the real one would. All the observers shared their reactions in a chat group on the encrypted messenger app Signal, and at the end Dunn would synthesize the feedback and convey it to Harris herself, to avoid bombarding the candidate with a jumble of everyone's disparate opinions. Michael Sheehan, a Democratic speech coach who also worked with Biden, joined for a few sessions and gave Harris pointers about using facial expressions to take advantage of the time when she wasn't speaking since she would always be on camera. By Saturday night, when O'Malley Dillon arrived at Camp Pioneer from a staff meeting in Wilmington, the team felt they were in a good place. "There's a moment when it all clicks in," Clegg said. "She had a spectacular mock debate. She wiped the floor with Philippe."

Meanwhile the campaign was still wrangling with ABC over the rules. Harris's team wanted spouses to be able to watch in the studio, but

Trump's campaign objected (Melania wasn't coming). Families could stay backstage in the hold rooms with the staff. But the only restrooms that the candidates could use during commercial breaks would require them to leave the stage and cross through their hold room. Harris aides said that would be too tempting for someone to give a word of advice or slip a note. ABC said they would clear the hold rooms before the candidates left the stage, but Harris's side thought that was still too easy for a Trump aide to leave a note behind. They suggested the candidates walk through the *other*'s cleared-out room so there would be no opportunity to cheat. The Trump team objected to that. The resolution they came up with on debate day was for no bathroom privileges during the commercial breaks.

The day before the debate, Harris wanted to leave the Pittsburgh hotel and wake up in Philadelphia on game day. On the afternoon of the debate, she took a call from Biden, who was ostensibly calling to wish her good luck. But he also wanted to share concerns that some of his friends were questioning her loyalty to him because of the way she was campaigning. Biden framed the concerns as political advice, warning that he remained popular in Pennsylvania, and efforts to distance herself from him could hurt her in the critical battleground state. At the staff level, Biden's aides conveyed to Harris's aides that the vice president should do whatever she needed to win—essentially giving the campaign license to break with the president as they needed to. But Harris felt the president clearly saw it differently, and his comments annoyed her. Still, his intervention contributed to her reticence to criticize Biden or his record, despite his deep unpopularity.

She had one last prep session that afternoon, in a meeting room at her hotel. Reines used his closing argument to deliver a comedic monologue about how well Harris had done and how well she was going to do, delivered in Trump's voice. He called her extreme and crazy for being so punctual. He said he would yell on the screen but she should just look at him as a little man. "I'm a little mouse," he said. He finished with: "You are a radical. You are radically ready. You got this." Harris cracked up.

At her walk-through of the studio set, Harris asked if the candidates had always begun by shaking hands. Her staff informed her that Biden and Trump did not shake hands at the July debate. They didn't in 2020 either, because of COVID. In 2016, Trump and Clinton shook hands at the first debate, but not the next two. Harris decided she wanted to do it, as the proper way to greet someone, and especially since it wasn't a given, so it would make a statement if she initiated. She had never met Trump in person before.

"I have been doing this for twenty years, and you're the most pre-pared person that I've ever worked with," Dunn told Harris as she stepped onto the stage. "Kick his ass."

For Trump's flight to Philadelphia from Palm Beach, he invited the MAGA blogger Laura Loomer to tag along, as she had for big nights throughout the campaign. Many of Trump's advisers viewed Loomer as too conspiracy-minded and pugilistic, but he liked her. "Is she too fringe to be press secretary?" he asked aides once.

This time, Loomer showed him allegations circulating online about a community of thousands of Haitian immigrants resettled in the Ohio town of Springfield, accusing them of stealing geese and cats for food. Loomer showed him a call to the county sheriff complaining of Hai-tians carrying geese away from a public park* and a woman arrested for eating a cat.† She showed him a video of her associate confronting Ohio

---

*This isolated complaint was never verified.

†The woman was an American, not a Haitian immigrant, and lived in a different Ohio town.

Senator Sherrod Brown outside the Capitol. ("Would you be happy if an illegal alien ate your dog, Senator Brown?") The state's other senator, JD Vance, had also been promoting the allegations, to the chagrin of some local Republicans.

On the plane to Philly, Trump responded by joining in the online frenzy. He posted several memes on Truth Social alluding to the mania: a computer-generated image of him on his plane surrounded by grateful-looking cats and ducks; and another of cats equipped with assault rifles and MAGA caps.

When Harris aides saw Loomer get off Trump's plane in Philly, they called the vice president to brief her on the Springfield rumors so she would be prepared if Trump brought them up.

W hat the fuck!" LaCivita exclaimed in the conference room where the Trump staff was watching the debate. Trump had just said people were eating dogs and cats in Springfield, and moderator David Muir interjected that the city manager had said there were "no credible reports of specific claims of pets being harmed, injured, or abused by individuals within the immigrant community." The Trump campaign believed the network had agreed to no fact-checking. The official written debate rules did not actually specify, but Jason Miller said he'd gotten an assurance from an ABC journalist that the moderators would replicate CNN's hands-off approach at the first one.

Miller and LaCivita went into the hallway demanding to speak to ABC politics producer John Santucci. They even asked to talk to the moderators, while the debate was still going on.

"What the fuck is this?" LaCivita said again, now to Santucci's face.

"We are trying," Santucci said.

"What does that mean?" LaCivita said. "That's a fuck job."

Santucci said the crew was trying to convey their concerns to the moderators. "We are in the control room," he said. "We are in the ears. We are trying."

"There's a huge fucking problem," LaCivita said.

"Tell them to knock it the fuck off," Miller told Santucci.

Wiles called the president of ABC News to complain. "This is not what we agreed to," she said. "This is wrong."

When Trump left the studio, the first thing he said, as one aide recalled, was "Test the data," meaning he wanted to know what viewers thought. Others said that he said it went great, his best debate ever. Several advisers tried to talk Trump out of going to the spin room, but he insisted, saying he wanted to dominate the coverage.

To many of his aides, that decision meant he felt unsure about his performance. Before his first debate with Biden, he'd also wanted to go to the spin room, but then decided to let his performance speak for itself. This time, he barged in and declared that he won under unfair conditions. In the spin room, Trump's aides said he was looking forward to another debate. But Trump walked onto Sean Hannity's show and refused a rematch. "If you won the debate, I start to think maybe I shouldn't do it," he said. "Why should I do another debate?"

Trump was watching Fox News when Brit Hume said, "Make no mistake about it, Trump had a bad night. He rose to the bait repeatedly when she baited him, something I'm sure his advisers had begged him not to do . . . and we heard so many of the old grievances that we'd long thought Trump had learned were not winners politically." Trump didn't understand. "What is he talking about?" he erupted. "Why is this guy still on TV?" He told his team to change the channel to CNN. He liked commentator Scott Jennings's performance there better.

On the plane, over helpings of McDonald's, Wiles and LaCivita tried to reassure Trump that what mattered now was winning the postdebate:

arming influencers and surrogates with his best clips and Harris's worst moments, pointing out the questions she dodged and the answers she fumbled. They would channel Republican angst toward the moderators, casting the debate as a biased, three-on-one pile-on. The debate audience was not the one they cared most about anyway; anyone who watched the debate, or the media coverage of it, was definitionally a higher-information voter.

Loomer said she had no regrets about the dogs-and-cats outburst. She thought it was a defining moment of the campaign, like when Trump told Clinton at the second debate in 2016 that if he were in charge, "You'd be in jail." Trump's pet-eating line was the debate's most memorable, launching thousands of memes and becoming a TikTok trend. It put the focus on immigration, Trump's most comfortable terrain, and did so in a way that appealed especially to young voters. Illegal immigration was core to the campaign's economic argument on what to blame for pushing down wages and driving up housing costs, and how Trump was going to address the struggles Americans were feeling—through mass deportations.

In the days to come, Lindsey Graham, Kellyanne Conway, Wiles, and others encouraged Trump to stay away from Loomer. Conway told him Loomer had attacked her daughter online. Trump said he was surprised by how many people despised her, but he also seemed taken aback when allies showed him some of her most incendiary posts. "She's a fighter," he said. But he conceded she did not need to come on the plane again.

Whatever pundits thought of Trump's performance, the debate didn't move the polls. Fabrizio told others on the campaign that he was surprised. His advisers lined up against another debate, figuring that no matter how well Trump did, Harris would get positive coverage and land some blows against him. They could never be sure how he would behave in response. It was more risk than reward. His team agreed that Harris needed another breakout moment more than Trump did. When Mar-a-Lago members and other advisers tried to convince Trump to do another debate, he would listen but say it was not to his advantage. He said refusing to debate had proven to be a smart bet in the Republican primary.

For the Harris campaign staff, watching her with the Democratic surrogates next to the spin room was like being in a bar watching the home team winning a championship—cheering and hollering. The energy was the opposite of the silent, stunned looks they'd traded during Biden's debate. Harris's aides were sure she was winning from the first fifteen minutes of the debate. In every moment that called for an exchange they had rehearsed, she consistently delivered it. The communications staff had teed up videos they could use to highlight key moments, but as the debate went on, they saw them as unnecessary. Harris's performance *was* the story. By the sixty-minute mark, the team decided their message coming out of the debate would be to challenge Trump to a second one, as a show of how well Harris did. "There was no narrative we were trying to push," one adviser recalled. "We didn't have to home in on a single thing."

The catering attendants who delivered food to the Harris campaign's space agreed with their assessment. "She beat his ass," one said. The staff rewarded them with coveted camo Harris-Walz caps.

Harris herself, in the studio without any audience, didn't have any immediate feedback to assess how it went. As soon as it was over she asked her advisers. Allen and Dunn showed her X posts praising her performance as one of the most successful debates ever. Voles started crying, which others saw as a sign of how far Harris had come after being underestimated for so long. Harris went over and hugged her. She saw Reines and called him over, then gave him a hug and a kiss on both cheeks.

Minutes after the debate ended, Taylor Swift surprised the campaign with a full-throated endorsement posted on her Instagram. She shared a photo of her with her cat, Benjamin Button, and signed it "Childless Cat Lady," a dig at JD Vance. Harris asked if she should mention the endorsement when she spoke to supporters at a watch party. They said that would sound too thirsty, but agreed to change her walk-off song to Swift's "The Man."

Harris spoke at the watch party and then flew to New York, where she (like Trump) would visit Ground Zero for the September 11 commemoration the next morning. Most of the debate prep team did not usually travel with her and stayed behind in Philadelphia. By then most of the bars were closed except one dive bar with no seats, so a few aides went back to their hotel, bought beers at the minimart behind the front desk, and took them back to the staff holding room to watch MSNBC.

The high did not last very long. In the weeks leading up to the debate, Harris's senior campaign advisers fretted about the lack of other potential inflection points in the final sprint to Election Day. Voters still said they had questions about Harris. Polls showed she had a narrow lead, but there were still eight weeks to go. They needed Harris in front of big audiences. They needed more "moments." That hunger became even stronger after the debate, when the data showed the race barely moved. Voters said Harris won the match, but the overall race remained largely unchanged. The campaign continued to try to bait Trump into a second debate, to no avail.

In strategy meetings after the debate, they started brainstorming other opportunities. A Fox News interview. An event with big-name Republican endorsers. A trip to the U.S.–Mexico border. Anything that was visually arresting and might cut through the noise. Anything to get eyeballs on Harris. Even the vice president, who preferred extensive prep before agreeing to an event or interview, let down her guard a bit. "What else do you think I could be doing?" she asked aides. "I'll do whatever I need to."

Paranoia

Two days after the debate, Susie Wiles and Chris LaCivita sat down with Trump in the library at Mar-a-Lago. They had to talk about Corey Lewandowski.

LaCivita said he thought Lewandowski was coming on board to work only on New Hampshire, but now he was claiming total power. Wiles told Trump she was prepared to leave the campaign if Lewandowski stayed. She had brought a sixteen-page presentation to defend her spending, responding to every allegation, justifying every expense, to give to Trump if he asked.

Trump did not want to blow up his own campaign anymore. He said he didn't know where Lewandowski was getting his ideas. He did not want people quitting, but he didn't want to fire anyone. "You guys are in control," he told Wiles and LaCivita. "You guys run my campaign."

There was one catch. He wanted them to cut commissions and mail ads to spend $50 million more on TV (the number Lewandowski had alleged was being misspent).

Later that day, they got on the plane for a trip to Tucson. Lewandowski was already on board. Trump called him over to sit down with

Wiles and LaCivita, and told him, "They're in charge. They're running the campaign." He told Lewandowski to go on TV and worry about winning New Hampshire. Lewandowski got off the plane at the next stop. Wiles told others she was shaken by going through the showdown.

On Friday, September 13, Trump held a news conference at his golf club in Los Angeles. California was obviously not a swing state, but even in the peak season of the campaign, he wanted to check on the property. He was always interested in how his courses and hotels looked and how busy they were. He ordered a bowl of New England clam chowder, recommended the soup to others, and inspected the merchandise at the pro shop before venturing outside to face the press. When Trump spoke, his Secret Service detail usually stood still and stoic, moving only their eyes to scan for threats. This time, Danielle Alvarez noticed the agents began to move around and talk to each other on their radios.

Alvarez rushed inside to find Wiles, who was working at a table overlooking the news conference. "Look at how the agents are moving!" she said. There was talk of pulling Trump from the stage. Wiles went outside. Soon they realized there had been a drone in the area, putting everyone on high alert. It turned out not to be a threat.

Two days later, on Sunday, September 15, Trump was back in Florida, enjoying a round of golf with his friend Steve Witkoff on his course in West Palm Beach. For years, the Secret Service had warned Trump about the challenge of protecting him on the links. Officials told him his routine was too predictable—he golfed almost every weekend morning, and some weekdays too—and his courses often bordered heavily trafficked public roads, including the one in West Palm Beach. To make their point, officials showed him news photographs of him on the greens, arguing that if photojournalists could find him with a zoom lens, so could snipers with a rifle scope.

Trump didn't want to give up his game, and he complained that there were too many agents on the course. "The only thing I don't like about Secret Service, they're all over the golf holes," he told amused donors at a private fundraiser. "I hit a ball down the fairway, it's in a little rough, and there's a guy standing behind a tree, 'Good morning, sir.' And I got a ball with a horrible lie, I'd go like this, nobody would know the difference," he said, pretending to move the ball to a better spot (something he was known to do frequently, as documented in a sports journalist's book called *Commander in Cheat*). "I can't because he's standing—they're all looking down at me. It's horrible."

In general, the Secret Service worked by establishing a secure bubble around the protectee. The size of the bubble depended on the threat level and available resources. The danger to Trump was already high, based on his status as a former president and major-party nominee, even before the Butler shooting. National security officials had also determined that Iran's government wanted to kill Trump, as revenge for the 2020 Soleimani strike. But the Secret Service was running security details for more than two dozen people, with limited funding, and leading up to the Butler rally, the agency had repeatedly denied the Trump campaign's requests for more resources. After the assassination attempt, Biden ordered the Secret Service to boost Trump's protection, and Trump started receiving the same level of security as a sitting president, except for the assistance of the military. For weeks the Secret Service resisted outdoor rallies, saying they were too hard to secure, and limited the campaign to indoor arenas. By late August, Trump was able to speak outside again, surrounded by panes of bulletproof glass, which had to be transported on special trucks because they couldn't withstand too much jostling.

That Sunday, the Secret Service did not shut down the entire golf course. The golf outing wasn't on Trump's schedule. He and Witkoff had fixed the date last minute, on a call the night before. The protective bubble around their party had a radius of three to five hundred yards, with an officer leading one or two holes ahead.

At around 1:30, Trump and Witkoff were standing in the fairway of the fifth hole. They hit balls about ten yards from one another. Then both men heard the unmistakable pop-pop-pop noise from one hole over—the sixth hole, which ran along a busy road.

Secret Service agents swarmed Trump, tackling him to the ground, covering him and then rushing him to a golf cart specially built to whisk him away in an emergency. Witkoff stayed standing; he later told others that he did not know why he did not jump to the ground. For several minutes, he watched and listened before getting into his own golf cart and returning to the clubhouse.

When Witkoff arrived, the men's room was swarming with local police, Secret Service agents, and others. "Are you okay, Steve?" Trump asked.

Wiles was in a nail salon getting her nails done on a rare quiet Sunday afternoon. Suddenly she received multiple back-to-back calls from the Secret Service and realized something must be wrong. The agents downplayed the danger, saying their officer had shot at the shooter. Then Eric Trump called her and asked what was happening. He was driving south on I-95 and saw a high-speed police chase on the northbound side of the highway.

The Secret Service kept Trump in the golf club's safe room for hours—long enough to make sure Mar-a-Lago was secure for his return. Trump spent the afternoon calling friends, joking that he wished he could have finished the round because he was playing two under par after five holes. He watched the news coverage of the shooting and became outraged at a TV segment suggesting it could have been an unrelated gunfight near the course instead of an assassination attempt. He called into Sean Hannity's show, enraging other Trump aides and the Secret Service, who did not want the public to know where they were.

When Trump finally returned to Mar-a-Lago, he saw House Speaker Mike Johnson, who had been on his way to see him and had to wait at the airport for thirty minutes because of the shooting. Johnson had been planning to try to talk Trump out of calling for a government shutdown before the election, bringing polling to show how it could hurt him in the election. Instead they discussed the assassination attempts (now plural) over fried shrimp and meatballs. The Secret Service hid them in the far back of the dining room even though the club was entirely cleared out. Trump wondered if he'd ever be able to play golf again, his favorite activity. Johnson told Trump about a book called *The Bulletproof George Washington*, which argued that God protected the future founder during the French and Indian War. Johnson said Trump, too, had been saved by "divine providence," and Trump, who'd never shown much interest in talking about religion with him before, said he agreed.

The suspected gunman, identified as Ryan Wesley Routh, left a note declaring his intent to kill Trump and offering a reward to anyone who finished the job. He had a long history of violent crimes and unstable behavior, and he'd spent the past several years trying (uninvited) to recruit soldiers to fight in Ukraine. Unlike Thomas Crooks, who remained an enigma, Routh left ample online footprints to let Republicans portray him as a radical left-wing lunatic ginned up by overheated anti-Trump rhetoric. But there was another possible interpretation that, after two close calls, became too much for some of Trump's advisers to ignore—that Routh had been manipulated by a hostile foreign power.

Iran's desire to kill Trump was real, and the regime's M.O. was to hire cutouts. In 2022, a hitman tasked with assassinating an Iranian dissident living in Brooklyn got as far as her front door with an assault rifle. That same year, the Iranians figured out where Trump's last secretary of state, Mike Pompeo, was staying in a European hotel. The Iranians also held Pompeo responsible for the Soleimani strike, and they tried to capture him in the hotel. He narrowly escaped. In June 2024, undercover FBI agents posing as hitmen met with a Pakistani man in Brooklyn who was looking to assassinate an American politician (prosecutors didn't specify who, but his targets included Trump) on Iran's behalf. Authorities arrested him on July 12, which turned out to be the day before Trump's Butler rally.

Investigators had not found any evidence of a connection between the Butler shooter and Iran, but many on Trump's team did not think it was such a stretch to wonder. The second attempt looked even more suspicious.

They were always on edge now. When Trump spoke at a Bitcoin conference in Nashville, he was delayed for more than an hour because someone slipped past the security screening and disappeared into the crowd. Trump waited impatiently, periodically asking the agents for an update. There had been a time during the primaries, when if Trump wanted to visit a football game or a frat house and the Secret Service would object, he wouldn't care. If he wanted to go, the agents would have to deal with it. Not anymore. This wasn't security theater, this was life and death. In Nashville, when the agent told Trump they were still clearing the area, he nodded and said, "I'm gonna listen to my guys." Wiles became a little emotional. She had mostly stayed resolute during the assassination attempt and the convention, but for some reason in Tennessee that day, it was all catching up with her.

When Trump had visited the southern border in August, local police searched the desert for a man who threatened the former president on social media. Another time, a man who'd had too much to drink stumbled toward Trump on the Mar-a-Lago patio, prompting agents to physically escort him away. Officials warned the Trump campaign about poison and drones. Trump needed to stop touching the phones of people seeking selfies, they said, because it could be a way to expose him to chemical weapons. The campaign stopped doing rope lines altogether.

Three days after the scare on the golf course, on Wednesday, September 18, while leaving a rally on Long Island, the Secret Service told Wiles and LaCivita that they were on alert for someone trying to shoot at the motorcade* and would be scrambling the cars, driving faster and taking a different route. "I wish I had my fucking rifle," LaCivita said in the car. "Give me my M4." Wiles, with fast-food fried chicken on her lap, reclined her seat all the way back to get away from the windows, half joking, but only half.

It was clear how much their world had changed when Trump's team got a new directive: Instead of meeting at the airport for a campaign swing as they always had, everyone needed to come first to Mar-a-Lago for security sweeps. They took a different route than usual to the airport, and the plane was parked in a different spot, where no one had ever seen it before. "Get on the plane as fast as you can!" an agent yelled to the staff as they boarded. "Keep your head down!" The aides found out later that agents were worried about snipers and missiles.

On a trip to a farmers' event in western Pennsylvania, the campaign had to take country roads an hour southeast of Pittsburgh. On the way back, Wiles got a call from the Secret Service saying there was an unknown drone overhead, and they couldn't shake it. They might have to split Trump from the rest of the motorcade. Wiles thought to herself,

---

*The threat arose from a social media post relayed by local law enforcement.

This is it. The drone followed them for almost the entire drive but never did anything.

Wiles demanded to know what the authorities were doing about the Iran threat. She started corresponding with Jeff Zients, the White House chief of staff, and Annie Tomasini, Biden's deputy chief of staff who oversaw operations. Trump advisers spoke with Erik Prince, the founder of notorious military contractor Blackwater, whose advice included asking for protection from Delta Force commandos.

On September 24, national security officials came to Mar-a-Lago to brief Trump on the Iranian threat. U.S. intelligence suggested Iran had multiple kill teams inside the U.S. It was possible the regime hired drug cartels to carry out the murders. Trump repeatedly asked if Iran was behind the gunmen in Butler and West Palm Beach, and he didn't get a definitive answer. The intelligence officials said they had no evidence but wouldn't rule it out. Agents told him they couldn't access all of Crooks's phone. Trump got fed up with the acting director of the Secret Service, Ron Rowe, who Trump felt flattered him but would not answer his questions. Trump's team began discussing how excited they'd be to fire Rowe, if they could just win.

Wiles's aggravation with Rowe boiled over in an October 2 email. They had met and talked repeatedly, and she felt like the campaign had been patient. They had just needed to reconfigure an event because of a shortage of Secret Service personnel. The intelligence briefings had left the Trump campaign extraordinarily concerned that they and Trump were in danger, and she did not feel like the Secret Service was doing much about it. "The apparent reluctance of our own government to address this situation immediately and with grave seriousness is concerning, to say the least," Wiles wrote. She asked for military planes but never got them.

Secret Service agents on Trump's detail were especially concerned about Trump's jet, which lacked the defensive systems of Air Force One and could be vulnerable to surface-to-air missiles. They started flying decoys. Secret Service agents would drive down the runway behind Trump's plane as it took off, in case someone might be shooting at it. Snipers patrolled every roof wherever Trump landed and took off. On board the plane, agents might occupy up to twelve seats. On a September 28 trip to Prairie du Chien in remote western Wisconsin, the rural airport runway couldn't accommodate Trump's jet, so the campaign had to charter a smaller plane. The charter couldn't fit the full detail that the Secret Service required, so the agents decided to fly separately, and the campaign would have to wait on the runway until the agents arrived at the next destination. But the agents' government plane couldn't fly as fast as the campaign charter, leaving Trump on the runway for more than an hour. For a while the staff kept him busy with tele–town halls, afraid to tell him why they were behind schedule. Finally, he asked, "What's going on?" and got angry about the delay.

On one trip, the campaign staff boarded Trump's plane and waited for him to join, but he never did. The door shut. LaCivita got on with the staff instead of flying with Trump so he could explain what was happening. "The boss isn't flying with us today," he said. He had switched to Witkoff's plane, part of a new procedure to use two planes and sometimes two motorcade routes.

"So we're the bait?" one staffer said.

LaCivita said no, but that it was important to make more unexpected moves. "Right now, we're too predictable," he said. In the air, LaCivita snapped a picture of Trump's empty chair.

Trump had a chemical weapons detection device installed in his office. A bomb-detecting robot started roaming the lawn at Mar-a-Lago, amusing the guests. Some campaign staff began bringing guns to the office, fearful of intruders. James Blair borrowed an armored vest from a friend in the military and kept it underneath his desk. He told staff that they should keep the blinds closed at all times so no one could see through the windows. Armed guards were stationed downstairs.

For one month, Alvarez's husband told her she could not travel after overhearing her calls about security and becoming too concerned. A toy listening device planted in the office as a prank prompted an evacuation and full-scale bug sweep. Three death threats to LaCivita's house in Virginia led the RNC to post armed guards on his driveway for the last several months of the campaign. Fabrizio told others that at least half the campaign's time was spent on security and logistics. Aides worried that Trump would be in a worse mood and self-sabotage more often because he couldn't play golf.

The physical transformation of Mar-a-Lago into an armed camp seemed to finally shake him out of his summer funk and strengthen his resolve. One of the same visitors who saw him despondent over the summer visited him at the club, newly fortified by Secret Service. "I have to win," Trump said. "Stay alive and win. Because if I don't, we are fucked."

A Man's World

This is a man's world, this is a man's world.

James Brown, as heard at almost every Trump rally

The weekend before the vice presidential debate on October 1, the power went out in Cincinnati as the remnants of Hurricane Helene ripped through the region. JD Vance was in the middle of a mock debate with former Fox News contributor Monica Crowley playing the moderator and Minnesota Congressman Tom Emmer playing his former Democratic colleague, Tim Walz. In the blackout, the group switched to using their cell phones for timers and continued the prep session by lantern light.

Emmer studied videos of Walz's past debates to anticipate how he would act and what he would say, while Vance studied policy books and met for strategy sessions with his advisers. His two months since the RNC had been rocky. Surveys rated him the least liked vice presidential nominee on record, eleven points underwater, even worse than Trump. His campaign trail debut caused so many negative news cycles—from his admission that the substitution of Harris for Biden was a "sucker punch," to the resurfacing of his insult to Democratic women leaders as "childless cat ladies"—that some old Republican hands were reminded of Dan Quayle, George H. W. Bush's widely derided running mate in 1988.

Vance's team disputed that he was doing anything wrong. They blamed the pile-on on a special hatred that they thought reporters and official Washington reserved for Vance, viewing him as a class traitor; he hadn't turned out to be the Ivy League–educated ambassador to Trump's America that they imagined when they'd read (or at least pretended to have read) his memoir. Trump would acknowledge that Vance was taking heat, but the former president and his team never expressed any dissatisfaction to him. Running mates often get assigned new advisers, who are loyal to the top of the ticket and then get micromanaged by the campaign leadership. But Trump's circle let Vance keep his own team and run their own race.*

For the debate, Vance had two chief objectives. He had to appear reasonable, relatable, and normal, to show the country he was not the angry "weirdo" Democrats had made him out to be. The second, more important task was to take the fight to Kamala Harris. Beating Walz didn't matter.

Vance's team rejoiced from the first exchange, when he appeared composed and Walz stammered with nerves. Vance repeatedly offered to agree with Walz, which seemed to catch him off guard. His team's favorite line of the night was when he took pity on Walz for having to defend the indefensible: "You've got to pretend that Donald Trump didn't deliver rising take-home pay, which, of course, he did. You've got to pretend that Donald Trump didn't deliver lower inflation, which, of course, he did. And then you've simultaneously got to defend Kamala

---

*The autonomy had drawbacks too: Vance's team wasn't informed that Iranian hackers had obtained his vetting dossier until the news became public.

Harris's atrocious economic record, which has made gas, groceries, and housing unaffordable for American citizens."

The first thing Walz said when he walked off the stage was, "I'm so glad it's over." His wife, Gwen, said, "You could have done better." The staff would have to talk to her about positive reinforcement. Democratic aides cringed throughout the debate because Walz had been better prepared. He wasn't confident. He was so anxious heading into the debate that he barely ate and then got woozy on a run.

Walz had a history of constantly scrolling on social media, seeing what people were saying about him. Harris told him, "You should get off the internet," and shortly after becoming her running mate, he deleted X, formerly known as Twitter, from his phone. He sometimes said he wanted to be more like her and wall himself off. He was thin-skinned. Some people around him fed his ego by focusing on the comments and coverage.

The upside of being "too online" was that Walz was eager to court influencers and go on podcasts, in search of voters who took only a casual interest in politics—especially men. He went on the *SmartLess* podcast with Jason Bateman, Sean Hayes, and Will Arnett, and *The Dan Le Batard Show*. He played Madden with Representative Alexandria Ocasio-Cortez on Twitch, went running in Central Park with a popular TikTok user, and talked about hardware stores on the "SubwayTakes" social media account. He brought influencers into his photo lines and set aside time to call them like politicians usually did with donors.

Progressives imagined Walz could be their emissary to middle America. As a Midwestern veteran, teacher, and hunter, he fit their idea of someone moderates would like, and he brought a plainspoken charm to articulating progressive values, with mottos like "Mind your own damn business." But where progressives heard one of their own who could speak moderates' language, moderates still heard a progressive. Walz had a liberal governing record in Minnesota, and Republicans attacked him as a nod to the left, not to the center. In September, the Harris campaign was planning an event in Pennsylvania and contacted a farmer to inquire if they would host an event with "the governor." The family gladly accepted. A day before, when the advance teams arrived, the family discovered the event was for Walz, not Josh Shapiro. They balked and pulled out. The Harris campaign scrambled, and with the help of Shapiro's office, found a different farm to host Walz.

Harris was also trying to get on podcasts that could help her with people who only sporadically followed politics. But her team kept hearing "no." Travis and Jason Kelce wouldn't take her. Neither would Bill Simmons. There was a general aversion to bringing politics into nonpolitical spaces. The campaign asked Jeffrey Katzenberg for help getting on Sean Evans's celebrity talk show on YouTube, *Hot Ones*. He couldn't help there, but he offered instead to assist with *Call Her Daddy*, Alex Cooper's advice show advertised as the most popular podcast with women. Some Harris advisers came to fear that Democrats lacked a way to connect with disengaged voters through nonpolitical cultural communities like Trump was doing with sports and men.

By the fall, both campaigns understood that Trump's path to victory lay in running up the score with men. "We were going after men big-time. We made a real push for men," Chris LaCivita would later tell donors, according to an audio recording. "The Democratic Party is a bunch of Karens."

With Wiles's approval, Trump aides Alex Bruesewitz and Danielle Alvarez called the former president one afternoon to pitch him on appearing with Theo Von and other influential podcast hosts. Trump picked up on the golf course and listened as Bruesewitz highlighted the shows' massive reach.

"Call Barron," Trump said, referring to his eighteen-year-old son. "See what Barron thinks." He then hung up and returned to playing golf.

Barron Trump had largely stayed out of the public eye during his father's first term, but in the past couple of years he'd started joining Trump at rallies and fundraisers and giving him ideas for things to say. Barron had already recommended Trump do an interview with Adin Ross, a video-game streamer who was banned by the Twitch platform over offensive language. Still, the younger Trump was not a known quantity to campaign staffers. Bruesewitz asked other family members for help contacting him. From then on, Trump told his team he would agree to the appearances as long as Barron said it was smart. "How many people are listening?" the elder Trump would ask.

Trump had long been obsessed with ratings. Every morning he'd want to know how many millions of people were watching him on a TV show. He partly sabotaged his first presidency with daily coronavirus briefings that he continued against the advice of almost all of his aides because they got big audiences. This time, his team was trying to get him to think differently. The reach of linear TV was shrinking. Alvarez told Trump that his appearance on a Spaces event with Elon Musk had gotten millions of views. Trump processed that for a second and replied, "That's big."

Trump barely did any interviews with the national press, but he spent hours sitting down with internet personalities who were unknown to many of Trump's own advisers. LaCivita consulted his own son about the Nelk Boys, a group of YouTube pranksters who sold clothes, had millions of viewers, and promoted Zyn, a brand of flavored nicotine pouches that became a MAGA status symbol. Some staffers had more familiarity. Steven Cheung, the pugnacious, sometimes profane campaign spokesman, had worked for the Ultimate Fighting Championship before Trump, and many of the "manosphere" podcasts grew out of mixed martial arts fan bases. The job of keeping in touch with some Trump-endorsing rappers fell to Wiles. Trump himself often seemed bemused by the array of surrogates. At a September rally in Las Vegas, he struggled to pronounce the name of mixed martial artist Henry Cejudo but complimented his hair, and he introduced Reggaeton artist Nicky Jam by saying "she's hot," then played down his surprise when the musician, who is a man, approached the stage.

The podcasts, along with attending UFC matches and a Formula One race, were meant to impress young men who didn't usually vote or care about politics by reaching them in nonpolitical settings. For Trump, the interactions came naturally, a return to the celebrity socialite/playboy mode that dominated most of his life. Not every seventy-seven-year-old politician could flip burgers and toss around a football at a frat house's pregame tailgate in Iowa, as Trump did in September 2023. But for younger Americans who didn't remember Trump as a cultural icon before he entered politics, the exposure to that side of him was new, and it brought the chance to change their view of him.

Trump had been skeptical of TikTok, even proposing a ban in his first term. Kellyanne Conway and others working on behalf of the company brought Trump data showing he had more supporters on the app than Democrats did. Conway showed Trump funny videos of people promoting him and told him he had twelves times as many followers on TikTok as Biden. Jason Miller pitched it as an effective campaign tool. Trump agreed to join the platform, but the campaign's TikTok account was largely dormant until August, when two men in their twenties joined the staff and started growing the audience. The leader was Jack Fuetterer, a twenty-two-year-old known on the campaign as "TikTok Jack." For one video, the campaign brought a camera to a graveside ceremony in an especially sacred section of Arlington National Cemetery, which ordinarily does not allow political activity. (When a cemetery employee tried to prevent filming at the graveside, Justin Caporale and another staffer brushed past her, then left in the motorcade as police sought to investigate the altercation. Cheung released a statement attacking the cemetery employee as having a "mental health episode.") Before long, the Trump TikToks were routinely fetching a million views, and by Election Day the account would surpass Harris's in followers. The clips were meant to humanize Trump, showing how he lived and what he was like. Campaign officials privately regretted they did not have a better plan to make even more videos.

The fratty antics flowed neatly from the campaign's data analysis that defined Trump's target voters as disproportionately young and male; but it fit just as well with the personalities of the candidate and many of his advisers, whose idea of authenticity was often talking smack. Ronna McDaniel, the deposed RNC chair who had been one of the party's most prominent women leaders, described the campaign to friends as a "bro show." Even Roger Stone, Trump's longtime consigliere not known for his sensitivity, asked on one conference call why the campaign didn't have more women surrogates.

Nikki Haley kept offering. She repeatedly went on TV warning Trump and Vance to reconsider how they spoke to women and cautioning that the campaign's focus on men could not come at the expense of repelling the other, slightly larger half of the electorate. When asked about Haley, Trump usually resumed badmouthing her, still mad about the primary. Aides eventually got him to agree to campaign with her, and they held talks about a joint town hall with Sean Hannity, but it never came together. This was a freeze that even Trump's personal peacemaker, Steve Witkoff, could not thaw entirely. He visited her at her house in South Carolina, asking, "Tell me what you want." She told him, "There's nothing I want."

Trump's advisers saw no sign of their outreach to young men backfiring with women. It was true that public polls showed a historic gender gap, but not because he was performing any worse with women than in 2020. It was because he was running even stronger with men. The gender gap cut both ways. Trump could afford to lose women by 8 points if he was winning men by 10, 11, or 12 points.

One of the fruits of the campaign's deep dive into the RNC's Harris video library was a clip of her speaking with the National Center for Transgender Equality Action Fund in 2019, highlighting her work on transgender care for inmates in California. Trump's advisers, especially LaCivita, viewed the clip as a bombshell and were eager to turn it into an attack ad, with the memorable tagline, "Kamala Is for They/Them. President Trump Is for You."

Pat McCarthy, one of the campaign's ad makers, delivered the spot to LaCivita for review. "Why do you hate the trannies so much?" LaCivita asked jokingly. Trump liked the ad, and he wanted the team to show more of the transgender woman interviewing Harris in 2019. They also added footage of other transgender employees in the Biden-Harris administration.

The ad would never have worked without the video of Harris in her own words; voters would have dismissed it as too far-fetched. It scored well in audience tests, but pollster Tony Fabrizio had qualms. He didn't want to interrupt the argument their ads were building on the economy. As a compromise, the campaign decided to split a week's ad buys between an ad about taxes and the trans ad.

The trans ad generated so much attention that LaCivita added airings during sports programs. He noticed the ad was resonating especially well with Black and Latino men. Radio host Charlamagne Tha God discussed the ad on his show. LaCivita hadn't heard of the host before and refused to call him "Tha God," but he eagerly used the clip to make a new version of the ad specifically targeting Black men.*

"She's sitting here and she's being interviewed by a dude dressed as a woman, he's six foot six, a big guy with a voice like mine," LaCivita would tell a group of donors and activists, according to an audio recording. "And he goes, 'Oh Kamala, do you support taxpayers paying for transgender surgeries?' And she says, 'Oh, absolutely. Every prisoner should have access to gender-affirming care, as well as every illegal immigrant.' So Juan, who crosses the border, decides he wants to be Juanita, and we got to pay for it. Yeah, that's just not gonna work. We knew we were onto something."

The impact was not limited to men. LaCivita made a third version of the ad that connected Harris's position to trans athletes, this one targeting suburban women. In the final days of the race, he went further, with an ad saying Harris's support for transgender equality plus her hawkish foreign policy would lead to drafting women. "President Trump won't draft your daughter," a female voice-over said. Since the ad ran digitally, it didn't cause much media attention, but LaCivita beamed it directly at persuadable women.

Harris's team agreed that the ad was devastating because it showed her speaking in her own words. Grow Progress, a consulting firm working for the Harris campaign, tested almost every ad against her, and this was among the most devastating they saw. The Harris campaign considered and taped a number of proposed responses, from attempting to explain she had moderated her position since 2019, to pivoting to the economy, to attacking Trump for his administration's allowing gender-affirming care in prisons. But none of them tested that well.

*Charlamagne Tha God, a Harris supporter, said the Trump campaign took his clip out of context, since he was summarizing the ad's message rather than endorsing it. He said the campaign continued running the ad after he sent a cease-and-desist letter.

Even before the trans ad, the Harris campaign had identified the issue as a vulnerability. In debate prep, Harris workshopped an answer in which she would say she was uncomfortable with trans girls playing sports against other girls, she understood parents' concerns, and she would let school districts decide. But the topic never came up at the debate.

Harris later addressed the issue of transgender care for prisoners in an interview with Fox's Bret Baier, arguing that the procedures were available in the federal prison system under Trump. "He spent twenty million dollars on those ads trying to create a sense of fear in the voters because he actually has no plan in this election that is about focusing on the needs of the American people," she said. "Twenty million dollars on that ad, on an issue that, as it relates to the biggest issues that affect the American people, it's really quite remote."

One Harris adviser recalled visiting home for a college football weekend in a swing state and seeing the trans ad during every commercial break. The Trump campaign was running entirely negative ads (or ads contrasting Harris with Trump), wearing down her ratings and making her less acceptable to independents and young men. By comparison, the Harris campaign largely ran positive ads about her, and attack ads against Trump that turned out to be largely ineffective. She never directly tackled the attacks against her—a mistake that reminded one adviser of Mike Dukakis's 1988 campaign, which ended in a landslide defeat.

The Trump team was reimagining the MAGA coalition for the long term. They understood the Republican Party could not survive as a party of old white people, and the campaign had to decide which constituencies to bring into the fold. They picked union workers and young Black men; RFK Jr. brought them crunchy parents; and Vance brought some peaceniks—none of whom were traditional Republicans. When Black men in Atlanta started receiving mailers from the Trump campaign, some Democrats viewed that as a sign that the Republicans' targeting was off. But to Blair and data guru Tim Saler, that reaction proved their theory that the Democrats didn't see the same battlefield they did.

Much of the political press shared Trump's fixation with broadcast and cable ads, partially because they were easier to track and claimed large chunks of campaign budgets. But cable service was concentrated in cities and suburbs, not Trump's friendliest turf, and many of the low-information, low-propensity voters whom Republicans were hoping to mobilize were cord-cutters. One aide described them as people opening YouTube for instructional videos on how to change their own oil. The pro-Trump super PAC Preserve America, funded largely by megadonor Miriam Adelson, bet on forty-five-second vertical videos designed to watch on phones, made by influencers paid to discuss why they were supporting Trump. The ads cost just eleven dollars per thousand impressions, versus a going rate of about seventy dollars for thirty-second slickly produced, skippable YouTube ads that Democrats were buying. The PAC's data found a quarter of viewers stayed for more than fifteen seconds. Using the same type of studies as corporate advertisers, the PAC could see that people who saw the ads were more likely to support Trump than similar users who didn't, according to internal documents. The campaign's metrics were so impressive that Google used a Preserve America ad as an example in a presentation to political clients showing how they could expand their reach on YouTube.

The biggest outside boost came from Elon Musk. The July 13 assassination attempt tipped his support from tepid to unabashed. He pumped more than $100 million into a super PAC that hired paid door knockers at fifty dollars an hour, taking over in Wisconsin for the field program started by Turning Point Action. In North Carolina, where rural western counties were hard hit by Hurricane Helene, the PAC offered free rides to the polls. Every battleground got a state director who knew the territory. Senior staff went into the field to see how the programs were working in practice. The door knockers focused exclusively on encouraging people to vote for Trump and to vote early, not bothering with the rest of the Republican ticket when talking to voters who were often eager to close the door. There were some isolated instances of door knockers faking their work, people involved in the effort said, but overall it was surprisingly effective.

Across the swing states, Musk began offering forty-seven dollars to refer registered voters to sign a petition, then raising the bounty to one hundred dollars, plus a million-dollar daily raffle for one lucky voter. He did not stop when the Justice Department warned that the sweepstakes could violate federal election law. He did not stop when the Philadelphia DA accused him of violating state lottery rules.*

Musk viewed Pennsylvania as the one pivotal state, so he moved there and began headlining his own rallies. He started regularly talking with Trump and his top advisers about the strategy and messaging for ads. Some advisers found him difficult to have a conversation with at first, especially around women, but they came to view him as crucial.

Musk liked to bring up "censorship" with Trump, who remained mad about being banned from social media platforms after January 6. They also started talking about ideas to cut government spending. Trump recognized Musk's contributions by promising him an advisory role in the administration and inviting him to speak at an October 5 rally in Butler, returning to the site of the first assassination attempt. Wearing a black MAGA hat and "Occupy Mars" T-shirt, Musk hopped on stage, baring his midriff and a Tesla belt buckle. The crowd cheered, and Trump pledged to reach the red planet of Musk's obsession within four years.

Less conspicuously but perhaps just as important, some of the politi-

---

*The PAC argued the million-dollar checks were not prize winnings but PR contracts.

cal consultants behind Musk's America PAC (ironically, many of them alumni of DeSantis's primary campaign and super PAC) ran another operation focused on deterring voters from turning out for Harris. The $45 million effort ran through an entity called Building America's Future, which also received money from Musk, as well as from billionaire investor Ken Griffin. The consultants found ads tested better if voters thought they were hearing a friendly message meant for them—or accidentally receiving a message meant for someone else. They went after Bernie bros with ads comparing Harris unfavorably to Sanders, noting her abandonment of Medicare for All: "Bernie would never," two guys in a bar watching Harris on TV said in one ad. They went after Muslims in Michigan with ads appearing to praise Harris for supporting Israel and marrying a Jewish man. Meanwhile, they went after Jews in Pennsylvania with ads accusing Harris of wanting to stop weapons shipments to Israel. They went after Black voters by criticizing the Biden administration for trying to ban menthol cigarettes, and Midwestern white men by saying Harris would ban Zyn nicotine pouches. Another PAC, also run by the same people and funded by Musk, placed online ads showing women saying Trump would not sign a national abortion ban. Across all the outfits, Musk's spending on the election topped a quarter of a billion dollars.

The gift that, in the Trump campaign's view, rivaled the trans clip was Harris's interview on *The View*, on October 8. His advisers brimmed with speculation over why she spent weeks avoiding interviews, wondering what she must be hiding, and leaning into the contrast with Trump's go-anywhere, say-anything adventurousness. Their suspicions that Harris and her team were terrified of letting her make a mistake appeared to be confirmed.

Harris had repeatedly dodged opportunities to offer up any policy disagreements with Biden, in part spooked by Biden's private warning on the day of her debate with Trump. On *The View*, she was asked for any regrets, anything she wished she'd done differently in their administration. She paused, and stammered, "Nothing comes to mind." Harris had an ability to laugh off uncomfortable questions, but this time she spoke with no authority in her voice. Trump's advisers could not believe she was caught unprepared for such an obvious question.

Backstage on *The View*'s set in Manhattan, Rob Flaherty, a deputy campaign manager, put his head into his hands and swore. During the next commercial break, Stephanie Cutter went to cohosts Whoopi Goldberg and Ana Navarro to ask them to try the question again, but Harris didn't get a second chance. After the interview, Harris knew she'd messed up and asked how big the problem was.

One adviser called *The View* answer "the defining error of the campaign." Some aides blamed a lack of preparation. But Harris was not unprepared for the question. She just answered the literal question instead of using the answer she had prepared with aides to the effect of: "I'm the sitting vice president of a president who has done great things for this country. I am not going to be a vice president who looks back to critique what we did. But I will tell you, I am my own person. I'm from a different generation. I'm not from Washington. I didn't build my career in Washington. I understand the future challenges, and I know that the best ideas don't come from Washington. Throughout my career, I have collaborated. I have focused on what makes sense." Aides also encouraged her to mention that she planned to appoint a Republican to her cabinet.

Harris wouldn't lie and pretend she wasn't part of the Biden administration. She did genuinely believe Biden had done a good job. She also wouldn't say what aides told her to say just because they told her to. Like many politicians, she needed to work with staff to develop an answer that felt true to her. One aide compared the process to therapy. Harris couldn't convincingly deliver an answer she wasn't comfortable with. Top Harris advisers began discussing how to clean up her answer on *The View*, offering several proposals. But she followed Biden's warning and did not want to do anything that would be seen as critical of him.

The Trump campaign's digital team immediately cut the *View* clip and started promoting it online. It became at least as popular in Trump's ads as the trans clip for how it summed up their argument of tying her to the unpopular incumbent. The Trump team had sometimes struggled for weeks to settle on an argument against Harris, and suddenly she was making it for them.

Trump himself was fixated on a perceived phoniness about Harris. He started questioning her story that she'd briefly worked at McDonald's, and when no documentation emerged to prove her temporary employment four decades earlier, Trump took that as proof that she was lying. For months, he wanted to drive home the point by going to a McDonald's himself. "I'll work the deep fryer," he'd say.

It took a while for the campaign to find a willing restaurant owner, set up an available time, and accommodate all the security arrangements. They eventually found a franchise location in a Philadelphia suburb, where prescreened supporters practiced going through the drive-thru window ahead of Trump's arrival. For Trump, the visit was another throwback to his younger years, when he would bring his sons around his hotels to show them the jobs and meet the staff in the kitchens and laundry rooms. His turn at the fryer was hardly working a real shift, but it looked like one when images of Trump wearing a yellow-and-blue apron waving out the drive-thru window rocketed across the internet.

When Harris saw the video of Trump working the deep fryer, she told aides he was doing it wrong. An aide suggested she could point that out in an interview, but she never did. Some franchise owners were mad that a McDonald's hosted Trump but not Harris, and the corporate parent did not want to look like the company was favoring him. McDonald's sells a varsity-style jacket for alumni, embroidered with "One in Eight"—the fraction of Americans the company says its restaurants have employed. A franchise in Atlanta invited her to come and receive one there, but aides didn't want her to visit a restaurant and look like she was copycatting.

Her aides debated for weeks whether they should respond to Trump's attacks about McDonald's. The facts were not especially favorable. She worked there in the summer of 1983 in Alameda, California, alongside her sister, Maya, while Harris was a student at Howard University, but only for two or three weeks. Given the short stint, most advisers didn't want to lean into her time at McDonald's, but it polled well. Aides discussed making available Maya Harris, who had worked alongside Harris in the restaurant, for a feature story with a lifestyle magazine, but others viewed the story as too risky. They learned that at least one major mainstream news outlet was investigating her McDonald's employment, causing alarm inside the campaign. They agreed on a statement rehashing her past comments about her time at McDonald's. In 2019, she'd modestly told striking McDonald's workers on the picket line, "There was not a family relying on me to pay the rent, put the food on the table, and keep the bills paid by the end of the month. But the reality of McDonald's is that the majority of the folks who are working there today are relying on that income to sustain a household and a family."

The Harris team also spent weeks agonizing over whether she should sit for an interview with Joe Rogan, the blockbuster podcast host who wanted to have both candidates. Harris aides held at least six discussions about whether to go on Rogan's show. Some of her advisers believed he would take cheap shots at her. Others alleged he might say something racist. But they eventually decided—and convinced Harris—that his podcast was worth doing.

Harris aides reached out to Spotify, which hosts Rogan's podcast, to coordinate an interview. Rogan's team made three demands, which they require of every guest. The interview would have to be taped in Austin, Texas. Harris had to be in the studio alone. And she would have to agree to at least one hour, with no topic restrictions. The Harris campaign initially thought it was absurd for a podcast host to demand the vice president travel to him. But they relented, coming up with a rally in Houston about abortion rights to justify the trip to a noncompetitive state. It helped that Beyoncé, a Houston native, agreed to speak at the rally. But the Harris campaign didn't give Rogan's team advance notice of the rally; the producers found out about the Houston trip on the day it was announced. Rogan's team offered the Harris campaign a time slot after her evening rally or at 8:00 a.m. the next morning. The campaign declined.

Instead, Harris recorded a podcast with Brené Brown, a researcher who studies courage, vulnerability, shame, and empathy. One aide observed it was about as far from Rogan as you could get. Rogan interviewed Trump and went on to endorse him.

22

Warnings

In early October, Trump's senior campaign advisers took a meeting at their headquarters with Markwayne Mullin, the senator from Oklahoma perhaps best known for flying to Greece in 2021, against State Department advice, hoping to evacuate refugees from Afghanistan on a rented helicopter. Mullin brought two men he said were former CIA operatives. Staffers believed one of them was a foreign national. The senator vouched for them, and they went on to give an extensive presentation that argued Trump would probably lose the election because voting machines were shaving off votes in Republican-heavy areas. The operatives claimed the machines suffered from foreign infiltration stemming from business relationships in Venezuela going back to 2004.

The campaign advisers were left speechless. The presentation was intriguing but seemed to have holes. Even if the information was true, what was the campaign supposed to do with it? The operatives claimed they were already too late to save this election and they should start getting ready for the next one.*

---

*A spokesperson for Mullin disputed this account but declined to specify.

Everyone in the briefing agreed they would never discuss the information publicly, because if Republican voters heard about it, they might conclude their votes wouldn't count and stay home. They also agreed not to bring the information to Trump, at the risk of derailing the end of the campaign.

Aides were vigilantly looking out for an "October surprise"—anything that could upend that race in the final weeks. Some were searching for one of their own, including seeking a copy of the nondisclosure agreement from Doug Emhoff's acknowledged affair during his first marriage.

Trump's senior staff did not want any mischief that could hurt them in a race they thought they were winning. They worried about what they did not know, but all the evidence they saw looked good for Trump. The investments in early voting appeared to be paying off. In recent elections, Republicans had gotten used to spinning the Democratic turnout in early voting and hoping to make it up on Election Day. This time, Trump won the first day of statewide early voting in Michigan by about 21 points, according to the campaign's internal tracking. In Wisconsin, the early vote was about tied. There was a moment when Trump advisers thought the Democrats were giving up on North Carolina and Arizona (which they thought might have been a good move), but the Democrats turned out to be just moving their ad buys around.

"The trends are showing exactly what we want them to show," LaCivita told Trump. "Things are in a good fucking spot. We're heading in a good direction."

Trump would ask for a probability of winning, but LaCivita had run too many campaigns to project too much certainty. He put it at 65 percent.

"Oh, only sixty-five," Trump said.

"If you'd have told me a year ago that your chances of winning were sixty-five percent?" LaCivita said. "Come on."

Wiles and Fabrizio gave similar assessments. "Talk to me on election night," Wiles would say. She encouraged him to relax. Depending on what the surveys showed, Trump called his pollster either "Fabrizio" or "Fucking Fabrizio." Trump sometimes complained about Fabrizio, particularly how much his polls cost. But Fabrizio was usually right.

Eventually Trump stopped asking his advisers because he knew what they'd say. But he kept seeing troubling TV coverage. He would ask everyone he talked to whether he would win or lose, and their answer would determine his mood.

On an October 13 flight to a town hall outside Philadelphia, Trump was joined by South Dakota Governor Kristi Noem, who would be moderating the event.* Noem was often publicly seen with Corey Lewandowski, at all times of the day and night, though they both denied having a romantic relationship. On the flight, Noem spoke up to tell Trump that Republicans were behind in voter registration. Trump looked surprised, since his advisers had been telling him the opposite. LaCivita jumped up and walked over to Trump to correct her. "Where are you getting your information?" LaCivita asked Noem. "Because it's all wrong." He was convinced she had gotten the idea from Lewandowski.

Two days later, on October 15, some of the allegations that Lewandowski had been circulating about LaCivita's compensation were published in *The Daily Beast*. Three tense days passed before LaCivita faced the boss in person. He came ready with a stack of receipts and tax filings documenting where the campaign payments went and how they didn't total anywhere near the sum reported in the article. They went over the article for twenty minutes in the small office at the front of Trump's plane. LaCivita told Trump he'd made about $2 million over two years, not $22 million. "I'm still waiting for the $20 million check to appear in

---

*The town hall would be best remembered for turning into a thirty-minute dance party when Trump decided to stop taking questions and instead request some of his favorite songs.

my house," LaCivita said. Trump told him he should sue and agreed to move on.

The top aides running Biden's presidential campaign long believed that the more voters saw Trump, the more his approval ratings would go down. Their theory of the case always rested on the premise of a binary choice—when voters had to choose between Biden and Trump, they would choose Biden. Most of those aides were now running Harris's campaign and were finding out their theory of the case was wrong. By the fall, Trump's popularity was increasing, not decreasing. It didn't matter that Harris's popularity had steadily increased too—from the high thirties when Biden dropped out to the high forties a few weeks later. Trump had halved his unfavorable numbers, and Harris's advisers knew they needed to reverse the trend.

They scheduled three Zoom meetings in September and October to try to figure out how to dent his approval ratings. But just like his Republican opponents in the primary, Harris's aides struggled to find a message that stuck. The meetings, which included roughly two dozen senior staff, turned into wide-ranging brainstorming sessions. The campaign's pollsters advocated for a messaging campaign that labeled Trump "dangerous." O'Malley Dillon, among others, had concerns. Hillary Clinton used a similar moniker ("Dangerous Donald") in 2016, without success.

After weeks of debate, the Harris campaign leaders settled on what became known as the three "Uns": Unhinged. Unchecked. Unstable. Some thought the lengthy meetings were a waste of time—the adjectives weren't all that different from each other. Even more people were frustrated it took until October, less than a month before Election Day, to fully settle on an attack against the opponent Democrats had been running against since 2015.

The campaign's painstaking search for the right words was quickly overshadowed by John Kelly, a former Marine general who served as Trump's White House chief of staff. Over eighteen months in the role, Kelly developed an extraordinarily low opinion of Trump. He spent 2021 and 2022 telling others that Trump could not get reelected; Trump was too venal and corrupt, and the legal system would run its course. But he had largely declined to say anything publicly, concluding "it doesn't move his numbers" or expressing concern about speaking out as a retired general. (He also did not like Trump attacking him.) As the election approached and Kelly saw Trump stood a real chance of winning, he gave a series of interviews warning the country not to reelect him, saying the former president met the definition of a "fascist."

Harris had a CNN town hall scheduled the next day, and staff knew she would be asked about Kelly's comment. Advisers encouraged her to tell voters to trust the assessment of people who worked with Trump closely and knew him best. But the truth was Harris didn't disagree with Kelly's assessment, so when she was asked point-blank, she said so. Advisers felt like they'd been cornered into inadvertently making fascism a bigger part of their closing message than intended. Trump aides, for their part, saw a burst of interest in the word "fascist" online as a sign not that the story was breaking through but that people didn't know what the term meant.

At the same time, Harris campaign officials were growing increasingly frustrated with Future Forward, the main outside super PAC supporting the presidential campaign. Founded by Obama campaign veterans, the group billed itself as the future of political advertising. With nearly $1 billion in funding, the group tested thousands of messages with millions of voters in search of the most effective ways to persuade and mobilize them. But the group saved the vast majority of that money until the final weeks of the campaign, citing research that television ads closer to Election Day are more effective. Back in January, Future Forward started reserving hundreds of millions of dollars of advertising in battleground states to secure the best time slots at better rates. Harris campaign officials weren't allowed to tell the super PAC what to do, but they complained among themselves that Future Forward did not spend earlier to introduce the vice president to voters, as Trump and his allies unleashed vicious attacks on her. Future Forward officials said they put up new positive ads for Harris within days of her becoming the nominee and spent more than $50 million. Campaign officials also disagreed with Future Forward's decision not to run any strictly negative ads about Trump. Officials at the super PAC would argue that purely negative ads about the former president were less effective than contrast ads.

As part of the anti-Trump messaging campaign, Harris was betting on winning over disaffected Republicans. Harris aides believed there were a significant number of Americans, particularly in swing counties, who previously voted for Trump but were now turned off by his conduct. The Harris campaign wanted to create a permission structure to convince these voters that they could support Harris. Central to that effort was securing the endorsements of prominent Republicans who broke from Trump. Atop that list was Liz Cheney, the former Wyoming congresswoman and daughter of former vice president Dick Cheney. Following the January 6 attack, Cheney transformed from a stalwart of the Republican establishment to one of Trump's fiercest critics. She voted to impeach him after the attacks, which led Republicans to remove her from her House leadership role. She accepted Nancy Pelosi's appointment to serve as the vice chair of the House committee investigating the Capitol riot, and then she lost her seat in the 2022 primary.

The Cheney endorsement was such a priority that it was handled directly by O'Malley Dillon, who quietly courted her support for months, beginning when Biden was still running. Over multiple phone calls, O'Malley Dillon told Cheney that the campaign appreciated her warnings about Trump as she gauged her interest in an endorsement. Once an endorsement appeared to be within reach, and Harris took over the campaign, the vice president called Cheney directly. Cheney and her father both endorsed, and the younger Cheney became a top surrogate for the campaign. Two weeks before the election, Harris and Cheney toured the battleground states together, sitting for moderated discussions in the suburbs of Philadelphia, Detroit, and Milwaukee. As a capstone, the Harris campaign announced that she would deliver her closing argument speech, a week before Election Day, from the Ellipse, the lawn behind the White House where Trump spoke to supporters on January 6 before they stormed the Capitol.

Harris's team also tried to secure endorsements from other top Republican critics of Trump, including Mitt Romney and Chris Christie. The campaign hired the chief of staff of former Congressman Adam Kinzinger, the other Republican who'd served on the House January 6 committee, as well as Maria Comella, a top Christie aide, to work on Republican outreach. In the final weeks of the race, Comella worried the Harris campaign's strategy was not working. "It doesn't give a reason to vote for Harris," she said in one of a series of memos. Comella recommended focusing less on Cheney and instead finding male moderators and surrogates to appear with Harris. She encouraged Harris to appeal to Republicans by differentiating herself from Biden and acknowledging where the Democratic Party had been wrong, such as "missing the mark" on urban crime, transitioning too quickly to electric cars, neglecting border security, and backing away from Israel. She recommended Harris address the trans issue by framing it as an issue of fairness: "There are clearly physiology differences." Comella was also nervous about the Ellipse speech and told O'Malley Dillon after reviewing a draft that it wasn't an effective closing message. "You do not want the dominant takeaway to be, Harris closes campaign invoking January 6th," she wrote. Comella told others she did not feel like her ideas were listened to.

While Comella worried about falling short with Republicans, other staffers feared neglecting Democratic constituencies. "We're spending all this money on persuasion, but isn't the problem that we still have voters left to mobilize?," Mitch Stewart, who joined the campaign as a senior adviser after Harris became the nominee, said on one of the campaign's Zooms. "Do we really think we're going to peel some Trump voters away?"

Tony West, Harris's brother-in-law, was also actively escalating concerns internally. He spent much of the final weeks traveling around the country as a surrogate, speaking especially to Black men. He kept hearing from groups that needed more money to reach first-time or occasional voters and receiving calls from anxious Democrats reporting the same problems around the country. West relayed the concerns to O'Malley Dillon and other senior campaign leaders in Wilmington, warning that get-out-the-vote efforts in the Black community were underfunded. He saw little follow-up, so in the final weeks of the campaign, he started connecting donors directly to the groups on the ground.

Obama had also been barnstorming the battleground states imploring Americans to support Harris, at times admonishing Black men specifically for considering Trump. On October 24, he made his first joint appearance with Harris. The musical guest for that night's rally outside Atlanta was Bruce Springsteen, a longtime Democratic booster (and friend of Obama's). But staffers on the ground in Georgia were flummoxed by Wilmington's decision to send Springsteen, whose fan base is overwhelmingly white and whose oeuvre is closely associated with New Jersey, to Clarkston, Georgia, a city whose population is 70 percent Black and 50 percent foreign born, proudly calling itself the Ellis Island of the South. The predominantly white press corps seemed more interested in Springsteen's performance than the twenty-three thousand mostly Black attendees.

Obama and Harris met in a trailer before taking the stage. The conversation turned to her closing argument, planned for the address a few days later at the Ellipse. Obama encouraged her to infuse more of her background and vision for the country into the speech. It couldn't just be an anti-Trump diatribe that warned Americans about Trump, he said. Harris needed to say what she was for, not just what she was against.

Garbage In, Garbage Out

As far back as January, Trump had been saying he could win his home state of New York, and he wanted to do a rally at Madison Square Garden. The urge only grew with the time Trump spent in Manhattan for the trial. Many of his advisers viewed the event as a waste of time and money, but they realized they would have to oblige him. According to a friend, Trump wanted to be "like Elvis or Sinatra." He told donors, "It's going to be a hell of a show."

The big night came two Sundays before Election Day, on October 27. Trump became ebullient as his motorcade charged across Fifty-Seventh Street from Trump Tower. Tens of thousands of people filled New York's streets to see the hometown boy who had a tortured relationship with his city. "I haven't seen a crowd like this since the pope," Wiles told others in the motorcade.

The event cost at least half a million dollars, picked up by a super PAC funded by Trump's transition cochair, Linda McMahon. Legally, the super PAC was able to pay for the rally by having it double as a fundraiser. During the preprogram, Trump gathered with major donors in the Rangers locker room. Glowing, he asked if they had seen the crowds clogging the Manhattan street grid. He grinned for photos with familiar faces: Brian Ballard and the Reynolds American lobbyists who'd become a regular presence at his home, his club, and his fundraisers. "My tobacco guys," he called them. Over the course of the campaign, Reynolds American gave about $10 million to Trump's efforts, dispatched political operatives to battleground states to help his campaign, and ran ads attacking Harris on menthol.

McMahon and the other transition cochair, Cantor Fitzgerald CEO Howard Lutnick, looked to be enjoying the glad-handing more than Trump, who said he was going to be quicker than usual because he wanted to go upstairs and watch the show. He suggested wrapping up unless anyone had questions, and then a few donors piped up with "questions," which were really just compliments.

Since Trump was not yet watching the preprogram, he missed the warm-up act by a comedian named Tony Hinchcliffe, host of the podcast *Kill Tony*. During his set, Hinchcliffe told offensive jokes about African Americans, Jews, Arabs, and Puerto Ricans. "There's literally a floating island of garbage in the middle of the ocean right now," Hinchcliffe said. "I think it's called Puerto Rico."

Campaign staffers immediately got slammed with calls from members of Congress, allies and outside advisers, and Latino political operatives. The senior team met to address the emerging crisis. Danielle Alvarez argued against apologizing, believing it would show weakness and turn a joke from the early stages of a six-hour rally into a much bigger story. "When do we ever apologize?" She said humor was often crass and inappropriate and people were going to vote on Trump's record, not a joke.

Other aides pushed back. Two of the country's largest Puerto Rican communities were in Philadelphia and Allentown, both in Pennsylvania. Jason Miller wanted a statement out before Trump took the stage.

LaCivita ended the debate. "We're putting out a fucking statement," he said. It appeared under Alvarez's name and said the campaign did not support the comedian's remarks. (After fighting so much initially, LaCivita and Alvarez had come to like and respect each other. He called her "my Cuban killer.")

In his own speech, Trump gave a shout-out to House Speaker Mike Johnson, alluding to "our little secret . . . He and I have a secret." The blogosphere exploded with speculation that Trump and Johnson, who'd recruited lawmakers to petition the Supreme Court to reject the 2020 election results, had a new diabolical plan to subvert the 2024 outcome. Johnson later asked Trump to clarify that the secret was nothing nefarious, but Trump didn't want to.*

The secret he was referencing was tele-rallies. Trump was convinced they were a secret weapon that would help Johnson grow his congressional majority. Trump spent the last forty-five days of the race participating in seventy-eight tele-rallies for all competitive Senate candidates and many battleground House contests. He loved the tele-rallies because he thought the technology was cutting edge (even though it was actually decades old, just a massive conference call), and he thought he was the only politician who could draw so many interested participants on such a call. He kept telling Johnson that no other celebrity could get such a turnout.

Trump often made the calls from his plane or between events, demanding them so frequently that they exhausted his aides. Before the audiences joined the calls, Trump would spend a few minutes chitchatting with the candidates, often teasing them with quips like, "You say you love me now, but you'll probably impeach me in a few months."

The morning after the Madison Square Garden rally, Trump came

---

*A Trump spokesman denied that Trump didn't want to clarify.

downstairs in his Manhattan triplex angry that Hinchcliffe had distracted from his big night. "Who the fuck is this guy?" he said to aides and allies gathered in the apartment. "Why the fuck did we have a comedian? We got thirty congressmen that are dying to get up there and talk. We don't need a fucking comedian. Who picked a comedian?" He began quizzing Wiles about who approved the speakers list. "Now I've got to deal with this and it could actually hurt us," he said. "And we had a great night."

Trump wondered why all his advisers said he was winning but national news shows like *Morning Joe* said the opposite. "He's a smart guy," Trump said of Scarborough.

Trump's advisers doubted that after years of outrageous provocations from Trump's own mouth, he would finally be undone by something someone else said. But Democrats piled onto Hinchcliffe's Puerto Rico insult as a spoiler for Trump's closing message and a scandal that could break through to voters who didn't usually follow the news. Coincidentally, Harris had spent that Sunday rolling out an agenda for Puerto Rico—part of an effort to secure the endorsement of Puerto Rican superstar Bad Bunny. Several Puerto Rican celebrities who'd endorsed Trump, including Nicky Jam, took back their support, while Bad Bunny, Ricky Martin, and Jennifer Lopez threw in for Harris.

On Tuesday, seven days before Election Day, Biden joined a video call with Latino activists to rally their support behind Harris. He lit into Trump, saying, "The only garbage I see floating out there is his supporters. His—his demonization of Latinos is unconscionable, and it's un-American."

Trump advisers couldn't believe their luck. They thought Biden's gaffe was even better than when Hillary Clinton notoriously disparaged Trump supporters as "deplorables." The blowback for Democrats worsened when Biden aides got caught pressuring the White House

Stenography Office—a team of nonpolitical professionals who officially transcribed the president's remarks—to add an apostrophe ("supporter's"), which would direct Biden's criticism to Hinchliffe's remarks rather than Trump's supporters.

The next day, Trump was flying to a rally in Green Bay when his deputy campaign manager, Justin Caporale, proposed, "Can we get a garbage truck?" Caporale, the same aide who pushed past the Arlington National Cemetery employee in August, had a combative personality and occasionally clashed with other campaign officials. Because of his big attitude and small stature, LaCivita would call him "Napoleon," and he told Caporale to his face, "If you weren't so good at your job, you'd have been fired a fucking long time ago."

He was good at his job. Somehow Caporale found a garbage truck, fresh off the assembly line, and the owner drove it two hours to meet Trump's plane at the airport. Trump got an orange reflective vest and tried it on in anticipation. The original plan was to bring the garbage truck along in the motorcade, but then Trump suggested climbing in and talking to reporters on the tarmac. LaCivita knew they had another magic viral moment, like the McDonald's stunt. Trump was thrilled too. "We wouldn't have had that great garbage moment if we hadn't had garbage earlier in the week," he said.

The garbage gaffe was not the first time Biden had vexed Harris aides, leading them to largely sideline him from the campaign trail. A week earlier, while speaking at a local Democratic field office in Concord, New Hampshire, Biden said Trump was a threat to democracy and "we got to lock him up." He quickly caught himself and added, "Politically lock him up. Lock him out." The slip fueled Trump's claims that the government was politically persecuting him. The month before, while visiting firefighters in Pennsylvania, Biden briefly put on a "Trump 2024" hat, prompting MAGA memers to speculate that he was tacitly endorsing the Republican, or that he'd proven he was senile. But Biden thought he was a political asset and complained that Harris's campaign wasn't deploying him enough, especially to Pennsylvania. Trump aides began wondering if Biden was really trying to sabotage Harris and joked that he was their best surrogate.

His "garbage" controversy also stepped on Harris's closing argument speech, which started just moments after video leaked of Biden's Zoom call with Latino activists. Heeding the advice of Obama and others, Harris and her aides cut down the portion of the speech about Trump. Still, she spent most of the speech outlining her and Trump's contrasting visions, promising to enter the Oval Office with a "to-do list" while calling Trump a "petty tyrant."

Anthony Bernal, Jill Biden's top aide, had other concerns about the speech on the Ellipse, scheduled for October 29. The Harris campaign wanted the White House in the background, but the first lady's office had planned extensive Halloween decorations that staffers would have to set up before the speech, meaning the White House facade would be lit up in orange. Bernal asked if the speech could be rescheduled. When he was told no, the White House had to dramatically scale back the Halloween decorations.

The next day, the guests for the White House Halloween party included veterans of past administrations and campaigns. Democrats milled around the South Lawn enjoying each other's costumed children and sharing intel on Harris's campaign. They all had friends working on the effort, especially those who joined in the final few weeks for "late help," as they called it, when veteran staffers who had other jobs volunteered as extra hands in battleground states. The reports coming back from the front lines were disheartening. Democrats consoled themselves that the dysfunction they'd heard about must be limited to that one department or territory. But as they swapped stories, an unsettling trend emerged. A data director in a battleground state had to be replaced. A policy person relayed a bad interaction with a campaign policy aide. There was a lack of Spanish-language materials for voter contact. The leadership structure was still in shambles. They realized the problems weren't isolated—the whole operation was a mess. Harris was in trouble.

The senior leadership of Harris's campaign saw it differently. They were both publicly and privately messaging that she would win, though they expected it to be close. When Jen O'Malley Dillon ran Biden's campaign in 2020, her mantra was "We can do hard things." Four years later, as Harris's campaign chair, she repeatedly said, "We're going to win this." Days before the election, she said on MSNBC that she was "very confident" Harris would defeat Trump. Harris, too, dropped the framing that she was the underdog, telling voters, "Make no mistake: We will win." Gwen Walz was telling people, "We have to win. I think we're going to win." Sometimes she'd add, "I'm not sure I want us to win"—she was overwhelmed by thinking about the impact on her family.

The campaign's internal polling had Harris leading Trump slightly across the must-win Blue Wall states and still competitive in the other battleground contests. Trump, they believed, was closing the race in ways that reminded voters what they liked least about him. The Harris campaign's top leaders did not expect to know the winner on election night, assuming states would be slow to count and Harris might not be declared the victor for a few days, like with Biden in 2020. Democratic lawyers spent years preparing to fight against any efforts to subvert the results. When Biden launched his campaign, Dana Remus, his former White House counsel and a senior adviser to the campaign, started building a robust legal effort, culminating in more than four hundred lawyers across the country and more than five hundred draft pleadings for a wide range of possible litigation for Election Day and the days after. Among their biggest concerns was that Trump would prematurely—and inaccurately—declare victory. To prepare for that, Harris associates made outreach to top CEOs, imploring them not to go along with Trump, to exercise patience before recognizing a new president. They conveyed it would be a close election and likely days before all the votes were counted.

Harris's team also sought out major economic figures such as Warren Buffett to embrace her economic plans and endorse her. But when they asked Buffett's team, Buffett said he wasn't aware of what her economic plan entailed and didn't plan to endorse.

The Saturday before Election Day, Harris made a surprise detour from North Carolina to New York City to appear on *Saturday Night Live*. While waiting backstage, she called Yohannes Abraham, the chair of her presidential transition. Abraham had served as a senior White House aide in the Obama administration and was the executive director of Biden's transition in 2020. He joined Biden's national security council before the president nominated him to be ambassador to the Association of Southeast Asian Nations. Harris, like many other presidential candidates, wanted to focus on the race and leave important personnel decisions until after she won. But she was preparing to be president.

During the campaign, she and Abraham would squeeze check-in calls between campaign events to review transition memos, so the vice president could give guidance to Abraham's team of roughly eighty people. By Election Day, the transition team had a short list of roughly three to five people for every cabinet position and top White House job to present to Harris if she won. She decided that Denis McDonough, Biden's secretary of veterans affairs and Obama's White House chief of staff, would serve as her own White House chief of staff. Obama and others had told her she should choose someone with extensive West Wing experience. Harris promised a Republican in her cabinet, and Abraham's team vetted a number of candidates, including Liz Cheney, former Nevada Governor Brian Sandoval, former Massachusetts Governor Charlie Baker, former Illinois Congressman Adam Kinzinger, and former Georgia Lieutenant Governor Geoff Duncan. Some top aides, however, were skeptical Cheney would get the slot, as they struggled to figure out which agency she could run given her vast disagreements on most policy matters with Harris. Harris wanted Lloyd Austin, Biden's secretary of defense, to stay on in his position, and he signaled interest in doing so. Bill Burns, Biden's CIA director, was in line for another big national security job.

Hours before Harris walked on stage in Studio 8H, *The Des Moines Register* published the final preelection Iowa survey from famed pollster J. Ann Selzer, who had accurately predicted every presidential election since 2008. Her poll, this year, had Trump trailing Harris by 3 points. Some Harris aides thought it was a joke. The senior staff were in an hours-long meeting when the news was published, and it immediately torpedoed the meeting. David Plouffe worried it was a bad omen, as staff started pouring over the crosstabs. The poll showed Harris held an enormous 28-point lead over Trump among independent women, while also winning senior women by more than a two-to-one margin. The campaign's internal polling did not align with those findings. Still, it sent Democrats outside the campaign into euphoria. Aides received a flurry of messages from Iowa Democrats asking them to send Harris there to campaign. Tom Vilsack, Biden's secretary of agriculture and the former governor of Iowa, texted O'Malley Dillon directly to make the pitch for Walz to travel there. The campaign didn't even consider it.

Trump woke up on Sunday morning jittery and exhausted. His voice was almost shot. He'd barely slept in days. And no matter how much his advisers told him why the Selzer poll was wrong, it filled him with dread. Advisers said he was set off by an early-morning phone call with ABC's Jonathan Karl. He had a packed day with rallies in Pennsylvania, North Carolina, and Michigan. "Why am I doing three rallies?" he shouted at Caporale. By the first stop, they were already running more than an hour late.

Half an hour into the speech in Lititz, Pennsylvania, Trump started critiquing the stage setup. He didn't like how the bulletproof glass he now had to use caused glare in the television shot. He didn't understand why the glass didn't go all the way around. "I have a piece of glass here," he said, pointing to his right, as the crowd laughed. "And I don't have a piece of glass there. And I have a piece of glass here," he added, looking straight ahead. "But all we have really over here is the fake news, right?" People were cracking up. Someone shouted, "We love you, President Trump!"

"And to get me," he went on, "somebody would have to shoot through the fake news, and I don't mind that so much because—I don't mind. I don't mind that."

"Did you just fucking hear that?" LaCivita said to Jason Miller backstage. "That's a fucking problem."

Miller and LaCivita went to Wiles freaking out that Trump could jeopardize everything in the final hours. Wiles was on the phone with NBC and Comcast executives trying to negotiate a time slot for free Trump advertising to compensate for Harris's appearance on SNL. She needed Trump to get off the stage and approve the message they would air.

Trump had a timer on the podium, which he ignored. The staff put a message on the teleprompter for him to stop, and he ignored that too. He was now an hour and half behind. Wiles, wearing mirrored sunglasses, walked out into the secure buffer zone between the stage and front-row seats. She had never done that before. She stood there silently, where Trump could see her.

Finally, he left the stage, and his advisers told him they were getting swamped with questions and bad headlines about his reference to shooting the press. Trump said he didn't say that. As aides tried to explain how the remark was being interpreted, Boris Epshteyn started clapping, jumped in, and told Trump, "It was such a great speech!" He described part of the speech as a "religious experience."

"What is the matter with you?" Wiles snapped at Epshteyn.

Miller had out a laptop with a cleanup statement for Trump's approval. It said his comments had nothing to do with harming the media, only the danger that Trump himself was in. "There can be no other interpretation of what was said." Trump agreed to the statement. Hannity called and urged Trump to tone it down.

Trump was shorter in the next speeches. But he was driving his staff batty. Wiles repeatedly told him to relax; he was going to win. Just stick to the plan. But he was snappy and mercurial, even more than usual. His team tried to occupy him with presentations showing him leading in early vote totals and on track to win the swing states. They put lawmakers on the phone who would express enthusiasm about the outlook in their states.

Backstage at the final rally in Grand Rapids, Michigan, the senior staff had finished almost every can of soda, every bottle of water, every piece of candy, every scrap of food. They sat and wished it would end. How much longer could he talk? How much longer could this last? Would they get home before the sun rose on Election Day? On the last flight back to Palm Beach, LaCivita hid in the back of the cabin with the Secret Service detail so he could sleep. They arrived in West Palm Beach around sunrise.

The Ballroom and
the Boiler Room

On the evening before Election Day, the senior staff of Kamala Harris's campaign gathered for one of their final conference calls. Meg Schwenzfeier, the campaign's chief analytics officer, presented her team's final projections. The campaign had Harris down in Arizona, Nevada, North Carolina, and Georgia. They projected Harris with a slight advantage in Michigan and Wisconsin—0.6 and 0.2 percent, respectively. In Pennsylvania, they projected Harris to lose by 0.1 percent. With margins that tight, Schwenzfeier called the race a toss-up. The margin of error spanned from Harris losing with 226 electoral votes to winning with 306. Schwenzfeier then explained why her team's projections could be too optimistic (because surveys often underestimated Trump's strength) or too pessimistic (because data showed voters who made up their mind closer to Election Day were breaking Harris's way). Most staffers were not too fazed by the presentation. They knew it would be close, and they remained hopeful that she would win.

Later that night, Harris arrived in Reading, Pennsylvania, to join volunteers going door-to-door. Rumors flew that the town's most famous daughter, Taylor Swift, would join Harris there or perform at a last rally in Philadelphia. Low-level Harris aides did nothing to tamp down the speculation.

The Harris campaign had dedicated huge resources in the final month to massive rallies with celebrity guests. The vice president was drawing Trump-size crowds, and the sense of enthusiasm pulsing through the party gave Democrats a high. Harris and Walz said they were bringing joy back to politics, and massive celebrity-filled rallies—Megan Thee Stallion performed in Atlanta, Maggie Rogers in Ann Arbor, Gracie Abrams and Mumford & Sons in Madison, Wisconsin—were key to that strategy. But privately, some campaign staff raised concerns that the major rallies may not be worth the millions of dollars they cost to stage or the staff investment. There was scant evidence that the rallies were persuading voters or necessarily boosting turnout.

Swift proved to be a special challenge. Staffers who worked on celebrity appearances were instructed not to make any outreach to her universe; Doug Emhoff was handling it. Before Harris became vice president, Emhoff had had a lucrative career as an entertainment lawyer in Los Angeles. He and Swift's lawyer, Doug Baldridge, were both partners at the firm Venable. Before Swift's surprise endorsement, Emhoff had reached out to Baldridge to convey that the campaign would appreciate any efforts the pop star could make to help Harris. Baldridge said Swift would do what Swift thought was best. Nothing more than the endorsement ever materialized. Instead, the final night featured performances by 2 Chainz in Raleigh, Christina Aguilera in Las Vegas, Jon Bon Jovi in Detroit (another head-scratcher for many Black voters), and, in Philadelphia, Lady Gaga, reprising the role she played in both 2016 and 2020.

In the morning, Trump showed up to vote at a gymnasium in Palm Beach, then visited a place he had never seen before: his campaign's headquarters. In the drab rooms, he thanked his staff, who'd packed to-gether to get a glimpse of their boss, and asked what they thought of Wiles. They responded with a raucous cheer. He praised the team who made his digital content. Then Trump did something Wiles had spent months trying to get him to stop doing. Now that early and mail-in vot-ing were over, he railed against them again, saying everyone should vote only in person on Election Day with paper ballots.

As the day went on, the Trump campaign received live turnout re-ports by precinct and party registration for many Florida counties, as well as almost real-time updates from the largest counties in Arizona and Nevada, allowing analysts to see who'd voted. The campaign also had staff on the ground in Detroit and Philadelphia who could dispute Democratic rumors of high turnout in urban precincts. Philadelphia in-dependents who cast mail ballots were splitting down the middle, not breaking for Democrats like Harris needed.

Around 5:00 p.m., James Blair, Tony Fabrizio, and Tim Saler got into a car to head to the election night war room at Mar-a-Lago. Just then, CNN reported the first exit polls. The surveys said the issue that the most voters called their top priority (35 percent) was democracy. "If those are true, we've got a major problem," Blair said in the car.

One of Saler's senior employees at his firm was from Fort Wayne, Indiana, and knew that the polls there closed at 6:00 p.m. and the county posted all its early voting results by 6:15, offering an instructive early data point. In 2020, Trump lost the early vote there; this time he was winning—an 8-point net swing in his favor. The more Fabrizio looked at the incoming data, the better the campaign felt.

The Mar-a-Lago ballroom had TVs set up for donors and VIPs to watch the coverage. The staff was originally working in the dining room but decided to seek more privacy. Too many people were milling around, and it was becoming unproductive and impossible to follow the results.

They snuck upstairs and turned off the lights behind them so no one would follow. When Boris Epshteyn found them, LaCivita, munching on pigs-in-a-blanket, told him they were trying to keep the room small and Epshteyn should leave. The two argued, and Epshteyn went back downstairs to be with Trump.

On past election nights, Trump would haunt the counting room. This time, he mostly stayed downstairs at the party. The television coverage was making him nervous. "Why are none of the national pundits saying we're going to win?" he said. "Even Fox." He called governors and state lawmakers around the country who he thought might have insights. He called into the Pennsylvania war room around 8:30. An aide named Alex Meyer answered the phone and told Trump they were going to win Wisconsin and Michigan. He said Pennsylvania looked good too, but it was too early to say for sure.

"Just make sure they don't steal the votes in Philadelphia like they did the last time," Trump said.

Wiles told him it would be a long night, but he was going to win. He said he understood but he was still anxious and irritated. He came up to the office for a few minutes to check in on the count. The staff said all the data was pointing his way, the campaign was hitting all their benchmarks. They knew they were in better shape than the news coverage was suggesting.

"You better fucking be right," Trump said.

Harris spent election night at the vice president's residence with her family and a few close friends, including Laurene Powell Jobs, the billionaire widow of Steve Jobs, and Reg and Chrisette Hudlin, who set Harris and Emhoff up on a date. The group ate in the dining room and then roamed around the lower floor of the residence, where televisions were set up. One room showed CNN, another showed MSNBC, and Fox News played in a room in the back, where people spent the least time. Harris's family and friends were prepared for a long night. They figured they would make their way over to Howard University, where the party was being held, around 10:00 p.m. They doubted the outcome would be clear on election night. It took four days for the networks to project a winner in 2020, and Harris's team thought this election would be even closer.

A few of her top aides, including Lorraine Voles and Sheila Nix, were also at the residence, but they did not interact with the vice president. They spent most of the evening in a back office, in contact with senior campaign leaders in the boiler room, set up in the bowels of the Marriott Marquis in Washington. A few times, Emhoff dropped by their office to get updates. For one of their check-in calls with the boiler room, Harris's aides decamped to Voles's car, which was parked by the back door, for privacy.

During the day, campaign officials were optimistic based on reports from the ground, especially signs of high turnout on college campuses. On one check-in call, during a discussion about hours-long lines at colleges in Pennsylvania, a Harris campaign official shared they had sent Paul Rudd to Villanova University to entertain the students.

Inside the boiler room, the mood shifted around 8:00 p.m. Voices became more hushed. People in the room started texting each other under the table, acknowledging the bad vibes. Social media posts became more dire. Democratic commentators known for being upbeat ("hopium" accounts) went silent. Staffers barely used the full open bar set up in an adjacent room, so the bartenders closed up early. Some of the hotel workers seemed to catch on before campaign officials. One of the bartenders said the staff were going to need a drink that night. A security guard observed, "Looking pretty bad out there."

Around 9:30, David Plouffe and Mitch Stewart sought to reassure the senior staff. They still had hope in the Blue Wall. Quentin Fulks, who managed Raphael Warnock's 2022 Senate race, said there were still votes out in Gwinnett County in Georgia. But the numbers had worsened by the 10:00 p.m. check-in call. Schwenzfeier said Harris would lose Georgia and North Carolina. The turnout in Dane County, Wisconsin, was soft, and the numbers in Philadelphia were problematic. She didn't have enough data for Detroit yet, but the trend was clear. Around 10:30, O'Malley Dillon directed the staff to start working on the concession speech.*

At the vice president's residence, as the first returns started to come in and Trump established an early lead, people stayed largely calm. They were told to expect Trump would perform well in the early results. As the night dragged on, the mood quickly turned solemn.

Harris's family and friends were incredulous. Many of them had spent the past several weeks crisscrossing the country, witnessing the massive crowds and enthusiasm for the vice president. They were having trouble comprehending what the anchors were announcing on the televisions.

"They're going to call Pennsylvania," Harris told her family at last, "so Jen is telling me I need to concede."

West urged caution. "Hold on," he said. "Let's first check with folks on the ground so we don't have concerns. We don't need to rush into a concession."

Some Harris aides were at the White House preparing to motorcade with the vice president from the vice president's residence to Howard. The cars never moved.

Staffers decided to send Cedric Richmond, the former Louisiana

---

*One Harris aide had started a draft of the concession speech weeks earlier.

congressman and cochair of Harris's campaign, to Howard and have him deliver a brief statement, sending him scrambling to find a suit to wear. Shortly before 1:00 a.m. on Wednesday morning, he took the stage at Howard and told the crowd they would not hear from the vice president tonight. "We still have votes to count. We still have states that have not been called," he said. "You will hear from her tomorrow."

Saler had already briefed the AP and the network decision desks not to get too caught up in the Democrats' fears that Trump could declare victory prematurely. The scenario he argued they should be prepared for was that Trump would win on election night and the Democrats would pressure the decision desks to wait. Saler just wanted the data scientists to believe their own eyes, trust their own professional judgment, and not get spun.

He called and texted the networks urging them to start calling states, warning them of getting lapped by their competitors if they held out. Around 10:00 p.m., the networks started to call North Carolina for Trump, but they hesitated on Georgia, even though the campaign was confident Trump would win both. It was getting close to the point where they thought Pennsylvania was clear enough to call too.

By 11:00, Wiles went downstairs to find Trump and tell him she was 100 percent certain he was going to win. Sitting in the middle of the ballroom, Trump had spent the evening talking to Steve Wynn, Elon Musk, and hundreds of well-wishers. He told Wiles he wanted to believe her. She said they needed to get ready to move to the Palm Beach Convention Center, where the main election night party was being held. It would take some time to get everyone together and motorcade over. But Trump wanted to stay and keep watching the returns.

Everyone started coming up to Trump and congratulating him: his detail, club staff, his family. He asked if they were sure. No one had called it.

Finally, around 12:15 a.m., the team began loading into the motorcade for the short drive across Lake Worth Lagoon to the convention center. Trump turned to the small group of aides and smiled.

"You know," he said, "if we'd been in office for the last four years, we'd be getting ready to leave right now. We'd be kind of sad, and they'd be rid of us. But we're just getting started."

Epilogue

At the victory party, Trump called up Susie Wiles to speak, and she demurred. In the past, Trump had complained that his co-campaign managers wouldn't go on TV to defend him, but now it was Wiles's big chance to take credit, and she passed. That meant a lot to him. He called her "the ice maiden," which she'd never heard him say before, and she wondered where it came from. It would soon be her regular nickname.

LaCivita happily accepted his turn to take a bow. Backstage, he spurned Corey Lewandowski's offer of congratulations and vowed to destroy him. LaCivita would not go into the White House; he was a mercenary who went home at the end of the war. He would decamp to the mountains to shoot elk and send the remains back home as sausages, then give paid speeches, work for a cryptocurrency company, and return to his collection of Italian wines. The security guards would finally leave his house in Virginia. On New Year's Eve, he would stand by a cigar bar at the British Embassy, drinking rare scotch and holding court. He would see Terry McAuliffe, the former Virginia governor and longtime Democratic power broker he'd worked against. McAuliffe would approach him saying, "What a campaign you guys ran," and take a selfie together.

Harris didn't concede the night of the election, even though the campaign knew they had lost. Once she was ready to call Trump, her team at first could not get through. Wiles missed the call. When Harris's aides finally got Trump on the phone, they couldn't manage to merge the call with Harris. "Phone service isn't what it used to be," Trump quipped. Aides ended up holding two phones together on speaker so that the rivals could talk.

"You're a tough cookie," Trump told her. He complimented her husband. He did not compliment her campaign, but he acknowledged she'd given him a run for his money. Even her aides described him as gracious.

Harris was professional but not warm. She had considered alluding to his failure to concede when things turned out the other way, but in the end she just said the country was too divided, and she hoped he would be a president for all Americans.

Biden called to congratulate Trump and invite him to visit the White House—the same customary courtesy that Trump had refused him four years earlier. Now Trump accepted amicably. "In another life," he told the president, "we would be friends and go golfing."

No one had expected the election to be over and decided already. Even the Trump advisers who were confident of their victory thought they'd be spending the days after the election dealing with lawsuits and recounts. James Blair had deployed operatives to key states. Instead they had to start staffing the administration. Wiles told others that Trump had not asked her to be his chief of staff, and she didn't know who he would pick.

He summoned her to Mar-a-Lago on Thursday morning. When she arrived at the club, Trump asked her why she didn't want to be his chief of staff, as he claimed people were telling him. It wasn't true, she said. "I would be honored." The two shook hands, and it was settled in less than two minutes.

Trump had resisted formal transition planning before the election, since he wanted to focus on the campaign, and because he was superstitious, not wanting to jinx the outcome. But he had already thought through who he wanted in his cabinet and jotted down some names. With Wiles in place, he swiftly started announcing nods: Elise Stefanik for the UN, Lee Zeldin for EPA, John Ratcliffe for CIA, Marco Rubio for secretary of state. He named his friend Steve Witkoff as a special envoy to the Middle East. As he considered who to pick for homeland security, all the border hawks he trusted uniformly recommended Kristi Noem. The South Dakota governor was not a natural choice, and it became obvious to Trump aides that Lewandowski had put others up to promoting her. Trump assented, viewing her as a gentler face for deportations than Stephen Miller.

Wiles left town for the weekend, flying to Las Vegas for a Republican donor retreat with other top aides, including Fabrizio. At a hotel on the Strip, she realized strangers were recognizing her. She had never sought the public eye and told others she would prefer to live without a security detail, but she eventually took one, as was customary for the White House chief of staff.

To Wiles's surprise, Trump picked a White House counsel and staff secretary while she was gone. She needed to get back to Florida and get things more under control. Eventually, she got Trump to reverse course and pick a different White House counsel whom she preferred. She soon flew to Washington, where she had dinner with Jeff Zients and other former White House chiefs of staff, saw much of the West Wing for the first time, and received her first daily intelligence briefing. She described the learning curve as "daunting."

Trump struggled with the position he cared most about: attorney general. He viewed his first-term AGs as disloyal and wanted someone who would purge everyone connected to the Smith probe and investigate fraud in the 2020 election. Earlier hopefuls such as Matt Whitaker and Jeffrey Clark had drifted out of favor. Trump repeatedly interviewed Missouri AG Andrew Bailey, who was being pushed by his mentor, Missouri Senator Eric Schmitt, but Trump saw him as too conventional. "We need someone who is tough," Trump said.

He remained undecided on November 13 when he flew to Washington to meet Biden at the White House. The thick curved hidden panel door opened and Trump stepped back into the Oval Office. The rug with the presidential seal was blue, instead of the white he'd picked eight years earlier. The paintings and busts were different: Benjamin Franklin instead of Andrew Jackson; Cesar Chavez instead of another Andrew Jackson. The Resolute Desk was still there, and behind it, surrounding the three great eleven-and-a-half-foot windows that reliably brightened the cornerless room, the same gold drapes.

Biden and Trump talked for nearly two hours. Their chiefs, Wiles and Zients, joined for most of the time. Biden hugged Wiles and complimented her blue eyes. The outgoing president extensively discussed foreign affairs, especially Ukraine and the Middle East. Trump listened politely. He asked what Zelensky and Xi were like to deal with, getting Biden's perspective on negotiating and interacting with them. Biden conveyed his understanding of those leaders and their priorities. There were no contentious moments. They touched on the need to formalize the transition and fund the government during the lame-duck session of Congress.

Trump kept asking what Biden thought of Harris's campaign, or her performance as vice president, trying to uncover any daylight between them. Biden wouldn't say anything bad about her. Trump mentioned wanting to get politics out of the Justice Department, alluding to Biden's own experience with that through his son Hunter, but Biden didn't engage with that either.

Biden spoke softly, but he showed no signs of confusion, and he went into detail on a variety of topics. He never needed any assistance or intervention to stay on topic. At one point he stood to fetch some pictures from a console table, and his gait was labored. But mentally he seemed sharp and smart. Trump left astonished, remarking he didn't understand what had happened at the debate. It didn't seem like the same guy.

Trump's staff waited outside in the Roosevelt Room, and some White House employees who remembered them from the Trump years stopped by to say hi. Walt Nauta, Trump's valet and codefendant, was particularly popular. Some of the aides began quarreling with Boris Epshteyn.

Epshteyn had also begun clashing with Trump's new best friend, Elon Musk. Once, Musk made an impassioned case for Trump to consider aid to Ukraine. Epshteyn interrupted. "With all due respect . . ." Musk cut him off. Those who start sentences that way, he said, are not usually trying to show respect. He then went back to arguing his case to Trump.

Congressman Matt Gaetz tagged along for Trump's trip to Washington. On the plane, Wiles left the president's side while Gaetz and Epshteyn started talking to him about attorney general. Trump said he wasn't excited about any of the candidates he'd seen, and Gaetz told him those conventional picks wouldn't get him what he wanted. Trump offered Gaetz the job. Epshteyn agreed, and Gaetz accepted.

Trump called Wiles over to share the news. She liked Gaetz, but she thought they were joking. "You've got to be kidding me," she told others, saying she had no idea it was coming.

When the news broke, top officials at the Department of Justice thought it was a mistake because it seemed so preposterous. They viewed Gaetz as unfit for the role not just because the department had investigated him for sex trafficking, but after prosecutors *declined* to bring charges, Gaetz relentlessly accused the department of persecuting him.

Trump knew about the investigation, which was widely publicized, but he did not know the House Ethics Committee was preparing to release a damning report that concluded Gaetz used illegal drugs and paid for sex. Nine days later Gaetz offered to withdraw.

Other Trump aides caught wind that Epshteyn was asking for money from people seeking cabinet posts, and the boss tasked a lawyer to investigate. The review, conducted by campaign attorney and incoming White House counsel David Warrington, found that Epshteyn asked Scott Bessent, a hedge fund billionaire seeking to become treasury secretary, for a monthly stipend of at least $30,000 and a $10 million investment in a three-on-three basketball league. When Bessent declined, and came to believe Epshteyn was blocking him, Epshteyn said Bessent should have paid him. "I'm Boris Fucking Epshteyn," he said. The review found Epshteyn also approached a former Trump administration official turned defense contractor for $100,000 a month. (Epshteyn denied the allegations.) Warrington's report recommended that Trump fire Epshteyn and stay away from him.

But Trump kept Epshteyn around. "They didn't kill me," Epshteyn told others. He walked about the club with Trump, telling people he'd turned down a White House job and wanted a role analogous to Vernon Jordan, Bill Clinton's outside fix-it man.

Trump proceeded to install his own lawyers in the Justice Department, starting with Todd Blanche as deputy attorney general. He specifically wanted Blanche to make sure nothing like the Smith investigation ever happened again. Smith submitted his final report concluding he had enough evidence to convict Trump at trial, but also accepting the reality that he had run out of time. Trump's incoming DOJ and FBI officials prepared to find out every employee who touched a January 6 case in any way and scrutinize their conduct.

Even midlevel administration jobs required exhaustive loyalty tests. Had they ever criticized Trump? Worked for a rival? Worked for a group or politician Trump didn't like? Donated to any cause that Trump didn't support? Outside consulting firms helped vet candidates to make sure they were committed to Trump's agenda. Experience mattered far less than loyalty. Trump suspected military leaders of undermining him in his first term, so for secretary of defense he chose the Fox News host Pete Hegseth, an Army National Guard veteran who'd prominently pushed him to pardon officers charged with war crimes.

Hegseth was never fully vetted, and after his announcement the transition team received a letter accusing him of a sexual assault in 2017. He denied it, but more reports detailed his problems with drinking and with women. Trump himself was rattled by the publication of an email from Hegseth's own mother excoriating his behavior. The president-elect saw DeSantis at a police officer's funeral and began seriously discussing swapping him in for Hegseth. But DeSantis's many enemies who remained on Trump's staff weighed in against it, circulating clips of DeSantis criticizing Trump. Hegseth showed resolve to weather the scandal, and Trump decided to stick with him. Vance would cast the tie-breaking vote.

Trump nominated RFK Jr. and Tulsi Gabbard, who some Trump allies called the "X-Men" because of their unconventional place in the Republican coalition and their comic-book-like appearances, for health secretary and director of national intelligence, respectively. Kennedy galled some advisers by casting an even wider influence, including promoting his daughter-in-law for deputy director of the CIA. But Trump loved having Kennedy around, calling him "a star."

Musk moved into a cottage at Mar-a-Lago and almost never left the president-elect's side. They went to Washington together for the Oval Office meeting. They went to Paris together for the rededication of Notre Dame. Together they torpedoed a government spending package, almost causing a government shutdown before Christmas. Musk also started freelancing with his own calls to lawmakers and business leaders seeking input for his advisory board for cutting government programs. He called it the Department of Government Efficiency, or "DOGE," after an internet meme of a Shiba Inu. Other tech executives flocked to join the effort; the only thing they didn't want was anyone from Washington with government experience.

The CEO of Coca-Cola came with a commemorative inauguration Diet Coke, Trump's favorite drink. Trump was grateful but had a lot of questions. He asked why the company didn't use cane sugar, and the CEO said there wasn't enough supply. Trump called José Fanjul, the Republican donor and sugar magnate, put him on speakerphone, and asked if that was true. He also called his son Eric during the meeting to ask how Coca-Cola was treating his properties and whether he needed anything.

The incoming president showed occasional flashes of aftereffects from his several near-death experiences. While attending the Army–Navy football game in December, he looked around the crowded skybox, filled with Vance, senators, and other dignitaries, and asked, "What if a drone hit this suite?" Another time, when meeting with Vance and Johnson at Mar-a-Lago, he joked that the three of them should not be in the same room.*

A t Harris's concession speech, held at Howard University the day after the election, many of the staff who worked for her sighed

---

*A Trump spokesman denied both remarks.

that the party might never nominate another woman. Most campaigns paid staff through the end of the year, providing a cushion for finding a new job. The Harris campaign, which raised more than $1 billion, finished $1 million in debt, and staff received their last paychecks in November, a bitter end to a long year.*

The top officials on the Harris campaign wrestled with how to account for their loss. They decided to try friendly terrain: *Pod Save America*, the podcast hosted by former Obama aides who also happened to be their friends and former colleagues. Some Harris aides thought nothing good could come from it. On the show, four of the campaign leaders, including Jen O'Malley Dillon and David Plouffe, blamed the outcome largely on the truncated timeline—Harris had only 107 days to make her case to the American people. "In a one-hundred-and-seven-day race, it is very difficult to do all the things you would normally do in a year and a half, two years," O'Malley Dillon said. They also pointed to the broader political and economic climate, arguing the lingering effects of the pandemic and global inflation contributed to an anti-incumbent sentiment that doomed Biden and Harris. None of them conceded any strategic mistakes, infuriating many Democrats. Some of the Harris aides said they were being discreet because they wanted to protect Harris and her future ambitions, which could include a run for California governor or president in 2028. They also genuinely believed Harris did a great job.

Harris knew the race would be close, but she really thought she would win. As she prepared to move back to Los Angeles, sprawling wildfires rapidly approached her home, but it stayed just outside the evacuation zone. She made no immediate decisions about her political future, but her first stop upon returning to Los Angeles was a visit with firefighters

---

*Campaign officials noted they provided employees with health care until the end of the year.

and volunteers, helping them distribute free meals. A few weeks later, she reemerged in public to tour areas damaged by the fire alongside local officials. Reporters followed along, capturing photos of Harris amid the wreckage. Asked about running for governor, she did not rule it out, saying she had been back home for only two weeks.

It was true that Harris inherited a campaign limited by earlier strategic and personnel choices. Whether or not she could have assembled a stronger operation herself, she never had the chance. Perhaps most consequentially, her advisers underestimated the public's anger toward Biden, and she was unwilling to separate herself from him, in part because he pressured her not to.

Democrats also suffered from conceptual and tactical messaging failures. Their overconfidence in the merits of Biden's policy accomplishments and in improving macroeconomic indicators led to an economic message that, to the extent it ever took shape, came across to struggling Americans as out of touch and unempathetic.

The Democrats limped out of the election on the unpopular side of most top issues. Trump, through a combination of popularizing his own views and running toward the middle, monopolized the center on contentious issues from trade and foreign intervention to transgender participation in sports. Even on abortion, Trump staked out a centrist position that took the sting out of Democratic attacks and even won him some pro-choice voters. Some Democrats concluded that ballot initiatives protecting abortion in battleground states backfired on them, allowing pro-choice voters to protect rights they valued while still voting for Trump. He targeted the Democrats' long-standing weaknesses on taxes and crime to brand them as the party of open borders, foreign wars, transgender rights, and anti-Zionism. The Democratic congressional candidates who ran stronger than Harris in battlegrounds did so by distancing themselves from the rest of their party and more closely resembling Republicans. Many Democratic strategists left 2024 calling for the party to recalibrate for the rightward shift of the national mood.

But mimicry has never amounted to much electoral success. For the bulk of the last century, Republicans responded to the New Deal consensus by offering a milder, watered-down version of the Democratic platform, belittled as a party that said "me too" rather than offering its own ideas. The result was four decades spent almost entirely out of power in Congress and often out of the White House—until Ronald Reagan delivered a new vision of conservatism that redefined the political landscape. Now that Trump has redefined the political landscape again, he has succeeded in tilting the field such that as long as the Democrats are playing on his terms, they seem inclined to lose.

At the same time, Trump's new coalition on its face relies on his personal appeal to less frequent voters. As much as many opponents have tried and failed to take the shine off Trump, many followers have tried and failed to reproduce his unique place in American cultural and political life. The flip side of Trump's new MAGA GOP is that he has driven away many more reliable voters who used to tilt Republican. That offers the Democrats a potential advantage in the 2026 midterms, which are likely to see lower turnout than in 2024, on top of the usual historical pattern of a two-year backlash to the sitting president, and the risk that Republicans will use their unified control in Washington to overreach.

Harris, who declined to be interviewed for this book, quietly made clear she wanted a stake in the future of her party. As Democrats were choosing a new national party chair, Harris kept her options open by withholding an endorsement, and called the top candidates to say she expected to work closely with the eventual winner. For the party election, Harris sent in a prerecorded video, and delegates responded with loud cheers, in contrast to a tepid response to a video from Biden.

———

In the weeks after the election, Biden repeatedly told allies that he could have won if he'd stayed in the race, even as he publicly questioned whether he could have served another four years. Aides scoffed that if they'd been trying to cover up his condition, they hadn't done a very good job, since everyone had seen him for themselves every time he appeared in public. They also pointed to his long-standing habit of rambling and putting his foot in his mouth.

Biden and his advisers blamed other Democratic leaders for pushing him aside. He refused to speak with Nancy Pelosi, and sometimes swore when discussing her role in turning the party against him. Jill Biden, too, remained furious at Pelosi, feeling she had betrayed the Bidens. "We were friends for fifty years," she told *The Washington Post*.

"It was an act of insanity by the Democratic leadership," Mike Donilon said in an interview for this book. "Tell me why you walked away from a guy with eighty-one million votes. Why you walked away from the only Democrat in recent years who has split men. The only one who has run ahead among seniors. A native of Pennsylvania. Why do that?"

A few days before Thanksgiving, Hunter Biden arrived in Washington ahead of the family's annual trip to celebrate the holiday on Nantucket. At the White House, Hunter told his father that his legal team had prepared a fifty-two-page document titled "The Political Prosecutions of Hunter Biden." They planned to release it publicly after Thanksgiving, ahead of his sentencing hearings the following month in Delaware and California, where the judge told him he could face up to seventeen years in prison. The president asked to see the document and appeared surprised by some of the specifics, asking Hunter and his legal team follow-up questions. The document argued that Hunter would not have faced the charges if he were not the president's son. The legal team largely rehashed the arguments they unsuccessfully made in court for years and provided a detailed timeline of the investigations. The document also warned that Trump's election posed an even graver threat to Hunter. "There is no disputing that Trump has said his enemies list includes Hunter," the report said. "The prospect that Trump will turn his vengeance on the Special Counsel prosecutors if they fail to take a harder line against Hunter no doubt exerts considerable pressure on them not to let up on Hunter."

Until this point, Biden and his aides repeatedly and emphatically ruled out pardoning Hunter. Privately, the president had been grappling with the idea, especially after Hunter was convicted in June. Many of the president's closest allies thought it was obvious he should pardon Hunter after the election. The president had already lost one son to cancer; they could not imagine he would allow his other son to serve a day behind bars—especially on charges they thought were largely bogus. But Hunter Biden told friends that he never discussed the prospect with his father, and he believed he would still win both cases on appeal. He thought his father would never have pardoned him if Biden was reelected or Harris had won. But Trump's victory, and especially his nomination of Kash Patel to run the FBI, changed the calculus, Hunter told friends.

On Nantucket, Biden, alone with his family, reached his decision. He would grant Hunter a full and unconditional pardon. No staffers were involved in the process. When the president returned to Washington on the Saturday after Thanksgiving, he called his senior staff to tell them. He announced the pardon on Sunday with a blistering statement he wrote personally. He referenced "an effort to break Hunter" with "unrelenting attacks and selective prosecution," arguing those efforts would continue. "Enough is enough," he said.

But that wasn't enough for Biden. He then turned his ire on the Department of Justice: "I believe in the justice system, but as I have wrestled with this, I also believe raw politics has infected this process and it led to a miscarriage of justice." Even some of the president's staunchest defenders were appalled. Top officials at the Department of Justice were shocked. Biden had spent the last several years pushing back on Trump's attempts to delegitimize federal prosecutions as politicized. Now Biden was agreeing. After years of condemning Trump for putting his own interests before the country, Democrats started criticizing Biden for the very same thing. His damage to the credibility and independence of the justice system, in the view of many Democrats, went further with last-minute pardons for his three siblings and two of their spouses, as his last act in office.*

Biden's aides declined to make the president available for an interview. They said they worried it would conflict with the memoir he planned to write. Reached directly on his cell phone on March 25, Biden said he would be willing to speak for this book the next day. The next morning, he answered and said he was running late to catch a train. He said he had a "very negative" view of Trump's second term, his first public comments about his successor since leaving office. "I don't see anything he's done that's been productive," he said. Asked if he had any regrets about dropping out of the presidential race, he said, "No, not now. I don't spend a lot of time on regrets." He quickly hung up to get on the train.

After the first call, Biden's aides repeatedly called and texted the reporter. After the brief second call, his aides blocked the reporter's calls to the former president. Two days later, a message from Verizon Wireless replaced Biden's voicemail: "The number you dialed has been changed, disconnected, or is no longer in service."

---

*Biden also preemptively pardoned people who were likely targets for Trump's revenge, including Anthony Fauci, Mark Milley, and Liz Cheney.

The inauguration festivities were unbridled for the first time in twelve years. Trump's first inauguration was shunned by much of corporate America, upstaged by a defiant women's march the next day, and best remembered for a tantrum over crowd size. The occasion in 2021 was confined by the pandemic and the intense security after the Capitol riot. This time, Trump's revelers took over Washington's watering holes, sipped champagne on a triple-decker gilded yacht called the *Liberty*, and bolted around town in black cars from one gala to another. Cryptocurrency executives threw a black-tie affair, tech companies held brunches with caviar bars, and tech billionaire Peter Thiel held a VIP soiree at his Washington home. Fans jockeyed to get close to Trump and his team, with some driving all the way to Trump's golf course in the outer Virginia suburbs to watch fireworks with him.

Mark Zuckerberg, whose company reached a $25 million settlement for banning Trump from its platform, threw a party at Mastro's Steakhouse in Trump's honor, along with Miriam Adelson, restaurant mogul Tilman Fertitta, and Chicago Cubs co-owner Todd Ricketts. Zuckerberg sat in the back, behind a velvet rope, and greeted Republican lawmakers, billionaires, and other donors who were now part of his world. Zuckerberg told others he had no relationship with Harris and had not met with or spoken to Biden throughout his entire presidency.

Trump's top aides gathered at a posh Italian restaurant two nights ahead of the inauguration to salute Wiles and LaCivita. There were jokes about Lewandowski, who was not present, and how much money LaCivita made. Fabrizio toasted Wiles's understated management style and her way of expressing disappointment. "Did you really think you were being helpful when you did that?" he said to laughter.

An Arctic chill swept through the mid-Atlantic, and the inauguration planners nervously took briefings from the National Weather Service every three hours. They did not want to move the ceremony inside. They did not want to disappoint the fans who'd traveled far to see Trump—not the high-dollar donors, they would be fine, but the people who'd saved up for this. They also braced for sneering headlines and sniping pundits who would surely accuse them of moving indoors to avoid being embarrassed by an underwhelming crowd. But the blowback never came. All the coverage focused on the weather. Aides were baffled that, for once, Trump wasn't getting skewered. What world were they living in?

The high-dollar donors were, in the end, not fine. The streets were so choked with traffic that some donors had to walk for blocks in the cold to reach a candlelit dinner the night before the swearing-in, only to learn there was no room for them. Fewer people no-showed than expected—a nice problem to have, except the tables were squeezed too close together, leaving no room for the servers to pass. Hundreds of guests, including some top officials and their spouses, did not have seats. At least one cabinet nominee had to wait forty-five minutes for a glass of water. Some attendees left hungry after 10:00 p.m. because their food never arrived. One senior Trump appointee screamed at staff because he did not have a military escort.

All the hours of planning and millions of dollars spent on the outdoor grandstand were for nothing. The committee had to throw together a new program overnight. The Capitol Rotunda wasn't configured for a large ceremony, and the Architect of the Capitol, which manages the facility, lacked modern sound equipment. The inaugural committee, awash with cash, unleashed the advance team to tear down the existing setup and bring in all new gear. They joked that their orders to transform the Rotunda were to "go J6 on it."

Just before the swearing-in, Trump was making final edits to his address when he learned that Biden had preemptively pardoned his family members. Trump wanted to add a swipe at Biden to his script. "I feel like I should talk about that," he said to senior House Republicans Mike Johnson, Steve Scalise, and Tom Emmer.

They urged him to reconsider. "I would keep it as lofty and aspirational as possible," Johnson said.

"Are you sure about that?" Trump said. He consulted his staff, who agreed he should not attack Biden. They also convinced him not to mention pardoning January 6 rioters.

The Rotunda had far fewer seats than outside, relegating many VIP ticket holders to an overflow room in the underground Capitol visitor center. Trump chose billionaires he'd spent little time with to be close to him onstage over others he'd known for decades. He invited Zuckerberg and Jeff Bezos to join Musk on the dais. Trump began regularly speaking with Bezos, saying they commiserated over critical stories about them in *The Washington Post*. "He's concerned about it," Trump said in an interview. "They actually write bad stories about him."

After the formal address Trump went down to the overflow room to treat the crowd there to the speech he really wanted to give. He lashed out at Liz Cheney, said he looked forward to pardoning January 6 defendants, mocked Biden's last-minute pardons, described the border wall in detail, and chastised his advisers for wanting him to focus on the economy throughout the election. How many times, he asked, could he say the cost of an apple had doubled? He spoke for forty minutes, as long as his official remarks. After finishing with a tangent about Melania's sore feet, he declared himself satisfied. "I think this was a better speech than the one I made upstairs," he said.

LaCivita was not able to make it to the inauguration because he got stuck at a security checkpoint near the White House. After waiting for forty minutes, he declined help from other Trump aides and returned to the Waldorf Astoria (the former Trump hotel). Jason Miller, the president's longtime spokesman, was blocked from getting into the Capitol complex for about an hour while wearing a Secret Service pin. "He's friends with Mogul," an agent eventually told a Capitol Police officer, using Trump's code name. Even that didn't work. Eventually, Miller was let in but escorted by an officer all the way to the Rotunda.

The designated blowout for the foot soldiers of Republican politics (professional operatives and party officials) was the Liberty Ball in the convention center. It became the catch-all for sundry attractions, including a live "Christian worship artist" who painted Trump under a cross, a tailgate section sponsored by DraftKings, and a golf simulator. The Village People, the disco legends who once objected to Trump's reappropriation of their cruising anthem, now said their music was apolitical and performed four songs: "YMCA," "Macho Man," "In the Navy," and a fourth song that they apparently also sang.* At the swankier Starlight Ball, the Secret Service closed the indoor bathrooms because they were in Trump's walking path, and the lines for porta-potties got so long that some revelers took to relieving themselves outside of Union Station.

Trump wanted to show his supporters he was serious about making good on the dozens of day-one promises he'd made during the campaign. Aides discussed signing a stack of executive orders before leaving the Capitol, or taking the oath in the Oval Office and signing orders right then and there. He ended up signing some in front of cheering fans at the hockey and basketball arena downtown, then more upon returning to the White House. Within days, his administration would officially withdraw the menthol cigarettes ban that the Reynolds American donors opposed.

Trump granted blanket clemency for all January 6 defendants: about

---

*Lead singer Victor Willis was the only original member still in the band.

twelve hundred pardons, three hundred dismissals, and fourteen commutations for the violent extremists convicted of seditious conspiracy. Some aides pushed Trump to pardon only nonviolent criminals, but he wasn't interested. He decided it would be too hard to sort them all out. People who had beaten police officers, smashed windows, and defiled the Capitol were free within hours.

Trump hung up his mug shot in a gold frame just off the Oval Office. Epshteyn stood by as the new president scratched his distinctive signature in Sharpie onto the procession of pages, sometimes without stopping to read them or listen to his aide describe them. Instead he took far-ranging questions from a scrum of reporters.

"President Trump, there was a lot of concern about this during the campaign," one of the reporters said. Throughout 2023 and 2024, Trump had repeatedly responded to concerns about his authoritarian tendencies by saying he didn't want to be a dictator—"except for day one . . . I want to close the border, and I want to drill, drill, drill." Sometimes he said he was joking, but he was completely serious about halting unauthorized immigration and expanding oil production. Now that his first day in office was here, he'd just finished officially invoking emergency powers to do both things. The reporter asked, "Are you a dictator on day one?"

Trump, resting one arm on the Resolute Desk, looked away from the reporter and directly into the camera, breaking the fourth wall. "No," he said softly. He shook his head, puckered his lips. "I can't imagine even being called that."

He began ordering deportation raids, firing government workers, eliminating diversity programs, raising tariffs, and revoking security clearances. He started flying migrants out of the country on military planes, in shackles. He directed federal agencies to take away protection for John Bolton, his former national security adviser turned critic; his former secretary of state, Mike Pompeo; former chief medical adviser Anthony Fauci; and Hunter Biden.

On a weekend trip back to Mar-a-Lago in February, reporters saw staff loading boxes onto Air Force One. Trump said they were the same boxes that the FBI had seized from the club in August 2022, now returned to him by the Department of Justice under his control. He said he was bringing the boxes home with him, to someday be part of his presidential library.

ACKNOWLEDGMENTS

We are all deeply appreciative to the many sources who helped with this book. Without your time and insight, this book would not be possible. Thank you for talking even when it was not convenient or helpful—and, at times, for risking your jobs. We cannot overstate how much we appreciate you and your commitment to helping us tell the accurate and comprehensive account of this historic election.

Thank you to Ann Godoff and her team at Penguin Press. Ann is a legendary editor whose list of titles is awe-inspiring. We appreciate your belief in the project and your steady hand and wisdom in seeing it through. Thank you to Will Heyward, Casey Dennis, Sarah Hutson, Christine Johnston, Matthew Boyd, Darren Haggar for the brilliant jacket design, Jane Cavolina, and Ryan Boyle. We had the best time we've ever had getting lawyered with Claire Leonard.

Elyse Cheney and Isabel Mendía helped bring this project to life and shepherded us through this entire process. We are grateful for your support and advice at every step of the way.

We are indebted to Julie Tate, who corrected errors we never would have even thought to check, and who worked with tremendous speed. Our favorite was Sheff G's grills, plural.

Devon Spurgeon and Ziad Ojakli allowed us to spend a few days at their home on the Eastern Shore. Those were the most productive days of our time writing this book, and we are not sure we could have finished this project without that time. Thank you for your generosity, friendship, and support of the project.

We are grateful to *The Washington Post* for bringing the three of us together and supporting this project. The book is an outgrowth of our years covering Washington and national politics at the *Post*, and we were lucky to work with so many talented editors and reporters. Thank you to Steven Ginsberg for hiring us and encouraging us to think big about stories. Thank you to Sally Buzbee for being a trusted editor and giving us leave to complete this work. We all feel tremendous gratitude to have worked for Matea Gold, a singular editor who embodies the best of journalism with her brilliance, tenacity, and kindness. We also feel incredibly lucky to have worked with Phil Rucker, a true mensch and leader. And we are all grateful to Dan Eggen, who spent many mornings, nights, and weekends helping us land difficult stories while making work fun and rewarding.

One of the hallmarks of the *Post* is the collaboration and collegiality in the newsroom, and the three of us tremendously benefitted from working closely with journalists across the *Post*.

There are few people we worked more closely with than Ashley Parker and Michael Scherer, and they deserve a special thank you. Ashley and Michael are two of the best in Washington, and they elevated our work with their deep source networks and brilliant writing. They are also tremendous human beings, who are some of our closest friends. We dearly miss sharing a newsroom with you both. We also want to thank Dan

Balz, a stalwart of the *Post* for [redacted] years. He is the most gracious and generous man in Washington.

Dawsey

First of all, I am deeply thankful to Isaac and Tyler. We emerge from this process as actual friends, which may surprise us all. You both have spent countless hours on this book trying to make it perfect. We also had some fun. I finish this process with admiration and respect for you both. This process is over, right?

Most of this book was reported at *The Washington Post*, where I am grateful for a number of terrific colleagues and friends during my 7.5 years there. That group includes but isn't limited to: Jackie Alemany, Devlin Barrett, Phil Rucker, Ashley Parker, Roz Helderman, Shane Harris, Michael Scherer, Matt Zapotosky, Isaac Stanley-Becker, Juliet Eilperin, Theo Meyer, Dan Balz, Nick Miroff, Ben Terris, Nick Baumann, Sarah Ellison, Marianne LeVine, Caroline Kitchener, Tom Hamburger, Amy Gardner, Damian Paletta, Karen DeYoung, Manuel Roig-Franzia, Yasmeen Abutaleb, Lauren Weber, Lena Sun, David Fahrenthold, Peter Wallsten, Brady Dennis, Perry Stein, Matt Viser, Amy Fiscus, Jeff Stein, and many others. To those of you still there, keep the faith.

Thank you to Mary Jordan and Kevin, Kate and Tom Sullivan. You all have been a second family to me in Washington. I have been honored to be friends with the singular Sally Quinn: you make life here infinitely more interesting. Thank you to Katharine Weymouth and your wonderful family for being generous and welcoming.

I am eternally thankful to *The Wall Street Journal* for giving me my start in journalism after college and for bringing me back on staff earlier this year. I am thrilled to be working with you all, and thanks for supporting this book. I also am thankful for the Allbritton Journalism Institute, where I've gotten to work with a lot of terrific young journalists who want to make the world a better place.

I was initially skeptical of moving to Washington. But it has turned into a wonderful life with so many of you in the world. They include Zolan Kanno-Youngs, John Hudson, James Adams, Nate Evans, Meridith McGraw and John Beasley, Evan Hollander and Eli Yokley, Beverly Leslie, Katie Benner and Jed Miller, Tarini Parti and Ryan Barber, Jonathan and Betsy Fischer Martin, Betsy Klein and Jeff Solnet, Ted Mann and Annie Karni, Kaitlan Collins, Devon Spurgeon and Ziad Ojakli, Shawn McCreesh, Maureen Dowd, Eli Aguayo, Matt Moore, T. W. Arrighi, Matt Mowers and Cassie Spodak, Mark Bailey, Pascal Confavreux, Brooke Lorenz, Tammy Haddad, Jeff Zeleny, Andrew Restuccia, Sam Wright, and Sean Dugan, among others. At the risk of leaving someone important out, a special thanks to a few people who have made my life incredibly meaningful in various chapters: Amanda Riley, Samantha Ward, Mara Gay, Nick Wagner, Andrew Patterson, Barin Powell and the Powell family, Gareth Rhodes, and Matt Jarzemsky.

I must credit Maggie Haberman, Jonathan Swan, Rebecca Ballhaus, Katherine Faulders, Tim Alberta, Mike Bender, and other indefatigable reporters on the Trump beat for being such talented and fierce competitors and colleagues.

I am notoriously a joy to edit, but I would never be anywhere without so many good mentors and editors over the years. Thanks to Chrysti Shain, Fitz McAden, Carolyn Callison Murray, Charles Bierbauer, Rob Wells, Gabby Stern, Kirsten Danis, Michael Amon, Carrie Melago, Mike Siconolfi, Bob Rose, Carrie Budoff Brown, Dan Eggen, Dave Clarke, and Aruna Visawantha among others.

Friends at the Garden District (shoutout to James, Reed, Ben, and

Tracy) and Jefferson Hotel fueled much of this book. Thank you for always being so accommodating.

A huge thank you to my parents, particularly my mom, who edited this book with a red pen and found every misplaced comma. Is anything wrong with this sentence, Mom? I love you both. My cousin Denise has been like a sister to me. I have been lucky to have so many aunts, uncles, and cousins play an important part in my life. I love you all. And, finally, to my beloved and psychotic rescue dog, Pepper, thank you for making life better. You have been there for it all. I hope you never start talking.

Pager

This project began when Isaac approached me at a party and proposed collaborating on a book about the 2024 election. He and Josh were covering Donald Trump, and I was covering Joe Biden. Even though we had never shared a byline, he thought the three of us were uniquely positioned to write this book. It didn't prove to be a historic rematch, as we originally pitched it, but Isaac was prescient about this partnership. It has been an incredibly rewarding experience to work so closely with both of you. I am deeply grateful for your friendship and for all that you brought to this project.

Josh: Thank you for your unparalleled reporting abilities, the analytical perspective you imbued throughout the manuscript, for hosting and feeding us at your home, and for ensuring we always had fun. A true highlight of this project was our joint source meetings, during which I became a better reporter from watching you work.

Isaac: Thank you for proposing this idea. Your lyrical writing transformed this project, and your investigative reporting chops combined with your limitless historical knowledge deepened the narrative and the analysis. Our countless conversations about structure and storytelling made me a better writer.

I never thought Ann Godoff would edit my first book. It was an honor to have her brilliance shape this project at every step of the way.

I had the most incredible four years working at *The Washington Post*. Naftali Bendavid, my editor at the *Post*, is a reporter's dream. He made every single story of mine better while simultaneously being an empathetic manager. His influence shines throughout this book. Ashley Parker and Michael Scherer are two of the best journalists I have ever worked alongside. They made me a better reporter and person. My closest partners on the White House beat, Yasmeen Abutaleb and Matt Viser, are tremendously talented and somehow even more kind. They are cherished friends and gifted collaborators.

The *Post* newsroom is filled with so many talented and collegial journalists. A special thank you to those who helped with and supported this project: Dan Balz, Devlin Barrett, Ruby Cramer, Dan Diamond, Dan Eggen, Amy Fiscus, Amy Gardner, Anne Gearan, Matea Gold, Shane Harris, Rosalind Helderman, Molly Hensley-Clancy, John Hudson, Greg Jaffe, Caroline Kitchener, Marianne LeVine, Toluse Olorunnipa, Beth Reinhard, Phil Rucker, Robert Samuels, Marianna Sotomayor, Jeff Stein, Perry Stein, Sean Sullivan, Lena Sun, Ben Terris, Kara Voght, Peter Wallsten, and Cleve Wootson.

I am thrilled to now be part of *The New York Times*, and I am grateful to work under the leadership of Joe Kahn, Carolyn Ryan, and Marc Lacey. In the Washington bureau, I'm thankful to work for Dick Stevenson, Matea Gold, and Elizabeth Kennedy and to be part of the incredible White House team: Peter Baker, Luke Broadwater, Erica Green, Maggie Haberman, Zolan Kanno-Youngs, Shawn McCreesh, Katie Rogers, David Sanger, Michael Shear, and Jonathan Swan.

Since I participated in the Medill Cherubs program at Northwestern University, I've had the support of two mentors: Roger Boye and Charles Whitaker. Their guidance throughout my career has been instrumental, and I am indebted to them for constant encouragement and support. Gina Centrello was the first person to tell me to write a book and provided crucial support from the start of this process.

Writing a book requires a lot of patience and support from those around you. I am privileged that three of my best friends live in Washington, D.C. Josh Goldstein, Alex Herkert, and Bryan Rosenberg accompanied me on runs, indulged in late-night ice cream trips, and joined for dinner parties—providing necessary reprieves from this all-consuming process.

Mary Jo and Dan Viederman welcomed me into their home with bountiful generosity and regularly treated me to the best home-cooked meals. They were unceasingly supportive of this project, even when it interrupted holidays and vacations. And thank you, Dan, for taking our author photo.

Naomi Cohen and Lida Hamber, my incredible grandmothers, remain my biggest cheerleaders and are simply the best. My brothers, Dylan and Austin Pager, whose professional successes are a constant source of inspiration and motivation, and my sister-in-law, Morgan Pager, who is also a new author and generously shared her publishing expertise, provided unending support during this process.

This book is dedicated to three people: my parents, Debbie and Clark Pager, and Hannah Viederman. I decided I wanted to be a journalist while taking an introduction to journalism class during my freshman year of high school. Since then, my parents have supported that dream in every way possible. Thank you for championing this passion without reservation. I couldn't ask for anything more, and for that, I am forever indebted. This book is just as much your accomplishment as it is mine.

Hannah, this book would not have been possible without your constant love and support. You are a brilliant writer and thinker with more self-discipline than anyone I've ever met. You taught me how to write a book and inspire me with your own creative process. You enrich my life in a way I could have never dreamed of. This project—as everything always will be—is for you.

Arnsdorf

From the start of this project, the only goal that was a must for me was that we would still be friends at the end. By that measure, the only one I care about, it was a success.

Working with the legendary Ann Godoff and the entire top-flight team at Penguin Press has been a career highlight and a thrill. So has being part of the *Post*'s politics team and the traveling campaign press corps: Michael Scherer, Ashley Parker, Isaac Stanley-Becker, Beth Reinhard, Robert Samuels, Marianne LeVine, Hannah Knowles, Dylan Wells, Maeve Reston, Sabrina Rodriguez, Kara Voght, Nick Baumann, Annah Aschbrenner, Amy Gardner, Martine Powers, Jeff Stein, Roz Helderman, Dan Diamond, Jackie Alemany, Cat Zakrzewski, Michael Birnbaum, Jabin Botsford, Kate Sullivan, Vaughn Hillyard, Jake Rosen, Jake Traylor, Olivia Rinaldi, Lalee Ibssa, Alayna Treene, Soorin Kim, Libbey Dean, Jillian Frankel, and Michael Gold.

Marilyn Thompson, a cherished friend and mentor for a decade now, reprised her role as expert reader and adviser. Margy Slattery somehow made time to read as well, and her edits were spot-on as always.

Thank you to Liz for generously sharing me with Josh and Tyler. We are so fortunate we got the timing right.

NOTES

We covered the Trump, Biden, and Harris campaigns in real time as reporters for *The Washington Post*. This book is based on more than 350 additional interviews with people across the political spectrum, including those at the senior-most levels of the White House and the campaigns. Where possible we relied on contemporaneous notes, emails, calendar entries, and recordings. Many of the interviews were conducted on the condition of anonymity in order for people to speak candidly; we agreed we could use the information without identifying where we heard it. In most cases we confirmed information with multiple people. Verbatim quotes reflect recordings, notes, transcripts, or firsthand recollections. We gave the people named the opportunity to respond for fairness and accuracy. We provided the Trump White House with thirty pages of detailed points to fact-check and more than a month to review.

Introduction

ix **Trump's personal lawyer, Boris Epshteyn:** Isaac Arnsdorf and Josh Dawsey, "Trump Aide Sought Payments from Job Seekers, Internal Legal Review Found," *Washington Post*, November 25, 2024, www.washingtonpost.com/nation/2024/11/25/trump-epshteyn-legal-review-conflicts.

Chapter 1: Point of No Return

3 **Trump could recount:** Dan Bongino, "Interview with Donald Trump," *Don Bongino Podcast*, May 30, 2024, https://rollcall.com/factbase/trump/transcript/donald-trump-interview-dan-bongino-radio-show-may-30-2024/; "Speech: Turning Point Action Sponsors a Town Hall with Donald Trump in Phoenix—June 6, 2024," *Roll Call*,

NOTES

June 6, 2024, https://rollcall.com/factbase/trump/transcript/donald-trump-speech
-town-hall-turning-point-phoenix-june-6-2024/; "Speech: Donald Trump Holds a
Political Rally in Robstown, Texas—October 22, 2022," *Roll Call*, October 22, 2022,
https://rollcall.com/factbase/trump/transcript/donald-trump-speech-political-rally
-robstown-texas-october-22-2022/; "Press Gaggle: Donald Trump Speaks to Reporters Before Court in New York—October 17, 2023," *Roll Call*, October 17, 2023,
https://rollcall.com/factbase/trump/transcript/donald-trump-press-gaggle-before
-court-new-york-october-17-2023.

5 **He and a few loyal aides:** "Superseding Indictment, United States v. Trump, Nauta,"
Department of Justice, July 23, 2023, www.justice.gov/storage/US-v-Trump-Nauta
-De-Oliveira-23-80101.pdf.

5 **Briefings, memos, maps:** Perry Stein and Devlin Barrett, "Golf Shirts and Classified
Docs: New Court Filings Show Trump's Clutter," *Washington Post*, June 25, 2024,
www.washingtonpost.com/national-security/2024/06/25/trump-classified-photos
-boxes-mar-a-lago.

5 **a phone list, a menu, a napkin:** Ashley Parker, Jacqueline Alemany et al., "15 boxes:
Inside the Long, Strange Trip of Trump's Classified Records," *Washington Post*,
February 12, 2022, www.washingtonpost.com/politics/2022/02/12/trump-15-boxes.

5 **The National Archives started bothering:** Rosalind S. Helderman and Dan
Rosenzweig-Ziff, "A Timeline of What Led to Trump's Classified Documents Indictment," *Washington Post*, June 11, 2023, www.washingtonpost.com/national
-security/2022/08/30/mar-a-lago-timeline-trump-documents.

5 **couldn't they just tell the archives:** Helderman and Rosenzweig-Ziff, "A Timeline
of What Led to Trump's Classified Documents Indictment."

6 **mimed plucking a paper:** Helderman and Rosenzweig-Ziff, "A Timeline of What
Led to Trump's Classified Documents Indictment."

6 **taped-up folder containing the thirty-eight documents:** Rosalind S. Helderman, Josh Dawsey et al., "Trump's Legal Team Divided over How to Handle Mar-
a-Lago Case," *Washington Post*, September 30, 2022, www.washingtonpost.com
/national-security/2022/09/30/trump-lawyers-kise-corcoran-bobb; Helderman and
Rosenzweig-Ziff, "A Timeline of What Led to Trump's Classified Documents Indictment."

6 **"I should have given them dinner":** "Speech: Donald Trump Addresses an NRA
Event in Harrisburg, Pennsylvania—February 9, 2024," *Roll Call*, February 9, 2024,
https://rollcall.com/factbase/trump/transcript/donald-trump-speech-nra-event
-harrisburg-pennsylvania-february-9-2024.

8 **"It made me more resolute":** Donald Trump, interview with Josh Dawsey, January
10, 2025.

8 **Besides the documents investigation:** Shayna Jacobs, David Fahrenthold et al.,
"Prosecutors Allege a 15-Year Tax Fraud Scheme as the Trump Organization
and CFO Allen Weisselberg Are Arraigned on Multiple Criminal Charges,"
Washington Post, July 2, 2021, www.washingtonpost.com/politics/trump-business
-weisselberg-indictments/2021/07/01/e2b774a0-da15-11eb-bb9e-70fda8c37057
_story.html.

8 **federal prosecutors were interviewing former White House officials:** Carol
D. Leonnig, Devlin Barrett et al., "Justice Dept. Investigating Trump's Actions in
Jan. 6 Criminal Probe," *Washington Post*, July 26, 2022, www.washingtonpost.com
/national-security/2022/07/26/trump-justice-investigation-january-6.

8 **The Manhattan district attorney wound down a probe:** Jonah E. Bromwich, Ben Protess et al., "Manhattan Prosecutors Move to Jump-Start Criminal Inquiry into Trump," *New York Times*, November 21, 2022, www.nytimes.com/2022/11/21 /nyregion/trump-bragg-stormy-daniels.html.

8 **The district attorney in Fulton County:** Matthew Brown, "GOP Fake Electors 'Targets' in Georgia Election Fraud Inquiry," *Washington Post*, July 19, 2022, www .washingtonpost.com/national-security/2022/07/19/georgia-fake-electors.

9 **"I decided to start the campaign then":** Donald Trump, interview with Josh Dawsey, January 10, 2025.

12 **went on a rampage:** Isaac Arnsdorf et al, "Inside the Collapse of the Trump-DeSantis 'Alliance of Convenience,'" *Washington Post*, February 18, 2023, www .washingtonpost.com/politics/2023/02/18/trump-desantis-relationship-2024 -election.

15 **He froze, tricked and cornered:** Tim Alberta, "Trump Is Planning for a Landslide Win, *The Atlantic*, July 2024, https://archive.is/aejQq.

16 **Trump polled his confidants:** Isaac Arnsdorf, Josh Dawsey et al., "Trump Team Pushes to Delay 2024 Launch as DeSantis Star Rises in GOP," *Washington Post*, November 9, 2022, www.washingtonpost.com/politics/2022/11/09/trump-presidential -announcement-delay.

18 **"the Chickenshit Club":** Jesse Eisinger, *The Chickenshit Club: Why the Justice Department Fails to Prosecute Executives* (New York: Simon & Schuster, 2017).

19 **"Enough is enough'":** "Remarks: Donald Trump Addresses the Appointment of a Special Counsel - November 18, 2022," *Roll Call*, November 18, 2022, https://roll call.com/factbase/trump/transcript/donald-trump-remarks-special-counsel -appointment-palm-beach-florida-november-18-2022/#25.

Chapter 2: Not Dead

21 **former aides had launched a PAC and a nonprofit:** Ashley Balcerzak, "Murphy Allies Launch Two Political Fundraising Groups to Back Candidates, Push Agenda," NorthJersey.com, February 7, 2022, www.northjersey.com/story/news/2022/02/07 /gov-phil-murphy-stronger-fairer-forward-pac/6691560001.

22 **J. B. Pritzker, who had deployed his family's hospitality:** Elena Schneider, "The Dem Governors Who Could Run in 2024 if Biden Doesn't," *Politico*, June 23, 2022, www.politico.com/news/2022/06/23/democratic-governors-2024-presidential -election-00041614.

22 **Senator Bernie Sanders was open to another run:** Sean Sullivan, "Sanders 'Has Not Ruled Out Another Run for President' if Biden Doesn't," *Washington Post*, April 20, 2022, www.washingtonpost.com/politics/2022/04/20/sanders-president-2024.

26 **raised the president's age as a concern:** Reid J. Epstein and Jennifer Medina, "Should Biden Run in 2024? Democratic Whispers of 'No' Start to Rise," *New York Times*, June 11, 2022, www.nytimes.com/2022/06/11/us/politics/biden-2024 -election-democrats.html.

26 **Biden was a man who'd first introduced himself:** Evan Osnos, "Why Biden Didn't Run," *New Yorker*, October 21, 2015, www.newyorker.com/news/news-desk/why -biden-didnt-run.

28 **indecisive and secretive:** Christopher Cadelago, Daniel Lippman, and Eugene Daniels, "'Not a Healthy Environment': Kamala Harris' Office Rife with Dissent,"

Politico, June 30, 2021, www.politico.com/news/2021/06/30/kamala-harris-office
-dissent-497290.

30 **"You all . . . declare me dead"**: Gabriel Debenedetti, "The Vindication (for Now) of
Joe Biden Being Underestimated Is Not New to Those Who've Been with Him
from the Start," *New York*, November 11, 2022, https://nymag.com/intelligencer
/2022/11/midterm-results-the-vindication-for-now-of-joe-biden.html.

34 **Lowell's hiring prompted Josh Levy**: Kenneth P. Vogel, Maggie Haberman et al.,
"Abbe Lowell Built Ties to Trump World. Now He's One of Hunter Biden's
Lawyers," *New York Times*, February 28, 2023, www.nytimes.com/2023/02/28/us
/politics/abbe-lowell-hunter-biden-ivanka-trump-kushner.html.

Chapter 3: Just Business

35 **"A Massive Fraud of this type"**: Donald J. Trump, Truth Social post, December 3,
2022, https://truthsocial.com/@realDonaldTrump/posts/109449803240069864.

39 **"They told me anybody wearing Trump"**: Laura Loomer, X (formerly Twitter) post,
February 28, 2023, https://x.com/LauraLoomer/status/1630723636263878656.

41 **A story appeared in *The Daily Beast***: Zachary Petrizzo and Jake Lahut, "The GOP
Campaign Trail Is Already Getting DeSantis Proofed," *Daily Beast*, March 16,
2023, www.thedailybeast.com/the-republican-2024-presidential-campaign-trail
-is-already-getting-gov-ron-desantis-proofed.

42 **He took up the term "groomer"**: Kimberly Leonard, "Trump Shares Photos of Desantis Alleging He Parties and Drank with High School Girls When He Was
a Teacher," *Business Insider*, February 7, 2023, www.businessinsider.com/trump
-shares-photos-of-desantis-alleging-partied-with-high-schoolers-2023-2.

42 **He dramatized the story**: Lauren Sforza, "Trump Says Desantis Came to Him
'with Tears in His Eyes' to Ask for an Endorsement," The Hill, March 26, 2023,
https://thehill.com/homenews/campaign/3918896-trump-says-desantis
-came-to-him-with-tears-in-his-eyes-to-ask-for-an-endorsement.

42 **told reporters that if not for his endorsement**: Donald Trump, interview with Isaac
Arnsdorf, March 13, 2023.

Chapter 4: Inevitable

45 **Trump started joking**: Ashley Parker and Josh Dawsey, "Trump and Advisers
Caught Off Guard by New York Indictment," *Washington Post*, March 31, 2023,
www.washingtonpost.com/politics/2023/03/30/trump-indictment-suprised.

46 **they were informed that Trump had been indicted**: Parker and Dawsey, Trump and
Advisers Caught Off Guard by New York Indictment."

47 **In the 1970s, federal prosecutors accused Trump**: Michael Kranish and Robert
O'Harrow, "Inside the Government's Racial Bias Case Against Donald Trump's
Company, and How He Fought It," *Washington Post*, January 23, 2016, www.wash
ingtonpost.com/politics/inside-the-governments-racial-bias-case-against
-donald-trumps-company-and-how-he-fought-it/2016/01/23/fb90163e-bfbe
-11e5-bcda-62a36b394160_story.html?itid=cb_box_QAIWCOSQQFDY5P77
SABPADUIII_2.

47 **In the '80s, he worked closely with an FBI informant**: Robert O'Harrow, "Trump's
Ties to an Informant and FBI Agent Reveal His Mode of Operation," *Washington*

Post, September 16, 2016, www.washingtonpost.com/investigations/trumps-ties
-to-an-informant-and-fbi-agent-reveal-his-modes-of-operation/2016/09/16
/6e65522e-6f9f-11e6-9705-23e51a2f424d_story.html.

47 **The '90s and 2000s brought more state and federal scrutiny:** Rosalind S. Helderman, "Judge Approves $25 Million Settlement in Trump University Cases," *Wash-
ington Post*, March 31, 2017, www.washingtonpost.com/news/post-politics/wp/2017
/03/31/judge-approves-25-million-settlement-in-trump-university-cases/?itid=cb
_box_QAIWCOSQQFDY5P77SABPADUIII_3.

49 **He was tying their fates together:** Donald J. Trump, X (formerly Twitter) post,
August 12, 2024, https://x.com/realDonaldTrump/status/1822890929855811931
?lang=en.:.//www.youtube.com/watch?v=2nimBA71Y.

49 **"'This case is ridiculous'":** Donald Trump, interview with Josh Dawsey, January 10,
2025.

53 **One allied effort found that voters' affinity:** Benjamin Wallace-Wells, "The Ron
DeSantis Slump," *New Yorker*, August 14, 2023, www.newyorker.com/news/the
-political-scene/the-ron-desantis-slump.

54 **Trump criticized DeSantis for signing a ban on abortions:** Allan Smith, "Trump
Criticizes Republicans Pushing Abortion Bans with No Exceptions: 'You're Not
Going to Win,'" NBC News, September 16, 2023, www.nbcnews.com/politics
/donald-trump/trump-bring-country-together-abortion-meet-the-press
-rcna105311.

54 **A *Des Moines Register* poll:** Michaela Ramm and Stephen Gruber-Miller, "Economy, Immigration Most Often Listed as 'Extremely Important' Issues by GOP Cau-
cusgoers," *Des Moines Register*, November 1, 2023, www.desmoinesregister
.com/story/news/politics/iowa-poll/caucus/2023/11/01/iowa-poll-how-republican
-caucusgoers-rank-issues-from-the-economy-to-abortion-israel-ukraine/71328
389007.

54 **News reports said a pro-DeSantis outside group:** Julia Manchester, "Group Backing Desantis Rolls Out Ad Campaign Hitting Trump over Abortion Remarks," The
Hill, October 23, 2023, https://thehill.com/policy/healthcare/4284202-group
-backing-desantis-rolls-out-ad-campaign-hitting-trump-over-abortion-remarks.

56 **Seven inmates had died there:** Ben Brasch, "Trump Could Be Booked in Violent
Atlanta Jail with Crumbling Walls," *Washington Post*, August 18, 2023, www
.washingtonpost.com/national-security/2023/08/18/fulton-jail-trump-indicted
-mugshot.

Chapter 5: Sleepwalking

64 **He started wearing sneakers:** Alex Thompson, "Scoop: Biden Team's Don't-Let-
Him-Trip Mission," *Axios*, September 26, 2023, www.axios.com/2023/09/26/biden-
trip-2024-campaign-sneakers.

65 **Katzenberg had encouraged the president:** Ken Thomas and Catherine Lucey, "Jeffrey Katzenberg's Very Hollywood Advice for Joe Biden," *Wall Street Journal*, June
26, 2023, www.wsj.com/articles/joe-biden-jeffrey-katzenberg-advice-b268d2ec.

65 **Donors often left satisfied:** Tyler Pager and Michael Scherer, "Biden Holding Private Meetings at White House to Reassure Supporters," *Washington Post*, January
10, 2024, www.washingtonpost.com/politics/2024/01/10/biden-holding-private
-meetings-white-house-reassure-supporters.

68 consumer prices rose 8.2 percent: Gwynn Guilford, "Inflation Sits at 8.2% as Core Prices Hit Four Decade High," *Wall Street Journal*, October 13, 2022, www.wsj.com/articles/us-inflation-september-2022-consumer-price-index-11665628037.

69 appropriate the name "Bidenomics": Reid J. Epstein, "Biden Struggles to Make 'Bidenomics' a Plus, Not a Minus," *New York Times*, September 2, 2023, www.nytimes.com/2023/09/02/us/politics/biden-economy-inflation-voters.html.

70 When the plea deal collapsed: Tyler Pager, "Hunter Biden Stays Close to Father at White House amid Criminal Probe," *Washington Post*, August 17, 2023, www.washingtonpost.com/politics/2023/08/17/hunter-biden-investigation-white-house.

Chapter 6: Capitulation

77 "Bye, bye," she posted: Susie Wiles, X (formerly Twitter) post, January 20, 2024, https://x.com/susie57/status/1748924190831354002.

78 he predicted backstage on a hot mic: Madison Fernandez and Alex Isenstadt, "Christie Caught on Hot Mic: Haley Is 'Gonna Get Smoked,'" *Politico*, January 10, 2024, www.politico.com/news/2024/01/10/christie-caught-on-hot-mic-haley-is-gonna-get-smoked-00134887.

79 Her case became harder to doubt: Holly Bailey and Amy Gardner, "Trump Co-Defendant Jenna Ellis Pleads Guilty in Georgia Election Case," *Washington Post*, October 24, 2023, www.washingtonpost.com/national-security/2023/10/24/jenna-ellis-plea-deal-georgia.

80 he and Willis were in a romantic relationship: Amy Gardner and Holly Bailey, "How a Sleuth Defense Attorney and a Disgruntled Law Partner Damaged the Trump Georgia Case," *Washington Post*, March 16, 2024, www.washingtonpost.com/national-security/2024/03/16/fani-willis-misconduct-accusations-ashleigh-merchant.

80 many lawyers, including Trump's, were skeptical: Gardner and Bailey, "How a Sleuth Defense Attorney and a Disgruntled Law Partner Damaged the Trump Georgia Case."

80 He told his attorney: Gardner and Bailey, "How a Sleuth Defense Attorney and a Disgruntled Law Partner Damaged the Trump Georgia Case."

83 calls to pressure: Craig Mauger, "Trump Recorded Pressuring Wayne County Canvassers Not to Certify 2020 Vote," *Detroit News*, December 21, 2023, www.detroitnews.com/story/news/politics/2023/12/21/donald-trump-recorded-pressuring-wayne-canvassers-not-to-certify-2020-vote-michigan/72004514007.

84 McDaniel maintained there were some "problems": Todd J. Gillman, "GOP Chair Ronna McDaniel Concedes That Joe Biden Beat Donald Trump, Sort Of," *Dallas Morning News*, November 18, 2021, www.dallasnews.com/news/politics/2021/11/18/gop-chair-ronna-mcdaniel-concedes-that-joe-biden-beat-donald-trump-sort-of.

Chapter 7: A Poor Memory

91 For Hatch Act purposes: Tyler Pager and Michael Scherer, "Biden Campaign to Open Office near White House," *Washington Post*, January 26, 2024, www.washingtonpost.com/politics/2024/01/26/biden-campaign-washington-office.

92 fourteenth-best president: Peter Baker, "Poll Ranks Biden as 14th-Best President, with Trump Last," *New York Times*, February 18, 2024, www.nytimes.com/2024/02/18/us/politics/biden-trump-presidential-rankings.html.

NOTES

93 **The news website *Axios* had reported:** Alex Thompson, "Biden's Team Bracing for Special Counsel's Report on Classified Docs," *Axios*, February 4, 2024, www.axios.com/2024/02/04/biden-special-counsel-classified-docs-trump.

93 **"a sympathetic, well-meaning, elderly man":** Robert K. Hur, "Report from Special Counsel Robert K. Hur February 2024," U.S. Department of Justice, February 5, 2024, www.justice.gov/storage/report-from-special-counsel-robert-k-hur-february-2024.pdf.

96 **Biden twice mistakenly referred to the late German Chancellor:** Matt Viser and Tyler Pager, "Special Counsel Report Paints Scathing Picture of Biden's Memory," *Washington Post*, February 8, 2024, www.washingtonpost.com/politics/2024/02/08/biden-memory-special-counsel-report-robert-hur.

96 **turning down an audience of tens of millions:** Ashley Parker, Michael Scherer et al., "'Hair on Fire': Democratic Worries Grow over Claims About Biden's Memory Lapses," *Washington Post*, February 9, 2024, www.washingtonpost.com/politics/2024/02/09/biden-memory-age-hur-documents.

97 **his aides handpicked reporters:** Paul Farhi, "The Dirty Little Secret of White House News Conferences," *Washington Post*, April 27, 2023,www.washingtonpost.com/media/2023/04/27/white-house-press-conference-questions-biden.

97 **the president received his annual physical:** Darlene Superville and Will Weissert, "Biden 'Continues to Be Fit for Duty,' His Doctor Says, After President Undergoes Annual Physical," Associated Press, February 28, 2024, https://apnews.com/article/biden-physical-health-oldest-president-reelection-trump-05668d241d1a67b51b2a91c302c38985.

97 **Sometimes it was thirty-six hours:** Matt Viser, "As Biden and Xi Meet, Can Their Old Connection Avert a Clash?," *Washington Post*, November 12, 2022, www.washingtonpost.com/politics/2022/11/12/biden-xi-meet-avert-clash.

98 **Harris expressed concerns:** Adrian Carrasquillo, "'Can I Just Vote for Her Instead of Biden?': Inside Kamala's Scramble to Win the Latino Vote," *Politico*, August 26, 2024, www.politico.com/news/magazine/2024/08/26/kamala-harris-latino-voters-00173976.

99 **she had been privately telling her aides:** Cleve R. Woodson Jr., Tyler Pager et al., "Harris Takes More Public Role Criticizing Israel's Actions in Gaza," *Washington Post*, March 4, 2024, www.washingtonpost.com/politics/2024/03/04/harris-gaza-israel-ceasefire-humanitarian-aid.

99 **she delivered a major speech:** Erica L. Green, "Harris Calls for an 'Immediate Cease-Fire' in Gaza," *New York Times*, March 3, 2023, www.nytimes.com/2024/03/03/world/middleeast/kamala-harris-cease-fire.html.

100 **largest Muslim communities:** Yasmeen Abutaleb, "Michigan Arabs and Muslims Deeply Split over Supporting Harris," *Washington Post*, October 24, 2024, www.washingtonpost.com/politics/2024/10/24/kamala-harris-arab-american-muslims-michigan.

100 **200,000 registered voters:** Mohamed Gula and Aysha Ahmed, "Impact 2020: The Million Muslim Votes Campaign Voter Turnout Report," Emgage, https://emgageusa.org/wp-content/uploads/2022/06/Emgage-ImpactReport-2020-v2.4-lr-1.pdf.

101 **Days before the speech:** Shane Goldmacher, "Voters Doubt Biden's Leadership and Favor Trump, Times/Siena Poll Finds," *Washington Post*, February 3, 2024, www.nytimes.com/2024/03/02/us/politics/biden-trump-times-siena-poll.html.

101 "The speech is good. Let's practice": Tyler Pager, "Joe Biden's Obsessive Search for the Right Words," *Washington Post*, March 15, 2024, www.washingtonpost.com /politics/2024/03/15/joe-bidens-private-speech-prep-can-be-scary-his-aides.

102 Biden never spoke Trump's name: President Joseph R. Biden, "State of the Union Address," White House Briefing Room, March 8, 2024, www.whitehouse.gov /briefing-room/speeches-remarks/2024/03/08/remarks-by-president -biden-in-state-of-the-union-address-3.

103 launched an independent bid: "2024 Race for President Remains Tied Between Former President Trump and President Biden," Reuters/Ipsos Poll, March 18, 2024, www.ipsos.com/en-us/2024-race-president-remains-tied-between-former -president-trump-and-president-biden.

103 first-ever team dedicated to counter third-party: Alex Seitz-Wald, "Democrats Prepare to Go to War Against Third-Party Candidates," NBC News, March 14, 2024, www.nbcnews.com/politics/2024-election/dnc-war-third-party-candidates -rcna143290.

103 more than four dozen members of the Kennedy family: Kerry Kennedy, Instagram post, March 21, 2024, www.instagram.com/p/C4yXOxov9I-.

103 RFK Jr.'s siblings endorsed Biden: Tyler Pager, "Kennedy Family Members' Embrace Carries Deeper Meaning for Biden," *Washington Post*, April 21, 2024, www .washingtonpost.com/politics/2024/04/21/biden-kennedy-family-members -endorsement-catholic-tragedy-rfk-jfk.

Chapter 8: A Takeover

113 allegations of fraud in the 2020 election weren't true: Josh Dawsey and Michael Scherer, "Top RNC Lawyer Resigns After Rift Grows with Trump," *Washington Post*, May 4, 2024, www.washingtonpost.com/politics/2024/05/04/trump-rnc -spies-election-fraud.

Chapter 9: Criminal

120 The penalty announced: Shayna Jacobs and Mark Berman, "Judge Orders Trump to Pay More Than $350 Million After Civil Fraud Trial," *Washington Post*, February 16, 2024,www.washingtonpost.com/politics/2024/02/16/judge-engoron-ruling -trump-ny-civil-fraud-trial.

120 $83.3 million penalty: Jonathan O'Connell, Shayna Jacobs et al., "Clock Is Ticking for Trump to Post Bonds Worth Half a Million Dollars," *Washington Post*, February 26, 2024, www.washingtonpost.com/investigations/2024/02/26/trump-money -bonds-engoron-carroll.

125 give him $1 billion: Josh Dawsey and Maxine Joselow, "What Trump Promised Oil CEOs as He Asked Them to Steer $1 Billion to His Campaign," *Washington Post*, May 9, 2024, www.washingtonpost.com/politics/2024/05/09/trump-oil-industry -campaign-money.

130 opposed letting Epshteyn come to the trial: Indictment, *State of Arizona v. Kelli Ward, Tyler Bowyer, Nancy Cottle* et al., www.azag.gov/sites/default/files/2024-05 /PHX-%2312079639-v1-TRUE_BILL_-_INDICTMENT_93_SGJ_81.PDF.

131 Trump invited on stage two rappers: Kate Sullivan, "Trump Shares Stage at Bronx Rally with Rappers Indicted over Alleged Conspiracy to Commit Murder,"

CNN, May 24, 2024, www.cnn.com/2024/05/24/politics/trump-rappers-bronx -rally-indicted/index.html.

Chapter 10: The Block

135 **Polls showed Biden trailing:** Lenny Bronner et al, "Who Is Ahead in Harris vs. Trump 2024 Presidential Polls Right Now?" *Washington Post*, November 5, 2024, www.washingtonpost.com/elections/interactive/2024/presidential-polling -averages.

136 **Hunter Biden reported to the J. Caleb Boggs Federal Building:** Matt Viser, "Hunter Biden's Trial Unfolds in a City Deeply Tied to His Family," *Washington Post*, June 4, 2024, www.washingtonpost.com/politics/2024/06/04/hunter-biden -wilmington-trial.

137 **he could be unnecessarily harsh:** Alex Thompson and Tina Sfondeles, "Jill's En- forcer Has a Mean Streak," *Politico*, August 2, 2021, www.politico.com/newsletters /west-wing-playbook/2021/08/02/jills-enforcer-has-a-mean-streak-493812.

137 **"fire you on the spot":** Shawna Chen, "Biden to Staffers: 'I Will Fire You on the Spot' for Disrespecting Others," *Axios*, January 20, 2021, www.axios.com/2021/01 /21/biden-fire-staffers-disrespecting-others.

138 **Jill Biden's seventy-third birthday:** Kara Voght, "At Hunter Biden's Trial, Jill Biden Can Only Watch," *Washington Post*, June 6, 2024, www.washingtonpost .com/style/2024/06/06/jill-biden-hunter-biden-trial.

138 **Ashley Biden cried:** Voght, "At Hunter Biden's trial, Jill Biden can only watch."

139 **"I'm really sorry, dad":** Eileen Sullivan, Glenn Thrush et al., "Hunter Biden's Daughter Naomi Testifies on His Behalf in Gun Trial," *New York Times*, July 6, 2024, www.nytimes.com/2024/06/07/us/politics/hunter-biden-trial-naomi-testimony .html.

139 **The verdict came:** Perry Stein, David Nakamura et al., "Hunter Biden Found Guilty in Gun Trial That Exposed Dark Parts of His Life," *Washington Post*, June 11, 2024, www.washingtonpost.com/national-security/2024/06/11/hunter-biden-verdict -gun-trial.

139 **It happened so quickly:** Glenn Thrush, Eileen Sullivan et al., "Rapid Verdict Took Biden Family by Surprise as They Rushed to the Courtroom," *New York Times*, June 11, 2024, www.nytimes.com/2024/06/11/us/politics/biden-family-verdict-court room.html.

143 **Clooney complained about it directly:** Tyler Pager and Ashley Parker, "George Cloo- ney Called White House to Defend Wife's Work on Israel Warrants," *Washington Post*, www.washingtonpost.com/politics/2024/06/06/george-clooney-biden-criminal -court-israel.

Chapter 11: "We're F—ed"

148 **"Love *War Room*":** Grace Chong. X (formerly Twitter) post, June 17, 2024. https:// x.com/gc22gc/status/1802728255558160414.

154 **At the party, a DJ:** Alan Binder, "At One Post-Debate Party, President Biden Found a Jubilant Reception," *New York Times*, June 28, 2024, www.nytimes.com/2024/06 /28/us/biden-debate-watch-party.html.

155 **"Let us not decide the outcome of who's going to be president":** "Kamala Harris

Reacts to Pres. Biden's Debate Performance: He 'Did Not Get Off to a Strong Start,'" ABC News, June 27, 2024, www.youtube.com/watch?v=Rx3GecStvos.

159 The *New York Times* editorial board: "To Serve His Country, President Biden Should Leave the Race," *New York Times*, June 28, 2024, www.nytimes.com/2024/06/28/opinion/biden-election-debate-trump.html.

159 "The last time Joe Biden lost the *New York Times* editorial board's": Patrick Svitek, "New York Times Editorial Board Calls on Biden to Drop Out of the Race," *Washington Post*, June 28, 2024, www.washingtonpost.com/politics/2024/06/28/new-york-times-editorial-biden-drop-out.

159 Even Joe Scarborough, who Biden watched almost religiously: Michael M. Grynbaum, "One by One, Biden's Closest Media Allies Defect After the Debate," *New York Times*, June 28, 2024, www.nytimes.com/2024/06/28/us/politics/biden-media-allies-debate.html.

162 Biden arrived at the $137 million home: Katherine Clarke, "Hedge Fund Exec Barry Rosenstein Lists Hamptons Estate for $70 Million," *Wall Street Journal*, November 16, 2017, www.wsj.com/articles/hedge-fund-exec-barry-rosenstein-lists-hamptons-estate-for-70-million-1510784795.

162 encouraging the president to eat vegetables: Alex Thompson, "The Food Fight in the White House: Biden's Diet," *Axios*, May 8, 2023, www.axios.com/2023/05/08/food-fight-white-house.

163 She wanted to know why they allowed: Katie Rogers, "As Her Husband Faces Tumult, Jill Biden Is a Protective Force," *New York Times*, September 2, 2024, www.nytimes.com/2024/02/09/us/politics/jill-biden-joe-biden.html.

163 He then confused Italy for France: "Remarks by President Biden at a Campaign Reception, East Hampton, NY," White House Briefing Room, June 29, 2024, https://web.archive.org/web/20240805071950/https://www.whitehouse.gov/briefing-room/speeches-remarks/2024/06/29/remarks-by-president-biden-at-a-campaign-reception-east-hampton-ny.

164 An internal memo in May had outlined scenarios: Alex Isenstadt, "Trump Campaign Began Preparing for Biden Exit in May, Confidential Memo Shows," *Politico*, July 22, 2024, www.politico.com/live-updates/2024/07/22/kamala-harris-campaign-biden-drop-out/trump-kamala-harris-biden-00170471.

Chapter 12: The Drumbeat

167 OpenLabs found Biden trailing: "Post-Debate Landscape," Puck News, June 30, 2024, https://puck.news/wp-content/uploads/2024/07/SUNDAY_Post-Debate_Landscape_2024_06_30__1_-1.pdf.

171 Governor Janet Mills of Maine: Maggie Haberman, Shawn Hubler et al., "Biden Tells Governors That He Is Staying in the Race," *New York Times*, March 7, 2024, www.nytimes.com/2024/07/03/us/politics/biden-governors-presidential-election-debate.html.

171 The president said he was fine: Matt Viser, Tyler Pager et al., "Biden Told Governors He Needs to Get More Sleep, Avoid Events After 8 P.M.," *Washington Post*, April 7, 2024, www.washingtonpost.com/politics/2024/07/04/biden-independence-day-message-trump-values.

172 Biden, seeming to jumble serving as Obama's vice president: Hannah Abraham, "Biden's Bad Week Just Got Worse After He Said He Was the 'First Black Woman

to Serve with a Black President," *Business Insider*, July 5, 2024, www.businessinsider
.com/joe-biden-proud-first-black-woman-serve-white-house-slip-2024-7.

172 **group of senators going over to the White House:** Leigh Ann Caldwell and Liz
Goodwin, "Sen. Mark Warner Works to Gather Senate Democrats to Ask Biden to
Exit Race," *Washington Post*, July 5, 2024, www.washingtonpost.com/politics
/2024/07/05/mark-warner-joe-biden-exit-race-democratic-senators.

174 **"tell me it's a toss-up":** "ABC's George Stephanopoulos' Exclusive Interview with
President Joe Biden," ABC News, July 5, 2024, https://abcnews.go.com/Politics
/abc-news-anchor-george-stephanopoulos-exclusive-interview-biden/story?id
=111695695.

175 **another House Democrat:** Riley Hoffman and Ivan Pereira, "Congressional Democrats Respond to Biden's Interview with ABC News," ABC News, July 6, 2024,
https://abcnews.go.com/Politics/congressional-democrats-respond-bidens
-interview-abc-news/story?id=111708326.

176 **He sent a two-page letter:** "Letter to the Democratic Party on Intention to Accept
the Presidential Nomination," American Presidency Project, July 8, 2024, www
.presidency.ucsb.edu/documents/letter-the-democratic-party-intention-accept
-the-presidential-nomination.

178 **top donors and bundlers had given up:** Elena Schneider, "Dems Fear Biden's Fundraising Is 'Cratering,'" *Politico*, October 7, 2024, www.politico.com/news/2024/07
/10/dems-fear-biden-fundraising-cratering-00167496.

179 **"I want him to do whatever he decides to do":** "Nancy Pelosi: It's Up to Biden to Decide if He's Going to Run. Whatever He Decides, We Go With," MSNBC, July 10,
2024, www.msnbc.com/morning-joe/watch/nancy-pelosi-it-s-up-to-biden-to-decide
-if-he-s-going-to-run-214554181531.

180 **George Clooney published an op-ed:** George Clooney, "I Love Joe Biden. But We
Need a New Nominee," *New York Times*, July 10, 2024, www.nytimes.com/2024
/07/10/opinion/joe-biden-democratic-nominee.html.

182 **Senator Peter Welch of Vermont published an op-ed:** Peter Welch, "Biden Should
Withdraw for the Good of the Country," *Washington Post*, July 10, 2024, www
.washingtonpost.com/opinions/2024/07/10/welch-biden-withdraw.

183 **two independent neurologists should evaluate Biden:** Carl Hulse, "How Biden's
Senate Allies Helped Push Him from the Race," *New York Times*, August 29, 2024,
www.nytimes.com/2024/08/29/us/politics/senate-democrats-biden-drop-out
.html.

184 **It didn't help that he answered a question:** Michael D. Shear, "In News Conference,
Biden Has Slips but Shows Strength on Foreign Policy," *New York Times*, July 11, 2024,
www.nytimes.com/2024/07/11/us/politics/biden-high-stakes-news-conference
.html.

Chapter 13: July 13, 2024

194 **asked his father for his AR-15:** "Butler Investigation Evidence Photos," Federal
Bureau of Investigation, August 28, 2024, www.fbi.gov/news/press-releases/butler
-investigation-photos.

194 **He said he was going to the gun range:** "Final Report of Findings and Recommendations of the Task Force on the Attempted Assassination of Donald J. Trump,"
United States House of Representatives, December 5, 2024, https://taskforce

.house.gov/sites/evo-subsites/july13taskforce.house.gov/files/evo-media
-document/12-5-2024-Final-Report-Redacted.pdf, 18.

194 **Crooks had taken the day off:** John Miller, "Trump Shooter Requested Saturday Off from Work and Told Colleagues He'd Be Back at Work Sunday, Officials Say," CNN, July 16, 2024, www.cnn.com/2024/07/16/politics/trump-shooter-requested -saturday-off-from-work/index.html.

194 **He didn't leave a manifesto:** John Woodrow Cox and Steven Rich, "A 20-Year-Old's Perplexing Place in the Catalogue of American Gunmen," *Washington Post*, July 21, 2024, www.washingtonpost.com/investigations/2024/07/21/thomas-crooks-adam -lanza-shooters-assassins.

194 **He was quiet, did well in school:** Emily Davies, Devlin Barrett et al., "Trump Rally Shooter Appears to Have Acted Alone, FBI Says," *Washington Post*, July 14, 2024, www.washingtonpost.com/nation/2024/07/14/thomas-matthew-crooks -trump-shooting-suspect.

194 **a black SwissGear backpack:** "Butler Investigation Evidence Photos."

194 **packed a drone and improvised bombs:** "Final Report of Findings and Recommendations of the Task Force on the Attempted Assassination of Donald J. Trump," 24.

195 **red-carpeted stage and bunting-adorned bleachers:** Elon Musk, X (formerly Twitter) post, October 29, 2024, https://x.com/elonmusk/status/1851359164259582178? s=46.

195 **it looked like an angel:** "Butler Rally Survivors Tell Their Story: 'We All Prayed,'" *The John Fredericks Show*, https://rumble.com/v5hgee5-roundtable-butler-rally -survivors-tell-their-story-we-all-prayed.html.

196 **took out a range finder:** "Final Report of Findings and Recommendations of the Task Force on the Attempted Assassination of Donald J. Trump," 31.

196 **"how far was oswald from kennedy":** "Final Report of Findings and Recommendations of the Task Force on the Attempted Assassination of Donald J. Trump," 17.

196 **The sniper Crooks had spotted:** "Final Report of Findings and Recommendations of the Task Force on the Attempted Assassination of Donald J. Trump," 34.

196 **Several police officers started searching:** "Final Report of Findings and Recommendations of the Task Force on the Attempted Assassination of Donald J. Trump," 36.

196 **Nicol reported the sighting:** Shawn Boburg et al., "'We Lost Sight of Him': Radio Traffic Shows Failed Search for Trump Rally Shooter," *Washington Post*, August 3, 2024, www.washingtonpost.com/investigations/2024/08/03/trump-rally-police -radio-transmissions.

197 **"He's got a gun!":** "Final Report of Findings and Recommendations of the Task Force on the Attempted Assassination of Donald J. Trump," 41–42.

198 **It was misleadingly labeled:** Philip Bump, "A Look at Trump's Misleading, Inaccurate Graph of U.S. Immigration," *Washington* Post, May 23, 2024, www.washing tonpost.com/politics/2024/05/23/look-trumps-misleading-inaccurate-graph-us -immigration.

198 *My God*, **Biden thought:** "Joe Biden Interview with Lester Holt," NBC News, July 15, 2024, www.nbcnews.com/politics/2024-election/transcript-read-full-biden -interview-lester-holt-nbc-news-rcna162029.

200 **the agency had established an emergency plan:** Hannah Webster, "Pa. Hospital

Had a Response Plan in Place Years Before the Trump Rally Shooting," *Pittsburgh Post-Gazette*, July 15, 2024, www.post-gazette.com/news/health/2024/07/15/butler -memorial-hospital-trump/stories/202407160009.

200–201 **The medical center went into lockdown:** Ron Southwick, "Pa. Hospital That Treated Donald Trump After Assassination Attempt Relied on Preparation and Focus," *Chief Healthcare Executive*, July 18, 2024, www.chiefhealthcareexecutive .com/view/pa-hospital-that-treated-donald-trump-after-assassination-attempt -relied-on-preparation-and-focus.

201 **in the ER:** Disrespected Status, X (formerly Twitter) post, December 25, 2024, https://x.com/disrespectedthe/status/1872023815678812658?s=42.

201 **He didn't want the visual:** Donald Trump, interview with Josh Dawsey, January 10, 2025.

201 **"bleeding like a bitch":** Trump interview, January 10, 2025.

202 **buy a lottery ticket:** Trump interview, January 10, 2025.

Chapter 14: Unity

205 **Why wouldn't they try and kill you:** "Tucker Carlson Interview with Donald Trump," Rev.com, August 23, 2023, www.rev.com/transcripts/tucker-on-x-debate -night-interview-with-donald-trump-transcript.

206 **constitutional amendment banning abortion:** "Reagan-Mondale Presidential Debate," Commission on Presidential Debates, October 7, 1984, www.debates.org /voter-education/debate-transcripts/october-7-1984-debate-transcript.

207 **which ran for sixty-six pages:** 2016 Republican Platform, https://prod-cdn-static .gop.com/media/documents/DRAFT_12_FINAL%5B1%5D-ben_1468872234 .pdf.

207 **fit on sixteen pages:** 2024 GOP Platform Make America Great Again!, American Presidency Project, July 8, 2024, www.presidency.ucsb.edu/documents/2024 -republican-party-platform.

207 **"based on thin air":** Donald J. Trump, X (formerly Twitter) post, July 11, 2019, https://x.com/realDonaldTrump/status/1149472282584072192?lang=en.

209 **platform was toned down on abortion:** "Statement on Proposed 2024 Republican Party Platform, Faith and Freedom Coalition," www.ffcoalition.com/statement -on-proposed-2024-republican-party-platform.

212 **Vance stunned him by apologizing:** Jonathan Swan and Maggie Haberman, "How JD Vance Won Over Donald Trump," *New York Times*, July 16, 2024, www.nytimes .com/2024/07/16/us/politics/trump-vance-vp-decision.html.

213 **"I have to get off this train":** Ross Douthat, "What JD Vance Believes," *New York Times*, June 13, 2024, www.nytimes.com/2024/06/13/opinion/jd-vance-interview .html.

213 **Trump was keeping close track:** JD Vance, "Trump's Best Foreign Policy? Not Starting Any Wars," *Wall Street Journal*, January 31, 2023, www.wsj.com/articles /trumps-best-foreign-policy-not-starting-any-wars-ukraine-russia-war-rocket -nuclear-power-weapons-defense-1167518695.9

220 **Trump spoke for ninety minutes:** "Trump Delivers Longest-Ever Convention Acceptance Speech," NBC News, July 19, 2024, www.nbcnews.com/politics/trump -delivers-longest-ever-convention-acceptance-speech-politics-desk-rcna162569.

Chapter 15: Lord Almighty

221 **In an interview with NBC's Lester Holt:** "Joe Biden Interview with Lester Holt," NBC News, July 15, 2024, www.nbcnews.com/politics/2024-election/transcript -read-full-biden-interview-lester-holt-nbc-news-rcna162029.

225 **It took him longer to descend the steps:** Zolan Kanno-Youngs, "From Buoyant to Frail: Two Days in Las Vegas as Biden Tests Positive," *New York Times*, July 18, 2024, www.nytimes.com/2024/07/18/us/politics/biden-covid-democrats.html.

226 **Biden started to feel better on Friday:** Katie Rogers, Michael D. Shear et al., "Inside the Weekend When Biden Decided to Withdraw," *New York Times*, July 21, 2024, www.nytimes.com/2024/07/21/us/politics/biden-withdrawal-timeline.html.

227 **sixteen additional members of Congress:** Derek Hawkins, Hayden Godfrey et al., "The Democrats Who Called on Biden to Drop Out of the 2024 Election," *Washington Post*, July 3, 2024, www.washingtonpost.com/politics/interactive/2024/calls -for-joe-biden-drop-out-election-2024/; June Kim, Blacki Migliozzi et al., "How Pressure Grew for Biden to Drop Out," *New York Times*, July 21, 2024, www.nytimes .com/interactive/2024/us/elections/biden-drop-out-democrats.html.

228 **He joined a call:** Peter Baker, "With Prisoner Swap, Biden Scores a Win as His Term Nears Its End," *New York Times*, August 1, 2024, www.nytimes.com/2024/08 /01/us/politics/biden-hostage-swap.html.

Chapter 16: Unburdened

237 **a signal that she was taking over the campaign:** Michael Scherer and Tyler Pager, "How Kamala Harris Took Control of the Democratic Party," *Washington Post*, July 28, 2024, www.washingtonpost.com/politics/2024/07/28/kamala-harris-control -democratic-party.

241 **The new memes promoted Harris phrases:** Scherer and Pager, "How Kamala Harris took control of the Democratic Party."

241 **"kamala IS brat":** Charli XCX, X (formerly Twitter) post, July 21, 2024. https:// x.com/charli_xcx/status/1815182384066707861?lang=en.

Chaper 17: Cruel Summer

245 **"I didn't know she was Black":** "Trump Addresses National Association of Black Journalists," NABJ, July 30, 2024, www.rev.com/transcripts/trump-addresses -national-association-of-black-journalists.

246 **They found old headlines:** "California's Kamala Harris Becomes First Indian- American US Senator," Associated Press, November 9, 2016, www.businessinsider .com/californias-kamala-harris-becomes-first-indian-american-us-senator -2016-11.

247 **"to all my fans":** Chris LaCivita, X (formerly Twitter) post, August 1, 2024, https:// x.com/ChrisLaCivita/status/1819140317271986505.

247 **Kemp, whose wife had told a local TV reporter:** Greg Bluestein, X (formerly Twitter) post, April 3, 2024, https://x.com/bluestein/status/1775689493925769552.

249 **he used the time to call and scream:** Maggie Haberman, "Trump Claims He Has Helicopter Trip Records and Threatens to Sue," *New York Times*, September 8, 2024, www.nytimes.com/2024/08/09/us/politics/trump-helicopter-landing.html.

251 Trump's team publicly cut ties with Lewandowski: Beth Reinhard and Isaac Stanley-Becker, "Loyalty to Trump Helped Corey Lewandowski Survive Harassment Scandal," *Washington Post*, August 31, 2024, www.washingtonpost.com/politics/2024/08/31/corey-lewandowski-trump-sexual-harassment.

Chapter 18: Honeymoon

256 Cooper's lieutenant governor: Richard Fausset, Danny Hakim, and Eduardo Medina, "How a Knack for Provocation Fueled Mark Robinson's Rise," *New York Times*, October 22, 2024, www.nytimes.com/2024/10/22/us/how-a-knack-for-provocation-fueled-mark-robinsons-rise.html.

257 lawyers vetting Shapiro did flag some comments: "Gov. Shapiro: Peaceful Protests Can't Be Excuse for Antisemitism," *The Lead with Jake Tapper*, CNN, April 24, 2024, www.cnn.com/videos/politics/2024/04/24/the-lead-josh-shapiro-college-protests-israel-hamas-democrats-primary-2024-jake-tapper.cnn.

260 "Would you be my running mate?": "Kamala Harris Calls Tim Walz to Offer Running Mate Role," MSNBC, August 6, 2024, www.youtube.com/watch?v=VIutnSouxLM.

260 The new Democratic ticket: Darlene Superville, "Early Harris-Walz Rallies Feature Big Crowds, Talk of 'Joy' and Unsolicited GOP Counterprogramming," WHYY.com, August 11, 2024, https://whyy.org/articles/kamala-harris-tim-walz-early-rallies.

262 country was on the wrong track: "July 2024 Times/Siena Poll of Registered Voters Nationwide," *New York Times*, July 3, 2024, www.nytimes.com/interactive/2024/07/03/us/elections/times-siena-poll-toplines.html.

266 Rumors started spreading that Beyoncé: Amie Parnes, "Beyoncé Does Not Appear at Democratic National Convention," The Hill, August 22, 2024, https://thehill.com/homenews/campaign/4843083-beyonce-dnc-vice-presidential.

Chapter 19: "Kick His A—"

268 he would be in charge: Corey Lewandowski, email to Susie Wiles, September 7, 2024. "I wanted to memorialize our conversation regarding the campaign budget process going forward . . . I will be reviewing and authorizing final approval on all spending . . . please send for final approval all new contracts, agreements, or hires made by any committee."

272 She received encouragement: Annie Karni and Katie Glueck, "Hillary Clinton and Kamala Harris: Inside Their Quietly Close Bond," *New York Times*, August 19, 2024, www.nytimes.com/2024/08/19/us/politics/hillary-clinton-kamala-harris.html.

275 "if an illegal alien ate your dog": Laura Loomer, X (formerly Twitter) post, September 9, 2024, https://x.com/LauraLoomer/status/1833320587038474627.

275 chagrin of some local Republicans: Aaron Blake, "Local Republicans Decry Hurricane Falsehoods—as Trump Spreads Them," *Washington Post*, October 7, 2024, www.washingtonpost.com/politics/2024/10/07/trump-misinformation-hurricane-springfield.

275 grateful-looking cats and ducks: Trump Posts on X, X (formerly Twitter) post, September 10, 2024, https://x.com/trump_repost/status/1833620373914718379.

275 **cats equipped with assault rifles:** Trump Posts on X, X (formerly Twitter) post, September 10, 2024, https://x.com/trump_repost/status/1833616582477812204.

275 **people were eating dogs and cats:** "Harris-Trump Presidential Debate Transcript," ABC News, September 10, 2024, https://abcnews.go.com/Politics/harris-trump -presidential-debate-transcript/story?id=113560542.

276 **"There's a huge fucking problem":** Justin Wells, "Art of the Surge," season 1, episode 4, October 29, 2024, https://tuckercarlson.com/art-of-the-surge-episode-4.

276 **"Why should I do another debate?":** Accountable GOP, X (formerly Twitter) post, September 10, 2024, https://x.com/AccountableGOP/status/183371433366 8311515.

276 **"Make no mistake about it":** "Brit Hume: 'Make no mistake about it, Trump had a bad night,'" Fox News, September 10, 2024, www.foxnews.com/video/636181 9534112.

278 **Allen and Dunn showed her X posts:** Michael Beschloss, X (formerly Twitter) post, September 10, 2024, https://x.com/BeschlossDC/status/1833696775552594201.

Chapter 20: Paranoia

282 **Lewandowski got off the plane:** Tim Alberta, "Inside the Ruthless, Restless Final Days of Trump's Campaign," *The Atlantic*, November 2, 2024, https://archive .is/pO0El.

282–83 **news photographs of him on the greens:** Carol D. Leonnig, Josh Dawsey et al., "Trump's Golf Outings Have Long Concerned Secret Service," *Washington Post*, September 16, 2024, www.washingtonpost.com/politics/2024/09/16/trump-golf -courses-secret-service-protection.

286 **assassinating an Iranian dissident:** Ryan Lucas, "She Was the Target of an Iranian Assassination Plot. She Now Lives in Its Shadow," NPR, July 10, 2024, www.npr .org/2024/07/10/g-s1-8835/masih-alinejad-iran.

286 **police searched the desert:** Josh Dawsey and Michael Scherer, "How the Trump Campaign Has Been Forced to Adapt to Assassination Threats," *Washington Post*, September 18, 2024, www.washingtonpost.com/politics/2024/09/18/trump -threats-campaign-security-assassination.

Chapter 21: A Man's World

291 **prep session by lantern light:** Paul Steinhauser, "Power Outage Doesn't Slow Down Vance's Prep for Tuesday's VP Debate with Walz," Fox News, September 30, 2024, www.foxnews.com/politics/power-outage-doesnt-slow-down-vance-prep -tuesdays-vp-debate-walz.

291 **Surveys rated him the least liked:** Hanna Panreck, "CNN's Harry Enten Says JD Vance Has 'Nothing to Lose' in Debate with Walz Because of Low Favorability Ratings," Fox News, October 1, 2024, www.foxnews.com/media/cnns-harry -enten-says-jd-vance-has-nothing-lose-debate-walz-because-low-favorability -ratings.

292 **Vance's team rejoiced:** "Vice Presidential Debate Transcript," CBS News, October 2, 2024, www.cbsnews.com/news/full-vp-debate-transcript-walz-vance-2024.

295 **had millions of viewers, and promoted Zyn:** Shane O'Neill, "How Zyn Became 'in' amid Right-Wing Fervor for Nicotine," *Washington Post*, August 15, 2024, www

.washingtonpost.com/style/of-interest/2024/08/15/zyn-nicotine-pouches -culture.

296 **The leader was Jack Fuetterer:** Samuel Benson, "The Utahns That Helped Trump Go Viral," *Deseret News*, December 25, 2024, www.ksl.com/article/51217824/the -utah-bros-that-made-trump-viral.

297 **"There's nothing I want":** Kristen Holmes, X (formerly Twitter) post, November 14, 2024, https://x.com/KristenhCNN/status/1857068910555677064?lang=en.

298 **Charlamagne Tha God discussed:** Preezy Brown, "Charlamagne Files Cease and Desist Order Against Donald Trump Over Campaign Ad," *Vibe*, October 21, 2024, www.vibe.com/news/politics/charlamagne-files-cease-desist-trump-campaign -ad-1234934198.

299 **"President Trump won't draft your daughter":** "2024 Trump Draft Daughters Ad," YouTube, October 30, 2024, www.youtube.com/watch?v=lttBMu63Fvg.

300 **addressed the issue of transgender care:** Glenn Thrush, "Under Trump, U.S. Prisons Offered Gender-Affirming Care," *New York Times*, October 16, 2024, www .nytimes.com/2024/10/16/us/politics/trump-prisons-transgender-care-harris .html.

302 **Justice Department warned that the sweepstakes:** Perry Stein and Trisha Thadani, "DOJ Warns Musk His $1 Million Petition Contest Could Violate Election Laws," *Washington Post*, October 24, 2024, www.washingtonpost.com/national-security /2024/10/24/doj-elon-musk-1-million-giveaway-election-laws.

302 **Musk viewed Pennsylvania:** Michael Scherer and Josh Dawsey, "Elon Musk Is the October Surprise of the 2024 Election," *Washington Post*, October 29, 2024, www .washingtonpost.com/politics/2024/10/29/elon-musk-october-election-trump.

303 **They went after Black voters:** Michael Scherer and Josh Dawsey, "Inside the Republican False-Flag Effort to Turn Off Kamala Harris Voters," *Washington Post*, November 15, 2024, www.washingtonpost.com/politics/2024/11/15/republican-ads -false-flag.

303 **Another PAC, also run by the same people:** Trisha Thadani and Clara Ence Morse, "Elon Musk Gave $20M to Mysterious Group Defending Trump's Abortion Stance," *Washington Post*, December 6, 2024, www.washingtonpost.com/technology /2024/12/05/elon-musk-rbg-pac-trump-abortion.

304 **"Nothing comes to mind":** Patrick Svitek, "On Differences with Biden, Harris Says 'Not a Thing That Comes to Mind,'" *Washington Post*, October 8, 2024, www .washingtonpost.com/politics/2024/10/08/harris-biden-differences-view -howard-stern.

Chapter 22: Warnings

308 **a rented helicopter:** Tyler Pager and John Hudson, "Oklahoma Congressman Threatened Embassy Staff as He Tried to Enter Afghanistan, U.S. Officials Say," *Washington Post*, September 1, 2021, www.washingtonpost.com/politics/mullin -afghanistan-trip/2021/08/31/62f63bb0-0a90-11ec-a256-709238a1404d_story .html.

310 **Noem was often publicly seen with Corey Lewandowski:** Ashley Parker and Michael Scherer, "Corey Lewandowski Is Too Controversial—Even for Trump," *The Atlantic*, February 14, 2025, www.theatlantic.com/politics/archive/2025/02/corey -lewandowski-is-too-controversialeven-for-trump/681694.

310 **about LaCivita's compensation:** Michael Isikoff, "Trump in Cash Crisis—As Campaign Chief's LLC's $19.2m Pay Revealed," *Daily Beast*, October 15, 2024, www .thedailybeast.com/donald-trumps-campaign-manager-chris-lacivitas-llc -multi-million-payday-revealed.

311 **It didn't matter that Harris's popularity:** "Do Americans Have a Favorable or Unfavorable Opinion of Kamala Harris?" fivethirtyeight.com, retrieved August 8, 2024 from the Internet Archive, https://web.archive.org/web/20240809002706/https:// projects.fivethirtyeight.com/polls/favorability/kamala-harris.

312 **former president met the definition of a "fascist":** Michael S. Schmidt, "As Election Nears, Kelly Warns Trump Would Rule Like a Dictator," *New York Times*, October 22, 2024, www.nytimes.com/2024/10/22/us/politics/john-kelly-trump-fitness -character.html.

312 **the group billed itself as the future:** Theodore Schleifer, "Harris's Main Allied Group Raised over $900 Million to Aid Her Bid," *New York Times*, November 15, 2024, www.nytimes.com/2024/11/15/us/politics/harris-future-forward.html.

314 **the vice president called Cheney:** Tyler Pager, "Harris Team Quietly Courts Big-Name GOP Endorsements," *Washington Post*, September 29, 2024, www.washing tonpost.com/politics/2024/09/29/harris-campaign-courts-prominent-republican -endorsements.

315 **Ellis Island of the South:** "Clarkston, Georgia: A Small Town with a Big Heart," City of Clarkson, www.clarkstonga.gov/about-clarkston/history#:~:text =The%20City%20has%20embraced%20the,Ellis%20Island%20of%20the %20South.%22

Chapter 23: Garbage In, Garbage Out

319 **"our little secret":** Annie Karni, "Trump Hints at 'Little Secret' with House Republicans, Setting off a Panic," *New York Times*, October 28, 2024, www.nytimes.com /2024/10/28/us/politics/trump-secret-house-republicans-panic.html; www.thenation .com/article/politics/little-secret-trump-johnson-election.

320 **blowback for Democrats worsened:** Aamer Madhani and Zeke Miller, "White House Altered Record of Biden's 'Garbage' Remarks Despite Stenographer Concerns," Associated Press, November 1, 2024, https://apnews.com/article/biden -garbage-transcript-puerto-rico-trump-326e2f516a94a470a423011a946b6252.

321 **"we got to lock him up":** Peter Baker, "Biden Quickly Backtracks After Saying Trump Should Be Locked Up," *New York Times*, October 22, 2024, www.nytimes .com/2024/10/22/us/politics/biden-trump-lock-him-up.html.

321 **Biden briefly put on a "Trump 2024" hat:** Tim Balk, "Biden Briefly Put on a Trump Hat, and MAGAWorld Flipped Its Lid," *New York Times*, September 13, 2024, www.nytimes.com/2024/09/13/us/politics/biden-trump-hat.html.

322 **His "garbage" controversy:** Katie Rogers and Reid J. Epstein, "In Closing, Harris Casts Herself as the Unifier and Trump as a 'Petty Tyrant,'" *New York Times*, October 29, 2024, www.nytimes.com/2024/10/29/us/politics/harris-speech-ellipse -trump.html.

323 **"We're going to win this":** "Harris Campaign Chair Jen O'Malley Dillon on Why She's 'Very Confident,'" MSNBC News, October 27, 2024, www.youtube.com /watch?v=KYMRu_DHaSg.

323 **building a robust legal effort:** Amy Gardner and Tyler Pager, "Could Trump Un-

dermine the Vote Again? Harris's Legal Team Says It's Prepared," *Washington Post*, October 21, 2024, www.washingtonpost.com/politics/2024/10/21/trump -overturn-vote-kamala-harris-lawyers.

325 **the final preelection Iowa survey:** Brianne Pfannenstiel, "Iowa Poll: Kamala Harris Leapfrogs Donald Trump to Take Lead near Election Day. Here's How," *Des Moines Register*, Novemerb 7, 2024, www.desmoinesregister.com/story/news/politics/iowa -poll/2024/11/02/iowa-poll-kamala-harris-leads-donald-trump-2024-presidential -race/75354033007.

Chapter 24: The Ballroom and the Boiler Room

331 **Pennsylvania war room:** Peter Deutsch, interview with Josh Dawsey, December 19, 2024.

Epilogue

341 **Warrington's report recommended:** Isaac Arnsdorf and Josh Dawsey, "Trump Aide Sought Payments from Job Seekers, Internal Legal Review Found," *Washington Post*, November 25, 2024, www.washingtonpost.com/nation/2024/11/25/trump -epshteyn-legal-review-conflicts.

342 **his problems with drinking:** Michael Kranish Dan LaMothe et al., "Hegseth's History with Alcohol Shadows Pentagon Selection," *Washington Post*, December 4, 2024, www.washingtonpost.com/politics/2024/12/04/pete-hegseth-drinking -defense-secretary-nomination.

342 **and with women:** Michael Kranish et al., "Trump Team Weighs Pentagon Pick After Sexual Assault Allegation Surfaces," *Washington Post*, November 15, 2024, www .washingtonpost.com/politics/2024/11/15/pete-hegseth-sexual-assault -investigation.

342 **excoriating his behavior:** Sharon LaFraniere and Julie Tate, "Pete Hegseth's Mother Accused Her Son of Mistreating Women for Years," *New York Times*, November 29, 2024, www.nytimes.com/2024/11/29/us/politics/pete-hegseth-mother-email.html.

342 **discussing swapping him:** Maggie Haberman et al., "As Hegseth Vows to Fight, Trump Considers DeSantis for Defense Secretary," *New York Times*, December 4, 2024, www.nytimes.com/2024/12/04/us/politics/hegseth-trump-defense.html.

342 **Musk moved into a cottage:** Maggie Haberman, Jonathan Swan et al., "How Elon Musk Has Planted Himself Almost Literally at Trump's Doorstep," *New York Times*, December 30, 2024, www.nytimes.com/2024/12/30/us/politics/elon-musk -trump-mar-a-lago.html.

344 **"In a one-hundred-and-seven-day race":** "Exclusive: The Harris Campaign on What Went Wrong," *Pod Save America*, November 26, 2024, https://crooked.com /podcast/exclusive-the-harris-campaign-on-what-went-wrong.

346 **Harris sent in a prerecorded video:** Adam Wren, Lisa Kashinsky et al., "Ken Martin and Kamala Harris Were Winners Saturday. Billionaires and the Old Guard Took a Hit," *Politico*, February 1, 2025, www.politico.com/news/2025/02/01/dnc -chair-election-takeaways-ken-martin-00201948.

347 **he publicly questioned:** Joe Biden, interview with Susan Paige, January 5, 2025, "Read What Joe Biden Said During His Exclusive Interview with USA Today: Transcript," *USA Today*, published January 8, 2025, www.usatoday.com/story /news/politics/elections/2025/01/08/joe-biden-interview-transcript/77490912007.

347 **Jill Biden, too, remained furious at Pelosi:** Kara Voght, "Jill Biden Still Hopes for a Good Ending," *Washington Post*, January 15, 2025, www.washingtonpost.com/style/power/2025/01/15/jill-biden-interview-first-lady.

347 **planned to release it:** Matt Viser, "Hunter Biden's Team Issues a Fiery Defense Ahead of Sentencing, Possible Pardon, *Washington Post*, November 30, 2024, www.washingtonpost.com/politics/2024/11/30/hunter-biden-defense-sentencing-pardon.

349 **"very negative" view:** Joe Biden, interview with Tyler Pager, March 26, 2025.

350 **party at Mastro's Steakhouse:** Zeke Miller and Colleen Long, "Mark Zuckerberg Will Cohost Reception with Republican Billionaires for Trump Inauguration," Associated Press, January 14, 2025, https://apnews.com/article/trump-zuckerberg-inaugural-reception-gop-billionaire-donors-bb9663cc352b78d89ec927fe65d334bd.

355 **reporters saw staff loading boxes:** Haisten Willis, "WHCA Travel Note 1" and "WHCA Travel Note 2," The American Presidency Project, February 28, 2025, www.presidency.ucsb.edu/documents/pool-reports-february-28-2025.

INDEX

INDEX